John Tribe

Buckinghamshire College
a college of Brunel University

Corporate strategy
for tourism

THOMSON

THOMSON

Tourism and Public Policy

Contents

Figures

Tables

Case studies

Acknowledgements

I would like to thank those tourism students at Buckinghamshire College who have shared their ideas and enthusiasms for this subject.

I would also like to thank the Barclays Economic Review for its generous policy of allowing text and data to be used, as well as British Airways and the British Airports Authority for permission to reproduce their mission statements.

Series Editors' Foreword

The International Thomson Business Press Series in Tourism and Hospitality Management is dedicated to the publication of high quality textbooks and other volumes that will be of benefit to those engaged in tourism, hotel and hospitality education, especially at degree and postgraduate level. The series has two principal strands: core textbooks on key areas of the curriculum; and the *Topics in Tourism* and *Hospitality* series which includes high focused and shorter texts on particular themes and issues. All the authors in the series are experts in their own fields, actively engaged in teaching, research and consultancy in tourism and hospitality. Each book comprises an authoritative blend of subject-relevant theoretical considerations and practical applications. Furthermore, a unique quality of the series is that it is student oriented, offering accessible texts that take account of the realities of administration, management and operations in tourism and hospitality contexts, being constructively critical without losing sight of the overall goal of providing clear accounts of essential concepts, issues and techniques.

The series is committed to quality, accessibility, relevance and originality in its approach. Quality is ensured as a result of a vigorous refereeing process, unusual in the publication of textbooks. Accessibility is achieved through the use of innovative textual design techniques, and the use of discussion points, case studies and exercises within books, all geared to encouraging a comprehensive understanding of the material contained therein. Relevance and originality together result from the experience of authors as key authorities in their fields.

The tourism and hospitality industries are diverse and dynamic industries and it is the intention of the editors to reflect this diversity and dynamism by publishing quality texts that enhance topical subjects without losing sight of enduring themes. The Series Editors and Adviser are grateful to Steven Reed of International Thomson Business Press for his commitment, expertise and support of this philosophy.

Stephen J. Page
Massey University – Albany
Auckland
New Zealand

Roy C. Wood
The Scottish Hotel School
University of Strathclyde
UK

Series Adviser
Professor C.L. Jenkins
The Scottish Hotel School
University of Strathclyde
UK

Preface

There exist many excellent, comprehensive texts on strategy, so this small text sets out with a clear mission and a distinctive strategy to achieve what Michael Porter has called a competitive advantage.

Its mission is to provide an accessible introduction to strategy within the tourism sector. The rationale for a book which concentrates solely on tourism is not hard to find. The World Travel and Tourism Council estimated that in 1995, the tourism industry employed over 210 million people directly or indirectly and accounted for 12.5 per cent of world export earnings. By 2005 it is expected to produce a gross output of $7.2 trillion

Its strategy is a hybrid one – low price with high value added. Its brevity enables a lower price and thus puts it within the reach of more students. However, brevity also enables the overall idea of strategy to come through more strongly, without getting unduly bogged down in detail on the way. Value added is offered by way of:

- chapter objectives
- case studies from the tourism sector
- extensive use of graphics and data
- chapter summaries
- review questions
- an international outlook
- extensive bibliography

The international aspect of this book particularly reflects developments in tourism, where new markets are opening up in the Asia/Pacific regions, Latin America and Central and Eastern Europe. Students are encouraged to use the bibliography as a point of departure into more detailed readings of specific concepts.

Whilst much of the emphasis of this book is on strategy in large profit-maximizing organizations, it also stresses that strategy is an important concept for non-profit organizations such as national and local tourism organizations, trade associations and pressure groups.

It is recognized that few students of corporate strategy will become Directors of Strategy. However, strategy brings a holistic approach to the study of tourism organizations and it is hoped that students will find this useful in their future roles. It will enable them to see the broad view when working within a traditional organization. It will enable them to bring strategic skills to bear when working in pressure groups to change aspects of tourism. Finally, it may give them the motivation to work towards positions of strategic influence.

John Tribe

Part 1: Introduction

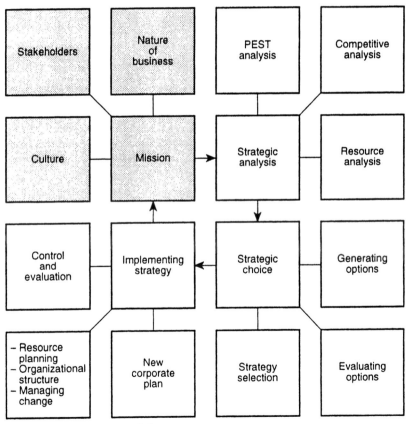

Figure 1.1 The framework for corporate strategy

This section provides an overview of tourism corporate strategy. Figure 1.1 provides the framework for examining the whole strategy process and Chapter 1 explores the four key component parts of the strategic process:

- mission
- strategic analysis
- strategic choice
- strategic implementation.

Chapter 2 examines in detail the mission of tourism organizations and analyses their aims and purposes. Thus these initial chapters provide the essential toolkit to engage in the first part of this strategic process.

1
Corporate strategy for tourism: introduction and overview

Chapter objectives

The aim of this chapter is to give students an overview of the strategy process. By studying this chapter students will be able to:

- define and explain the concept of strategy
- distinguish between the different elements of the strategy process
- utilize a simple model for strategic planning
- identify the rationale for corporate strategy
- interpret corporate developments in terms of the strategy model
- understand the complexity and debate surrounding the concept of strategy.

What is strategy? An example

Case Study A: The Disneyland, Paris Roller Coaster

'We have taken an important step forward since the beginning of this year [1995]. We have come out of a downward spiral and are

Case Study A (*continued*)

in a much more favourable environment,' said M. Bourguignon, President Directeur Général, Disneyland, Paris S.A., in the company's interim report.

Disneyland, Paris, S.A is an indirect wholly-owned subsidiary of The Walt Disney Company. The downward spiral had been all too painfully highlighted in the newspapers with captions such as *Euro-Dismal*, *Euroflop*, and *Magic Rubs Off*.

There had been initial optimism over Disneyland, Paris. Early forecasts had predicted profitability from the first year. The issue of 86 million shares in the Company in 1989 was oversubscribed and share prices had reached £7.37 by March 1992 just ahead of its opening in April. But the financial figures contained in the company's reports showed how quickly Disneyland, Paris had reached crisis point. Share prices also reflected the Company's poor performance and had slumped to 78p in October 1994.

Net Profit/(Loss)	1992	1993	1994	1995
FF millions	(1893)	(5337)	(1797)	114
£ millions (£1 = FF7.9)	(240)	(676)	(227)	14
$ millions ($1 = FF5.1)	(371)	(1046)	(352)	22

(*Source*: Euro Disney Annual Reports)

Commentators blamed high prices, a poor choice of site in terms of climate, the recession, high royalty charges to the parent company, the strength of the franc and hotels that were just too up market. It looked like the strategy that had been successfully followed in California, Florida and Japan had failed.

The Euro Disney 1993 annual report was a watershed which stated bluntly that 'in the face of an unprecedented recession which is affecting every sector of the economy, we are thoroughly revising our business strategy and entire staffing structure'. As the following timetable shows, Disneyland moved quickly to re-appraise its position.

- Spring 1992: Euro Disney opened

Case Study A (*continued*)

- Spring 1993: In depth review of operations and financial structure
- Winter 1993: Negotiations with banks
- Spring 1994: Financial restructuring, and new marketing strategy
- Winter 1994: New prices and new name announced.

Speaking in 1994, M. Bourguignon said, 'Over the last 18 months no stone has been left unturned to improve the Company's performance and our actions are beginning to pay off. . . Our financial problems, an unprecedented economic recession in Europe and rumours surrounding Euro Disney have only strengthened our resolve.'

Specific changes included the introduction of alcoholic drinks into restaurants, a reduction in hotel rates of 20 per cent, a reduction in admission prices from FF 250 to FF 195 (high season) and FF 175 to FF 150 (low season), a waiver of royalties to the parent company, a reduction in the labour force from 11,865 in 1993 to 10,172 in 1994 and the opening of a new £82 million attraction – Space Mountain.

Thus Euro Disney's 1994 report ended on an upbeat note: '. . . management continues to believe that its strategies to improve the Group's marketing effectiveness and operating efficiency will reposition the resort to increase annual attendance and operating margins despite the difficult economic environment the group faces. In addition, the positive effects of the financial restructuring, combined with the operating cost reductions, will help to improve the Group's financial results over the coming years.'

In 1995 Disneyland Paris's first profits were reported as £14 million for the year during which park admissions rose by 22 per cent from 8.8 million to 10.7 million. Share prices recovered to £2.01. The 1995 Annual Report felt able to say '1995 was the year of Renaissance for Disneyland, Paris'. It also alluded to the difficult period of change saying, 'our management philosophy and organization have undergone a deep review, reaching every department of the company'.

Case Study A (*continued*)

1995 was also an important year for Disneyland, Paris's parent company, The Walt Disney Company. It was the year in which it bought ABC, the American Broadcasting Company. Chairman Michael Eisner explained how this represented an important step in the evolution of the company by finding a distribution network for Disney's entertainment products. This type of vertical integration, between producer and distributor, had previously been outlawed by US law, forbidding production studios from owning networks and it was the deregulation of this sector that had allowed the move to take place. The purchase of ABC looks likely to change further the balance of Disney's portfolio which has seen a gradual shift away from the importance of theme parks and hotels towards filmed entertainment as illustrated in Figure 1.2.

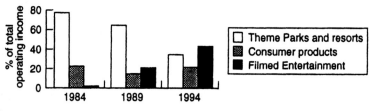

Figure 1.2 Contribution of sector to Disney's operating income (*Source*: Annual Report)

Case Study A illustrates some of the key features of corporate strategy for a tourism attraction. First, the initial development of Disneyland, Paris was part of continuing strategic review of The Walt Disney Company. The agreement between The Walt Disney Company and the French government was signed in March 1987, and thus the planning for Disneyland, Paris can be traced back to the early 1980s.

There had been earlier plans to expand the Disney theme park concept out of the US and into Europe. However, financial difficulties within the organization coupled with a joint-venture offer from a large financial group from Japan meant that The Walt Disney Company's preferred strategy for the 1970s was to concentrate on the development of Tokyo Disneyland.

The successful inauguration of Tokyo Disneyland meant that strategic factors once again favoured the development of a European theme park by the early 1980s. What were the key strategic factors?

- The concept of Disneyland had proved successful in California, Florida and Japan and it was therefore felt that success could be readily replicated in Europe.
- The company had the resources available for expansion, both in terms of finance (from internally generated profits and external sources) and in terms of expertise.
- Europe was considered to be a market which was already familiar with Disney products such as books, magazines and animations.
- The European Union had a population base of about 250 millions – similar in size to that of the US, and the population had relatively high levels of disposable incomes.

Thus a survey of 200 possible sights within Europe was made, culminating in a short list of Belgium, Spain and France. France was eventually chosen for a number of reasons. It was central to the key markets of Germany, the UK and the Netherlands, as well as having a large domestic market. There was a large site available. The site had excellent potential in terms of transport infrastructure. The proximity of the site to Paris meant that a ready supply of labour was available. Paris itself was an established visitor destination (30 million visitors in 1991) and last but not least, the French government offered attractive financial incentives to attract Euro Disney. In all, the government invested about FF 2.5 billion in the site and its surrounding area of which a third was of direct benefit to the project.

Strategic plannning: The elements

Figure 1.1 illustrated in schematic form the four key elements of corporate strategy:

1 mission
2 strategic analysis
3 strategic choice
4 strategic implementation.

What do each of these stages mean and how do they relate to The Walt Disney Company (TWDC)?

Mission

We start by considering the mission of an organization. The mission can be thought of as:

- what the organization is trying to achieve
- what its purpose or aim is
- where it is trying to head in the medium to long term.

The people who have key interests in the organization (its stakeholders) will fashion its mission. In common with most profit-making organizations, the most influential people determining the mission of TWDC will be the owners. Thus the key aim of The Walt Disney Company is to make money for shareholders. The Walt Disney Company has been highly successful in this and Table 1.1 shows how both share prices and dividends have shown strong growth.

But most organizations give expression to a complex range of interests. For example, Walt Disney, the founder of The Walt Disney Company, had and still has, a significant influence on the company's mission. He was always keen to promote a wholesome image for the company and thus, in line with company policy, Disneyland, Paris opened with the traditional prohibition of the selling of alcoholic drinks. This was an example of the established culture of The Walt Disney Company holding sway over pure profit motive.

Disney is also historically associated with entertainment and thus its general mission might be expressed as generating a profit through the provision of entertainment. It would be difficult though to imagine Disney being associated with just any type of money making entertainment. Pornography would not fit in with the Disney way of doing things and so the mission statement should be qualified by reference to family entertainment.

Table 1.1 Disney shares: price and earnings (*Source: Financial Times*)

Year	Share price ($)	Earnings per share ($)
1984	2	0.27
1989	30	1.28
1994	39	2.00

Strategic analysis

This involves consideration of the major influences upon the organization's success in terms of:

- resources
- environment.

Strategic analysis is concerned with analysing the strengths and weaknesses of an organization's internal resources and the opportunities and threats posed by its external operating environment.

The external operating environment in Europe held great promise. There was a large, high income population, the French government were prepared to provide financial inducements, there was a strong family visitor market and the Disney brand was well known. Additionally, the European Union was free from political upheaval.

Analysis of The Walt Disney Company's internal resources showed that the Disney theme park was still a successful brand which could be promoted further. The company had gained expertise in all aspects of park development and was able to assemble the financial resources for further expansion.

Strategic choice

This is concerned with:

- generation of strategic options
- evaluation of strategic options
- selection of strategy.

In simple terms, an organization seeks to gain advantage over its competitors either by selling a cheaper product than the competition, or a better product than the competition, or a cheaper and better product. These are the key strategic options available.

The strategy followed by The Walt Disney Company in theme park development has been to offer a better product than the competition and indeed to attempt to make the Disney product unique.

The chosen method was to develop the market (by overseas expansion) for an existing concept. Thus rather than extending the US parks, or opening a new park in the US, or perhaps diversifying into a network of motels, The Walt Disney Company chose to develop its potential market in Europe.

During any phase of strategic review a number of strategic options will be generated from strategic analysis. The preferred option will pass the tests of suitability, feasibility and acceptability. The choice of Disneyland, Paris as the key strategy for the development of The Walt Disney Company in the 1980s and 1990s appeared suitable in that it fitted in favourably with the outcomes of the organization's strategic analysis. It appeared feasible as both financial and other resources could be arranged. It also appeared acceptable in that it fitted in with the organizations' mission and promised a good rate of return on the investment.

Strategic implementation

This is concerned with:

- resource planning
- organizational structure
- logistics and implementation timetable
- timetable for implementation
- monitoring and review.

Implementation of the chosen strategy was relatively straightforward. The site was a greenfield one, and the concept was a tried and tested one. Thus the main task for successful implementation was the formulation of a project plan and the logistics exercise of ensuring that all the building, infrastructure, recruitment, training and finance were tackled in the right order, at the right time and according to specification.

In the event the construction and operations side of the project largely went according to plan. However, disaster struck from the start in terms of profitability and thus the company was forced into an early strategic review.

Lessons learned from Disneyland, Paris

Strategy does not guarantee success. In fact the general strategic method outlined above represents a standard cycle of strategic planning, but the success of a strategy depends on the accuracy of much of the analysis contained in the plan. Much of the analysis involves forecasting and the future is notoriously unpredictable. In particular, two parts of the Euro Disney strategy turned out to be inaccurate. First, the analysis of the external operating environment failed to predict the deep recession that coincided with the opening of the park. Second, the acceptability analysis was overly optimistic in its forecast of profitability. Customers failed to arrive as predicted and thus costs exceeded revenues resulting in huge losses.

However, the case study does illustrate the importance of strategic evaluation. The huge losses forced an early review of strategy in which costs were reduced and revenues boosted by a combination of price cuts and product development (Space Mountain).

What is strategy? Some definitions

The following examples illustrate a range of definitions of strategy by key writers in the area:

A strategy is the *pattern* or *plan* that *integrates* an organization's *major* goals, policies and action sequences into a *cohesive* whole.
(Quinn 1980, italics in original).

Strategy is the *direction* and *scope* of an organization over the *long term*: ideally, which matches its *resources* to its changing *environment*, and in particular its *markets*, *customers* or *clients* so as to meet *stakeholder* expectations.
(Johnson and Scholes 1993, italics in original).

Corporate strategy is the pattern of decisions in a company that determines and reveals its objectives, purposes or goals, produces the principal policies and plans for achieving those goals, and defines a range of business the company is to pursue, the kind of economic and human organization it is or intends to be and the nature of the economic and non-economic contribution it intends to make to its shareholders, employees, customers and communities . . .
(Andrews 1980).

Five definitions of strategy are presented . . . – as plan, ploy, pattern, position and perspective.
(Mintzberg 1987).

From the above it can be seen that a strategy is a master plan which has certain key features. It is medium to long term and is concerned with aims. But what then is an aim? To aim is to look towards and try to hit some target, and so an important part of a strategy is the careful scrutiny of the target. It needs to be clear to everyone involved in the strategic process exactly what it is they are aiming for, so the target needs to be carefully defined and described.

Consequently, the idea of an aim and a target is central to a strategy but does not fully explain the term. Targets can look quite different from one another and can be placed in different places, so we need to consider the form which a particular target will take. The process of considering strategic options and deciding which is the most appropriate one (strategic evaluation) is essentially the choosing between different targets.

However, merely having a target is not yet sufficient to be termed having a strategy. Part of strategy is the formulation of a plan of how to hit our target. For a simple target, like an archery target, this is straightforward. We take aim, we fire and we can see if we have hit the target by observing where our arrow has landed.

For a complex business target this process is far from simple. How do we know if we have hit the target? We need to express clearly what hitting the target means – it could be sales, or profit or market share or customer satisfaction or a combination of these things. It might take some time for us to find out how well we have hit the target since we have to collect, process and present complex data. So that is a key problem for strategists. Another problem is aligning or aiming a complex organization so that it is heading in the right direction to hit the target. This may be a particular difficulty if our strategy has involved moving the target to a new position or if the organization in question is a cumbersome one.

In summary, our strategy needs to address the following questions:

- Where are we trying to go?
- How can we get there?
- How do we know if we've got there?

Having given due consideration to the concept of 'strategy' we need to ask what the term 'corporate' means. Corporate comes from the Latin *corpus*, meaning body, and thus corporate means to do with the whole body of an organization and not a constituent part of it. So corporate strategy refers to that general strategy that steers the whole organization. There may be strategies going on at different levels, such as a marketing strategy and a staff development strategy. All of these lower level strategies should contribute to and inform the overall corporate strategy.

It should also be noted that the term corporate strategy is not confined to the narrow segment of organizations represented by large businesses. For it also covers small businesses and organizations that exist for non-profit making motives.

There are also a number of terms that cover similar ground to corporate strategy. These are 'business planning', 'management policy', 'organizational strategy' and 'strategic management'. The characteristics common to all these forms of analysis are that they involve decisions which

● are complex rather than simple
● are integrated rather than isolated
● are long-term rather than short-term
● are proactive rather than reactive
● have an impact on the whole rather than a part of the organization
● involve major rather than minor change
● involve grand design rather than marginal tinkering
● are made by those in positions of power in the organization rather than subordinates.

Another way to understand the meaning of the term strategy is to consider what it is not. Strategy is not 'flying by the seat of your pants', for this implies reacting to events as they happen, without a long-term plan. This approach is sometimes termed *ad hocism*, luck, or muddling through. For example, the development of the Spanish Mediterranean resort of Torremolinos lacked a clear strategy. The resulting, somewhat chaotic, development embraces an inharmonious juxtaposition of buildings.

Is a tactical approach the same as a strategic approach? It certainly implies more planning than *ad hocism* and more thinking things out in advance. But a strategy is more comprehensive than tactics. Tactics represent a way of dealing with a particular problem facing an organization, strategy involves a blueprint for the whole organization.

In summary a definition of strategy might be 'the planning of a desirable future and the design of suitable ways of bringing it about'.

The importance of strategy

Without strategy organizations are susceptible to strategic drift, particularly in today's turbulent environments and organizational fragmentation which might be likened to the headless chicken syndrome. Each of these ideas is now addressed.

Strategic drift

Strategic drift (Johnson 1988) occurs when an organization has failed to monitor and keep pace with its changing external environment. This is illustrated in Figure 1.3.

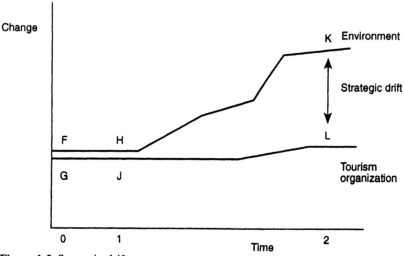

Figure 1.3 Strategic drift

An organization without a strategic view is likely to replicate current policy with perhaps a few minor changes. This is not a problem when environments are fairly stable, thus for example, between time periods 0 and 1 there is very little change in organizational policy, but this is not necessarily a problem since the environment has also witnessed little change either. However, between time periods 1 and 2, the environment has changed substantially from H to K. A tourism organization without a strategic view is likely to make only marginal change to its policy from J to L. Thus a gap opens up between the position of the tourism organization and its environment. This gap, KL in the figure, represents strategic drift.

Turbulent environments

The changing nature of the operating environment within which organizations work has also underlined the importance of strategic planning. It is possible to characterize business life as being relatively straightforward perhaps up to the end of the 1960s. Under this reading of things the external environment could' be expressed by the time period from 0 to 1 in Figure 1.3. It was essentially static. Thus, for example, The Walt Disney Company faced fairly predictable competition and the economic and political environments were generally stable. Technology advanced relatively slowly. Additionally many organizations tended to specialize in one product or service. Airlines, for example, tended to stick to the job of transporting passengers and thus they operated in a single environment. Similarly, The Walt Disney Company's main output was animated film. Thus, planning in these environments was a relatively simple exercise and these combination of features provided safe operating conditions for organizations.

Contrast this with the turbulent conditions that face the contemporary Walt Disney Company. The static environment has given way to the dynamic one where the pace of change is fast. Economies move from boom to recession, exchange rates and interest rates are volatile. Film-related technology has advanced via video, satellite and cable to the Internet. Organizations have moved from a single focus to a diversity of interests and thus have to operate in diverse environments. Disney, for example, spans the world of film animation and a whole range of associated merchandise. It owns theme parks and has moved into the area of network distribution. Planning has thus become more difficult because of the complexity of multiple product and service provision in fast changing environments.

The new condition that organizations find themselves in is therefore one of danger. Thus the environment previously characterized by the four Ss (static, single, simple and safe) is now characterized by the four Ds (dynamic, diverse, difficult and dangerous). This transition to conditions of turbulence is illustrated in Figure 1.4.

Organizational fragmentation

Organizational fragmentation is another symptom of lack of effective corporate strategy. The larger the organization, the more pronounced this problem may become. For a small tourism organization, such as a

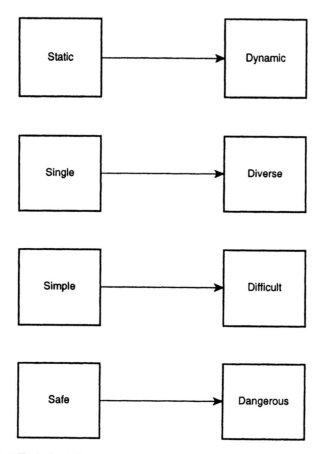

Figure 1.4 Turbulent times

family run hotel, most of the functions will be run or co-ordinated by one or two people. It is therefore relatively easy to ensure that the different functional areas of management are complimentary to one another and are pulling in the same direction. Thus a hotel that is seeking expansion will ensure that it has sufficient room capacity, a supporting marketing campaign, is able to field an increase in customer enquiries and is able to service a higher occupancy rate.

For larger organizations, the danger is that functional areas take up a life of their own and can therefore pull in different directions and frustrate each other's plans. The human body serves as a powerful

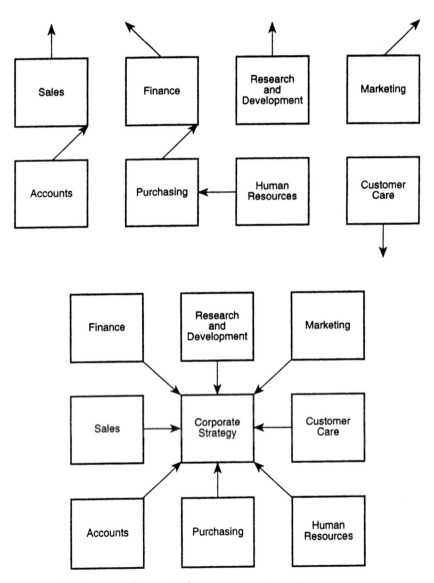

Figure 1.5 Corporate fragmentation vs. corporate strategy

metaphor here. Each of its constituent parts needs to be fulfilling the same objective. If different limbs, organs and senses do not act in concert, the result is chaos. Figure 1.5 illustrates how a corporate strategy acts as a powerful magnet to pull the different parts of an organization together.

The top part of the figure represents organizational fragmentation with different functions often operating in different directions. This is a caricature since in reality a typical hierarchical structure will impose some discipline over the organizational structure. The bottom part of the diagram shows corporate strategy as a unifying theme. A corporate plan offers a goal to which all the functional areas become oriented.

Scope of corporate strategy for tourism

Rovelstad and Blazer (1983) concluded that strategic planning was less advanced in tourism organizations than in manufacturing ones. However, a more recent study by Athiyamen and Robertson (1995) found 'a level of commitment to strategic planning in the tourism industry at least as strong as that in the manufacturing sector'. This latter study restricted its research to large tourism firms. However, use of the strategic approach is not confined to large firms and may be undertaken by the whole range of organizations in the tourism sector.

For example, organizations vary in size from sole proprietors and partnerships through to large, publicly quoted national and multi-national corporations. Second, organizations range from the private profit-making, through governmental organizations to voluntary associations. Third, organizations represent the key sectors of tourism – attractions, hospitality, transport and intermediaries, and national and local tourism organizations. Fourth, the scope of tourism strategy can be extended to destinations, which are not organizations, but rather a complex mix of individuals, organizations and natural and built environments. Finally, organizations operate from and in different parts of the world. Thus different organizations (in terms of size, location and ownership) will support different missions and thus seek different strategies to realize these differing missions.

We also need to distinguish between those organizations whose strategies are largely internally focused (i.e. an organization's own strategy which is a blueprint for how that organization will act) and those which are externally focused (i.e. an organization's strategy which is designed to co-ordinate or influence the strategies of others). Thus profit-seeking organizations such as Aerolinas Argentinas and Hilton International tend to have internally focused strategies, whereas organizations such as Tourism Concern and national tourism organizations tend to have externally focused strategies.

Athiyaman's (1995) survey of the literature on tourism strategy reveals that there has been little research specifically on strategy in tourism firms. However, there is a wealth of research on corporate strategy in general, much of which is readily applicable to tourism organizations.

Strategic interference

Strategies of different organizations will often have an impact on the possible strategy of others. We may term this interaction between strategies of different organizations strategic interference. First, this may come about because organizations are competing for similar markets. Thus competition between the cross channel ferry companies and Eurotunnel leads to a type of strategic interference which may be termed strategic feedback.

Stena Sealink may embark upon a particular strategy (strategy A in Figure 1.6), on the basis of its analysis of the competitive environment. However, strategy A may well affect the profitability of Eurotunnel and lead to a modification of the Eurotunnel strategy to strategy 1. This in turn will affect the market for Stena Sealink and thus a series of strategic changes may be set in action.

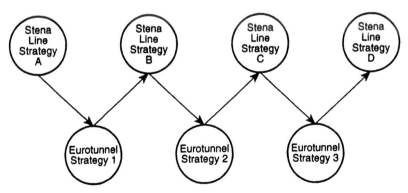

Figure 1.6 Strategic feedback

Second, the fact that some organizations have incompatible missions may cause deliberate strategic interference. For example, the mission of HAL (Heathrow Airport Limited), owners of London Heathrow Airport is to make profits for shareholders. However, the mission of Friends of the Earth is to protect the environment.

Thus Friends of the Earth will follow a strategy which is designed to frustrate that of HAL's attempt to increase profitability by the building of a new terminal five at Heathrow. Figure 1.7 shows the two competing strategies. They are incompatible since there is only space for one of them as a winning strategy and the adoption of one implies the frustration of the other.

Similarly, national and local government may have particular laws or planning restrictions which impose limitations on the strategies of tourism organizations. For example, the government of Bermuda has a policy to ensure that the island does not exceed its carrying capacity. This policy includes no planning permission for the building of new hotels and a high tax on cruise ships. Case Study A demonstrates how possible strategies of The Walt Disney Company were constrained by government industrial policy which prior to 1995 disallowed the ownership of network distribution companies by studio production companies.

Figure 1.8 shows how it was only after deregulation in this area that The Walt Disney Company was able to embark upon a strategy of vertical integration.

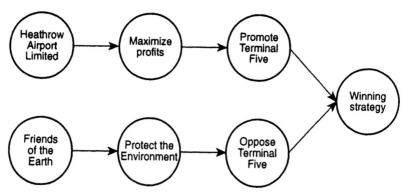

Figure 1.7 Incompatible strategies

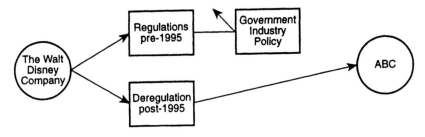

Figure 1.8 Constrained policy

Finally, national and regional tourism organizations (NTOs) have as their goal the co-ordination of the actions of a wide range of organizations. Figure 1.9 shows how they attempt to develop a strategy to encourage mutual development. The national tourism strategy might be to promote high value-added eco-tourism and it will attempt to co-ordinate the activities of individual tourism organizations towards this end. In the diagram the large square representing the NTO's strategy attempts to encompass parts of the individual tourism organization's strategies represented by the small squares. However, the directional arrows attached to the individual organization's demonstrate that this co-ordination task is a challenging one, as individual organization's strategies might run counter to the national strategy. For example, the aim of airline B might be to expand its cheap charter market.

Postscript: Strategy as a complex and contested concept

The explanation of strategy as presented so far in this text is designed to be clear and uncluttered. The purpose of this is to offer a relatively simple view on what is, for some, a new way of thinking. But in reality it would be wrong to portray strategy as being such a simple process or one about which there is universal agreement. There are in fact many different accounts of what strategy is. The four main approaches to strategy can be categorized as the Classical approach, the Evolutionary approach, the Processual approach and the Systemic approach (Whittington 1993).

The approach outlined in this chapter tends to follow the classical approach as developed by Ansoff (1965), Sloan (1963) and Porter (1985). This approach has a strong belief in the importance of strategy. It endorses a strong link between survival and profitability on the one

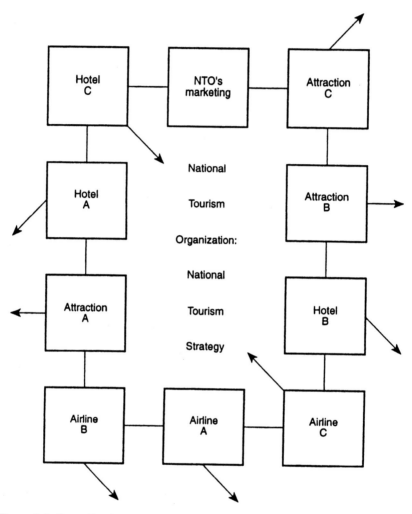

Figure 1.9 Co-ordination strategy

hand and the effective application by managers of the key strategic tools of analysis, policy choice and implementation on the other. It considers that an informed strategy can be formulated and will be important in determining the success of the organization.

Evolutionists include writers such as Alchian (1950), Friedman (1953) and Williamson (1991). They 'down-rate' the power of strategic managers to have much influence. Rather, they stress the power of market selection and the fact that corporate survival is at the mercy of the market. Market selection can be likened to biological selection – the fittest survive. Thus we might envisage dinosaur-type organizations which are unable to adapt fast enough to changing environments. These organizations give way to those best adapted to survival in particular market conditions.

In the world of airlines, companies such as People's Express (USA), Braniff (USA) and Laker (UK) failed the market test despite, in the latter case, the presence of a dynamic Chief Executive in Sir Freddie Laker. Whilst the Evolutionary theories may give little comfort to failed organizations and their planning procedures, from a whole market perspective consumers may be left with the fittest organizations. Of course, the Evolutionary dynamic is stifled in non-market economies and thus the far from fit Aeroflot managed to survive.

Processualists are also sceptical about classical planning. They stress that humans are imperfect cogs in the corporate machine in contrast to the classical model of the organization as a perfect machine.

Processualists such as Cyert and March (1963) stress that humans operate in 'bounded rationality' by which they mean that they cannot see a complete picture and only have the ability to process a number of factors. Thus they challenge the power of Classical analysis, which tends to assume that a comprehensive strategic picture can be composed and items within it readily manipulated to a strategic end. Furthermore they see the labour force as being motivated by a range of factors, only one of which may be the corporate plan. Thus they challenge the ability of managers to effectively operationalize a strategic plan (which they have already discounted as being flawed by the limited perspective of its authors).

The Systemic school emphasizes that an organization's labour force cannot be understood as simple automatons programmed to maximize the organization's well-being. It also stresses that there is no universal corporate goal shared by organizations across the globe. Rather, human resources have to be understood through their humanness and as members of a particular cultural group. Granovetter (1985) refers to this as the 'embeddedness' of economic activity within a social system. Thus psychological and sociological factors are important.

The Systemic school is significant to the international aspect of this book in that it cautions against a glib acceptance and interpretation of 'globalization'. Despite the communications revolution, different parts of the world still maintain distinct cultural identities and the Systemic approach suggests that strategies need to be understood as products of these cultures, and indeed that different strategies must be fashioned for different parts of the world.

The initial problems of Disneyland, Paris were a clear illustration of this point. Disneyland is a product of US culture. The strategy that the Disneyland package could be successfully implanted, lock stock and barrel, into France, a country with a very distinct culture, was clearly misguided. However, the strategists at The Walt Disney Company, like most of us, demonstrated an ethnocentric view of the world. They thus saw France as if it were populated by Americans, rather than as if it were populated by the French. They were thus considerably surprised at the lack of enthusiasm by French visitors for a cuisine of soft drinks and fast food.

Summary

Situr, Mexico's largest tourism developer with widespread hotel interests, is used to review some of the concepts developed in this chapter. In February 1995, Grupo Sidek, the parent company of Situr, defaulted on a $19.5 million payment on a loan. This was a point of crisis for the organization and the signal for a rethink in strategy.

1 **Mission**: In common with Disneyland, Paris, the mission of the organization became that of survival.
2 **Strategic analysis**: This provided the explanation for the sudden collapse in the company's fortunes: Its debt which had risen to $1.05 billion was readily identified as a crucial internal weakness. This was largely caused by turbulence in the external environment. The Mexican currency, the peso, had collapsed in 1994 causing an increase in interest rates and an increase in the burden of any debts denominated in dollars. These two factors had led to a 2000 per cent increase in Situr's costs of borrowing. As a short-term tactical response to this, the managing director of Situr, Mr Prysor-Jones, negotiated a rescheduling of some of the firm's short-term debt and this enabled the company to meet its February debt payments albeit a week late.
3 **Strategic Choice**: One strategic option available to Satur is that of cost-reduction by way of seeking a business partner. A proposal

under consideration is for AEW, a US insurance group to take an equity stake in 15 of Situr's hotels. This option is currently being evaluated. Would it provide sufficient funds? Would it eat too deeply into Situr's profits? Is it acceptable to Situr's owners? Can the two companies work together?

4 **Implementing Strategy**: If this option is selected, it will form a major plank in Situr's strategy for the next few years and the strategic process turns to that of implementation. How will the joint venture operate? What changes in the organizational structure are needed? How will AEW's interests be voiced on Situr's board? How will the success of this strategy be measured?

Review questions

1 Redraw the 'Framework for Corporate Strategy' (Figure 1.1) using the report on Situr in the text to illustrate the elements of the strategic planning process.
2 Define the term 'strategy' in your own words.
   (a) use examples;
   (b) explain the essential features which distinguish a strategy from similar concepts;
   (c) use counter-examples to clarify what strategy is not.
3 Explain how followers of the Systemic, Processualist and Evolutionist schools of strategic analysis might interpret the initial failure of Disneyland, Paris.
4 Explain the relevance of the terms 'strategic drift', 'turbulent environments' and 'organizational fragmentation' to a named tourism organization.
5 Map out the elements of strategy for a named tourism organization.
6 Explain, using examples, what Mintzberg (1987) meant when he described strategy as 'plan, ploy, pattern, position and perspective'. Do you think his definition is an appropriate one?

2
Aims, missions and objectives for tourism organizations

Chapter objectives

The study of the aims of tourism organizations must necessarily precede any further analysis of strategy, since it is impossible to have a strategy without having an idea of what the strategy is designed to achieve. A strategy is a means to an end, thus we need to state that desired end at the outset.

At first glance the aims of tourism organizations appear to be straightforward. Surely the owners of such organizations simply want the highest possible return on their investment, so that profit maximization is the universal aim?

However, two considerations make the further study of organizational aims worthwhile. First, the concept of 'stakeholders' is an important one, particularly for large organizations. A stakeholder is any person or group with an interest in an organization and the concept of stakeholders is a much broader one than that of owner or shareholder. This makes the study of aims a more complex issue, since stakeholders do not necessarily have identical aims. Second, many tourism organizations are non-profit making and so if their aims are not profit-maximization, we need to investigate what other aims are pursued and who decides what those aims are to be.

Missions and objectives are by no means static, and indeed the whole idea of corporate strategy is to engage in regular reassessment of an organization's mission and objectives to ensure that they remain appropriate. Thus mission and aims need to be understood as part of the circular nature of corporate planning. Figure 1.1 in Chapter 1 illustrates this cycle of planning. The starting point of this diagram is mission and objectives. Strategic analysis is then undertaken to test the continuing appropriateness of these. Such analysis may lead to a reformulation of the organization's mission and objectives in a new corporate plan for implementation over the next few years. The cycle of strategic planning will then recommence.

Finally, organizations develop their own distinctive cultures and are part of the wider culture of the society within which they operate. Cultural analysis is therefore necessary to complete the investigation into mission formulation.

By studying this chapter students will be able to:

● evaluate organizational missions and aims
● identify key stakeholders who influence the mission
● analyse sources of stakeholder power
● understand the relationship between culture and mission.

Aims, missions and objectives

Aims and missions

Many organizations work to a mission statement (David 1989). A mission statement is a concise expression of what the organization is trying to achieve and explains what it is in business for. Figure 2.1 reproduces the mission statement of the British Airports Authority (BAA) which owns key airports including Heathrow and Gatwick in the UK.

BAA's mission statement is a simple sentence. Of course, the word 'success' has many meanings and thus the meaning of the mission is qualified in three further sentences. Figure 2.2 illustrates the mission statement for British Airways. Readers will notice the similarity between the two missions and the trend towards similar mission statements across a range of organizations has led critics to dismiss the concept as a superficial one. However, a useful mission statement should have the following characteristics:

● it should be succinct
● it should be a visionary statement for the future

Our Mission Statement

Our mission is to make BAA the most successful airport
company in the world

This means...

Always focusing
on our customers'
needs and safety

Seeking
continuous
improvements in
the cost and
quality of our
services

Enabling our
employees to give
of their best

To achieve our mission we will...

Safety
and Security

Give safety and security the highest priority at all times.

Strategy

Concentrate on the core airport business, be prudently financed,
continuously improve quality and cost effectiveness, fully develop our
property and retail potential and achieve world class standards in
capital investment.

Customers

Ensure our customers receive excellence and good value for money
in the services BAA provides.

Employees

Provide a good safe working environment which attracts and
retains committed employees. Through training and two-way
communication allow them to fulfil their potential and contribute
directly to the success of the company.

Shareholders

Encourage shareholders to believe in our company by giving them
consistent growth in earnings and dividends.

Environment

Recognize the needs of the local communities and be seen as a good
neighbour with concern for the environment.

Figure 2.1 BAA's mission statement

- it should be an umbrella statement which can cover more detailed objectives
- it should be realistic and achievable
- it should describe the main aims of the organization.

Objectives

Objectives spell out the goals that have to be achieved to realize a mission. Thus objectives set out in more detail how a mission is to be achieved. There are two main levels at which objectives are set out. At one level there are corporate objectives. These tend to be framed at a fairly general level. For example, Figure 2.1 shows the six key ways in which BAA sets out to achieve its objectives in terms of safety and security, strategy, customers, employees, shareholders and the environment. Similarly, Figure 2.2 reveals BA's seven corporate goals (objectives) ranging from financial strength to good neighbourliness.

At another level there are unit objectives. These are much more specific and set out targets for operating units within an organization to achieve. For example, BAA sets targets for different areas of its operations and measures its performance against these targets. Recent survey data (Ferry 1995: 33) collected by BAA to monitor unit objectives records that:

- passengers rate catering at Heathrow and Gatwick as the best in Europe
- landing fees for airlines are in the lowest 25 per cent of those charged at world airports
- machinery such as ventilation systems, travelators, airbridges and escalators have achieved their target of being operational 98 per cent of the time.

Similarly, British Airways has set out unit objectives for each of its corporate objectives. For example, for its 'good neighbour' corporate objective specific unit objectives are set out, monitored and reviewed in its Annual Environmental Report (British Airways annually). They include the following objectives:

- to reduce the number of noise infringements
- to reduce the number of fuel jettison incidents
- to continue to increase the proportion of aircraft fleet complying with Chapter 3 (reduced noise) requirements.

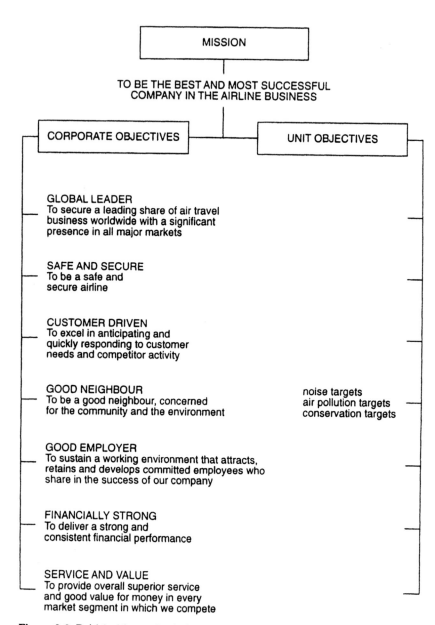

Figure 2.2 British Airways' mission statement

Figure 2.2 shows the distinction between the terms 'mission', 'corporate objectives' and 'unit objectives'.

Framing of objectives and missions

Objectives and missions may be framed as open or closed statements. Closed statements are written as a quantifiable target. This might be a financial target or an operating target. For example, BAA has a target for its airbridges to be 98 per cent operational. This is a closed,

---

THE NEW ZEALAND TOURISM DEPARTMENT

'To develop and market New Zealand as a tourism destination where this is beyond the interest of the private sector, and where this is a cost effective contribution to the Government's desired outcomes' (The government's outcomes are increased overseas earnings, increased employment and sustainable development)

THE NEW ZEALAND TOURISM STRATEGIC MARKETING GROUP

To secure 'a highly focused, profit orientated, internationally competitive inbound tourism industry' with targets of $10 billion foreign exchange earnings from 3 million visitors by the year 2000.

TOURISM AUCKLAND

'To be the focal point for the promotion of tourism in Auckland which best serves the economic and social needs of our members and the people of the Auckland region'

CANTERBURY (NZ) TOURISM COUNCIL

'To develop Christchurch and Canterbury as a major tourism destination; to solicit and service conventions and other group business and to engage in visitor promotions which generate overnight stays, thereby enhancing and developing the economic fabric of the community'

Figure 2.3 Mission statements of national and regional tourism organizations in New Zealand

operating target. It is readily measurable. Similarly the New Zealand Tourism Strategic Marketing Group (see Figure 2.3) has the closed financial objective of earning $10 billion foreign exchange earnings from 3 million visitors by the year 2000. Closed objectives should conform to the SMART principles, that is they should be:

- specific
- measurable
- agreed with those who must attain them
- realistic
- time-constrained.

Open statements are written in more qualitative terms. Missions are generally written as open statements and targets such as 'the most successful' are not measurable without further definition. Notice that many of the BA environmental targets are open (e.g. 'to reduce the number of noise infringements'). A closed statement would add a specific amount (e.g. 'by 10 per cent next year').

Types of mission

The aims and missions of organizations can be classified according to a number of types, where classification depends upon the significance of profit as against other aims. The following classification illustrates five main types.

Profit maximization

Many tourism organizations are exclusively profit-driven. If an activity does not contribute directly to profitability it will not be authorized by an organization in this grouping. Profit-maximization is assumed by neo-classical economic theory to be the key objective of private sector firms.

Tempered profit maximization

The next group of organizations may be termed 'tempered profit maximisers'. These organizations generally seek to maximize profits but their missions include some features which do not directly generate profits. Such features generally include social aspects and the good neighbour section of British Airways' mission (see Figure 2.2) is an example of this. In practice, BA's good neighbour policy may be viewed in several ways. It might be considered as a purely altruistic policy which is followed solely on ethical grounds. Alternatively, it might be viewed as good public relations with no instant payback, but improving the general image and attractiveness of the airline and thus adding to profitability in an indirect way.

Indirect profit maximization

Trade associations which promote the interests of their members may sometimes have their missions categorized in this group. Their missions are not to maximize their own profits, but to enhance the interests of their members. The Universal Federation of Travel Agents' Associations (UFTAA), for example aims to protect its members' interests through collective negotiation with principles. Similarly, the International Hotel Association (IHA) exists to promote the interests of, and provide services for, its members in the hotel and restaurant industry world-wide.

Some tourism trade associations and coalitions seek to promote 'good practice' in conjunction with profits. For example, the World Travel and Tourism Council (WTTC) exists to promote travel and tourism markets on behalf of its corporate members, but also promotes environmental tourism and co-sponsored the launch of the World Travel and Tourism Environmental Research Council (WTTERC)

Social aims

For some organizations, profit is not a major consideration. Instead, their mission is to serve some other end. An important grouping of organizations under this heading are those run by national and local government. Their missions generally embrace more general economic or social aims (O'Hagan et al. 1986) This can be seen in the mission statements of the New Zealand national and regional tourism organizations (see Figure 2.3). For example, the mission of the New Zealand Tourism Department has general economic aims such as generating more employment and foreign exchange earnings. These are aims which bring economic benefit to the wider population of a country rather than profit to shareholders.

Tourism Auckland's mission (see Figure 2.3) highlights the interests of the people of the Auckland region. These are aims which it would be difficult for a private sector organization to justify, since it is difficult to earn profits from them. The World Tourism Organization (WTO), an agency of the United Nations, has as its aim the promotion and development of tourism world-wide. This then is another example of seeking wider economic benefits rather than private profit.

The missions of voluntary and non-governmental organizations may take a number of forms. For example, for some organizations, e.g. Tourism Concern (UK), ethical considerations are paramount. The prime aim of Tourism Concern is to promote greater critical understanding of the impact of tourism. The mission of the Ecumenical Coalition on Third World Tourism (ECTWT) is to reduce damage caused by tourism by a programme of educating tourists and tour operators. The mission of the World Travel and Tourism Environmental Research Council (WTTERC) is to 'create a world-wide database and information network to further environmentally compatible growth in the Travel and Tourism industry' (WTTERC 1992: 1). The International Council on Monuments and Sites (ICOMOS) aims 'to further the conservation, protection, rehabilitation and enhancement of monuments, buildings and sites; bring together individuals and bodies involved in conservation; exchange information and promote interest in and protection of cultural heritage' (Medlik 1993: 286). The common aspect to all these missions is their commitment to wider social ends and lack of interest in making profit.

Organizations in communist states

Many organizations operating under Communist systems such as Cuba and China are also not primarily profit maximizers. Their role is to fulfil part of the state plan and these organizations' missions are therefore subordinate to the general aims of state or local planners. Such organizations might be required to have employment provision, or regional development as a key objective. However, private enterprise is gradually being permitted in Cuba and China and such organizations will exhibit profit-maximizing or tempered profit-maximizing missions.

Figure 2.4 locates a sample of tourism organizations on a grid which depicts the significance of profit on the vertical axis against social aims on the horizontal axis. It can be seen that there is a trade-off between profit missions and social missions. The ECTWT is able to sustain its pure social mission because it is funded through churches and does not therefore need to resort to profit making. Whilst the WTTERC has a

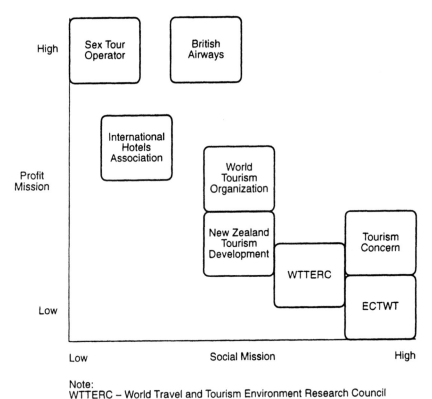

Note:
WTTERC – World Travel and Tourism Environment Research Council
ECTWT – Ecumenical Coalition on Third World Tourism

Figure 2.4 Classification of missions

strong social mission it is tempered by its need to satisfy the demands of its corporate sponsors and thus occupies a more intermediate position on the grid. BA's position reflects the fact that there is some social dimension to its mission but that profit is paramount.

Mission types and mission agenda

Each of the five main mission types outlined above can be roughly matched to a more particular agenda. This is illustrated in Table 2.1 where a distinct pattern emerges. Profit maximizing organizations have a well-focused agenda which is not diluted by any social responsibility.

Table 2.1 Mission types and mission agenda

Mission agenda	Mission type				
	1	*2*	*3*	*4*	*5*
Maximizing profits	✓	✓	✓		
Corporate success	✓	✓	✓		
Customer satisfaction		✓	?		
Employee welfare		✓			
Environmental sensitivity		✓			
Product safety		✓	?		
Employment policy		✓			
Community activity		✓		✓	
Ethical considerations		?	✓		
Benefits to society				✓	✓
Political considerations					✓

Notes:
1 = Profit maximizer   4 = Social welfare maximizers
2 = Tempered profit maximizer   5 = Communist organizations
3 = Indirect profit maximizer

Tempered profit maximizers incorporate a wider agenda which includes a range of possible social considerations. Those organizations which are not essentially profit maximizers have a mission which focuses on issues of social benefit, community activity and ethical considerations.

Mission and reality

The discussion of mission is concluded with two critical views of missions. Both the views suggest that missions are a side issue and that what we really need to consider is the actual track record of organizations to see their real goals. The first of these arguments is that mission statements are just a good public relations front which put an acceptable face on the cut-throat world of the activities of organizations in modern markets. This view would suggest that cost reduction and revenue enhancement are the universal unspoken missions of most private sector organizations, but that such a mission would make rather alarming reading.

The second argument stresses the divorce between ownership and control in the division between owners (shareholders) of large organizations and the professional managers who run them (Baumol 1959). Whilst the shareholders will favour a mission which generates a good rate of return on their capital, managers (who may not necessarily have a significant shareholding) may actually pursue a different mission which maximize their own benefits, irrespective of the published mission. Thus they may seek remuneration packages and a series of perks, including cars and travel, which detract from profitability. At other times they may seek to maximize particular targets, such as sales, at the expense of profit because of the personal prestige that is gained. However, the adoption of profit-related bonuses for directors may have lessened the significance of this point.

Stakeholders

Stakeholder analysis (Mitroff 1983; Freeman 1984) is a useful way of identifying the variety of different forces that act on an organization's mission. The term 'stakeholder' refers to a person or grouping with an interest in the operation of a particular organization. Figure 2.5 shows some of the key stakeholders which could be mapped for the Savoy Hotel.

Thus the neighbouring Savoy Theatre is a stakeholder, as some of its

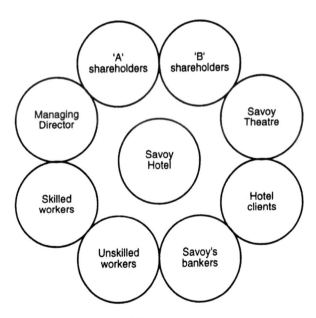

Figure 2.5 Savoy Hotel stakeholders

audience will use the hotel and it might be affected by noise from the hotel. Similarly, the Savoy's bankers have an interest in the financial health of the Savoy to protect their loan exposure. Shareholders are also stakeholders, with a keen interest in the Savoy's fortunes by virtue of their ownership, and thus financial stake in the company. Employees have a range of expectations from the organization with a particular interest in working conditions and job security. The hotel's clients too have an interest in the way in which the organization is run and managed.

We may further categorize stakeholders as those external to the organization and those internal to the organization. In the example of the Savoy Hotel, the Savoy theatre and its bankers are external stakeholders whilst the managing director and other employees are internal stakeholders.

Case Study B on the Savoy Hotel illustrates this and subsequent points.

Case Study B: The Savoy Hotel, London

There has been a battle taking place at the Savoy Hotel, London. It was a battle between the old guard and the new guard over the future of the hotel which was first opened in 1889.

Who are the old guard? They include the long-serving staff, the traditional clientele of the Savoy and some of the hotel's shareholders in the form of the Savoy trusts. And the new guard? Mr Ramon Pajares, the Savoy's managing director, is certainly a key member of this group. He was appointed in November 1994 and is only the sixth managing director in the Savoy's 100 year existence. He replaced Mr Giles Shepard (old guard and old Etonian). Forte – the largest hotel group in the UK – are part owners of the Savoy group and are certainly part of the new guard.

Change is anathema to the old guard. They are fighting to retain the traditions and standards which locate the Savoy more in the 1880s than the 1990s. Traditions include the wearing of full morning dress by reception staff, the serving of food from silver trays, beds made with Irish linen sheets and the discreet discouragement of the use of mobile phones. They fear that the Savoy will fall victim to the trend towards the standardization of

Case Study B (*continued*)

hotels and point to the dreary formula applied to hotels elsewhere in the Forte group. Some of their fears have already been realized. The specialist purchasing departments for meat, vegetables and wine have already been closed. So has the printing department.

The new guard are more preoccupied with financial statistics than with tradition. The Savoy made a loss in 1992. Its occupancy rate averaged 72 per cent in 1994, and its average achieved room rate was £174 – both lowish figures for the luxury hotel market in London. Mr Pajares has declared his main strategic aim as the improvement of occupancy rates. This, combined with a sustained attack on costs, is his key to improving profitability. Higher profits will, he says, provide the funds for investment. Higher investment leads to higher quality, pushing occupancy rates up further. A virtuous circle.

However, the battle has been in impasse for a while. This is because of a tactical move made by a previous chairman of the group, Sir Hugh Wontener. He created two types of shares back in 1955 in the form of A shares and B shares. B shares carried more voting rights than A shares and the board of the Savoy controlled a sufficient amount of B shares to carry more than fifty per cent of the total votes. This scheme, devised to protect the Savoy from take-over bids, has largely fulfilled its aim. Over recent years, for example, Forte accumulated 68 per cent of the shares of the Savoy group, but only 42 per cent of the votes. It has been frustrated in its quest for more profitability and persistently outvoted by the charitable trusts set up to protect the Savoy's independence. The turning point in the battle came with the losses made in 1992. This prompted a new period of co-operation between the Savoy trust and Forte as the very survival of the Savoy became the key issue. Both sides have not united behind Mr Pajares and have endorsed his strategy to improve the Savoy's fortunes.

Stakeholder power

Interest alone is insufficient to explain the relative influence of stakeholder groups on mission. We need to add another dimension – that of stakeholder power – to get the full picture of stakeholder influence (Mendelow 1991). Power may be defined as the ability to influence policy and Figure 2.6 maps the key stakeholder groups identified in the Savoy Hotel case study on a power/interest matrix.

The shaded area in the top right of the matrix represents the domain of most influence since here there is a concentration of both power and interest in the organization. Group B shareholders occupy a dominant position in this sector. As a group, B shareholders wield more power than A shareholders because of their superior voting rights. Shareholders derive their power from their ability to support or veto board policy, and blocs of shareholders can muster considerable muscle. Individual shareholders on the other hand have little power, as their votes are fairly insignificant in comparison with large shareholders. They probably have a variety of different shareholdings and thus little

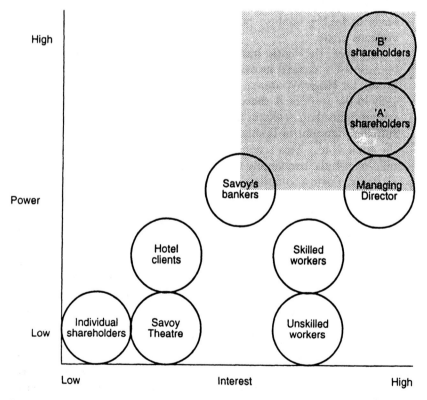

Figure 2.6 Stakeholder influence

interest in any one organization and can be seen to occupy a position of minimal influence in Figure 2.6.

The managing director however exerts considerable power, even as an individual. This results from his or her position at the top of the managerial hierarchy. This position gives unrivalled access to information in addition to the power of control and patronage of managers in subordinate roles. Turning to the Savoy's clientele, they can exercise little power as individuals, since their isolated decisions about spending have little effect on the overall revenue of the hotel. Unskilled workers are in a similar position of limited power although they clearly have a significant interest in the organization as it represents their livelihood. Trade union membership (a form of coalition) can enhance the power of workers.

In summary, internal stakeholders' power is enhanced by:

- position in hierarchy
- charisma
- comprehensive intelligence about the organization
- specialist knowledge
- patronage
- control of resources
- formation of coalitions.

On the other hand external stakeholders' power is enhanced by:

- control of resources (e.g. finance)
- constitutional role (e.g. shareholders' voting rights)
- public relations skills
- control of distribution links (e.g. outlets)
- formation of coalitions.

Stakeholders can increase their influence by forming coalitions. Such coalitions had an identifiable effect on changing the mission of the Savoy Hotel. The pre-1992 coalition had seen an alliance between the then managing director, Giles Shepard, the Savoy Trust B shareholders, workers and traditional customers. This coalition was largely able to resist the Forte drive for modernization and so the Savoy mission continued to stress maintenance of traditional standards. However, the 1992 losses saw a realignment of forces. The Savoy Trust B shareholders allied with Forte to replace Shepard with Pajares and subsequently follow a more profit-centred, modernizing mission.

Notice from the case study that the low power position of the work-force as individuals explains its inability to resist the closure of the centralized wine buying and in-house printing departments within the Savoy, with the subsequent loss of jobs.

Figure 2.7 shows four stakeholder groupings for a typical organization – shareholders, employees, the community and pressure groups. The outer circles represent the key objectives that each group wishes to incorporate in the organization's mission. Clearly, their success in incorporating their particular objectives will depend on their relative power. The mission statement of the British Airports Authority (BAA) illustrated in Figure 2.1 makes interesting reading in this respect. Its

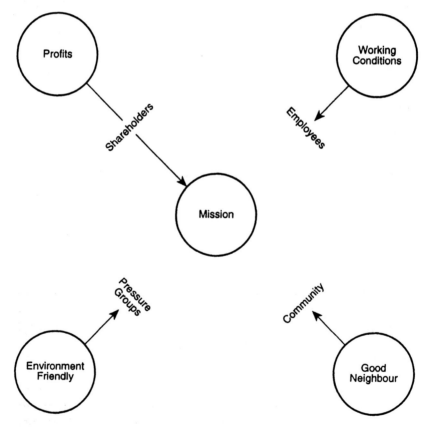

Figure 2.7 Inter-stakeholder dynamics

mission appears to appeal to a whole range of stakeholders – customers, employees, shareholders and environmentalists. There will, however, clearly be considerable tensions between the different claims of these groups on the mission. Is good value for money (customers) compatible with growth in earnings and dividends (shareholders)? Is cost effectiveness (shareholders) compatible with a good working environment (employees)? And is it possible for an expanding airport to be a good neighbour (community)? In reality it is likely that the priority given to the different elements of the BAA mission will depend upon the power of the relevant stakeholders.

Many missions represent a compromise between the conflicting demands of different stakeholders. The term 'profit satisficing' is used to describe organizational goals resulting from such a compromise. It is not profit maximization but rather it represents a level of profit which is sufficient to satisfy an organization's key stakeholders. Owners may therefore have to forego some profit in order to accommodate the demands of other powerful stakeholders. This acceptable compromise (Cyert and March 1963) represents a kind of bargaining between stakeholder groups.

Mission and culture

Cultural environment

We have investigated the influence of stakeholders on mission and analysed the significance of stakeholder role (i.e. owner, banker, employee, customer) in determining the type of mission and the form of the organization's more detailed objectives. However, the Systemic school of strategic theorists (see end of Chapter 1) emphasize that organizations and stakeholders need to be understood as part of the wider culture. Stakeholders are products of a particular culture and we therefore need to consider not just their roles, but also the values that they hold, which in turn have been fashioned by their cultural upbringing. Thus stakeholders in different cultures will hold differing values, which in turn will affect their expectations of an organization's mission.

As an example, Weiner (1981) argues that cultural values in England for much of the twentieth century have only given half-hearted support to business and profit making. He points to the development of a culture which was 'geared to the maintenance of a status quo rather than innovation, comfort rather than attainment [and] the civilised enjoyment, rather than the creation of, wealth'. This may be contrasted with the cultural values of the United States, where the capitalist ethic has been much more closely embraced and where making profits has been seen as a worthy aim. In England, according to Weiner, profits were viewed with distinct ambivalence. Under this reading of cultural differences, US organizations would have had clear profit-focused missions, whilst their UK counterparts would have had missions which were more socially conscious.

Of course, culture itself is not static and one of Mrs Thatcher's key aims for the UK in the 1980s was to create 'an enterprise culture'. This was a culture in which profit and enterprise would flourish. Taxation, legislation to curb union power and enterprise training in education were all used as part of the campaign to foster this culture.

The Savoy case study epitomizes this cultural transition in England. The values of the 'old guard' can be clearly located within Weiner's pre-1980 cultural norms which valued the status quo, comfort and civilized enjoyment. The values of the 'new guard' are more closely aligned with innovation, attainment and the creation of wealth – the hallmarks of the enterprise culture.

Business culture varies considerably between different countries. Japanese business practices are closely identified with the concept of *kaizen* or continual improvement, as well as having a comprehensive approach to the long-term care of employees. Business in some parts of Latin America suffers from 'the mañana culture' which describes an unhurried world where action can be postponed until tomorrow. Eastern European countries such as Romania retain lengthy bureaucratic procedures for business transactions. This is evident in the tourism sector in long queues at Bucharest airport for immigration clearance, as well as the near impossibility of hiring ski equipment for the independent traveller. Chinese business is still under the influence of attitudes of indifference which were a characteristic of state-run enterprises. The existence of shortages and hoards of customers do little to encourage a culture of customer service in China.

Cultural variance between countries in which tourism organizations operate can be understood by reference to differences in:

- attitudes to authority
- attitudes to work and leisure
- beliefs – religion, materialism

- traditions
- individual goals
- community goals
- definitions of good and bad, worthy and unworthy (moral and ethical system)
- sources of status.

and cultural norms are transmitted by and changed by:

- the family
- education
- mass media
- the arts
- government.

Stakeholders will tend to adopt values indifferent in different countries as the above influences vary from culture to culture, and research studies have been carried out into the effects of different national cultures on organizations (Schneider 1989; Schneider and Meyer 1991).

Individuals who work for organizations may also have their values coloured by membership of specific groups, such as political parties, or interest groups such as Greenpeace. Tourism organizations may find their values tempered by membership of professional bodies such as the Association of British Travel Agents (ABTA), or the International Hoteliers Association (IHA).

Organizational culture

It is also useful to consider culture at the organizational level.

Organizational culture refers to organizational beliefs, values and attitudes (Schein 1985; Martin and Siehl 1983). It describes how the way things are done in a particular organization and forms the basis for the rules of acceptable and unacceptable behaviour. Organizational culture is thus the arbiter of organizational norms and it therefore acts as a powerful force in encouraging or frustrating the emergence of new missions and strategies. This is particularly so where culture is deeply embedded.

The term cultural web (Johnson and Scholes 1993) is a useful device for highlighting the different strands of an organization's culture, symbols, rituals, stories and power, which add up to a paradigm – an agreed way of going about things. Figure 2.8 illustrates a cultural web for the Savoy, pre-1994.

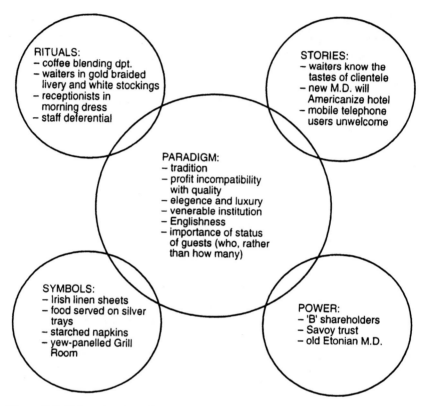

Figure 2.8 Cultural web at the Savoy Hotel (pre-1994) (Adapted from Johnson and Scholes 1993)

At this period the culture of the Savoy was deeply embedded, and each part of the cultural web supported and reflected the paradigm, which was that tradition should determine the way things are done. Now the more deeply embedded a culture is, the more self-perpetuating it will become and the less open to change or challenge. Factors such as continuity of management (Mr Shepard had been managing director for 15 years, and Mr Pajares was only the sixth managing director in the 100 year history of the Savoy) and low staff turnover ensured a deeply embedded culture at the Savoy, and recruitment policy would seek to perpetuate the existing culture by choosing new staff who fitted the existing culture. Training would also inculcate the existing culture.

Organizational culture also acts as a pair of cultural spectacles through which an organization interprets its environment. It is useful to be aware of this cultural bias in the way that organizations view things and the Savoy case illustrates the point well. The new managing director, Mr Pajares, is seen in a completely different way when viewed through the cultural spectacles of the old Savoy paradigm as compared with the paradigm of the Forte group. Thus the old Savoy paradigm sees largely negative qualities in him such as lack of aesthetic taste (by their definition), lack of Englishness (Mr Pajares was born in Barcelona, Spain), and a threat to standards and the status quo. On the other hand, the Forte group paradigm sees Mr Pajares' positive qualities such as his experience, his success in making the Four Seasons a highly profitable hotel group, and his seeking to improve occupancy rates and reduce costs. Figure 2.9 illustrates these contrasting views.

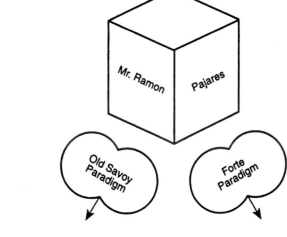

– lacking aesthetic judgement
– un-Englishness
– threat to standards
– threat to status quo

UNSUITABLE

– international experience
– previous success
– seeks cost reductions
– seeks improved occupancy

SUITABLE

Figure 2.9 Different views seen through different cultural spectacles

Miles and Snow (1978) distinguish between defender types, and prospector types of cultures in organizations. Their characteristics are summarized in Table 2.2.

Table 2.2 Defender and prospector type cultures

Defenders	Prospectors
● conservative	● outward-looking
● seek security	● responsive to environment
● cautious	● daring
● avoid change	● opportunistic
● inflexible	● flexible
● set in their ways	● adaptive
● reactive	● proactive

Defender type cultures (as illustrated by the pre-1994 Savoy) may represent a barrier to effective corporate strategy, since by their very nature they guard the status quo and thus seek strategies not on the basis of their suitability for the future of the organization, but based on how well they fit the current paradigm. Thus they are likely to seek cautious and conservative strategies. On the other hand the very nature of a prospector type culture is its open-mindedness. Organizational culture under this type is adaptive and flexible. The culture of the Forte group falls into this category.

A difficulty for defender type cultures is that they may not be aware of the fact that there is any problem, because the problem is not visible through their particular cultural spectacles.

Finally, we can identify different cultures in organizations relating to customer service. Employee indifference to customer satisfaction is legendary on some airlines. Aeroflot are a much quoted example, where little enthusiasm is shown for selling a ticket and on-board service is sullen. At the other extreme, Scandinavian Airline Systems (SAS), under Jan Carlzon, revolutionized their employee culture by 'empowering the front line' and encouraging front line staff to solve problems rather than to take refuge in the claim that 'it's someone else's job'. Heskett et al. (1990) provide an excellent example of how the Minneapolis Marriot City Center has fostered a culture of customer care. Its management has authorized employees to spend up to $10 at their discretion to satisfy guests' complaints.

Summary

1 An organization's mission and corporate objectives describe its general aim.
2 Stakeholder analysis, which considers stakeholder power and interest, can be used to analyse the relative influence that different stakeholder groups have on the formulation of an organization's mission.
3 Thus missions may be dominated by the pursuit of profit or have other, social goals as a priority, depending on the characteristics, power and alignment of stakeholder groups.
4 The cultural values of the society in which an organization operates will also be a significant factor in fashioning stakeholder expectations and organizational goals.
5 Organizations themselves display a distinctive culture and this culture will also play an important part in mission articulation and strategy development.

Review questions

1 Distinguish between external and internal stakeholders in Figure 2.6. Map the key external and internal stakeholders for a tourism organization with which you are familiar.
2 Distinguish between unit objectives, corporate objectives and the mission of a named tourism organization.
3 Specify some possible corporate and unit objectives that might underpin the mission statement of the Canterbury (NZ) Tourism Council (see Figure 2.3)
4 Locate some unit objectives to complete the spaces left in Figure 2.2 for British Airways. Distinguish between those objectives which are open and closed.
5 Construct a cultural web for a tourism organization of your choice.
6 Distinguish between defender and prospector type organizational cultures. Classify tourism organizations that you know according to this typology.
7 What is the problem of cultural spectacles for organizations with defender type cultures?
8 What are SMART objectives?

Part 2: Strategic analysis

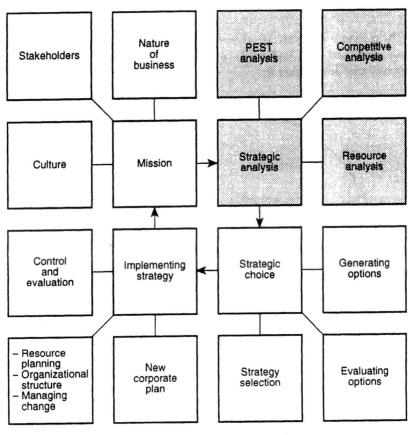

Figure 3.1 Strategic analysis in the strategic framework

The next stage of tourism corporate strategy is strategic analysis. Strategic analysis utilizes techniques for situational analysis. This involves reporting on the current and future opportunities and threats and strengths and weaknesses facing the organization.

Opportunities and threats summarize the external environmental factors that a tourism organization faces. The key elements of the external environment may be summarized as C-PEST factors which refer to the following environments:

- competitive
- political
- economic
- socio-cultural
- technological.

These external factors are shown in Figure 3.2. Of these, PEST factors are analysed in Chapter 3, whilst the competitive environment is considered in Chapter 4.

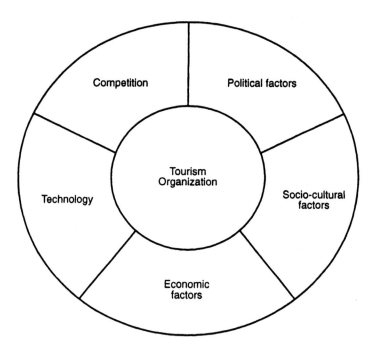

Figure 3.2 A tourism organization's external environment

Strengths and weaknesses analysis summarizes the state of the internal resources of an organization. Resource analysis is undertaken in Chapter 4.

All these factors are brought together in a comprehensive SWOT analysis at the end of Chapter 4, thus concluding strategic analysis and Part 2.

3
Analysing the external environment for tourism organizations: PEST

Chapter objectives

Chapter 1 suggested that the external environment of tourism organizations is a turbulent one. Under this reading, the external environment is characterized by the four Ds:

- dynamic
- diverse
- difficult
- dangerous.

By studying this chapter students will be able to undertake an initial analysis of the external environment. In particular they will be able to:
- distinguish between, describe and evaluate the features of the PEST (political, economic, socio-cultural and technological) environment.

The PEST environment

The political environment

The political environment is important to tourism organizations since it is here that changes in laws, regulations and policy are fashioned. It is therefore important to establish the location of political power, how political power may change in the future and the likely effects of this on policy. It is also important to identify the level of the political environment in which a tourism organization is working. For example, a tour operator situated in Belgium will face a political environment at local government level, at national government level and at European Union level. Additionally it will have to operate in the different political environments of the destination countries of its tours.

In democratic countries, therefore, it is instructive to know when the next election will take place, the alternative manifestos of competing parties, and the likelihood and implications of a change of government. Pressure group activity can also be important in influencing policy in democracies, and the activities of such groups as Greenpeace and Tourism Concern attempt to affect government policy as it relates to tourism.

In autocratic countries there is often careful monitoring of the circle of advisers of the leader in an attempt to ascertain possible successors and subsequent policy shifts.

Stability is an important factor in the political environment. Is the system of government a robust one or is it likely to be challenged and thus bring about a period of uncertainty or unpredictable change? There is also the important consideration of the extent of the government's writ. Are a country's laws generally respected or is there widespread lawlessness? This may be an important factor for tour operators who offer travel programmes in some parts of the world.

Opportunities and threats in the changing political environment

The following examples illustrate the effects of changes in the political environment on tourism organizations:

- The changing political environment has had a profound effect on the aims and mission of British Airways. Formerly a government owned airline, it was privatized in 1987 as part of the Conservative government's widespread privatization programme.
- The German airline, Lufthansa was also privatized in 1994 and, along with SAS (Scandinavia) and KLM (Holland), they now receive no state subsidy.
- Airlines such as Sabena (Belgium), Iberia (Spain), TAP (Portugal) and Air France are still in the public sector and have received

considerable amounts of state aid, but EU policy is now to ban state subsidy which it is felt allows unfair competition.

- The EU Trans-European Network (TEN) plans show a heavy bias towards rail travel and eighty per cent of the TEN budget is allocated to rail projects. Thus road and air transport face discrimination in European transport policy.
- In the United States, the 1980s saw the policy of deregulation of airlines. This made it easier for new airlines to set up and exposed the market to intense competition.
- The Gambia, in Africa, was a growing destination for winter-sun seekers from Europe until President Jawara was removed in a coup in 1994. This resulted in the British foreign office advising tourists to avoid the country and all but one UK holiday operator cancelled their programmes.
- The IRA cease-fire announced on 31 August 1994 led to an immediate increase in overseas tourists from Great Britain, Eire, North America and continental Europe. Visitor numbers for the first half of 1995 increased by 56 per cent compared to the same period in 1994, to a total of 156,000. The Northern Ireland Tourist Board aims that tourism should contribute 6 per cent to GDP by the year 2000 and calculates that 80 new hotels need to be built to provide 3,500 additional rooms.
- The separist Kurdistan Workers Party (PKK) is campaigning for an independent state within Turkey and a campaign of bombings has led to tourist injuries.
- In Peru, the arrest of the leader of the Shining Path guerrilla movement has lead to a reduction of terrorist incidents in the main areas of the country.
- Egypt suffered a steep decline in tourist arrivals in the mid 1990s as Muslim fundamentalists carried out a series of attacks on targets which included tourists.
- The ending of apartheid in South Africa has caused a sudden reversal in the country's tourism fortunes. From a position of isolation under the apartheid regime, it has become one of the world's fastest-growing holiday destinations. In 1995 an increase of about 100,000 visitors to South Africa over 1994 brought the total to around 800,000. The South African Tourist Board (Satour) forecasts an average rate of 15 per cent a year increase in foreign arrivals to the year 2000, with a doubling of foreign exchange from tourism.
- The transition of government of Hong Kong from the UK to China

has been a period of considerable uncertainty for tourism organizations operating in that area. The uncertainty has been exacerbated by the age and poor health of the Chinese leader and questions about possible policy directions of his successor.

- The Gulf war and the war in former Yugoslavia both had significant impacts in tourist movements. The former in particular led to a reduction in North American tourists to Europe.

The consequences of a change in government

Changes in government can bring about profound change to the political environment. For example, the Thatcher years in the UK and the Reagan years in the US signalled a turn to the political right in both countries and a radical package of new policies with less state intervention, lower tax rates, less government spending and an emphasis on private enterprise and profitability. Table 3.1 distinguishes between policy objectives of typical political parties of the left and of the right. The actual manifestos, speeches and policy documents of political parties can give a clearer guide to the consequences for a particular tourism organization of the electoral success of a particular party.

The economic environment

The economic environment affects different types of tourism organizations in different ways and examples of this are illustrated in Case Study C.

Table 3.1 Key differences between political parties

Left wing (e.g. Labour/Democrat parties)	Right wing (e.g. Conservative/Republican parties)
• need to control the free market	• belief in supremacy of the free market
• pro trade unions	• anti trade unions
• some state ownership of industry	• private ownership of industry
• progressive taxation	• proportional taxation
• regulation of industry	• minimal state interference
• higher government spending and taxes	• low taxes and government spending
• reduce inequality of incomes	• inequality of income as incentive
• provision of jobs a priority	• control of inflation a priority
• comprehensive welfare state	• minimal welfare state

Case Study C: The economic environment and tourism organizations

Disneyland, Paris

While we initially expected lower real interest rates . . . the impact of severe economic recession on tourism in France, combined with highly unfavourable exchange rates during the 1993 peak season . . . has resulted in lower guest spending and excessive interest costs.

(Source: Euro Disney SCA report 1993)

The economic environment although improving remains difficult, particularly in our industry . . . The continued lack of growth in European consumer spending, volatile and high short term interest rates and instability in the global currency markets remain important areas of uncertainty.

(Source: Euro Disney SCA report 1995)

Holiday boom in Asia

The World Travel and Tourism Council is predicting a rise in tourism output (tourism consumer spending plus tourism investment spending) in the Asia-Pacific region, from $800 billion in 1995 to $2 trillion in 2005.

Already, hotel operators are expanding their investments to share in this growing market. These include the Accor group (French, with brand names Novotel, Ibis and Mercure), Best Western and Choice hotels (American), Golden Tulip (Dutch), Forte (British), Inter-Continental (Japanese) and Hong Kong's Shangri-La group, operators of the Traders hotels.

(Source: WTTC/Press reports)

Eurotunnel

Eurotunnel's debt mountain had risen to £8 billion by 1995, which meant £2 million per day payments in interest charges before the company managed to negotiate an 18 month moratorium on payments.

Case Study C (*continued*)

The delay in opening the tunnel and disappointing sales revenues were both contributory factors to the growing mountain of debt, but is also reported that half of Eurotunnel's sterling borrowings are exposed to variable interest rates.

(Source: Press reports)

Korean Air and Asiana Results – 1994

South Korea's two rival airlines – Korean Air and Asiana – reported record profits in 1994. Net earnings in 1994 for Asiana were Won2.2bn ($3m) whilst those for Korean Air rose by 215 per cent to Won36.9bn ($48m).

As the South Korean economy continued to boom, Seoul's Kimpo airport became the world's fastest growing, with a 20 per cent increase in passenger traffic.

Both airlines recorded load factors of 67 per cent with predictions for 70 per cent loadings for 1995.

Results:

Year	Sales Won bn	Net profit Won bn
Korean Air		
1989	1,558	+31.9
1990	1,679	−7.8
1991	2,009	+16.0
1992	2,338	+1.2
1993	2,701	+11.8
1994	3,058	+36.9
Asiana		
1989	42.4	−31.4
1990	108.0	−46.2
1991	210.4	−35.6
1992	343.4	−45.6
1993	500.1	−51.5
1994	697.4	+2.2

(Source: Company reports)

Case Study C *continued*)

Torremolinos

Torremolinos, on the Mediterranean coast of Spain, is an international resort destination. Its main visitors come from Spain, the UK, France, Germany, the Benelux countries and Scandinavia. Records of visitors to Malaga province for the 1980s and 1990s show its mixed fortunes in attracting overseas visitors. Visitors from the UK, Scandinavia, Benelux and Germany all fell back in 1980. There was some recovery by the mid 1980s, but by 1991 quite a steep decline in visitor numbers from the UK, Germany and the Benelux countries had occurred again. Fortunately this latter decline was offset by an increase in domestic tourists. (Source: Pollard and Rodriguez 1993)

The success of an international tourism destination such as Torremolinos, Spain, will be affected by economic fluctuations in those countries which supply the majority of its visitors (tourism generating countries), as well as its economic attractiveness compared to competitive resorts. In line with this, national tourism organizations will seek to market destinations in countries whose economies are expanding. Of course, national tourism organizations themselves are often funded by the government and are therefore directly affected by government spending decisions.

Tour operators such as Kuoni (Switzerland) and Thomson (UK), face a number of economic environments. First, the domestic economic environment affects the expenditure patterns of their clients. Second, the variety of different international economic environments in which tourism is located affect the supply of the tourism package.

Providers of tourism services will find the international economic environment affects the demand for their services and the costs of supplying those services. Examples of services include hotels such as Best Western (USA) and Inter-Continental (Japan), transport operators such as Eurotunnel (UK/France) and Korean Air (South Korea) and attraction owners such as Disneyland, Paris (USA/France).

The key factors in the economic environment which affect tourism organizations are now set out before considering examples of how they affect particular types of tourism organizations:

- Economic growth – a measure of how much better (or worse) off a country is in economic terms over a period of time. It is defined more precisely as the increase in real output per capita of a country and often measured by Gross Domestic Product (GDP).
- Consumers' expenditure – the amount of money consumers actually spend. It is mainly determined by income level, but is affected by savings, taxation and government benefit payments, consumer credit and expectations about the future. We are interested in 'real consumer expenditure', or 'expenditure at constant prices' which is expenditure that has been adjusted to remove any changes which are just due to inflation.
- Investment expenditure – expenditure on capital goods such as hotel construction, aircraft and port facilities.
- Government expenditure.
- Exchange rates – the value of a country's currency in terms of other currencies.
- Interest rates – the cost of borrowing.
- Taxation – including taxes on income, spending and profits.
- Inflation – the change in the general level of prices.
- Unemployment – the number of people without jobs.

Tourism destinations, NTOs and the economic environment

Figure 3.3 shows how a tourism destination such as Torremolinos is affected by the international economic environment. In general terms it can be seen that the number of visitors to Torremolinos will be affected by changes in economic growth and consumers' expenditure in the tourist generating economies of its visitors.

Figure 3.4 traces changes in economic growth, as measured by GDP, for the UK, Germany and France over an 11 year period. These countries enjoyed economic growth in the late 1980s and during this period, growth led to rising consumer expenditure. It can be seen, however, that the UK moved into recession in 1990, followed by Germany and France in 1992, so consumers reduced their overall spending during at this time. A recession is defined as two successive quarters of falling output. The overall period of recession is shown by the arrow in the figure.

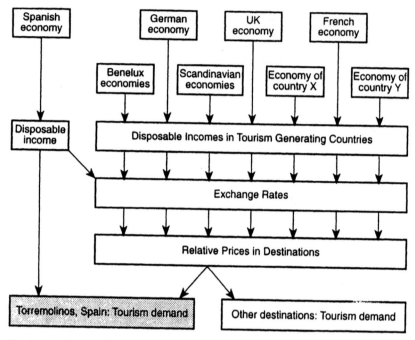

Figure 3.3 Economic environment of a tourism destination

However, tourists from abroad are also interested in the exchange rate, for this will affect their spending power in their destination country. Figure 3.5 plots the exchange rate of the peseta against the pound sterling. It can be seen that the UK economic environment posed a double threat to Spanish tourism in 1992 – not only was the UK suffering from a recession but the exchange rate against the peseta was at a low point, making Spain seem more expensive to UK tourists.

So, the fortunes of tourist destinations are closely tied with those of its tourism generating countries, and the exchange rate plays an important role too. The price level and inflation rate are also significant, since a combination of high inflation and a rising exchange rate can make a destination less attractive than its overseas competitors where such factors might be more favourable. This factor is shown in Figure 3.3 as 'other destinations' which can win over tourists in the face of more competitive exchange rates and domestic price levels.

It is therefore important for destinations, and the national and

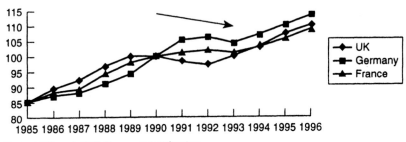

Note: 1995 and 1996 figures are estimates

Figure 3.4 Index of gross domestic product at constant prices (1990 = 100) (*Sources*: OECD; World Bank)

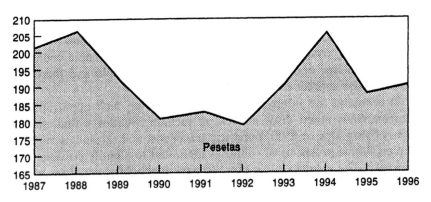

Note: 1996 figure is an estimate

Figure 3.5 Exchange rate: pesetas per pound sterling (*Source*: Barclays Economic Review)

regional tourism organizations which market destinations, to keep a careful watch on:

- economic growth
- consumers' expenditure
- exchange rates
- inflation.

Table 3.2 shows the arrivals of tourists from different generating countries at Malaga Airport (1990–1994), which gives a close approximation for visitors to Torremolinos. The fluctuations in the figures clearly

Table 3.2 Tourist arrivals at Malaga airport (*Source*: Malaga airport)

Country	1990	1991	1992	1993	1994
Germany	173,361	176,677	165,622	194,088	229,678
France	93,972	115,025	126,552	105,753	128,078
Holland	101,623	75,737	80,041	77,901	108,678
UK	765,519	760,715	838,461	882,587	1,039,358

reflect the changes in the economic conditions in tourism generating countries as well as changes in the exchange rates.

Figure 3.3, however, suggests that this scanning of the economic environment can alert destinations not only to opportunities and threats in existing markets, but also to opportunities emerging in new markets. In the figure, country X and country Y are used to denote countries where economic conditions might be more favourable and therefore possible new sources of tourists.

In scanning the international environment for such opportunities, Torremolinos might draw a circle to include counties within, say, 3 hours flying time or $500 round trip travel cost and carefully scrutinize the economic prospects of countries identified to identify possible new markets. The results of this exercise have highlighted countries which were part of the former USSR as being important new tourism generators for Torremolinos.

Of course, a tourist destination should not ignore its home market. The economy of Spain has achieved average growth of around 3 per cent per annum (1980–1992) (World Bank, yearly) and is now ranked as a high-income country by the World Bank. Its own population therefore provides a growing source of tourism income. Its more recent economic performance is illustrated in Table 3.3.

Finally in this section, it should be noted that national tourism organizations are generally funded by governments. Thus an important consideration in their operating environment is government spending plans. The English Tourist Board, for example, had its government grant cut from £13.9 million in 1993/94 to £11.3 million in 1994/95. Whilst the British Tourist Authority's grant over the same period remained unchanged, exchange rate movements and the falling pound led to a loss of £2 million in overseas spending power of its budget.

Tour operators and the economic environment

Tour operators are exposed to a variety of economic environments. They face an additional problem of time lags in matching booked capacity and holiday sales. We may classify their activities into client sales and purchase of tour components. Figure 3.6 illustrates some of the key factors in the external environment of a tour operator.

On the demand side a tour operator is selling to clients. The key variable influencing the level of sales will be the level of overall consumer expenditure. This in turn will be affected by earnings, taxes, and expectations about the future (if clients fear unemployment, their spending decisions will be more cautious). Interest rates will affect different groups of clients in different ways. Younger ones are more likely to have mortgage debt, whilst older ones are more likely to have savings. Thus a rise in interest rates will tend to stimulate expenditure of older groups and curb the expenditure of younger groups. Changes in the exchange rate will also alter patterns of consumer expenditure as different destinations become attractive due to weak currencies.

A tour operator's clients are not necessarily confined to one country and so expenditure data will need to be analysed for the main countries in which its clients reside. This is represented by countries A and B in the figure.

The tour operator itself will be affected by interest rate changes where capital is borrowed, and changes in company taxation will also affect it.

On the supply side, tour operators will find the costs they incur for transportation and accommodation affected by general inflationary pressures (wage levels and raw materials costs), as well as changes in interest rates and taxes. Where supplies are purchased from overseas, the exchange rate will also be significant. Since tour operators generally operate in a number of countries, economic data must be sought from these countries as represented by countries X and Y in the figure.

Tourism service providers and the economic environment

Figure 3.6 can also be used to analyse the economic environment for a tourism service provider, replacing the square marked tour operator with hospitality provider, attraction, or transport operator. Thus we can consider the effects of the economic environment on the fortunes of those organizations identified in Case Study C.

It is interesting to note that the economic environment differs from

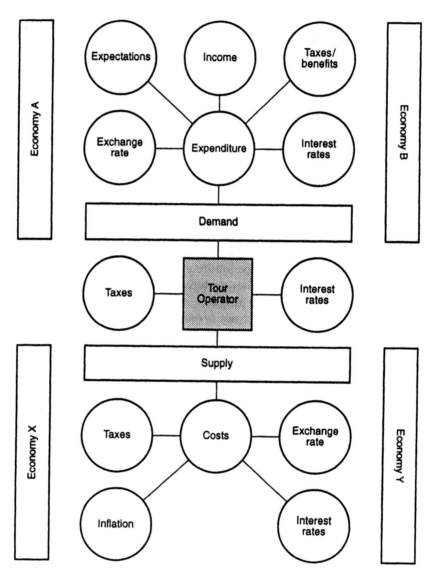

Figure 3.6 The economic environment of tour operators

one part of the world to the next and Table 3.3 compares growth rates in North America, South America, Europe and Asia for the period 1980–1997. Taking economic growth first, whilst Disneyland, Paris bemoans the lack of growth of consumer spending in Europe (confirmed by the data in Figure 3.4), growth prospects in Asia during the same period are very different. This means that domestic tourism organizations can benefit from increased sales (e.g. Korean Air and Asiana) and international organizations (e.g. Best Western and Inter-Continental hotels) are attracted to invest in the area.

China in particular has witnessed rapid economic growth, and with a population of 1.1 billion it is set to become a leading global economy in the twenty first century. Notice also the rapid growth of the economy of South Korea which is mirrored in the sales of Korean Air and Asiana. Hong Kong, Malaysia, Singapore and Thailand have also shown very strong growth in recent years whereas mature economies such as the US grew at a much more modest pace. It should be noted that economic

Table 3.3 Economic growth in selected economies (*Sources*: OECD, World Bank, Barclays Economic Review)

Country	GNP per capita ($) 1993	Average % growth in GDP pa					
		1980–1992	1993	1994	1995	1996	1997
China	460	7.6	13.0	11.8	10.0	9.0	8.5
Singapore	19,850	5.3	9.9	10.1	8.5	7.5	7.0
Thailand	2,110	6.0	7.8	8.5	8.8	8.5	7.3
Malaysia	3,140	3.2	8.5	8.7	8.5	8.2	8.0
S. Korea	7,660	8.5	5.8	8.4	8.5	7.0	7.0
Hong Kong	19,330	5.5	5.8	5.5	5.5	5.0	4.0
Argentina	7,220	–0.9	6.1	6.5	1.0	2.5	2.5
Brazil	2,930	0.4	5.3	5.7	4.5	4.0	4.0
Chile	3,170	3.7	6.3	4.4	4.8	5.0	6.0
Columbia	1,400	1.4	4.6	5.3	5.5	5.5	4.0
Peru	1,490	–2.8	7.0	12.5	8.0	6.0	3.5
Venezuela	2,840	–0.8	–1.1	–3.3	–1.0	1.0	1.7
UK	18,060	2.4	2.2	3.8	3.4	3.0	3.5
Germany	23,560	2.4	–1.1	2.9	2.9	2.7	2.5
France	22,490	1.7	–1.5	2.7	3.0	3.2	2.5
Spain	13,590	2.9	–1.1	2.0	3.0	3.2	2.8
US	24,740	1.7	3.1	4.1	3.2	2.3	2.5

Notes: Figures for 1995, 1996 and 1997 are estimates

growth figures by themselves may give a distorted view of the marketing prospects for a particular country. It is important to see what level of economic development a country is growing from. Therefore figures for GNP per capita are also included in Table 3.3. This puts China's growth in a more sober perspective. Since average income starts at a low point, even high levels of growth mean that the average consumer will not have an income on a par with those in developed countries for some years.

Interest rates are cited as problematic for Eurotunnel and Disneyland, Paris in Case Study C. Rising interest rates posed a problem to Eurotunnel since some of its sterling debt is subject to variable interest rates. Figure 3.7 shows just how volatile UK interest rates have been in recent years. A rise in interest rates to the levels of 15 per cent recorded in 1989 adds a significant burden to the costs of a heavily indebted organization. High interest rates can also affect the demand for attractions such as Disneyland. Consumers with mortgages have less money to spend, credit becomes less attractive and there is more incentive to save – all three factors tending to depress consumer spending.

Exchange rates have also been problematic for Disneyland, Paris. The French franc stood at £1 = FF9.32 when Euro Disney opened in 1992. But the value of the pound had fallen to £1 = FF7.75 by 1995. This meant that Disneyland prices seemed 16 per cent more expensive to an English visitor just because of currency fluctuations, a factor which would certainly depress demand.

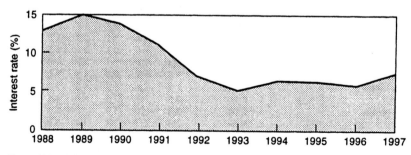

Note: 1996 and 1997 figures are estimates

Figure 3.7 UK interest rates (2 month interbank) (*Source*: Barclays Economic Review)

The socio-cultural environment

Factors in the socio-cultural environment of tourism organizations include the size and structure of the population, social class and attitudes and values.

Demographics

Demographics is the study of population and population is significant to tourism organizations for two reasons. First, the population is a key factor influencing the demand for tourism services. Second, the labour force which supplies tourism organizations is derived from the population. So, for example, a country with a large population represents a potential market for tourism services and one where economies of scale may be achieved. The age distribution of the population is also significant. A predominantly older population will perhaps seek less physically demanding holidays and perhaps more culturally focused holidays. This might mean a reduction in the demand for skiing holidays, for example. Table 3.4 illustrates the marketing profiles for different age groups.

Table 3.4 Tourism marketing profiles for different age groups

Life stage	Characteristics	Tourism income	Tourism time
Child	Tourism decisions generally taken by parent	Low	High
Bachelor	High propensity for travel. Independence asserted, budget travel popular, social aspects sought	Medium	Medium
Partnered	High tourism propensities underpinned by high income and free time	High	Medium
Full nest	Children become key preoccupation. Tourism must meet children's requirements. Costs per person important	Medium	Low
Empty nest	Children have left home. Opportunities for tourism increase. Exotic destinations and meaning of life sought	High	Medium
Old age	May lack partner, suffer from infirmity. Safer travel pursuits sought, package holidays popular	Low	High

Table 3.5 Population data for selected countries (*Source*: UN; World Bank)

| Country | Population (millions) | | | Annual growth 1992–2000 |
	1992	2000*	2025*	%*
China	1,162	1,255	1,471	1.0
Singapore	3	3	4	1.4
Thailand	58	65	81	1.3
Malaysia	19	22	30	2.0
S. Korea	44	47	53	0.8
Hong Kong	6	6	6	0.6
Argentina	33	36	43	1.0
Brazil	154	172	224	1.4
Chile	14	15	19	1.3
Columbia	33	37	49	1.4
Peru	22	26	36	1.8
Venezuela	20	24	34	2.2
UK	58	59	61	0.2
Germany	81	81	75	0.1
France	57	59	63	0.4
Spain	39	39	38	0.0
US	255	276	323	1.0

Note: * = estimate

   Similarly an ageing population will present different problems for training, as a labour force, than a young population. Table 3.5 illustrates population data for selected countries. Note that China's population exceeds one billion but that its growth rate has slowed down. In contrast, the populations of Malaysia, Venezuela and Peru are forecast to grow considerably. Note also that the German population is forecast to fall in the next century.

Inter-cultural differences

There are important cultural differences between different client groups of tourists. Thus if economic change demands a change in tourism marketing to new groups, the cultural differences of such groups need to be identified and addressed. For example, the alcohol aspect of tourism which is so important to the north European male is a religious taboo for Muslims. Whilst sun-based holidays are an attraction for many North American and North European tourists, it is not so for other groups. For example, the most important motivation for travel for the Japanese is to enjoy nature and scenery, whilst for Eastern European tourists visiting friends and relatives is the priority. European groups appreciate dining facilities al fresco in warm destinations. Asian groups expect air conditioned restaurants. In Bali, where Europeans want discos, Chinese, Koreans and Japanese want karaoke bars. European travellers to China often seek to get off the beaten track. The Chinese seek out crowded places since they equate popularity with quality in an attraction.

Other socio-cultural changes

The work of Greenpeace, Tourism Concern, Friends of the Earth and similar environmental groups continues to raise the public consciousness of the harmful environmental effects of economic growth and development. Changing attitudes to the environment may mean that tourists, on the demand side and host communities on the supply side, demand higher standards of impact containment.

The increased concern for healthy lifestyles means that tourists are becoming more cautious about sun-worship holidays. Scientific evidence points up the undesirable effects of exposure to the sun which include increased risk of skin cancer and premature ageing. The destruction of the ozone layer adds weight to these concerns.

Social class

Changes in the duration of paid holidays and hours worked will affect demand for tourism. Europeans have comparatively generous holiday entitlement, whereas two weeks' paid leave is common in the United States and Japan. This may help account for the fact that only one in ten Japanese travel abroad compared to one in two Britons. China has recently introduced a 5 day week thus extending the opportunities for travel. Currently, only 0.25 per cent of Chinese travel, 2 per cent of Thais and 5 per cent of Koreans. An increase in the Chinese travel rate to 1 per cent would generate 9 million extra tourists in the Asia region. Continued economic development in the Asian Pacific rim region suggests that travel rates for these countries will increase substantially.

Factors such as income distribution and unemployment can be important influences. Although for many countries average living standards have increased, this has often happened in an unequal way. Those who are unemployed or who rely solely on state benefits have generally not benefited from the fruits of economic growth. In some countries this has led to the development of an economic underclass – for example those living in shanty towns in Peru and Bolivia and those living on the streets in London and New York. This clearly poses a threat to such places as tourism destinations. Tourists to Peru are advised to line their handbags with chicken wire to stop them being slit open – hardly an alluring image for attracting tourists. Florida had a spell of very bad publicity in the early 1990s when tourists were murdered during robberies.

The term 'Generation X' has been used to describe a lost generation of youth emerging in the US who have refused to buy into the American dream and reject the cultural norms of 'work hard and play hard'.

Tourists are becoming more educated in, and assertive at obtaining, their rights as consumers. This may be underpinned by consumer rights legislation and, for example, a recent change to EU law has made tour operators liable for the provision of services (such as flights or hotels, or excursions) which are contracted from a third party.

'New Tourists'

Poon (1993) identified a change in values between 'Old Tourists' and 'New Tourists'. Her thesis suggests that tourism organizations need to be aware of the opportunities and threats resulting from this change in tourists' values, attitudes and aspirations.

Old Tourists are characterized by Poon as follows. They find security in large groups and seek a yearly pre-packaged tour to destinations which are not important in themselves but because of their location by the sea and in the sun. They see themselves as culturally superior to their hosts and demand home cooking and home facilities abroad. They often cause high impacts and are seeking relaxation.

On the other hand New Tourists avoid large groups and want something different. They travel more often and more spontaneously to destinations which are chosen because of their differentness from home. The differentness is sought and encouraged and they adapt their behaviour to fit in. They want to experience local cuisine and local life and understand a destination's culture and heritage. They are environmentally sensitive and are seeking new experiences. Figure 3.8 summarizes the key elements of this transformation.

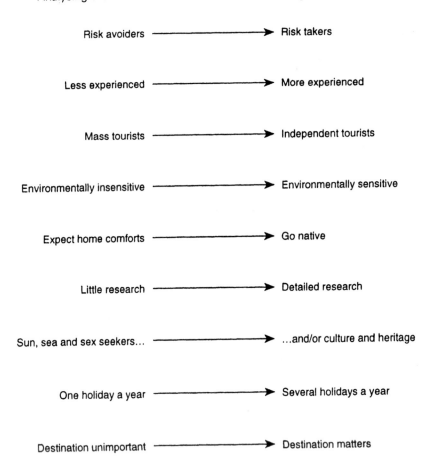

Figure 3.8 New Tourists (adapted from Poon 1993)

The technological environment

The technological environment offers both opportunities and threats to tourism organizations. The opportunities resulting from technological development may be found in cheaper provision, or improvements in goods and services or in better marketing. However, technology may result in an organization's product or service becoming obsolete, or subject to new forms of competition.

Computerized Reservation Systems

Case Study D: Computerized Reservation Systems

Sabre is the market leader in CRS – computerized reservation systems. It is owned by American Airlines and run from Tulsa, Oklahoma. By 1995, Sabre had reservation terminals in 26,000 travel shops in 184 countries and was processing up to 150 million requests a day.

A CRS is a system which links distant terminals to a centralized database and in Sabre's case allows booking primarily of air travel, car hire and hotel accommodation. Sabre's main competitor is Galileo, owned by a consortium of airlines headed by United and British Airways. There are clear advantages of such a system to travel agents who can offer a faster and better service to clients. CRS is also an important marketing tool for the organizations who use it to sell their services.

Tour operators have also developed CRS. In the UK, Thomson developed its own computerized booking system, which accounted for 85 per cent of agency bookings by 1985. By 1986, Thomson was able to withdraw telephone booking facilities to agencies and take advantage of productivity savings offered by its CRS. These are illustrated by the fact that an increase in passengers from 800,000 to 2.5 million between 1978 and 1986 was handled with no increase in reservations staff.

However, CRS continues to develop and its initial opportunity to travel agents may well turn into a threat. Developments in IT are fourfold. First, PCs are becoming more and more powerful and cheaper. Second, communication links between PCs are developing. Fibre optics and the digitalization of information mean that information can be cheaply exchanged at a global level. Third, the Internet has raised user consciousness of the potential uses of the PC. Fourth, the development of multi-media means that on-screen information is more interesting. For example, Sabrevision includes video footage and pictures of destinations to its CRS.

Thus new technology is set to link sellers directly with buyers and cut out the retailer, or the travel agent. CompuServe offers

Case Study D (*continued*)

access to Sabre to home subscribers. Holiday Inn has introduced a credit card booking service to the Internet. In France, the Mintel system of networked home computers is used to book over 40 per cent of travel reservations. In 1995, United Airlines and Microsoft entered into an agreement to provide an on-line travel service to turn PCs into 'desktop travel systems' where holidays, tickets, hotels and car rentals can all be booked from home.

The new system, United Connections was available to 75,000 of the airlines frequent flyers by 1996 and used to book two per cent of United's total flights. Mark Koehler, United's director of electronic distribution said, 'You put your floppy disc or CD-Rom into your computer and think of yourself as your own travel agent. The system allows you to choose flights and fares – not just on United – book your flight and your hotel room, hire car and whatever. All in real time.'

These developments seek to exploit a market which is estimated to be worth $21 billion a year This represents the expenditure by Internet users on air fares in 1995 according to CIC Research (a US Travel Consultancy). American Airlines launched a similar system in 1996 prompting a spokesman for the Association of British Travel Agents (ABTA) to say: 'It is potentially a real threat to travel agents.'

However, travel agents such as Going Places (UK) have responded to this threat by displaying package holidays on the Internet. Their brochure pages offer video images on resorts, tips on what clothing to take and details such as local prices. Customers can book directly through their PC using a credit card.

Case Study D shows that as computer reservation systems (CRS) develop, their associated opportunities and threats change. The first wave of development is clearly distinguishable from the second wave. In the first wave, CRS offered clear opportunities to travel agents. Labour costs in bookings could be saved and customers could be offered an improved booking service. However, the continued development of CRS may pose a significant threat. The development of the Internet means that suppliers can directly access their customers with the possibility that the agent's role will be redundant.

However, CRS continues to offer opportunities both for the providers of the service (SABRE is now more profitable to American Airlines than transportation) and subscribers to the services. Booking costs are reduced, marketing opportunities can be exploited and suppliers can build up useful profiles of their customers.

Other information technology changes

Gamble (1991) identified different stages of information technology usage in hotels. The clerical and administrative stages utilize IT for stock control, reservations, accounts and payroll. The tactical stage, however, harnesses developments in IT for activities such as yield management. Yield management uses records of room utilizations to suggest prices to maximize the yield for a given unit and thus allows variable charges to be made based upon a view of what the market will bear.

The hotel sector demonstrates a range of recent uses of IT to provide opportunities for better marketing. These include rapid registration and billing, smart keys, energy management systems and security management systems. In France the Hotel Première Classe, has taken IT to its current limits to provide a low price chain of hotels. Registration, key issue (a PIN number) and check-out are entirely automated, and bathrooms are cleaned automatically, resulting in lower costs and prices.

Technology also poses some possible threats to hotels and transportation in the form of video and computer conferencing. The development of this technology means that it is possible for conferences to take place without participants leaving their homes or offices, thus posing a possible threat to this lucrative source of income.

IT developments in virtual reality (VR) are bringing new opportunities to tourism. VR uses improved visuals (through 3-D vision), immersion (by making the participant the centre of things) and interactivity, to enhance the sense of 'being there'. Williams and Hobson (1995) analyse the effects of VR on tourism under three categories. First, the creation of virtual theme parks, second the use of VR as a sales and promotional tool and third, the creation of artificial tourism.

For example, Sega are developing theme parks in Japan with interactive attractions which will let people shoot and steer their way through adventures which appear to be real and have some 50 virtual theme parks planned for the Asian Pacific Rim by 1997. In Washington DC, Disney is planning to utilize virtual reality in its heritage theme park. Through utilization of this technology, visitors can have a virtual experience of life as a civil war soldier, or life as a slave. The future interpretation of heritage may well rely less on exhibits in glass cases and more on participation and interaction with virtual artefacts and virtual historical figures.

Other changes in technology relating to tourism

Technological change in transportation has generally led to faster and cheaper services. In air transport, jet travel and cheap fuel were the original drivers of mass tourism. The development of jumbo and super jumbo jets has resulted in a long-term reduction in the real price of air travel, as airlines have passed on the benefits of economies of scale to consumers.

Rail travel has also benefited from technological change, particularly in France and Japan. For example, the TGV, France's high speed train, has cut the journey time from Paris to Lyon to under 2 hours. The Channel Tunnel has added a new route between France and England.

These changes all have their opportunities and threats. Cheap mass air transportation has extended the frontiers of holiday destinations. In terms of European tourists, this may pose a threat to traditional destinations such as Spain, as cheaper fares allow tourists access to more distant destinations, for the same expenditure.

Summary

PEST analysis provides a framework for tourism organizations to analyse opportunities and threats as part of their external operating environment. The key factors are summarized in Table 3.6.

One of the outcomes of PEST environmental analysis is scenario planning. This is a technique, pioneered by Shell and the Organization for Economic Co-operation and Development (OECD), which sets out a number of different possible scenarios that might unfold in the external PEST environment. The point about scenario planning is that a proactive organization should plan ahead and have considered a range of strategies suitable to deal with different possible scenarios. McRae (1994) undertook an ambitious project in his book *The World in 2020*.

Table 3.6 Summary of PEST features

Political	Economic
● party politics	● economic growth
● political stability	● consumers' expenditure
● terrorism	● interest rates
● laws	● taxes
● regulations	● exchange rates
● change of government	● investment expenditure
	● government spending
	● unemployment
	● inflation
	● budget policy

Socio-cultural	Technological
● population growth	● IT development
● age structure	● communications development
● leisure time	● software development
● income distribution	● R & D spending
● environmentalism	● development cycles
● consumerism	● production technology
● lifestyles	
● attitudes	
● values	

In it he presents some plausible scenarios for the global PEST environment into the next century.

Review questions

1 Refer to Table 3.1. How would a change in government affect a named tourism organization?

2 Outline two possible future PEST scenarios for a major airline. Examine the consequences of each one and explain which is the most likely outcome.

3 Evaluate the economic environment for a named destination, using Figure 3.3 as a framework.

4 Explain how recent changes in
   (a) exchange rates
   (b) consumers' expenditure
   (c) taxation
   (d) interest rates
have affected the business of a named tour operator.
What other economic factors are relevant?

5 To what extent do you agree with Poon's (1993) hypothesis of 'New Tourists'? What other features might be added to the list in Figure 3.8 and how might these changes affect a major tour operator?

6 'Information Technology – opportunity or threat to the retail travel agent'. Discuss.

7 Which world markets provide the best opportunities for expansion for an international hotel group such as The Sol Group (Spain)?

8 Provide a PEST analysis for the provider of a major theme park, distinguishing between opportunities and threats.

4
Tourism organizations: competition, resources and SWOT analysis

Chapter objectives

By studying this chapter students will be able to complete their strategic analysis of tourism organizations. In particular they will be able to:

- describe and evaluate the competitive environment
- conduct a resource analysis
- summarize their strategic analysis by way of a SWOT report.

The competitive environment

The competitive environment of the tourism industry may be conceived of as the extent of influence of tourism organizations or destinations upon one another, in addition to the effects of suppliers and buyers.

The analysis of the competitive environment which follows is divided into three sections. First, the structure of the whole industry in which a tourism organization operates is examined for competitive pressures. Second, the concept of strategic group analysis is introduced to enable a tourism organization to identify its key competitors in specific markets. Third, techniques of competitor analysis are introduced so that profiles of key competitors can be constructed.

Structural analysis of an industry

An increase in competition within an industry generally leads to a loss of a firm's customers and/or a reduction in prices. Either way a reduction in profits is likely. Where an industry approaches the economists' model of perfect competition (no entry barriers, many sellers selling similar products) profits will be reduced to a level termed 'normal profits'. This is because any excess profits will attract new firms into the industry. Additional competition will cause prices, and profits, to fall until profits are no longer high enough to attract additional entrants.

Profit maximizing tourism organizations will therefore seek a position within an industry where competitive threats can be minimized and competitive opportunities exploited.

Porter's (1980) 'five forces' model is used to analyse the competitive environment. The five forces proposed by Porter are:

- the threat of new entrants
- the power of buyers
- the power of suppliers
- the threat of substitutes
- the degree of rivalry between competitors.

and these will be examined in the light of Case Study E on the US airline industry.

Case Study E: The US air industry

The early 1990s have been a disastrous period for many US airlines, with huge losses being made. Some analysts put this down to deregulation, others blame the nature of the product.

The American airline industry was deregulated in 1978. The industry then moved from a closely regulated environment, with prices and routes fixed nationally by the Civil Aeronautics Board, to an 'open skies' policy where airlines could fly between any airports at whatever price they chose.

The nature of the airline product is that airline seats are very similar, they are perishable and they have low marginal costs. The similarity of product means that customers are able to swap airlines, whilst the perishability of the product means that an

Case Study E (continued)

empty seat on a flight is a sale lost forever. The fixed costs of running an airline are high. They include aircraft depreciation costs, staff costs, access costs and fuel costs. But the marginal costs of selling a seat are very low. To fill an otherwise empty seat on an aircraft only requires a small administrative cost, a few drinks and a meal. So airlines will always be tempted to reduce prices to fill up empty seats on a flight.

This combination of freedom of entry into the industry, substitutability between services for consumers and a perishable product with low marginal costs has led to intense competition in the US skies. Some economists have applied 'core theory' to the airline industry. This refers to the conditions within some industries that makes unrestricted competition unstable.

Since deregulation, there has been a steady fall in average ticket prices. In 1994, 92 per cent of passengers bought tickets at discount prices, paying an average of 35 per cent of the full fare. There was an influx of new, low cost carriers post-1978, led by People's Express, but many airlines have gone bankrupt since deregulation. The 120 airline bankruptcies between 1978 and 1995 include large carriers such as Pan Am, Braniff and Eastern.

The larger airlines reacted to the competition by introducing 'hub and spoke' operations to cut costs and frequent flier programmes to attract customers. There was also a period of buying up of smaller operatives.

However, a new generation of low cost, no frills, carriers entered the market in the mid-nineties. These include Reno Air, Kiwi, South West and ValuJet. There are plenty of second-hand planes on the market making the start up costs of a new airline no real obstacle (but resulting in the fact that over a quarter of US planes are more than 20 years old). South West has a typical approach – it flies short haul routes between densely populated cities, uses only 737s to cut maintenance costs, has no assigned seating and charges well below its competitors' prices.

To keep costs low many of the small new players do not use CRS booking systems or issue tickets, preferring cheaper telephone bookings and allocating boarding passes as customers check in.

Case Study E (*continued*)

> Customers often have to carry their bags to planes parked in the (cheaper) fringes of airports.
>
> ValuJet has a small headquarters in a low rent office park and runs a fleet of 27 used DC9s. Its one way ticket from Jacksonville to Atlanta sells at $39, but now a new entrant, Air South, has an introductory fare of just $19.
>
> The large airlines are responding by cutting costs. Delta has reduced its labour force by 10,000 employees, it has capped the commission it pays to ticketing agents and is outsourcing some of its activities. United has introduced its own no frills service – Shuttle by United.

The purpose of five force analysis of the competitive environment is so that the corporate strategist can 'find a position in the industry where his or her company can best defend itself against these forces or can influence them in its favour' (Porter 1979)

The threat of new entrants

The threat of new entrants analyses the ease with which new firms may enter an industry. This largely depends upon the existence of barriers to entry that may exist in an industry.

Economies of scale

Large airlines should theoretically be able to fight off new entrants because their size confers economies of scale. Economies of scale occur where average production costs fall as a firm's size increases. For example, large airlines may save in fuel costs by bulk purchase. Size can allow sophisticated technology to be utilized (e.g. computer systems) and specialist managers to be employed which lead to more efficient operations whilst their costs can be spread against millions of ticket sales. Similarly, advertising costs per ticket become smaller as sales increase. The cost per seat of a jumbo jet is lower than those of smaller aircraft which are associated with smaller airlines.

However, small airlines are able to achieve economies in different ways. As the case suggests, they use their labour force more flexibly and have cut out many of the expenses such as CRS, ticketing and expensive corporate HQs. By concentrating only on popular routes they achieve higher load factors which cuts the cost per passenger.

Capital requirements of entry

High start up costs can restrict entry into an industry, thus the oil refining industry is difficult to enter. But as Case Study E notes, old aircraft can be leased relatively cheaply thus enabling potential entrants access to the US airline industry.

Availability of distribution channels

Airports and runway slots are key distribution channels for airlines. In the relatively uncrowded skies of the US this is rarely a problem. In the UK, however, there are few slots available at London (Heathrow) airport and this makes entry into the market difficult for newcomers. BA has built up rights to key slots over the years (so-called grandfather rights).

Expected retaliation: price and advertising barriers

Small airlines which compete with well-established ones may expect a period of sustained price and advertising wars. Laker Airways (UK) claimed that it was put out of business because of sustained predatory pricing by its major competitors (BA, Pan Am, and TWA) on the transatlantic route. However, price co-ordination is illegal in the US airline market.

Product differentiation

Product differentiation occurs where firms can build up customer loyalty to a particular brand. In Case Study E, large airlines sell their names strongly and encourage loyalty by frequent flier schemes. The creation of customer loyalty creates a barrier to entry since new firms must incur marketing costs to overcome existing brand loyalties.

Government policy

Before deregulation, the Civil Aeronautics Board limited access to the US airline industry, but this barrier to entry was removed in 1978. In

Europe, Government policies restrict entry in some parts of the EU airline industry but after 1997 the EU industry is expected to be fully deregulated. The changing policy of the EU is exemplified by a recent European Commission ruling that France must allow competitors to operate more routes out of Orly (Paris) airport – routes on which Air France had previously been allowed monopoly rights by the French government.

The power of buyers

Buyer power measures the relative power of customers of a particular organization.

Switching costs

Customers are not tied to any airline in any way and there are therefore no switching costs involved in moving to a cheaper supplier.

Large volume purchasers

Customers who buy in bulk can exercise considerable buyer power. Tour operators may exercise some power over prices because of their bulk purchasing of seats.

Homogeneous products

Despite attempts at product differentiation, there is little real difference between competing airlines. This enhances buyer power since they have a wide choice of suppliers, who are supplying basically similar services.

Buyer knowledge of competition

There is considerable buyer knowledge about prices of air tickets since comparisons can easily be made by a few telephone calls. Knowledge increases buyer power.

The power of suppliers

Suppliers to airlines include aircraft manufacturers, oil companies, airport operators and CRS owners. The ability of these organizations to make excess profits from their airline customers depends upon competition between suppliers. Whilst intense competition between aircraft manufacturers and oil companies keeps their supplies keenly priced, some airports are able to charge high prices from their near-monopoly position. The CRS giant SABRE is able to exploit its dominant position and charge high prices.

The threat of substitutes

Car, coach and rail may be substitutes for some air services. In Europe, the opening of the Channel Tunnel and the introduction of direct Eurostar trains between London, Paris and Brussels has had a considerable impact on airlines operating on these routes.

Technological advances in teleconferencing pose a potential threat to business travel.

The degree of rivalry between competitors

Degree of market leadership (dominant firm) and number of competitors

The US airline industry is characterized by a substantial number of competitors which means that competitive rivalry is intense. Whilst there are dominant players, such as United and American, deregulation and anti-trust laws make it difficult for these airlines to enforce price leadership.

Perishability of products

Airline seats, like package holidays and hotels rooms, are highly perishable since their capacity cannot be stored. Empty seat prices may therefore fall dramatically as the departure time nears. The existence of such last minute bargains can cause intense competitive rivalry in the industry.

Marginal costs of sales

The extra cost of selling an otherwise empty seat (marginal cost) is small and thus even a low achieved price will benefit an airline as the following example shows. The revenue gained from an empty trans-atlantic seat is zero. The cost of filling such a seat is perhaps $50 in drinks, security charges, meals and administration costs. Thus even selling the seat at $100 earns a profit of $50 that would otherwise be permanently lost. Again, such low prices exacerbate competitive rivalry.

Other factors

High exit costs, cross subsidization and slow market growth can intensify competitive rivalry, although none of these are evident in the US airline industry.

Strategic group analysis

It is often the case that the notion of 'an industry' is too wide to allow for useful consideration of an organization's competitive position. For example, within the UK package tour industry there is unlikely to be much competitive rivalry between China Travel Service (CTS) and Club 18-30 since their markets are segmented and distinct. It can also be the case that the level of 'an organization' may be too generalized. For example, the interests of Bass UK encompass the diverse brands of Bass beer and Holiday Inn.

In cases such as these, strategic group analysis can be used to focus on defined business units (which may be part of a larger organization) which compete on similar territory. The following list of characteristics may be used as a basis for establishing strategic groups which are in competition with each other:

- pricing policy
- quality of products
- product range
- extent of branding
- geographical coverage
- market segment served
- distribution channels used
- size of organization.

The choice of characteristics to use vary from industry to industry but two or three sets of characteristics will generally serve to differentiate between strategic groups. For example, it would be useful to use quality of service (using the national classification system) and degree of branding (standardized brand vs. individual unit) to differentiate between strategic groups in the hotel industry.

Figure 4.1 considers the strategic groupings that arise from such an exercise in the French hotel market. It enables hotel operators to limit their competitor analysis to competitors in the same strategic group. Thus, for example, there is considerable competitive rivalry between

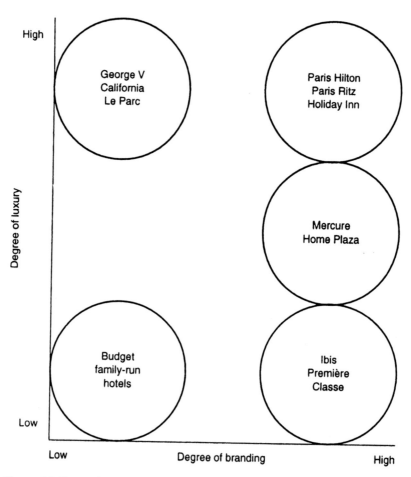

Figure 4.1 Strategic groupings in French hotels

the Paris Hilton and the Holiday Inn, Paris, but the Ibis and the Première Classe appeal to a different market segment.

Competitor analysis

Porter's five force analysis enables the level of competition within a particular industry to be monitored. It is therefore helpful for an organization in deciding where to position itself in the future to take account of the five forces. However, competitor analysis involves a more detailed look at a tourism organization's existing and potential competitors. It enables an organization to formulate a strategy in the light of an assessment of its key rivals, who have been identified by strategic group analysis.

Porter (1980) sets out a framework for competitor analysis which entails the construction of a response profile of competitive organizations. For example, Delta might prepare a response profile for ValuJet. The aim of this profile would be to forecast ValuJet's future plans and consider its likely responses to strategic changes that Delta might put into effect. Porter divides the competitor response profile into two sections.

The first section asks questions about the motives of competitors:

- What is ValuJet's mission?
- What are ValuJet's future goals?

The second section asks questions about the competitor's current and future activities:

- What is ValuJet's current strategy?
- What are ValuJet's capabilities for future change?

The detailed questions that need to be addressed within the response profile include:

- product lines
- buyers
- prices
- quality
- differentiation
- advertising
- market segment
- marketing practices

- growth and prospects
- financial resources
- human resources.

Table 4.1 examines what Delta's competitor response profile for ValuJet might look like. From this analysis it would be possible to evaluate ValuJet's likely response to strategic moves by Delta such as a reduction in fares, or an upgrading of its economy class cabin.

Table 4.1 Competitor response profile on ValuJet (1995)

Mission	● To run a profitable airline
Future goals	● 'Market dominance is not part of our formula' – Lewis Jordan, President, ValuJet·
Current strategy	● Based in Atlanta ● Flies to 23 destinations in South, East and Midwest ● No hub and spoke system ● Low frequency service ● Low fares ● No frills ● Low overheads
Capabilities	● Has only been operating for 17 months (lacks experience) ● Operates 27 used DC-9 jets (questions about safety) ● Small size allows flexibility and responsiveness

Resource deployment analysis

From strategic potential to strategic capability

Analysis of the external operating environment is useful in revealing strategic potential for an organization or destination. Attention is now turned to the organization or destination itself where resource deployment analysis considers its strategic capability. The main analytical techniques for conducting such a capability analysis include:

- resource audit
- performance monitoring and control
- evaluation of products.

These can be used to indicate the organization's current and potential strengths and weaknesses and reveal its core competences.

Resource audit

An audit (Buchele 1962) enables an organization to take periodic stock of its resources and is a good starting point for identifying strengths and weaknesses. Resources may be classified under four headings:

- physical resources
- human resources
- financial resources
- intangibles.

Physical resources

These include buildings, fixtures and fittings, machinery and transport fleets. Consideration should be given to age, compatibility, reliability, efficiency and fitness for purpose.

Human resources

An organization's labour force may be classified according to skills, costs and quantity. A probing audit will attempt to discover employees' undeclared skills and potential.

Financial resources

This should review an organization's liquidity and its overall debt or credit situation. Sources and costs of borrowings and exposure to debt should be included.

Intangibles

Intangibles (Hall 1992) include acquired knowledge and skills, patents and recipes, goodwill, brands and corporate image.

A resource audit is necessary preparation for the analysis that follows in this chapter and should also consider the following:

- Flexibility analysis – which considers whether an organization's resources are flexible enough to deal with the uncertainties of the external environment.
- Balance of skills analysis – which considers whether an organization's team can field a range of types such as innovators, leaders, doers and reflectors.

- Reliance analysis – which reveals whether an organization is over-reliant on key personnel and whether it could manage in the case of their departure.

Performance monitoring and control

Consideration of an organization's resources may include analysis of the way in which resources are being utilized and should ensure that systems are in place to monitor this aspect of an organization's activities and oversee performance monitoring and control. Techniques for such analysis can include:

- analysis of efficiency
- appraisal
- financial analysis
- value chain analysis.

An organization's performance with regard to resource utilization can be given a useful perspective by way of

- comparative analysis

Efficiency

Efficiency measures the ratio of outputs to inputs – the fewer inputs that are required to produce a given output, the more efficient an organization is. Specific indicators of efficiency include sales per square metre; sales per person; sales per outlet as well as output per person. In the tourism sector indicators may include average costs per passenger mile (transport), average costs per guest day (accommodation) and capacity utilization.

Appraisal

Monitoring of the performance of human resources is more complex than for other resources and involves qualitative as well as quantitative issues. Appraisal is a method where employees meet regularly with their line managers to review performance and set targets for the future.

Financial analysis

For profit-making organizations, profitability will clearly be a key indicator of performance. Here figures such as share prices, earnings per share, price/earnings ratio and return on capital will be important.

An organization's gearing ratio and liquidity position help in interpretation of its financial health. Additionally, a range of more specific financial ratios can monitor the use of specific resources, such as the employees wage ratio and the advertising expense ratio.

Value chain

The tendency to analyse organizations by reference to a narrow and visible aspect of its products resulted in analysts such as Porter (1985) developing the idea of the value chain. The product of a scheduled airline, for example, is not just a seat on an aeroplane, rather it is a complex set of connected activities that go to make up the total passenger experience – i.e. a value chain exists. Porter's initial model identifies primary activities and support activities in the value chain and is perhaps more appropriate to manufacturing than service industries. Primary activities are those directly concerned with product provision and include:

- inbound logistics
- operations
- outbound logistics
- marketing and sales
- service.

Support activities are the backroom activities which support product provision and include:

- infrastructure
- human resource management
- technology development
- procurement.

For this part of resource analysis the purpose of examining the links in the value chain is to identify where cost savings may be made. For example, some American airlines have recently focused on commission paid to travel agents as being too costly. This resulted in Delta Air Lines capping its commissions (previously 10 per cent) in 1994. The new structure pays travel agents 10 per cent commission but to a maximum of $25 for one-way domestic tickets costing more than $250, or $30 for a round trip costing over $500. Table 4.2 outlines the primary activities of

Table 4.2 Value chain for scheduled airline: costs

Element	Activity	Cost questions
Preparation	● Route availability ● Advertising ● Information ● Reservations ● Sales	● Are any routes unprofitable? ● Is advertising efficient? ● Can reservation costs be cut? ● Can IT reduce costs? ● Are commissions too high?
Pre-flight	● Arrival at airport ● Check-in ● Baggage handling ● Departure lounge ● Boarding	● What proportion are pre-flight costs to cost of product? ● Is this justified?
In flight	● Seat location ● Seat size/comfort ● Flight attendants ● Meal ● Entertainment ● Other provision	● Can catering costs be reduced by contracting out?
Post-flight	● Baggage reclaim ● Airport transfer	● What are costs of handling agents at overseas airports?
Follow up	● Customer requests ● Customer complaints	● Are passenger refund rules too generous?

the value chain for a scheduled airline and raises questions regarding possible areas for saving costs.

Comparative analysis

Comparative analysis can be made by reference to an organization's historical record, to other organizations in an industry (best practice) or to a benchmark. For example, an efficiency analysis for Thai Airways International in 1995 found an improvement in efficiency in historical terms. But industry comparison of capacity and revenues per employee found that Thai lagged well behind Singapore Airlines and Cathay Pacific. Thai's load factor had increased 3.4 per cent to 69.2 per cent – a historical improvement but still low in comparison with other industry players. Figure 4.2 illustrates comparative analysis of labour efficiency for airlines in Africa. Here best practice analysis reveals a big gap in labour efficiency between Lesotho Airlines and Air Namibia.

Evaluation of products

Part of an organization's capability review will focus on an evaluation of current products. There are several methods of analysis including:

- effectiveness
- value chain analysis
- portfolio analysis
- product life-cycle analysis.

Whilst effectiveness and value chain analysis focus on current analysis of the product, portfolio and product life cycle analysis consider products in more strategic terms.

Effectiveness

Effectiveness is a measure of how well a particular objective is achieved. Measures of product effectiveness may include:

- consumer satisfaction with product (measured by surveys or complaints analysis)
- analysis of matching between product and market need
- performance of product
- comparison with competing products.

Lewis (in Witt and Mouthino 1995) addresses these as issues of quality and lists the ten key aspects of SERVQUAL (Parasuraman *et al.* 1988) as:

- tangibles
- reliability
- responsiveness
- communication

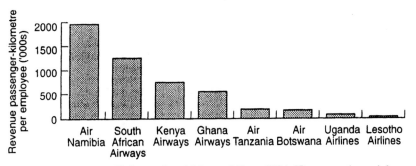

Figure 4.2 Labour efficiency for African airlines 1994 (*Source*: adapted from Endres 1995)

- credibility
- security
- competence
- courtesy customer knowledge
- access.

These may form the basis of research into an organization's service quality.

Value chain analysis

Value chain analysis can also be used to determine whether improvements or value added can be incorporated into a product's value chain. Table 4.3 adapts Table 4.2 and uses the value chain to raise questions relating to quality of service.

Table 4.3 Value chain for scheduled airline: quality

Element	Activity	Quality questions
Preparation	• Route availability • Advertising • Information • Reservations	• Is route system comprehensive and timings convenient? • Is reservation convenient for customer? • Are queries responded to quickly?
Pre-flight	• Arrival at airport • Check-in • Baggage handling • Departure lounge • Boarding	• Are there queues? • Are facilities comfortable? • Are staff helpful?
In flight	• Seat location • Seat size/comfort • Flight attendants • Meal • Entertainment • Other provision	• Is there a choice of meals? • Are there sufficient flight attendants • Is there a variety of entertainment? • Are seats comfortable? • Is there sufficient leg-room?
Post-flight	• Baggage reclaim • Airport transfer	• Is the destination agent efficient?
Follow up	• Customer requests • Customer complaints	• Are customer requests met? • Are complaints dealt with quickly?

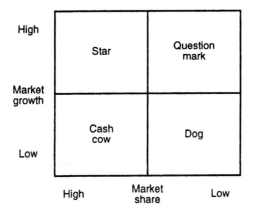

Figure 4.3 The Boston consulting group matrix

Portfolio analysis

Portfolio analysis considers whether an organization's range of products are well balanced with a particular view to the future. The Boston Consulting Group (BCG) matrix (see Figure 4.3) which considers products in terms of their market share and market growth, may be used to assess the balance of an organization's portfolio of products.

Star products are those with a high market share in a fast growing market and cash cows have a high market share in a slow growth market. The BCG matrix helps plan the cash cows and stars of the future since in many cases these will be the question marks of today. However, the development of question marks into future stars may require the profits that are derived from current stars and cash cows. Thus a balance of products across these parts of the matrix represents a strength for an organization. Products which are dogs should be withdrawn unless their future prospects are good.

It should be noted that profitability is not measured in the BCG matrix. It is thus implicitly assumed that cash cows and stars deliver profits from their high market share.

Product life cycle analysis

Product life cycle (PLC) (Vernon 1966; 1979) analysis is useful in considering the future path of sales of a product. Figure 4.4 depicts the

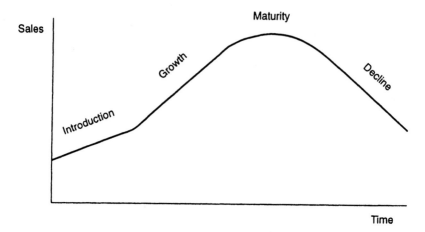

Figure 4.4 Product life cycle

four main stages of introduction, growth, maturity and decline, and the characteristics of these stages are tabulated in Table 4.4. Clearly, products which are entering decline may need rejuvenation or replacement whereas market development may be appropriate for those in the growth phase.

Case study F illustrates that whilst the ski industry in Europe and North America may be on the verge of its decline phase, in Japan growth prospects are still very good.

Other tourism products, such as the cruise holiday for younger age groups, can be placed on the growth phase of their product life cycle.

Therefore an organization's potential strengths and weaknesses in terms of products/services can be identified using PLC and the Boston Box. Clearly, there are also links between the PLC and the Boston Box. In many cases cash cows will be in the mature stage of the product life cycle and may be used to finance question marks which will correspond to the introduction phase. However, the Boston Box also serves as a warning that products do not necessarily follow the path into growth and maturity but may end up as dogs.

Butler (1980) applied the PLC model to destinations, substituting number of visitors for sales on the vertical axis. The stages identified in the destination life cycle were first exploration, characterized by a few initial visitors, followed by involvement where some facilities are

Table 4.4 Characteristics of product life cycle

	Introduction	Growth	Maturity	Decline
Customers	• Ignorance of product • Scepticism of product	• More awareness of product • Growing demand	• Mass market	• Seeking new products • Repeat customers
Competition	• None or little	• Growing	• Consumer choice	• Market saturated
Products	• Changing standards and design • Quality unproven	• Quality improves	• High reliability • Standardization	• Overtaken by new products
Production	• High costs	• Mass production and economies of scale	• Low production costs	• Over capacity
Marketing	• High advertising • High prices	• Marketing economies • Reduce price	• Segmentation • Competitive strategy vital • Reduce price	• Seek to re-launch

Case Study F: Skiing is *Kakko ii*

Sales of skiing holidays in both North America and Europe seem to have peaked, suggesting that the industry is in its mature phase in the 1990s and desperate attempts are being made to rejuvenate it by introducing new products such as snowboarding.

However, in Japan skiing took off relatively recently, in the 1980s, and is now, according to government statistics, the most popular sport for Japanese teenagers and first equal in popularity with tennis for those in their 20s. It is, according to one commentator, *kakko ii* (cool).

The sport is dominated by the Seibu Group owner and operator of a multitude of ski areas, seaside resorts and golf courses in Japan. Seibu capitalized on the sport in the early stages of its growth by buying up large tracts of Japanese mountains in the 1980s.

The most popular resorts are those within reach of Tokyo, and the resort of Naeba is the most popular of all. It is dominated by just one hotel – the Prince Hotel. The Prince chain is owned by Seibu, and the Prince in Naebu has accommodation for 4000 people and owns the 41 ski-lifts in the resort. The resort operates at or near capacity throughout the season and in 1994 around 2.8 million people skied at Naebu, just fewer than the peak of 3 million in 1991.

Marketing surveys suggest that more people are planning to go skiing in future years and that there is potential demand from those whose incomes are not yet high enough to afford to ski. In the light of skiing's continued appeal, Seibu is continuing to develop ski resorts.

Future questions for the Japanese ski industry revolve around the country's changing demographics. The birth rate has been falling and to sustain its growth the market will need to appeal to more people in the over 30s age group.

developed. Development involves perhaps more external investment and more sophisticated and comprehensive facilities. A consolidation and stagnation phase represents a destinations journey into maturity where tourism has become a major local industry. Butler suggests that this may be followed by decline, reduced growth, stabilization or rejuvenation, according to the policy chosen. Cooper (in Witt and Moutinho 1995) places destinations in this model as follows:

- parts of Latin America and the Canadian Arctic (exploration phase)
- the less developed Pacific and Caribbean islands (involvement phase)
- parts of Mexico and coastal Africa (development phase)
- North Mediterranean resorts (consolidation and stagnation phase)
- Atlantic City (USA) (rejuvenation phase).

Criticisms of PLC analysis are summarized by Witt, Brooke and Buckley (1995) and include the lack of empirical validation for its shape, and the determinism implied by the cycle (i.e. that maturity and decline are unavoidable). When applied to a destination it is asked whether this is an appropriate level of aggregation, since different geographical zones and market segments within a destination may reflect different stages of development. There is also evidence that the length of the PLC is shortening.

SWOT analysis

SWOT analysis is an executive summary of the different elements of strategic analysis. Under SWOT, the detailed analysis of an organization's external environmental and internal resource position is distilled and summarized into key factors. Table 4.5 summarizes the analytical techniques underlying a SWOT analysis.

Table 4.5 Components of SWOT analysis

Internal (resource) analysis	Strengths	Weaknesses
Resource audit	•	•
Performance monitoring	•	•
Evaluation of products	•	•
External (environmental) analysis	Opportunities	Threats
Competitive environment	•	•
Political environment	•	•
Economic environment	•	•
Socio-cultural environment	•	•
Technological environment	•	•

Table 4.6 SWOT analysis for Changi Airport, Singapore (1996)

Internal (resource) analysis	Strengths	Weaknesses
Resource audit	● Reclaimed land available for expansion (capacity = 80 million by 2002) ● $335 million earmarked for expansion and refurbishment	● Small size of Singapore – limited hotel rooms and restaurants ● Limited airspace around airport
Performance monitoring	● State-of-the-art terminals with top facilities ● Target for baggage retrieval = 30 minutes max. ● Target for immigration clearance = 8 minutes max.	
Evaluation of products	● Consistently voted one of top world airports	
External (environmental) analysis	Opportunities	Threats
Competitive environment	● Lack of space at Bangkok, Narita (Tokyo), Kuala Lumpur, (Kimpo) Seoul and Kai Tak (Hong Kong)	● Kansai (Osaka, Japan) opened in 1995 ● Chep Lap Lok (Hong Kong) to open in 1997 (capacity = 87 million by 2040) ● Sepang (Malaysia) to open in 1998 (capacity = 25 million) ● Yongjong (Seoul) to open in 2000 (capacity = 27 million) ● Non Hao (Bangkok) to open in 2003 (capacity = 80 million)

Political environment	• Integrated government approach to airport infrastructure planning: good road and planned rail links	• Other Asian governments keen to attract new business
Economic environment	• Annual economic growth of Singapore around 10 per cent per annum	• Growth in neighbouring economies provides the funds for investment in their infrastructure
	• High per capita income of Singaporians	
	• High growth rates of other 'Asian Tiger' economies	
	• Economies of China (pop = 1.1 billion), Vietnam and Thailand growing	
	• Continued investment of multinational organizations into Singapore	
Socio-cultural environment	• Singapore perceived as safe, well-disciplined country	
Technological environment	• Rapid production growth in region	
	• Super Jumbo Jets may relieve congestion in Singapore airspace	

Table 4.6 illustrates a SWOT analysis for Changi Airport, operated by the Civil Aviation Authority of Singapore (CAAS). It shows that the opportunities for increased passenger growth in the region are excellent and that Changi is currently in a strong position to exploit this growth largely due to the capacity and superior facilities which it offers. (In 1996 even first class passengers at neighbouring Kai Tak–Hong Kong have to wait on plastic seats as there is no room for airline lounges.)

However, a serious competitive threat is looming: By 2003, all the currently overcrowded Asian hub airports will have been replaced, matching (and possibly exceeding) the facilities provided at Changi and capacity will outstrip demand.

Once the key SWOT elements have been identified, it can be productive to prepare a grid with strengths and weaknesses along the vertical axis, and opportunities and threats along the horizontal axis. This helps to indicate the extent to which an organization has the capability to take advantage of opportunities, or whether its weaknesses will prevent these opportunities from being realized.

Identification of an organization's situational position by means of a SWOT analysis is an important phase prior to consideration of strategic options, which is the subject of the next chapter. Appropriate strategies are likely to:

- align opportunities and strengths
- transform weaknesses
- overcome threats.

Summary

1 This chapter has reviewed the remaining analytical techniques for conducting a situational analysis of a tourism organization, thus concluding the section on strategic analysis started in Chapter 3.

2 First, it has considered the remaining 'C' part of C-PEST analysis. Techniques such as five force analysis, strategic group analysis and competitor analysis have been identified as methods to evaluate the opportunities and threats in the competitive part of an organization's external environment.

3 Next, methods for internal resource analysis have been explored. Here an organization's strengths and weaknesses were scrutinized using techniques such as resource audit, performance review and product evaluation.

4 Finally, the two strands of Chapters 3 and 4 are brought together under a SWOT analysis which summarizes the key findings of a situational analysis.
5 Thus the stage of strategic analysis has been completed and the way prepared for the next stage of the strategy process – strategic choice.

Review questions

1 Conduct a five force analysis on the competitive environment for a named tourism organization. Explain how this will enable the director of strategy and planning of that organization to 'find a position in the industry where his or her company can best defend itself against these forces or can influence them in its favour' (Porter 1979)
2 Conduct a competitor analysis for a tourism organization. Identify a key competitor and prepare a competitor response profile to show how this organization may react to a low price strategy from your firm.
3 Use the SERVQUAL (Parasuraman *et al.* 1988) headings (tangibles, reliability, responsiveness, communication, credibility, security, competence, courtesy customer knowledge, access), to carry out a quality audit on a named tourism service. Identify any service gaps and make recommendations.
4 What is value chain analysis? Conduct a value chain analysis for a hotel which focuses on ways of either
   (a) reducing costs, or,
   (b) improving service.
5 Identify the position on a Boston Box of the main products of a named tourism organization. What conclusions can you reach about the balance of the portfolio of products and what points for future planning emerge from this exercise?
6 To what extent can the concept of product life cycles be used to analyse destinations (Butler 1980)?
7 What is the purpose of a SWOT analysis? Conduct a SWOT analysis for a tourism organization.

Part 3: Strategic Choice

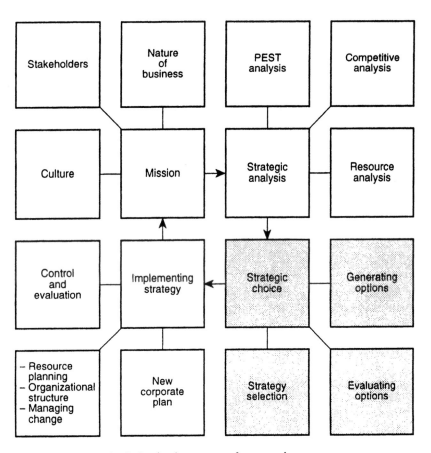

Figure 5.1 Strategic choice in the strategy framework

The next stage of tourism corporate strategy is strategic choice and by the end of Part 3 it should be possible to propose and justify a particular strategy for a tourism organization. Strategic choice follows logically from the previous two stages. Strategic analysis resulted in a summary of the opportunities and threats evident in the tourism organization's external environment and of its internal strengths and weaknesses, and it is in the light of this analysis that actual strategy will be formulated, guided by the organization's mission.

Strategic choice outlines a framework to assist the tourism organization in its development of an appropriate strategy. Chapter 5 introduces the main types of strategy, using Porter's (1980) generic strategies as a starting point. It then considers the directions and methods by which an organization can pursue its strategy.

Chapter 6 offers a framework within which different possible strategies can be evaluated and thus an appropriate strategy chosen. The appropriateness of a strategy will clearly depend on its ability to fulfil the organization's mission by exploiting strengths and opportunities and counteracting weaknesses and threats.

5
Tourism corporate strategies

Chapter objectives

By studying this chapter students will be able to develop a framework for generating a series of strategic options for tourism organizations. In particular, they will be able to:

- describe and utilize Porter's (1980) generic strategies of cost leadership, differentiation and focus
- describe and utilize adaptations of Porter's model
- analyse the directions and methods by which strategies may be pursued.

Generic strategies

A generic strategy is a strategy of a particular type or form designed to promote a lasting competitive advantage for an organization.

Porter's model

Porter (1980) identified three generic strategies that organizations could use to achieve competitive advantage. He argued that it was important for organizations to be clear about which strategy was being followed and that lack of a clear strategy could result in muddle and confusion. Porter's generic strategies are:

- cost leadership
- differentiation
- focus.

Cost leadership

This strategy involves an organization becoming the lowest cost provider in an industry. One of the key ways to achieve this is by offering a basic, standardized, mass-produced, no-frills product or service with inessential aspects stripped out. A cost-focused organization will be engaged in a perpetual struggle to minimize costs of inputs – mainly labour and raw materials. Economies of scale can also be an important element in cost leadership so that market share may be fought for to achieve the size that brings lower average production costs.

Porter's logic for this strategy is that if a firm can charge industry-average prices, but sustains below industry-average costs it will be an above average performer.

Differentiation

A differentiation strategy is where an organization seeks product uniqueness. It will attempt to establish real (by product design) or perceived (by advertising) differences between its products and those of its competitors so that a premium price can be charged without loss of customers.

Porter's logic for this strategy is that an organization will be an above industry-average performer if the price premium exceeds the extra costs of providing differentiation.

Focus

A focus strategy occurs where strategy is tailored towards a particular market segment rather than to the whole market and may take the form of cost focus or differentiation focus.

Problems with Porter

Problems with Porter's generic strategies arise first from their application to tourism and second from their internal logic.

Olsen (1991) notes that Porter's typology is more applicable to manufacturing and that problems arise with their direct application to tourism. Poon (1993: 239) concludes that 'Porter's generic strategies have little value in today's tourism industry.' Poon identifies four principles for an effective tourism strategy:

- put customers first
- be a leader in quality
- develop radical innovations
- strengthen the firm's strategic position within the value chain.

However, these principles can be accommodated in an adapted version of Porter, and price remains an important part of strategy which Poon ignores.

Next, the problems of the internal logic of Porter's typology are addressed. Cost leadership is a problematic concept for several reasons. First, many of the routes to lower costs are easily followed by competitors and therefore leadership may be elusive. It is perhaps only where a firm can achieve economies of scale by market leadership that costs may be reduced without compromising the quality of output. Second, where cost leadership is achieved by stripped-down products, consumers are unlikely to pay industry-average price. Price may well follow costs down thus reducing any extra margins. Third, there is a tendency for Porter to use the terms 'cost' and 'price' interchangeably. But they are very different terms – the first, measuring input costs (paid by firms) and the second, measuring market prices (paid by consumers).

Differentiation may be misinterpreted by managers as being merely a matter of improved technique of production. What is more important in terms of selling a product or service is the notion of consumer perception – does a particular product offer improved quality or value added over the competition in the eyes of the consumer?

Porter's typology also polarizes costs leadership and differentiation. There is evidence that many organizations seek to operate in a hybrid region which encompasses both low costs whilst attempting to market a distinctive product.

Porter adapted

Kotler (1988) and Bowman (1992) have sought to rework Porter's typology of generic strategies to take into account some of the issues raised above. In particular the typology is adapted to reflect the

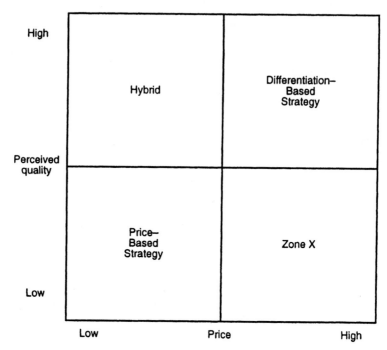

Figure 5.2 Price/quality matrix

consumer view of things. Thus consumers are more sensitive to prices than costs and consider perceived quality or value added rather than differentiation. Figure 5.2 illustrates a price/quality strategy matrix incorporating these ideas.

Price-based strategies

Price-based strategy is similar to cost leadership, but emphasizes the fact that low costs are passed on to the customer in the form of lower prices. Products are thus likely to be standardized and unnecessary but costly extras will have been stripped away. Eurocamp, the UK-based camping holiday operator reviewed its 1994 trading thus:

The competitive pricing strategy which we pursued in all our markets was a major factor in the achievement of increased volumes.

However, better camp-site occupancy levels and cost improvements enabled us to also realize a small increase in our sales margins.

(Eurocamp Annual Report 1994)

Value chain analysis can be a useful tool for highlighting extras which can be removed. Case Study G illustrates how this has been done for EasyJet, a recent arrival in UK air travel.

Case Study G: EasyJet

EasyJet is a classic example of an airline following a price-based strategy. In doing so the Greek-owned company, which operates on the London to Glasgow route, imitates many of the newer airlines that have developed in the US. The lowest fare on EasyJet is £29 single compared with the highest single fare on the route of £119.

EasyJet has looked hard at the typical value chain associated with air travel and reduced costs accordingly:

Advertising

- Major airlines run expensive campaigns promoting brand and image. Corporate design is expensive to maintain.
- EasyJet has its telephone number painted on the side of its jets. Advertising slogan: 'The airline that makes flying as affordable as a pair of jeans'.

Booking

- Major airlines must pay commission to travel agents with whom passengers book tickets. They also maintain comprehensive but expensive internal booking services which guarantee prompt answering of calls at peak times.
- EasyJet passengers can only book direct. It has taken passengers 30 minutes to get through at peak times.

Case Study G (*continued*)

Airports

- Major airlines fly out of convenient but expensive London-Heathrow.
- EasyJet flies out of London-Luton: Cheap but less accessible.

In flight facilities

- Free meals and refreshments with major airlines. Designer styled uniforms for cabin staff.
- Coffee at 50p and flapjacks at 70p with EasyJet. Cabin staff in jeans and sweatshirts.

Differentiation-based strategies

This is similar to Porter's differentiation strategy, but with an emphasis on providing extra qualities which are valued by the consumer. This value added may be provided by:

- design
- exploitation of the value chain
- advertising.

Investment in research and development is a route to providing products which are different from those of competitors in terms of better design or quality and durability.

The value chain can be used to indicate the range of activities associated with the delivery of a service or product where distinctive extras can be built in.

Advertising is an important tool in communicating product or service distinctiveness to consumers. It may emphasize real features (witness the advertisements comparing seat space for premium airline travel) or a particular brand image. The key to product differentiation is thorough market research to discover and deliver product differences which are important to the consumer. For example, first class passengers on British Airways can expect value to be added as follows:

- fully refundable/changeable tickets
- valet parking
- express check-in

- VIP lounges with office facilities, free drinks, entertainment and showers
- fast-track security clearance
- spacious cabin
- flexible meal times
- gourmet food
- limitless champagne
- vintage wines
- fine china
- spacious seating
- seating that converts into a full length bed
- limousine/helicopter transfer at destination.

Hybrid strategies

A hybrid strategy is an attempt to provide quality products and services at low prices. It seems contradictory because adding value adds to costs which should preclude low prices. The key to a successful hybrid strategy is therefore to reduce average costs.

The first route to this is achieving economies of scale, where average costs fall as output increases. Mass production, bulk buying, labour specialization and economies of increased dimensions become significant as output increases. Economies of scale are therefore open to firms which can achieve high market share and a virtuous circle, as illustrated in Figure 5.3, may become established.

The second route, important to service providers such as tourism organizations, is to ensure high load factors. Hotels, airlines and attractions all face high fixed costs and a perishable product. An unfilled room is revenue lost forever. Computerized reservation systems can help achieve high load factors and thus dissipate fixed costs, bringing average costs down.

The Spanish Tourist Authority in its Plan Futures document (Plan Marco de Competividad para el Turismo Español) seeks a hybrid solution to the recovery of the competitiveness of the Spanish tourist industry. It aims to 'maintain leadership in the sun-and-beach tourist market by improving the value for money ratio'.

Focused strategies

Price-based and differentiation strategies may each be focused on a particular market segment and it is increasingly common for organiza-

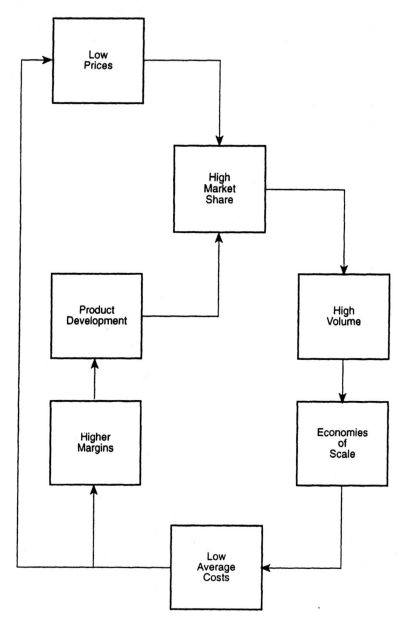

Figure 5.3 Route to hybrid strategy

tions to seek to serve a number of different market segments. Where this is the case it is important to identify distinct products or services so that there is no leakage between low price and high quality services. Branding is a key approach to this and Case Study H illustrates this for Thomson Holidays – the leading UK tour operator.

Case Study H: Thomson Holidays

Thomson adopts a broad range of strategies in the holiday market.

Hybrid strategy

Its key brand, Thomson holidays exemplifies a well-established hybrid strategy. This brand is associated with low prices but assured quality. Quality indicators include:

- free in-flight catering
- free in-flight entertainment
- representatives allowed to refund up to 10 per cent of holiday price in resort to ameliorate customer complaints
- comprehensive customer satisfaction monitoring through questionnaires.

Thomson defends its market share (31 per cent) aggressively against its key rivals First Choice (12 per cent) and Airtours (17 per cent) (1995 figures) so as to maintain the economies of scale which are crucial to a successful hybrid strategy. Thomson's size gives it unmatched buying power from suppliers such as hotels.

Price-based strategy (focused)

The following press advert demonstrates Thomson's focused strategy on the more price sensitive part of the market. In fact Portland is a company owned by Thomson. But Portland is a direct-sell company and so the main value added that has been stripped from the product is the service of a retail travel agent, enabling a lower price to be charged.

Case Study H (*continued*)

IF THE HOLIDAYS ARE THE SAME,
HOW COME ONE COSTS SO MUCH LESS?

17th July to 31st July –	17th July to 31st July –
Rhodes – Hotel Cosmopolitan,	Rhodes – Hotel Cosmopolitan,
Ixia – Direct from Gatwick	Ixia – Direct from Gatwick
FIRST CHOICE PRICE £688	PORTLAND PRICE £531

Differentiation strategy (focused)

Thomson à la carte represents a key differentiation brand. This offers holidays at a premium price in return for an emphasis on quality throughout the value chain, including:

- taxi transfers from airport
- flowers on arrival
- high grade hotels
- gourmet meals

Transport operators keep their focused strategies separate from each other by imposing conditions to stop a mass movement from high priced services to low price offers. The latter may include conditions such as:

- no refunds or changes
- minimum/maximum periods of stay
- advance booking
- availability on limited services.

Zone X

Zone X in Figure 5.2 represents a combination of high prices and low quality and will generally therefore lead to failure. However there are exceptions to this.

First, where an organization has a monopoly it can operate in Zone X without fear of losing customers, since they have no choice. Local transportation may operate under conditions of monopoly in some areas.

Second, where consumers have lack of information about quality, or competitive prices, Zone X strategies may persist. Generally, Zone X strategies will result in customers not returning and thus Zone X organizations will exist only in the short-term. But tourist areas represent a potential site within which organizations may operate such strategies since new and naive tourists are continually arriving. Restaurants, hotels and taxis may be able to operate Zone X strategies under such conditions.

Competition and strategy

The degree of competition within an industry will influence the position adopted by an organization on Figure 5.2. The greater the competition, the more an organization will be forced to deliver greater value added and/or lower price (away from Zone X). Less competition means more of a likelihood of strategy drifting towards Zone X.

Directions

This section considers the strategic directions an organization might take in pursuit of its overall strategy. The main directions are:

- withdrawal
- consolidation
- market penetration
- market development
- product development
- diversification.

In many cases a combination of these directions will be appropriate.

These directions are summarized and located in Figure 5.4 on the matrix developed by Ansoff (1965) in terms of market/product positioning. However, the boxes should not be viewed as having rigid boundaries – for example, current products are generally under a state of perpetual review.

Withdrawal

This does not appear in Figure 5.4, since it involves neither new nor current markets or products, but rather a position of retreat. There are

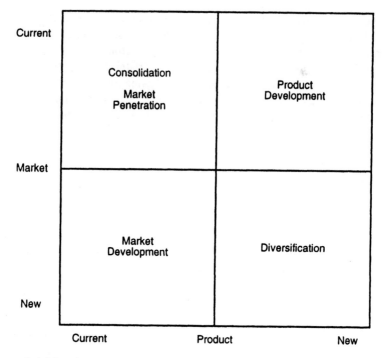

Figure 5.4 Mapping strategic directions (adapted from Ansoff 1965)

some cases in which an organization may withdraw from a particular market. These might include:

- de-cluttering
- contracting out
- raising money
- legal compliance
- competition
- market decline/economic prospects
- liquidation
- privatization.

De-cluttering

This occurs where an organization has grown into a range of diversified areas and now seeks to concentrate its efforts in its core business. For example, in 1994 Scandinavian Airline Systems (SAS) sold its travel group SAS Leisure to Airtours of the UK; its catering unit SAS Service Partner to Swissair's catering division; and Diners Club Nordic to Sweden's Skandinaviska Enskilda Banken. It intends to concentrate on its core businesses of airlines and hotel management. Similarly, Kaufhof, Germany's second biggest retailer, sold its 50 per cent stake in Kuoni travel to Swiss business interests in 1995.

Contracting out

Organizations may cease to provide a service related to their business, preferring to buy in the services from a contractor. This enables the service to be more flexibly provided. For example, British Airways contracted out its aircraft security services. Instead it specifies a level of service to a contracting company and can expand and contract the service more easily.

Raising money

Withdrawal may be used to raise money for expansion elsewhere or to fight off a take-over bid. For example, Forte, the UK's largest hotel and restaurant group planned to sell its roadside businesses – restaurants, service areas and Travelodge hotels – to Whitbread in 1996 for £1.05 billion, to help fight a £3.2 billion take-over bid from Granada.

Legal compliance

Monopoly or anti-trust legislation may require an organization to divest its holdings if it is acting against the public interest. The UK Monopolies Commission report on the brewing industry in 1989 set limits to the number of pubs that brewers could own and resulted in divestment. In 1996, British Airways considered giving up its partnership with US Air in order to win approval from the US competition authorities for an alliance with American Airlines.

Competition

Competition in an area may be so strong as to force an organization out of this particular market.

Market decline/economic prospects

Poor prospects for a particular market may cause an organization to make a partial or wholesale tactical withdrawal.

Liquidation

An organization may withdraw because of untenable losses.

Privatization

The government may wish to sell assets as part of a privatization programme. Examples of this in the tourism sector are:

- the sale by the government of Estonia of 66 per cent of the state-owned airline Estonia Air in 1966
- the sale by the government of Jordan of 54 per cent of the Jordan Hotels and Tourism Company and 62.3 per cent of its shareholding in the Intercontinental Jordan (1995/96).

Consolidation

Consolidation implies a period of concentrating an organization's efforts on existing products and existing markets. It may result from a period of rapid change to enable an organization to settle down or may result from a lack of resources to pursue a more active policy. This may result from lack of profits in the private sector or lack of government grants to a public sector organization such as a national tourism organization.

Market penetration

Market penetration involves increasing market share and is an important aim of generic strategies previously discussed. In the short-term, market penetration may be won by reducing margins and prices, but sustainable market penetration can only be achieved by price-based strategies that are coupled with cost reductions, or by differentiation or hybrid strategies. The exception to this is if a price war is successful in forcing a weaker competitor out of business.

There has been a continuing battle for market share in the UK package holiday industry. The managing director of Thomson, Mr Newbold, made the following pledge regarding market share:

To those competitors which think that Thomson's low prices in 1994
are just a short term measure and the umbrella of high prices will
return, think again. Thomson's low prices are here to stay. We intend
to be the number one choice well into the 21st century.

(Travel Trade Gazette: 4th May 1994)

Market development

Market development generally involves an attempt to take the existing
product range into new market areas which can include new geographical areas and new market segments. It may be that some product
development is required to adapt the product range to the new market
areas.

Eurocamp has recently been developing its market in Europe:

In Germany and Switzerland bookings increased by over 20% whilst
Holland and Belgium grew by approximately 10%. We already have
a small sales operation in Sweden and this is now complemented by
Denmark, where we promoted Eurocamp holidays for the first time
in 1994 . . . in co-operation with Larsen Rejser, an established
holiday tour operator.

(Eurocamp Annual Report 1994)

Case Study I illustrates how Icelandair follows the strategic direction of
market development to achieve its generic strategy which is mainly
price-based.

Case Study I: Icelandair

Iceland has a population of only 267,000 people. The domestic
market for Icelandair, its flag carrier and one of Europe's smallest
international airlines is therefore strictly limited. However, it has
been profitable in all but two of the last 10 years, earning profits of
$8.9 million on turnover of $227 million in 1994 and accounts for
about 4 per cent of Iceland's gross national product.

Icelandair's strategy is different from many scheduled airlines in
that it concentrates not on high fare business traffic, but on low-
fare tourist traffic for much of its revenue. For example, its
average fare is over a third less than a nearby rival, Scandinavian
Airlines System.

Case Study I (*continued*)

> To fulfil this strategy it needs to seek economies of scale and low average costs by achieving high seat sales. This means developing its market well beyond its limited domestic one.
>
> It did in fact carry 1.1 million passengers in 1994 – about four times its domestic population. It has achieved this first, by serving the growing market for tourism to Iceland. But more importantly, it exploits the 'fifth freedom' rights established by the Chicago Convention. This enables the setting down and picking up of passengers in the territory of a third country and means that Icelandair can carry foreign tourists from their home countries to other non-Iceland destinations. Thus its core business is its domestic routes and scheduled services to four US and 12 European cites. But in addition to this Icelandair:
>
> - carries more Swedes and Norwegians to holidays in Florida than any other airline
> - provides budget trips to Europe for Americans – with a stopover in Iceland
> - is the biggest 'fifth freedom' Airline operating from Amsterdam to the US.
>
> *The Financial Times* (London) recently summed up Icelandair's prospects as follows: 'Cost-consciousness and exploitation of niche foreign markets will continue to be the keys to its profitability.'

Product development

Product development encompasses the development of existing products and the development of completely new products.

The continuing development of existing products is almost an essential strategy in the dynamic environment which organizations operate in. For differentiation strategies, product development is necessary to maintain differences as competitors imitate previous innovations. Equally, price-based strategies require product development in order to maintain low production costs and even budget products or services must eventually incorporate recent innovations or they will fail to sell even at low prices.

New product development is a more risky strategy since research and development costs are expensive and only a minority of new products reach the market and succeed.

Eurocamp has recently launched three new products. First, EuroVillages and Les Maisons de Chantale. This represents a move from canvas to 'bricks and mortar' accommodation. These developments are explained as follows:

> This type of holiday is already well established in mainland Europe with a holiday season longer than for camping and represents a logical extension of Eurocamp's product range. As there are no fixed accommodation cost commitments and no capital requirements this represents a low risk diversification for the Group.
>
> (Eurocamp Annual Report 1994)

Second, Eurocamp has acquired Superbreak, a UK short-break business:

> In contrast to the overseas holiday market, UK short-breaks have been growing strongly . . . Superbreak provides an excellent complement and balance to other Group business.
>
> (Eurocamp Annual Report 1995)

Reference to product life cycle analysis (Are current products in the decline phase?) and the Boston matrix (Which products will be the cash cows of tomorrow?) (see Chapter 4) can be useful tools in judging the appropriateness and timeliness for product development within an organization.

Case Study J: Developments in cruising

In 1995, P&O launched the latest addition to its cruise fleet – the £200 million Oriana. It boasts:

- the biggest swimming pool afloat
- a waterfall descending the full height of its four-deck atrium
- a West End-style theatre with revolving stage, full orchestra pit and individually air-conditioned seats
- accommodation for 1,760 people

Case Study J (*continued*)

> ● and it is the fastest cruise ship built for more than a quarter of a century.
>
> The Oriana represents new capacity and new levels of appointment at the top end of the market.
>
> However, there are also developments at the lower-priced end of the market, with new players such as Airtours and CTC, a Ukrainian-owned cruise line, opening up affordable cruising to the mass market.
>
> Meanwhile, with more than 30 cruise liners worth a total of $7.5 billion on order around the world, the 69,000 tonne Oriana will soon be overtaken by several 100,000 tonners.

Case Study J examines product development in the cruise market. The Oriana represents continued product development and refinement in the luxury cruise market and may be seen as part of a classic differentiation strategy by its owners P&O who enjoy about 30 per cent of the cruise market, on a par with Cunard. However, the case also notes the entry of Airtours and CTC into the budget cruise market – a move which represents the development of new products for these companies. Airtours recently bought a cruise ship from Kloster cruises and such moves represent an attempt to capture the price conscious part of the cruise market.

Diversification

Diversification involves an organization moving into completely new products and markets which are unrelated to its present portfolio. The motives for this may be first, to take advantage of a new growing market – particularly if an existing product has a static or declining market. Second, diversification allows an organization to spread its risks. Third, economies of scope may be achieved. These are reductions in average costs that result from provision of a range of different goods and services. Such economies result from sharing marketing, or brand names, or customers, or outlets. Case Study K examines the International Thomson Organization – an example of a company whose diverse interests include tourism products.

Case Study K: International Thomson Organisation Ltd

The Canadian based International Thomson Organisation started life as a UK-based newspaper publisher with a commercial TV franchise. Between 1960 and 1990 four major phases of diversification can be detected.

Early 1960s

In this early period, Thomson faced two major problems. First, expansion in newspapers and TV were likely to be curbed by government legislation and second the company was over reliant on advertising revenue. In order to spread its risks more broadly Thomson acquired:

- educational and trade publishing interests
- consumer, professional and business journal interests.

Late 1960s

The mid-1960s took Thomson into a completely new area. It purchased three package tour companies and a small airline for under $3 million and started Thomson Travel. The logic behind move was to acquire a business:

- with good growth prospects
- with different cash flow characteristics to its publishing business
- with low initial investment.

This period also saw Thomson launch *Yellow Pages* in the UK.

The 1970s

In 1971 diversification took another turn when Thomson took a 20 per cent stake in a consortium drilling for North Sea oil. This project completely transformed the company as oil's contribution to group profits climbed to 70 per cent, compared to 25 per cent for publishing and 5 per cent for travel.

- The 1970s also saw Thomson expand its publishing interests in terms of titles and geographical spread.

Case Study K (*continued*)

- In 1978 the company became incorporated in Canada as International Thomson.
- In 1980, Thomson abandoned its Yellow Pages project and launched the competing *Thomson Local Directories*.

The 1980s

The 1980s represented a period when Thomson concentrated on acquiring information publishing businesses in the US with some smaller acquisitions in oil and travel in that market.

International Thomson are also the parent company of the publishers of this text.

Methods

This section examines the main methods by which a particular strategy may be developed which include:

- internal growth
- mergers and take-overs
- joint ventures and alliances.

Internal growth

Internal growth means that markets and products are developed without recourse to mergers with other organizations. This route may be chosen because:

- owners and managers wish to retain control of an organization
- organic growth is less disruptive and can be more readily accommodated
- finance may be limited
- there may be no suitable targets for mergers
- problems of cultural fit between merging organizations can be avoided.

However, internal growth may dictate a pace of adaptation which is too slow to keep up with environmental changes and does not preclude the possibility of a take-over bid. Also opportunities to benefit from already developed products and markets will be lost, as will the positive aspects of cultural change which can result from mergers.

Mergers and takeovers

Whilst mergers represent voluntary integration between organizations, take-overs may occur without the consent of the target company. Integration can be divided into three main types:

- horizontal integration
- vertical integration
- diversification or conglomerate integration.

Figure 5.5 illustrates the basis for different forms of integration. The vertical dimension of the industry represents a series of stages of production from raw materials or suppliers through to the consumer. Thus, there are three basic vertical stages in the package holiday industry – the supply of services (in this case the air transport), the packaging and the retailing. In the UK, Thomson represents a fully vertically integrated operation since it owns Britannia Airways, Thomson Holidays and the travel agency Lunn Poly.

The horizontal dimension of the industry represents a series of separate firms engaged in the industry at different stages. For example, in the UK the key retail travel agents are Lunn Poly, Going Places, Thomas Cook and AT May.

Horizontal integration

Horizontal integration occurs between firms operating at the same stage of production in the same industry. For example, in 1993 Airtours attempted a horizontal take-over of First Choice (then known as Owners Abroad). This was unsuccessful but it subsequently succeeded in a horizontal take-over of Aspro Travel, then the UK's seventh largest tour operator with 4 per cent market share. In 1994, Airtours bought SAS Leisure – the leading tour operator in Scandinavia and in 1995 it purchased Sunquest Vacations of Canada.

Motives for horizontal integration can include first, market development. Airtours' take-over of SAS Leisure, for example, represents an attempt to broaden its market base away from the volatile UK market

Vertical Integration

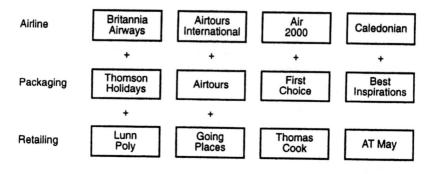

Horizontal Integration

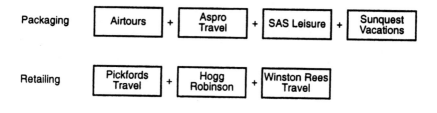

Diversification

Figure 5.5 The basis for integration

and embrace the Scandinavian market. Airtours plans to obtain half its future business from non-UK operations.

Second, market penetration can result from horizontal integration. Airtours' purchase of Aspro means that the customer database of Aspro is also purchased expanding Airtours' customer base and market at a stroke.

Third, there are economies of scale to be achieved by horizontal integration. Integrated firms can share the same management overheads and advertising and marketing campaigns may be merged. As Airtours grows larger, so its bulk purchasing opportunities grow. Larger turnover also justifies the use of more sophisticated specialized support (both in terms of staffing and technology). State-of-the-art computerization for reservations and yield management becomes more feasible. Financial economies in terms of access to cheaper capital are also open to larger firms. Rationalization can occur as firms merge and unnecessary duplication of services can be avoided. The result of such economies may be substantial reductions in average costs.

Horizontal integration can also be a short cut to product development as competitors' products and support systems are acquired as part of the business. For example, in 1994 Thomson purchased Country Holidays, the UK's largest holiday letting company, followed by the purchase of the cottage holiday letting business of Blakes Holidays in 1995. Thomson is thus able to broaden its product base (and by implication its market base) without developing these from scratch and bring its considerable marketing and promotional strengths to its expanded portfolio which now includes domestic as well as overseas holidays.

Finally, horizontal integration is a way of reducing competition. Less competition means that an organization needs to make less effort in terms of low prices or improved products.

First Choice (UK number three tour operator) announced three horizontal acquisitions in 1995. Purchase of UK base Skibound represented product development and gained First Choice a more balanced portfolio of operations and cash flow throughout the year. Market development was achieved through buying into Ireland (JWT Holidays) and Canada (Fiesta West).

Vertical integration

Vertical integration occurs where two organizations at different stages of production in the same industry merge. Airtours provides another good example of this. Having no existing retail outlets, Airtours bought Pickfords Retail Travel in 1992 for £16 million followed by another agent, Hogg Robinson, in 1993. A further 40 outlets were purchased in 1994 by the purchase of Winston Rees Travel, all these now trading under the name of Going Places.

The package travel industry in the UK has moved towards increasing vertical integration. Referring to Figure 5.5, Thomson is fully vertically integrated, owning its airline Britannia and travel agent Lunn Poly. Similarly, Airtours owns airline Airtours International and travel agent Going Places. First Choice is partially vertically integrated. It owns the airline Air 2000 and travel agency Thomas Cook owns a 14 per cent share in First Choice. Inspirations bought the charter airline Caledonian from British Airways and has a marketing alliance with travel agent AT May.

Market penetration has been an important motive for forward (towards the consumer) vertical integration in the UK package tour industry. Ownership of retail travel agents means that a tour operator can allocate its own brochures best rack space and offer its staff incentives to sell in house holidays. There has been particular rivalry as Airtours has boosted its outlets to 706, within reach of market leader Thomson at 783 outlets (1996 figures). Equally, forward integration ensures a ready market for airline seats, ensuring high load factors.

Product development is another important motive for vertical integration. Control of airlines means that tour operators can influence a key element in the value chain of the holiday package. Departure times and quality of service can all be directly controlled and this part of the service can help to support the overall corporate image and help add value to a product. Vertical integration also means that tour operators have close contact with their customers which can ensure that product development is customer-driven.

Diversification

This has been discussed previously in this chapter and can be illustrated by Figure 5.5. For example, diversification for Thomson represented a move from publishing to include package holidays and later oil and gas.

Problems with mergers

Some of the potential problems of mergers can also be noted. First, there is the potential problem of lack of fit in terms of products, or processes (information technology system incompatibility can be a problem here), or the culture of merging organizations.

Second, diseconomies of scale may arise. This may occur particularly if an organization becomes too big for effective management. Poor communications, ineffective control and co-ordination may arise, causing costs to rise.

Finally, there is monopolies and mergers and anti-trust legislation. Most countries have legislation to control .mergers where anti-competitive practices result in the interests of consumers being adversely affected. Vertical integration in the UK package tour industry has been criticized by the Consumers Association who allege that customers do not get unbiased advice when using vertically integrated travel agents. A proposed merger between ferry operators Stena and P&O was twice rejected by UK regulatory authorities.

Joint ventures and alliances

This method of strategic development represents a desire for the benefits of collaboration without complete merging of ownership and resources. It can take the following forms:

- franchising and licensing
- joint ventures
- alliances

Franchising and licensing

This can be appropriate when a successful product would benefit from rapid market development but funds for expansion are insufficient to cope with the product's development potential. The franchising concept has been successfully applied to hotels and restaurants. The owner of a successful brand undertakes marketing and is responsible for ensuring quality control, but outlets are franchised out in return for an initial fee and royalties. Thus the product can be expanded quickly as new capital is available and the brand owner can extend profits, whilst the franchise holder enjoys the marketing benefits of a well-known brand.

Case Study L illustrates the development of the Holiday Inn brand.

Case Study L: Holiday Inn Worldwide

Holiday Inn is the leading international hotel brand. We are committed to franchising as the way to grow our world-wide business

(Brian Langton, Chairman and Chief Executive Officer, Holiday Inn Worldwide)

Holiday Inn Worldwide has more than 1,770 hotels and 338,000 guest rooms, making it the largest single hotel brand in the world.

Approximately 90 per cent of Holiday Inn hotels are owned by franchisees, who choose Holiday Inn because it delivers a value proposition superior to other hotel brands. Hotel owners select the Holiday Inn name because they want the global marketing power of the strongest brand name in the hotel industry. They want the most advanced hotel reservation system to deliver the maximum number of room nights. They want and receive more training and service for their hotels than they would receive at any other hotel chain. They gain access to management services not found with any major competitor. Holiday Inn franchisees are in business for themselves but not by themselves.

Holiday Inn has the most highly developed communications network in the industry, with direct links to airline reservation systems and instantaneous satellite communications between reservation centres and hotels around the world.

Holiday Inn has recently signed a deal to franchise its name to Prague's Hotel Internacional and work started in 1996 on a 330 million koruna ($1 = 43 korunas) refurbishment of the 250 room hotel to three-star standards.

Targa Hotels has signed an agreement for exclusive franchise rights for the Holiday Inn Express brand throughout the Czech and Slovak Republics. It has commenced a 1.2 billion koruna investment programme which will result in a chain of 12–15 Holiday Inn Express hotels by the year 2002.

(*Sources*: Bass plc Annual Report and *The Guardian* newspaper)

Joint ventures

Joint ventures have typified tourism developments with governments of the ex-Soviet bloc of countries, and the governments of China and Cuba. Experienced companies provide expertise and finance with land and some labour being supplied locally. Case Study M illustrates recent joint ventures in China.

Case Study M: Accor Asia

The hotel group Accor Asia has recently announced an agreement for a joint-venture with the government of the People's Republic of China to upgrade state-owned hotels.

The agreement has set a target for the refurbishment of 100 hotels by the year 2000. Hotels are to be selected on their potential to fit into the budget to mid-market segment. The terms of the agreement are that Accor Asia will undertake refurbishment to 2 to 3 star standards and market them under the Ibis and Novotel brand names. In return the company will retain a 25 per cent interest in the hotels and a management contract for 25 years.

The chairman of Accor Asia, Mr David Baffshy stated 'Our charter is to provide clean, consistent and reasonably priced accommodation.' He added that the growing market in China represented an important strategic opportunity for Accor and that other joint ventures were under discussion in Vietnam and India.

Alliances

Strategic alliances are a way of capturing some of the benefits of globalization, that is, producing and marketing a product to a world-wide market. Alliances can therefore help to win global coverage for marketing a product and use the expertise that alliance partners have developed in different parts of the world. They can also reduce competitive pressures as former rivals seek to co-operate. Research and development costs may be shared.

Alliances may take many forms from partial share holdings, collaboration on specific projects to loose networks for marketing. They avoid the problems of full mergers such as expense and reorganization. They are easier to withdraw from and are more flexible in that they can be used to focus on particular aspects of an organization's strategy.

Strategic alliances have proliferated in the airline industry and Case Study N examines the issues involved.

Case Study N: Strategic airline alliances

1995 was a record year for airline alliances – there were 401 of them, 133 of which involved inter-continental agreements. They range from co-ordination of timetables through code-sharing agreements to equity links.

Thus looser code-sharing deals include **Delta–Virgin Atlantic, United–Lufthansa**, and **Air France–Continental–Air Canada–Sabena–JAL**. Slightly more formalized are **Delta–Singapore Airlines–Swissair** which have purchased between 1 and 5 per cent of each other's equity.

Another set of alliances exhibit closer financial integration. For example, British Airways is the dominant partner in its grouping, **BA–US Air–Qantas–TAT–Deutsche BA**, owning a 25 per cent equity share in the first two and a 49 per cent share of the last two. Similarly, within the **KLM–Northwest Airlines–Air UK**, KLM owns 25 per cent and 45 per cent respectively of its partners. Mixed alliances include **American Airlines–Canadian Airlines–British Midland–Gulf Air–LOT** where American owns 33 per cent of Canadian and code-shares with the others.

Alliances offer airlines both product and market development. The product is developed in that it becomes more comprehensive. BA's barely concealed ambition is to become a global airline so that passengers can pick up its flights from any one point to any other point in the world. This is what code-sharing is all about. Whilst BA does not fly from Denver to London through code-sharing with US Air, it appears to do so on reservation systems. Also, alliance airlines share their frequent flier programmes – increasing their attractiveness. Cost-savings arise from higher load factors and a single advertisement for a world audience can offer considerable economies.

Case Study N (*continued*)

Market development is also an important motive for alliances. It has been estimated that the **KLM–Northwest** alliance resulted in an increase of their combined market share of the transatlantic route from 7 to 11 per cent (1992–1995) and that combined revenue/cost savings amounted to $300 million a year. Northwest's loss of $60 million in 1991 has turned into a profit of $830 million in 1994.

Alliances offer a point of entry into distant markets with reciprocal benefits to the partners – so just as United finds a new market in Europe through Lufthansa, Lufthansa is able to develop its US market. The BA alliance has been criticized for failing to find a partner in the rapidly growing Asia market to complete its world-wide network and in this respect the Delta alliance (US–Europe–Asia) is perhaps the most comprehensive.

One important reason for the favouring of alliances over full mergers is the political regulation and state ownership of many airlines. There are widespread restrictions of foreign ownership of flag carrying airlines.

Not all alliances have been successful. For example, the **American Airlines–Aer Lingus** and **Qantas–Japan Airlines** agreements failed. Reasons for failure may include procrastination, differing objectives, mistrust, failure to integrate timetables and differing product standards – in summary, incompatibility.

BA's alliance, despite adding to overall profitability, has encountered problems. Co-ordination of board meetings across world time zones has been difficult and its partner US Air has been dogged by financial problems. This culminated in BA writing off £125 million from the value of its investment and US Air is seeking new partners in 1996 in an attempt to improve its prospects.

Summary

1 This chapter has reviewed the process of generating strategic options.
2 Generic strategies fall into the categories of price-based, differentiation-based or hybrid strategies which can operate at a whole market or focused on a particular market segment.

3 Strategic directions describes the development strategies that can be adopted to achieve these strategies. The Ansoff matrix is a useful tool for distinguishing between directions according to the degree of market and/or product development involved.
4 Strategic methods investigates the routes by which an organization can develop and grow to achieve a desired strategy.

Review questions

1 Review and discuss any recent cases of the policy of withdrawal in the tourism industry.
2 'Market share is crucial for a hybrid strategy.' Explain, using examples from tourism, what is meant by this statement.
3 Examine the advantages and disadvantages, to producers and consumers, of the strong vertical integration that is evident in the UK package holiday industry.
4 Locate two recent examples of horizontal integration in the tourism industry and critically evaluate the success of each.
5 Distinguish between market development, market penetration and product development in the tourism industry.
6 Choosing either Planet Hollywood restaurants, Hilton International hotels, or Walt Disney themeparks, explain which of the following methods would be most appropriate for a programme of international expansion:
   (a) internal growth
   (b) mergers
   (c) franchising
   (d) joint ventures
   (e) alliances.
7 Propose a suitable generic strategy for the future development of a named tourism organization.
8 Can the concept of generic strategies be usefully applied to tourism destinations?

6
Evaluation of tourism corporate strategies

Chapter objectives

By studying this chapter students will be able to utilize a framework for evaluating strategic options.

Figure 6.1 illustrates the main techniques for evaluation, and by studying this chapter students should be able to apply:

- suitability analysis (does it fit our situation?)
- acceptability analysis (do we want to do it?)
- feasibility analysis (can it be done?)

in order to rank strategic options, thus enabling informed strategic choice.

Case Study O illustrates strategic options open to the government of Mauritius. Option 1 represents a strategy of differentiation where the tourism product offered is differentiated from other destinations by its exclusivity. Option 2 represents a low price, mass tourism strategy. The tools of analysis developed in this chapter can help tourism organizations choose between competing options.

Case Study P illustrates Rank's strategy of a joint venture with MCA, to develop a new theme park – Universal City, Florida. This strategy embraced product development (the two companies already co-own a theme park in Florida) and market penetration. Aiming to provide

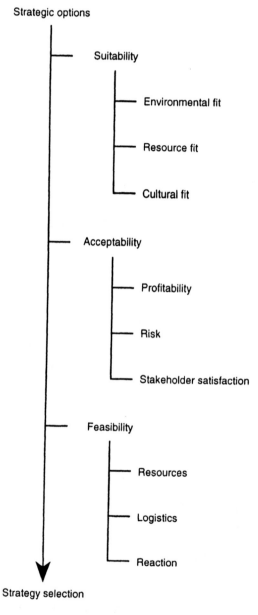

Figure 6.1 Strategic evaluation

Case Study 0: Tourism strategy for Mauritius

The Indian Ocean island of Mauritius, renowned for its shimmering white beaches and sparkling turquoise lagoons, is facing a dilemma for its tourism strategy.

The economy of Mauritius grew on average by 6 per cent per annum between 1985 and 1995, but rising wages and less favourable trade agreements under new General Agreement on Tariffs and Trade (GATT) arrangements have threatened the future of textiles and sugar, the island's key industries. Tourism, currently the island's third biggest earner of foreign currency is seen as a key to future economic development. The dilemma for tourism strategy can be seen in two competing options.

Under option 1 Mauritius would maintain its exclusive image by controlling the growth of tourism to a total of around 600,000 by the year 2000. Currently this policy has enabled the island to attract high-spending honeymoon couples and upmarket tourists. Supporting this view is Mr Sohun Ghoorah, manager of the government tourist office who says: 'We cannot survive if we lose our exclusive image, because no one will come on a 12-hour flight when they can get much cheaper holidays closer to home'.

Option 2 is to allow the rate of growth experienced in the early 1990s to continue by allowing more developments and flights. The ban on charter flights into the island would be lifted, for example. This policy would produce growth of tourists from 500,000 (1995) to around 1.5 million tourists by 2020. This option is favoured by hoteliers and those who see tourism as an important source of employment in view of the declining prospects for sugar and textiles. However, it is opposed by those who are worried about the effects of mass tourism on the social fabric of Mauritius and those who are sensitive to the encroachment of hotel developments onto public beaches.

families with 'value for money and a good day out' places the strategy as a generic hybrid one. This case will also be used to illustrate many of the following elements of strategic evaluation.

Case Study P: Universal City, Florida USA

In August 1995, Rank Organisation, the UK-based leisure group, and MCA, the US entertainment company, announced a new joint venture of a $2 billion (£1.3 billion) theme park to be built in Orlando, Florida. The park is expected to open in 1999.

The project – Universal's Islands of Adventure – will develop five individually themed islands to include Popeye, Spiderman, Jurassic Park and Dr Seuss characters. It will include four hotels and a 16-screen cinema with a capacity for 5000. A golf course and tennis complex will also be developed on the site.

The park will be built on land adjacent to Universal Studios, Florida, which is an existing cinema-based theme park and the two companies own both this park and the surrounding development land. The new complex, which has Disney World as a near neighbour, will be called Universal City, Florida.

In 1996, MCA announced plans to develop a new Universal Studios in Osaka, Japan. This is due to open in 2001 and Rank has an option to invest in this project. It would require an investment in the region of £45 million.

Suitability

Suitability analysis aims to test whether a strategy fits the situation facing a tourism organization or destination as identified by strategic analysis. Therefore suitability can be initially divided into:

- environmental fit
- resource fit
- cultural fit.

Environmental fit

The key questions relating to a strategy's fit with external environmental factors are whether the strategy exploits opportunities and whether it effectively counters threats. Therefore strategic options need to be evaluated against the factors which emerged from the C-PEST analysis.

The competitive environment

The main threats to Rank's strategy arise from competing theme parks in Florida, mainly Sea World, Wet n' Wild and Disney World. However, there is also a threat from global developments of theme parks. The USA was once the sole destination providing such attractions. But Disney now operates parks in Japan and France, Port Aventura has recently opened in Spain and Warner Brothers have opened their $255 million Movie World in Germany. Clearly, people now have more access to local regional theme parks as demonstrated by the fact that theme parks reached the £1 billion turnover level in Europe by 1993.

Second, competing theme parks continue to seek to add value to their products. For example, Disney has a $750 million project for the development of a wild animal theme park in Florida.

On the other hand the 'Honeypot theory' may well apply in Florida – the more theme parks in an area, the greater the attraction for tourists.

The political environment

The USA offers political stability and thus is a safe region for multinational investment. However, adverse international publicity on crime and violence affected Florida in the early 1990s following a wave of highly publicized muggings and murder of foreign tourists.

The economic environment

The economic environment appears to offer clear opportunities for development in Florida in the late 1990s. First, the domestic US economy has been improving. Second, the dollar is weak against European currencies and the Yen, making US prices attractive for foreign tourists. Third, European economies have recovered. These factors have contributed to a rise in admissions to Universal Studios of around 7 per cent per annum 1990–1995. The development of the Florida theme park will enable Rank to reduce its market exposure in the UK and seek greater geographical balance.

The socio-cultural environment

Three socio-cultural factors support the Universal City development. First, as economies grow richer a rising proportion of spending is committed to leisure. Second, children's leisure expectations are rising. Third, economic and cultural changes throughout the world mean that new potential markets emerge as tourists begin to flow from the Asia-Pacific region.

However, on the negative side, analysis of the population structures of the US, Europe and Japan, shows the average age of the populations are rising reflecting low birth rates. An ageing population is not advantageous for tourist attractions such as theme parks.

The technological environment

Possible threats to Universal City include competition from virtual leisure parks and the increasing sophistication of home-based leisure. However, technological developments in transportation seem set to continue the downward trend in the real price of air travel and thus Florida's international accessibility should improve.

Resource fit

Consideration of strategies in terms of an organization's internal strengths and weaknesses enables the degree of resource fit to be evaluated. This fit between strategy and reality can be analysed using:

- resource audit
- portfolio analysis
- product life cycle analysis
- value chain analysis.

Resource audit

An initial audit of an organization's resources may indicate whether a strategy is suitable in terms of current resources. In the case of Rank/MCA, suitable resources seem to be available.

First, the land for Islands of Adventure is already owned by the companies. Second, the organizations already have well-developed expertise gained through their joint development of Universal Studios, Florida and through running their respective individual enterprises – MCA in films and Rank in leisure management. Third, Rank's financial resources are strong, having raised £620 million in January 1994 from a partial sale of its holdings of Rank Xerox.

Strategic options do not always find such a ready fit in terms of existing resources and in many cases the acquisition of new resources will be necessary. Such issues are addressed later in this chapter under feasibility.

Portfolio analysis

Chapter 4 used the Boston Box to analyse the balance within an organization's product portfolio (refer to Figure 4.3).

Rank's portfolio of products at the time of this case included video duplication, film studios, cinemas, holiday centres, bingo and social clubs and restaurants (including the 'Hard Rock' chain). Market growth for some of these key products (particularly bingo and restaurants) was low, positioning them as deteriorating cash cows. Thus Rank's product portfolio was in need of refreshing. The Florida investment strategy represented the opportunity to participate in a question mark product (low market share/high market growth) with good prospects for transformation into a star (high market share/high market growth).

The General Electric Business Screen (Hofer and Schendel 1970) can also be a useful tool in assessing the suitability of a strategy. It analyses current and future products in terms of:

- the organization's competitive position (strong/weak)
- industry attractiveness (high/low).

Figure 6.2 places Rank's present and planned activities on a General Electric Screen, and illustrates the suitability of the Universal City project in terms of refreshing Rank's portfolio.

Note that bingo and social clubs are projected to become less attractive (largely due to competition from the national lottery) and holiday centres, which are largely UK-based, also face strong competition from overseas destinations. On the other hand, the theme park industry has high attractiveness and the prospects are good for Rank and MCA to improve their competitive position.

Product life cycle

Where does a theme park figure on a product life cycle curve (see Figure 4.4)? The basic product is well established and is thus probably at the growth/maturity phase. But the product is undergoing constant development which enables it to be repositioned in a growth phase. Thus theme

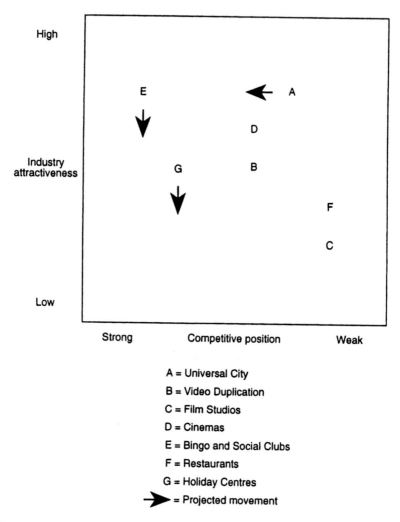

Figure 6.2 Rank's product profile on General Electric screen

parks invest considerably in new state-of-the-art attractions (Animal Park at Disney World, Space Mountain at Disneyland, Paris, Nemesis at Alton Towers), and Universal City is positioning itself towards movie-based themes. This project may be paced as being past the risky introduction phase of the product life cycle (theme parks themselves are well-established and Universal Studios is already successful) and into the growth phase where the prospects for the future are good.

Value chain analysis

This can be used to ascertain whether any enhancements in an organization's value chain will result from a particular strategy. There are several value chain enhancements that can result from the Rank/ MCA venture.

First, Universal City is an extension of the existing co-owned Universal Studios theme park. The addition of Islands of Adventure will result in additional value to the existing product in terms of more variety being offered to the customer. Second, MCA owns the rights to Jurassic Park, and therefore the development of the dinosaur theme in Islands of Adventure will exploit and develop that aspect of MCA's value chain. It adds an important new element to the exploitation and distribution of the product. Third, the development of recreational facilities such as golf, tennis and hotels represents an extension of the value chain attached to Universal City.

Thus value chain analysis for MCA/Rank suggests a logical fit where future product development fits well into present product ranges. In summary, these benefits may be termed as synergies. Synergies arise where the benefits of joint development by Rank and MCA exceed those attributable to the separate activities of those organizations – i.e. something extra is added in the process.

Cultural fit

Cultural fit considers how well a proposed strategy can be accommodated by an organization. Chapter 2 considered how an organization's culture gave rise to a particular paradigm – a way of seeing things and way of doing things.

Joint ventures, such as the Rank/MCA one, can result in difficulties of cultural integration where firms have markedly different paradigms. In this case, however, the dangers of a serious cultural clash are likely to be low. This is because Universal City is an extension of a joint project (Universal Studios, Florida) already well-developed between the organizations. It is therefore likely that cultural differences will have been resolved and that a shared paradigm has evolved.

Lack of cultural fit of a proposed strategy should not necessarily rule it out. It may be that an organization's existing culture is in need of change. The feasibility of effecting cultural change will need to be examined and this is addressed later in this chapter.

Acceptability

Acceptability scrutinizes strategic options in terms of whether organizational objectives are fulfilled and thus investigates factors such as:

- profitability (in the private sector)
- social profitability (in the public sector)
- risk
- stakeholder satisfaction.

Profitability

Since profit is a key element of the mission of most private sector organizations, profitability will be one of the most important ways of assessing the merits of a strategic option. Strategies with highest projected profitability will tend to be favoured. In the Rank/MCA case study, successful theme parks have a good track record at generating profits, hence the attraction of the Universal City project. The main tests for profitability include return on capital employed and payback period.

Return on capital employed

The formula for calculating return on capital employed (ROCE) is:

$$\text{ROCE} = \frac{\text{Profit before interest and tax}}{\text{Capital employed}} \times 100$$

It is likely that a date will be specified for a particular ROCE to be achieved.

Payback period

This method compares strategies by measuring the length of time it takes to repay the original investment from the revenues earned. Table 6.1 shows an example of the payback method.

Table 6.1 Payback period

Year	0	1	2	3	4
Costs	100				
Revenue	0	20	40	60	80
Cash flow	(100)	20	40	60	80
Cumulative cash flow	(100)	(80)	(40)	20	100

In this example, the project generates a positive cumulative cash flow in year 3. This method may favour projects with the quickest payback irrespective of overall profitability. On the other hand, the sooner the payback, the less a project will be subject to uncertainties, and some organizations may see speed of return as a priority over total return. This may be particularly true for theme parks where initial investment costs are high. For the Rank/MCA case study, it has been estimated that $690 million had been invested in the Universal Studios project by its completion in 1990 and that it had generated a net cash flow of $375 million by 1995.

A key problem with the simple payback method is that revenues are not discounted, so earnings within the payback period are given equal weight irrespective of the year in which they appear. This means that future earnings are overvalued. Discounted cash flow techniques are used to address this problem.

Payback method using discounted cash flow

Discounted cash flow takes into account the fact that future earnings have a lower value than current earnings. For example, if £100 today could be invested at a rate of interest of 10 per cent, it would be worth £110 in a year's time. Working this backwards, £110 in a year's time is only worth £100 today at a rate of interest of 10 per cent. In other words it has been discounted at a rate of 10 per cent to find its present discounted value. Discount tables exist to assist such calculations but there is also a formula for calculating present discounted value (PDV):

$$PDV = R_t/(1 + i)^t$$

R = return
t = year
i = rate of interest or discount rate (expressed as decimal)

Table 6.2 Payback period using DCF

Year	0	1	2	3	4
Costs	100				
Revenue (actual)	0	20.0	40.0	60.0	80.0
Revenue (discounted)		18.2	33.1	45.1	54.6
Cash flow (discounted)	(100)	18.2	33.1	45.1	54.6
Cumulative cash flow (discounted)	(100)	(81.8)	(48.7)	(3.6)	51.0

Table 6.2 applies this formula to recalculate the payback data from Table 6.1 to present discounted values using a discount rate of 10 per cent. Notice that this method pushes back the payback by one year.

Problems in using profitability analysis

Problems of using profitability analysis for strategy evaluation include first the fact that it may be difficult to isolate the costs and revenues that come from a particular strategy if it is not a clearly discrete project. Its costs and revenues may be inextricably mixed with other projects. Second, it is difficult to quantify the benefits of some strategy elements (e.g. investment in corporate image may lead to intangible benefits.) Third, there are the inherent dangers of uncertainty in forecasting.

Social profitability

Profitability analysis only includes expenditures and revenues which are internal to an organization (i.e. directly received or paid). Such a narrow view of profitability (i.e. private profitability), whilst appropriate to many private sector organizations, is not appropriate to the public sector or, for example, for evaluation of strategies of tourism destinations. In such cases social profitability will be a more useful indicator of acceptability. The technique used to determine social profitability is cost benefit analysis.

Social profitability attempts to measure the total costs and benefits of a strategic option beyond those that just affect the organization sponsoring the project. These external costs and benefits are not visible in an organization's profit and loss account but may have strong impacts on the wider community affected by an organization's activities. Thus an acceptable project in terms of private profitability would be one where

$$\Sigma Bp - \Sigma Cp \text{ is maximized,}$$

whilst an acceptable project in terms of social profitability would be one where

$$(\Sigma Bp + \Sigma Bs) - (\Sigma Cp + \Sigma Cs) \text{ is maximized,}$$

where,
Σ = the sum of
Bp = private (internal) benefits
Bs = social (external) benefits
Cp = private (internal) costs
Cs = social (external) costs

Table 6.3 considers the development of Changi Airport, Singapore in terms of its private profitability (net revenue generated for the Civil Aviation Authority of Singapore – CAAS), and its social profitability (overall acceptability to everyone affected by it).

Whilst calculating private costs and benefits is relatively straight-forward, it is more difficult to attribute monetary values for public costs and benefits (see Tribe 1995, Chapter 19).

Table 6.3 Changi Airport: private and social profitability

Costs	Benefits
Private costs	*Private benefits*
● Construction costs	● Revenue from airlines
● Finance costs	● Revenue from leases
● Running costs	
Social costs	*Social benefits*
● Noise pollution	● Employment provision
● More traffic generated	● Reduction in waiting time
● Air pollution	● More tourism to Singapore
● Loss of land to other uses	

Risk

The pursuance of a new strategy inevitably exposes an organization to some risk and an evaluation of the risk factors will help to determine the acceptability of a particular strategy. In particular, the risk of a strategy may be evaluated in terms of financial risk and sensitivity.

Financial risk

The financial risk inherent in a strategy will depend upon the capital cost of the project in comparison to the current capitalization and turnover of an organization. It is also important to consider the sources of funds to finance the project, its effects on the organization's overall liquidity position and the likely period of negative cash flow before a project breaks even. Thus a strategy which requires a large investment relative to current operations, which involves finance from banks and which has a distant break even point is likely to be of high risk. In short, failure of the strategy could jeopardize the whole organization.

In the Rank/MCA case the new investment in Universal City is large, at an estimated £1.3 billion. This can be compared to Rank's turnover in 1994 of £2.1 billion and operating profit of £227 million. However, the investment is shared between the two organizations and external sources of credit. Thus £780 million are being financed through bank credit, whilst Rank and MCA are providing the rest of the investment of £260 million each. This need not affect Rank's liquidity as it is a cash-rich company. It raised £620 million in February 1995 by selling 40 per cent of its share in Rank Xerox.

Sensitivity analysis

Taylor and Sparkes (1977) discuss the importance of sensitivity analysis in strategic evaluation. Sensitivity analysis considers how sensitive a project is to changes in the assumptions that underlie profitability forecasts. In particular, changes in the economic environment and competitor reaction may be important factors in causing actual prices and sales to deviate from predictions. Important factors to consider may include how the following affect profitability:

- changes in sales
- changes in prices
- changes in interest rates

- changes in costs
- changes in exchange rates.

A number of different scenarios may be considered and computer simulations can plot the predicted effects of changes revealed in these scenarios. Projects whose profits are sensitive to small changes, or for which the key assumptions are subject to a large degree of uncertainty will carry a high risk. Table 6.4 illustrates a sensitivity analysis conducted by Eurotunnel in 1994. It shows the sensitivity of the date of the first declaration of a dividend, to a number of different scenarios. It can be seen that under scenario 5, where Eurotunnel is unable to secure its desired level of refinancing, the declaration of first dividend is delayed considerably.

Stakeholder satisfaction

Stakeholder analysis, covered in Chapter 2, enables the key stake-holders who will be affected by a particular strategy to be identified. It may be recalled (see Figure 2.6) that it is important to identify stakeholder influence (as measured by stakeholder power) as well as stakeholder interest when assessing acceptability. Once again, those stakeholders with high power/interest will be the key players to whom stakeholder satisfaction analysis needs to be primarily addressed. In the Rank/MCA case, stakeholders that need to be considered for Rank include:

- shareholders (how will share prices/dividends be affected?)
- bankers (will the strategy affect Rank's credit worthiness?)
- unions (what impact will the strategy have on employment?)
- government (will the strategy infringe monopoly laws?)
- local people (how will local environment be affected?)

Table 6.4 Sensitivity analysis for Eurotunnel (1994) (*Source*: Eurotunnel)

Scenario	First dividend declared in the year . . .
1. Current projections (x)	2003
2. Revenue at x + 10%, costs at x − 3%	2000
3. Revenue at x − 10%, costs at x + 3%	2006
4. Real interest rates at x − 1%	2001
5. Only limited financing obtained in 1994	2014

Feasibility

Feasibility seeks to test whether a strategy can be realistically achieved and asks whether an organization already possesses or has access to the necessary resources. It therefore subjects strategic options to scrutiny in terms of:

- funding
- human resourcing
- timing/logistics
- competitive reaction.

Funding

Whilst profitability analysis tests whether a strategy yields an acceptable rate of return, funding analysis seeks to ascertain whether an organization can actually finance a particular strategy. Strategies will generally be funded from:

- retained profits
- disposals
- loans
- new share capital.

An organization may already have the necessary cash in hand to fund a particular strategy. Such assets may arise from profits retained from current and past activities or from cash generated by the disposal of companies, SBUs or brands. Where strategies can be financed from cash in hand, feasibility is clearly not a problem.

In the absence of sufficient funds at hand, organizations will need to seek new finance. Bank loans are a possible option. Here funding feasibility can be broken into two components. First, can funds be obtained? This will depend upon the bank's evaluation of the strategy to be financed as well as its assessment of the borrowing organization's overall credit rating. Second, how much will bank funding cost? A key issue here is how much the cost of loans (the rate of interest) adds to the costs of the project.

The other main source of new funds for public limited companies is by a rights issue. This is where new shares are sold to existing shareholders, thus raising new capital. The feasibility of a rights issue depends upon whether shareholders agree to a rights issue, the costs of the issue and whether shareholders are prepared to buy the new shares (i.e.

shareholder evaluation of a project's profitability and thus its potential to contribute to increased share prices and healthy share dividends into the future).

In the case of the Rank/MCA case study, funds are generated by the first three of the above sources. A bank credit facility provided by a syndicate of banks including JP Morgan, Nations Bank, NatWest Markets and Bank of Novia Scotia is supplying a loan of £780 million. Rank is sourcing the rest of the finance from profits retained from the operations of Universal Studios and cash in hand from its recent disposal of part of its share in Rank Xerox of £620 million. Thus the project is feasible in terms of funding analysis.

Human resourcing

The feasibility of a strategy may also be reviewed in terms of the skills of an organization's work-force. An audit can be useful in determining whether the skills necessary for the success of a particular strategy are available or accessible. Such audits need to consider several dimensions.

First, are skills available in the relevant functional area – e.g. marketing, operations management, financial management, purchasing. Second, it may be important to have personnel with knowledge of a particular market, e.g. hotels, airlines, theme parks, or geographical area. Third, the dynamics of a team assigned to a particular strategy are important. Here considerations include skills in project management as well as a range of team attributes. For example, is the project team balanced in terms of innovators, team workers, finishers, and sceptics?

Timing/logistics

Timing and logistics are crucial to some projects and timing has a knock-on effect on profitability. Therefore consideration needs to be given to the feasibility of a project's estimated scheduling. Here break even analysis can be a useful device. The question that needs to be asked is whether the assumptions underlying the initial analysis are realistic ones and what would be the effects on the break even point of a failure of a project to complete to its original timetable. Figure 6.3 illustrates a break even analysis for the Channel Tunnel and shows how its break even point has been profoundly affected by delay.

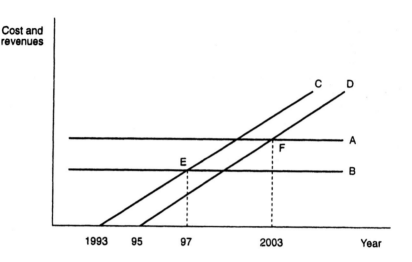

Key:

C, D = Total revenues

A, B = Total costs

For the Channel Tunnel project, the initial projections were that the tunnel would open in 1993, and that total revenues would then increase sharply (C) to achieve break-even (E) by 1997, with costs B.

However, construction and fitting delays meant that a full service did not occur until 1995. Thus the revenue curve shifts outwards to D and the cost curve shifts upwards from B to A as new borrowing is needed to finance the delay. Break-even (F) moves to around the year 2003. However, under some scenarios, break even is not achieved at all.

Figure 6.3 Break even analysis

Competitive reaction

Competitive reaction is an important consideration for the feasibility of any new strategy. This is perhaps most dramatically illustrated by developments in the Dover–Calais cross channel market (UK–France). When Le Shuttle (the channel tunnel service) opened in 1995, prices entered a period of intense competition. The main players in the market are the ferries – P&O, Stena Line, Sea France and Le Shuttle. 1996 was a bad year for consumers who booked up early. The original brochure price for a car and passengers with P&O was £339 for a peak return. Stena Line later promoted an early booking fare of £184. Le Shuttle undercut this with a peak return price of £129, but Sea France offered the lowest price of the season of £95 for their one price summer return. This forced companies such as P&O to abandon traditional marketing campaigns because published prices were soon out of date. Instead their 1996 advertising slogan became:

SNAP! Show us a competitor's discount and we'll match it instantly

Competitor reaction is likely to be fierce when there is a high degree of competitive rivalry (see Porter's (1979) five forces analysis, Chapter 4).

Choosing between options

The preceding analysis has surveyed some of the analytical tools available to assist in evaluating strategic options. However, it is likely that evaluation of options will generate a series of mixed results with each strategic option having a conflicting list of good and bad points. Under such a situation no clear winning strategy may emerge and resolution of this kind of stalemate requires prioritization of evaluation criteria.

This may involve listing some objectives that must be achieved (e.g. minimum ROCE) and some effects that must be avoided (e.g. loss of ownership and overall control of the organization). These may be classed as essential criteria. It is then possible to attach weightings to other criteria to reflect their relative importance. Thus an initial screening of options can rule out those which fail the essential tests and options may then be ranked according to their performance against the other, weighted criteria.

Ranking

Table 6.5 illustrates screening and ranking for the four strategic options available to Mauritius for tourism development. Most of the options are a mixture of pluses and minuses and evaluation is not clear. However, if protection of the environment is made an essential criteria then options 1 and 4 are screened out as not acceptable. Options two and three remain, each with a score of +8. If responsiveness of strategy to a

Table 6.5 Screening and ranking options

	Minimize resource costs of new investment	Generate extra employment	Protect environment	Achieve high economic growth	Responsive to changing external environment
1. Do nothing	+5	0	−2	0	0
2. Contentrate on exclusive image (sell to existing markets)	+5	0	+1	+1	+1
3. Concentrate on exclusive image (sell to new markets)	+3	0	+1	+1	+3
4. Lift ban on charter flights/ allow hotel development	−3	+4	−5	+2	0

Key:
<More unfavourable −5 −4 −3 −2 −1 0 +1 +2 +3 +4 +5 More favourable>

changing environment is thought to be a particularly important criterion of evaluation, it could be double weighted. This changes the overall scores to +9 for option 2 and +11 for option 3 which emerges as the most appropriate strategy.

Summary

1 There are three essential questions used to evaluate competing strategies:
   (a) does it fit our situation?
   (b) do we want to do it?
   (c) can it be done?
2 These questions are examined using
   (a) suitability analysis
   (b) acceptability analysis
   (c) feasibility analysis.
3 Suitability analysis considers the fit of a strategy in terms of C-PEST factors in the external environment, as well as considering an organization's resource capability and culture.

4 Acceptability analysis reviews strategy in relation to the aims and missions of an organization.

5 Feasibility examines whether an organization is able to muster the necessary resources to follow a particular strategy and scrutinizes plans in terms of their logistics and likely competitor reaction.

6 A ranking matrix can help in strategic decision-making particularly where strategic impacts are mixed. Here competing strategies are awarded scores according to how well they meet particular criteria.

Review questions

1 What is meant by cultural fit? Which factors suggest a good cultural fit and which suggest a poor one, between Rank and MCA?

2 Under what circumstances will cost benefit analysis rather than profitability be used to determine the acceptability of a strategy?

3 Use the framework in Figure 6.1 to carry out a full evaluation of the competing tourism strategies for Mauritius (Case Study O). Indicate what extra information is required and the likely sources of such information.

4 What is sensitivity analysis? Assume that Mauritius opts for a strategy of mass tourism. What variables would such a strategy be sensitive to, and how might they change in the future?

5 Identify a recent or proposed merger or take-over between tourism organizations. Evaluate the suitability of such a move.

6 What factors would make a strategy a high risk one?

Part 4: Strategic implementation

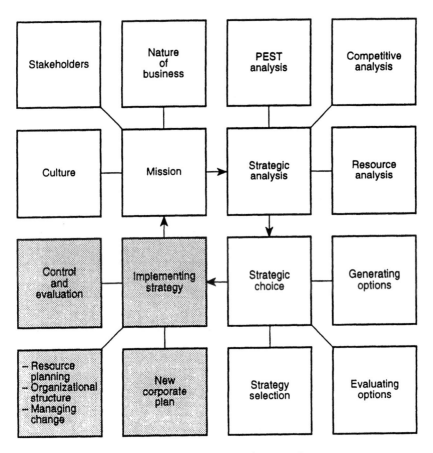

Figure 7.1 Implementation and the strategic framework

The final stage of tourism corporate strategy is strategic implementation. By the end of Part 4 it should be possible to construct a plan to operationalize a strategy for a tourism organization and systematically monitor that strategy. Strategic implementation follows logically from the previous three stages, where an appropriate strategy has been selected from a number of options after a comprehensive situational analysis of the tourism organization.

Chapter 7 introduces the concept of a corporate planning document and investigates the detail of planning in terms of financial, physical and human resources. Chapter 8 concludes the strategy process by examining the management of change and reviewing methods of control and evaluation of strategy.

7
Corporate planning

Chapter objectives

Case Study Q illustrates some practical issues of strategic implementation at Air France.

Case Study Q: Air France recovery strategy

Air France operates in a threatening environment. The key threats are twofold. First, it is a state-owned airline and the EU is committed to a policy of liberalization of the European airline market and a withdrawal of subsidies. Second, it is faced with intense competition from geographically close rivals British Airways and Lufthansa. BA in particular has become an efficient, service-driven airline since its privatization.

Air France began the 1990s in bad shape with annual losses of around FF 8 billion ($1.5 billion) per year and accumulated debt of around FF 40 billion ($7.5 billion). Attempts to implement a rescue-strategy had ended in strike action and the resignation of the chairman, Bernard Attali.

Christian Blanc became chairman of Air France at the end of 1993 and his major task was to put the rescue-strategy into effect. The strategy itself was fairly straightforward. It involved first an

Case Study Q (*continued*)

attack on costs and second a concentration on improvement in service quality in order to generate more revenue. In short, a classic hybrid strategy.

Central to the cost-cutting measures was a package which had little obvious attraction to the work-force. The proposals included a pay freeze, productivity gains of 30 per cent to be achieved by 1998 and the loss of 5000 jobs. Needless to say, this package was opposed by the majority of Air France's unions and there seemed little prospect of Blanc succeeding where Attali had failed. No action or strike action seemed inevitable.

Blanc responded to this impasse in a novel way by going over the heads of the trade unions and putting the package directly to the company's 40,000 work-force by way of a referendum. 30,000 of the employees participated in the referendum and more than 80 per cent of those who voted were in favour of the plan. This led to the eventual approval by a majority of the trade unions, enabling cost-cutting to be put into effect.

With regard to improving service quality, the structure of the company was diagnosed as being a key blockage. Structural difficulties were also seen as an important contributor to a dysfunctional culture where cost efficiency was given a low priority. Thus reorganization of Air France was seen as an important part of operationalizing the recovery strategy.

A team of consultants from SMG summarized the organizational problems as follows:

- a marked inability to adapt
- hierarchical and centralized management with little co-ordination between activities
- excellence in technical rather than commercial aspects of airline operations
- preoccupation by staff with their own job rather than service provision.

The SMG consultants recommended a reorganization of the company structure that would bring about decentralization and improved co-ordination. Decision-making was to be encouraged at

Case Study Q (*continued*)

the lowest possible level and smaller operating units were designed to improve team working and communications.

The original management structure which consisted of a few large managerial divisions such as the personnel, transport, airport and commercial divisions, was therefore replaced. Eleven profit centres were created to focus on more specific activities. These included distinct geographical markets such as America France, and the Paris airport services, as well as freight and maintenance operations. The new profit centres took responsibility for personnel, transport and airport responsibilities as it affected them.

The declared benefits of the new system included:

- stripping out of layers of management (from eight to three)
- improved responsiveness
- identifying accountability and responsibility of managers
- creation of client/supplier relationships between profit centres.

It was also felt that the destruction of the old system and its replacement with a new system facilitated cultural changes and encouraged new thinking and attitudes. However, François Dupuy, an SMG consultant, noted that while the organizational restructuring 'sent a powerful message of change . . . you can't alter attitudes just by redrawing the company organogram.'

Implementing change at Air France faced some profound difficulties. First, the entrenched nature of attitudes within such a large, previously bureaucratically organized company. Second, the nature of Air France itself. As a nationalized company it has lacked a commercial edge with losses being covered by state aid. Similarly there has been little incentive for personal initiative.

Thus two other important agents of change have been introduced. First, a share incentive scheme has been introduced. In return for a pay cut, employees have been offered shares in Air France – reducing costs and increasing incentives. Second, there has been a review of senior management. The executive committee of the company has been reduced from 40 to 25 and many of them are new appointments.

Case Study Q (*continued*)

In the financial year 1995–96, Air France made an operating profit of FF413 million ($77.5 million), its first since 1989. However, it made an overall net loss of FF2.9 billion ($544 million). This was largely due to the short-term effects of the rescue package which included the costs of voluntary severance packages to cabin crew of FF630 million ($118 million), and FF1.365 billion ($256 million) for ground staff.

The recovery strategy has itself come under recent review. M. Blanc said in 1996 that if it were to survive, Air France faced two choices – to be merged with Air France Europe or to turn itself into a low cost airline. The second option would involve cutting costs further, low pay, leasing of aircraft, withdrawal from many routes and no frills service. Reflecting that this was an impossible option for a 'traditional company'. M. Blanc announced that Air France Europe (formerly Air Inter) would be merged with Air France. A reduction in Air France Europe's costs to Air France's levels and a closer integration of international and national services 'would be a decisive factor in allowing the French flag carrier to compete with high performance US and European carriers.'

However, Serge Boulet, a spokesman for Air France Europe's union, warned: 'We're heading for a period of conflict . . . We aren't weak enough to allow ourselves to be gobbled up without a fight.'

The objective of this chapter is analyse the planning factors which enable a tourism organization's strategy to be successfully implemented.

By studying this chapter students will be able to identify and utilize the main planning techniques of strategic implementation which are:

- preparation of corporate strategy
- resource planning
- design of organizational structure.

Strategies that evolve in different organizations may well have different emphases between these elements. Thus the nature of the Rank/MCA

Universal City project (see Case Study P, Chapter 6), makes resource planning the key issue for implementation as it is a new project requiring significant new physical resources. On the other hand, organizational structure and management of change (see Chapter 8) were central to the Air France recovery plan, Here, the physical resources are in place but their management has been inefficient.

Preparation of corporate strategy

Central to the idea of corporate planning is the preparation of a corporate strategy. The key to this will be a master document which encompasses the main headings of this book. Thus a corporate strategy will have the following key sections:

- mission
- strategic analysis
- strategic choice
- strategic implementation.

This strategy will inform the organization's activities for the medium term – typically five years. However, most organizations have a rolling programme of strategic planning where the strategy is reviewed and amended yearly. Figure 7.2 illustrates a skeleton framework that could be used as a basis for a strategic planning document.

Resource planning

The evaluation stage of the strategy process involved analysis of the feasibility of an option in terms of finance and availability of resources. At the implementation stage, resource planning is concerned with:

- identification of resources
- resource fit
- formulation of a co-ordinating plan.

Identification of resources

Financial resources

At the financial level it is essential to have budgets prepared which show how an organization's strategy is to be financed. In particular plans need to show:

1 Introduction
  1.1 Executive summary
    1.1.1 Summary of main points of report
    1.1.2 Recommendations (proposed strategy)

2 Mission
  2.1 Nature of business
    2.1.1 Defining the business of the organization
    2.1.2 Identifying key strategic business units
  2.2 Mission and goals
    2.2.1 Statement of mission of organization
    2.2.2 Objectives set

3 Strategic analysis
  3.1 Analysis of external environment
    3.1.1 PEST factors
      3.1.1.1 Trends in political environment
      3.1.1.2 Trends in economic environment
      3.1.1.3 Trends in sociocultural environment
      3.1.1.4 Trends in technological environment
    3.1.2 Competitive environment
      3.1.2.1 Structural analysis
      3.1.2.2 Strategic group analysis
      3.1.2.3 Competitor analysis
  3.2 Analysis of capability
    3.2.1 Evaluation of product portfolio
    3.2.2 Resource audit (availability/effectiveness/efficiency)
      3.2.2.1 Human resources
      3.2.2.2 Physical resources
      3.2.2.3 Financial resources
      3.2.2.4 Intangibles
  3.3 SWOT summary and analysis

4 Strategic choice
  4.1 An outline of alternative strategies, directions and methods
  4.2 An evaluation of the alternative strategies under review
  4.3 The proposed strategy, direction and method

5 Strategic implementation
  5.1 Planning
    5.1.1 Resource implications of strategy
    5.1.2 Network analysis for strategy
    5.1.3 Review of organization structures
  5.2 Monitoring
    5.2.1 Setting and measuring objectives and key tasks
    5.2.2 Evaluation of strategy (assumptions testing and
      monitoring financial or other targets)

Figure 7.2 Strategic planning framework: strategic plan for XXX organization

- sources of finance
- logistics of finance (to ensure co-ordination between income and expenditure).

The Channel Tunnel project (UK/France) illustrated the importance of both these factors. Sources of finance were divided between bank loans and share issues, and phased so that additional sources were available as the project progressed. This is illustrated in Table 7.1. However, important problems of financial planning for Eurotunnel were the frequent extensions and rescheduling that were necessitated by slippages in the timetable for construction and opening of the project.

Physical resources

A change in strategic direction will generally require adjustments in physical resources at the level of plant and machinery or consumables. A tourism organization may have a dedicated purchasing department to co-ordinate the buying of physical resources. Important considerations in physical resources planning include:

- specification – this may involve a careful audit of the uses to which physical resources are to be put. The result will be a list of required specifications.
- fitness for purpose – this will examine the match between the specifications offered and the specifications required.
- cost – prices between suppliers need to be compared, taking into account running and maintenance costs.
- terms – is it more appropriate to lease or buy capital goods?

Table 7.1 Sources of finance for Eurotunnel (*Sources: Financial Times, Eurotunnel*)

Year	Loans	Equity
1986		● £46 million seed corn equity raised ● £206 million share placing with institutions
1987	● £5 billion loan agreed with 200-bank syndicate	● £770 million from public share offer in UK and France
1990	● £1.8 billion loan extension from bank syndicate ● £300 million loan from European Investment Bank	● £650 million rights issue of shares
1994	● £700 million additional bank loan	● £850 million rights issue of shares

For airlines, purchasing decisions range from the ordering of in-flight catering, through computer systems, to the ordering of aircraft and requirements will vary according to different strategic aims. For example, in-flight meals will be differently specified for the different strategies of low price, hybrid or high value added. Large airlines will have a powerful influence on suppliers and the specific requirements of the biggest carriers, such as Delta, American and British Airways, will be canvassed by aircraft manufacturers at the design stage for incorporation into the finished product.

Tour operators will similarly choose hotels to fit particular marketing strategies. Thus while price-based packages may well tolerate thin walls, high rise and Spartan service, high value-added packages would have more exacting specifications.

Human resources

Strategic implementation will have consequences for human resources, and manpower planning will need to address:

- manpower numbers
- skills
- recruitment and selection
- training and development
- grading and remuneration.

Strategic plans will need to determine both the quantity and the quality of the future work-force. In the Air France case, for example, the size of the work-force is a key issue. Productivity gains and 'downsizing' are central to the recovery plan in order to achieve the necessary reductions in costs. Careful consideration to the design of a redundancy programme is therefore central to this case. On the other hand the Rank/MCA Universal City plan (Case Study P) involves expansion and therefore particular attention must be paid to recruitment and selection of new personnel.

In both cases a programme of manpower training and development needs to be thought out. For Air France, the case study emphasizes the importance of cultural change and staff development may centre round programmes which communicate new strategic thinking with the work-force, and emphasize service quality and customer care. Worker re-education is more difficult here than for the Rank/MCA case, where new appointees may be more easily inducted into company practices and culture.

Burns (1995: 61) identified the particular problems of training which face the hotel industry in Romania in its transition from communism and central planning to capitalism and market forces. He noted that 'existing business culture has historically been focused on maintaining existing structures . . . [leading] to an operational culture unable to cope with the notion of customer-focused business activities'.

Finally, consideration needs to be given to grading and remuneration packages. It is interesting to note the element of share options which has been incorporated into the Air France recovery plan in order to increase motivation and incentives.

Resource fit

There are two potential problems of resource fit. First, the technical issue of how new resources will fit with existing ones? This is a particular problem for areas such as computer resources, where new software may just not technically operate on old systems, or the computer systems of two merging organizations may be incompatible.

The second problem of resource fit concerns fit between resources and organizational skills. An airline may be tempted, for example, to purchase planes from a different manufacturer offering better specifications and lower prices. However, the problem of integration of new planes into the existing fleet may be problematic in areas such as crew competence and maintenance expertise. Thus there are some clear manpower planning considerations in physical resource planning.

Formulation of a co-ordinating plan

A co-ordinating plan is a key to strategic implementation. It comprises the following elements:

- project logistics (planning)
- project objectives (operations).

Project logistics (planning)

The logistics of the Universal City (Florida) project (see Case Study P) are shown in Figure 7.3.

This is a large scale and complex project. Therefore each stage is assigned an estimated time slot so that an overall schedule for completion may be planned and a critical path is formulated. A critical

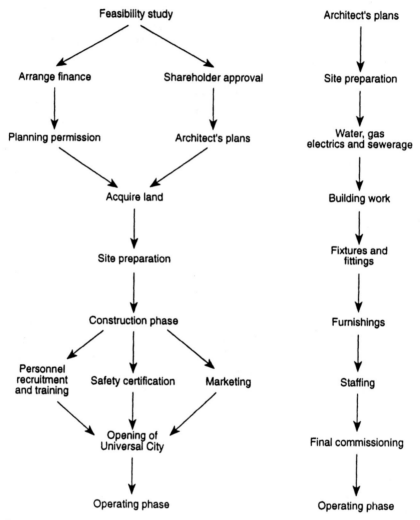

Figure 7.3 Project plan (logistics) Universal City – whole complex (left), single hotel (right)

path demonstrates the order in which the project must be executed, as well as showing those activities which may be programmed at the same time. It enables a project to be organized in the most efficient way. The importance of such analysis is first, to enable materials ordering and subcontracting to be co-ordinated and second, to highlight the impact of changes in one area on other areas. The Channel Tunnel exemplified these kind of knock-on effects. Delays in construction, fitting and safety certification meant that the initial marketing effort was largely wasted in trying to sell a service which was not opened in accordance with the original schedule.

It may be that the outcomes associated with some strategies could potentially be achieved at the same time. For example, there is no logistical obstacle to retraining managers in Romanian hotels (Burns 1995) in service delivery, personnel management and computer literacy. However, an attempt to achieve immediately all the desired outcomes will tend to lead to overload and superficial change. Here priorities need to be set to enable each objective to be properly met and monitored.

Project objectives (operations)

Management by objectives (MBO) is a system whereby strategy is translated into a number of clearly stated outcomes or objectives. The achievement of these objectives is assigned to specific personnel. MBO has been defined as:

> a system that integrates the company goals of profit and growth with the manager's needs to contribute and develop himself personally
> (Humble 1970: 21)

> directing each job towards the objectives of the whole business
> (Drucker 1968: 150)

Thus MBO can be an important contributor to strategic implementation. First, MBO helps to clarify the strategy – what does the strategy mean in terms of measurable performance targets? Second, MBO assists implementation since this now becomes attributable to personnel who have been assigned specific tasks. The key stages to effective MBO are:

- introduction of MBO – here, the purposes and the workings of MBO need to be explained
- setting of objectives – objectives should be generated from the strategic plan in consultation with relevant personnel. They should be prioritized, quantifiable and subject to time constraints
- performance review – participants require feedback about performance. Review, which may take the form of appraisal, should consider both past performance and future goal setting. There may be some form of performance related pay included

- monitoring – there should be periodic checking that objectives are being fulfilled and that strategic goals are being met.

Design of organizational structure

An organizational structure is the framework which describes how an organization's activities are arranged. It shows how its personnel are grouped together and the purposes of the groupings (e.g. marketing, human resource management). It shows lines of communications between groupings, organizational hierarchy and control. Mintzberg (1979) defines an organization's structure as '. . . the ways in which its labour is divided into distinct tasks and then its co-ordination achieved amongst those tasks.'

Organizational structure is a key consideration in determining how successful an organization is in achieving its aims. For this reason it has been said that 'structure follows strategy' (Chandler 1962; Sloan 1963; Child 1977). In other words, if a change in strategic direction has been decided, organizational structure will need to change to implement that strategy. However Mintzberg *et al.* (1995: 335) observe that 'Structure . . . no more follows strategy than the left foot follows the right in walking. The two exist interdependently, each influencing the other.' The point here is that any emerging strategy will itself be strongly influenced by the existing organizational structure.

Structural types

The main types of organizational structure include:

- simple
- functional
- multidivisional
- matrix structure
- holding company
- experimental.

However, it should be remembered that as well as the formalized organizational structure, informal structures generally also establish themselves. Whilst the formal structure is found in company manuals and handbooks, individuals within organizations frequently establish informal networks and ways of circumventing the formal structure.

Simple structure

This is typically found in small businesses and is often characterized by the absence of structure. There is little in the way of formalized division of responsibilities or clear lines of reporting. Such structures clearly can only operate when personnel are in close contact and therefore as an organization grows in size, formal structures inevitably arise.

Functional structure

The basic groupings within this form are those of functional areas, typically finance, production, marketing, personnel and research and development, as illustrated in Figure 7.4. This structure is often used in a single product, single market organization.

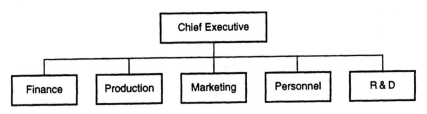

Figure 7.4 Functional structure

The benefits of this structure are that roles and responsibilities are clearly defined and that overall control by the chief executive is simplified. However, these are offset by the problem of horizontal communications between functional groups. This often involves the unnecessary referring up of relatively routine decisions. The focus of the organization on its customers may also be lost as functional groups compete with each other for power and status. Indeed, arrangement of Air France's structure on mainly functional lines (see Case Study Q) was seen as generating significant problems such as 'little co-ordination between activities', 'a marked inability to adapt', 'hierarchical . . . management', 'excellence in technical rather than commercial aspects' and 'preoccupation by staff with their own job rather than service provision.'

Multidivisional structure

A divisional structure groups activities according to a firm's products or services or geographical areas and is therefore more suitable for organizations with a diversity of products or services and markets. It avoids conflicts which are based on different functions (e.g. disputes between marketing and finance departments) and allows greater concentration on the customer. Also each division can be monitored as a separate unit encouraging a close supervision of costs and sales. However, although some functions (such as finance) may be provided centrally, others need to be provided within each division which may lead to duplication of effort. A typical divisional structure is illustrated in Figure 7.5.

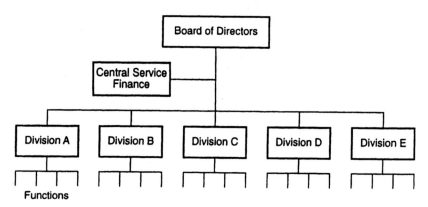

Figure 7.5 Multidivisional structure

The revised organizational form at Air France with its new focus on profit centres has moved more towards this type of structure. Divisions were formed for 'geographical markets such as America, France and the Paris airport services, as well as freight and maintenance operations.' Each division took its own responsibility for functional areas such as personnel.

Matrix structure

A matrix structure can be used where an organization wants to encourage collaborative tension between two arms of management. It may be appropriate if an organization has a number of products or services which are sold in a number of markets (product/market matrix) or to provide balance between the divisional organization of a firm and its functional operations (functional/divisional matrix). A product/market matrix for a multinational organization is illustrated in Figure 7.6.

It can be seen that this structure creates a number of units which report to different management arms. Its benefits include a more collaborative approach to decision-making. However, responsibility for decisions may become less clear. Members of units may prefer to have a single line manager rather than two potentially conflicting managers. Also resolution of disputes between the axes of the matrix may lead to overburdening of senior management, since co-ordination of the two

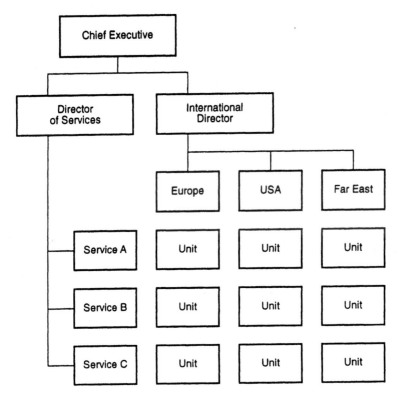

Figure 7.6 Service/market matrix structure

arms only occurs at a senior level. Decision-making may therefore involve a better quality of debate, but at the expense of increased time taken in reaching decisions.

Holding company

A holding company is an umbrella-type structure for the ownership and co-ordination of a number of clearly separated business units which are allowed a high degree of independence in decision-making. Control is exercised at arms length, with each unit having its own internal organizational structure. The benefits to the holding company are that it can spread its risks through its holdings of a cross-section of businesses. It can also adjust its portfolio, selling subsidiaries which do not meet profit targets and acquiring companies in growth sectors. The size of the overall group can enable cheaper finance to be obtained and temporary setbacks within individual markets to be weathered. Problems may include difficulties in managing such cumbersome organizations. Figure 7.7 shows some of the principle subsidiaries of Pearson plc, a UK holding type company whose subsidiaries include the Tussauds Group. This is a visitor attractions company whose interests include the Madame Tussaud's waxworks (London), the Alton Towers themepark (UK) and the Port Aventura themepark (Spain).

Experimental structure

Ricardo Semler, CEO of Semco, adopts an unorthodox organizational structure for his company. His thesis (Semler 1994) is that rigid, top down management is inappropriate for the conditions of the 1990s and beyond. He has therefore discarded secretaries, reserved parking spaces, executive dining rooms, dress codes and most rules. In their place he has introduced the guiding principles of democracy, common

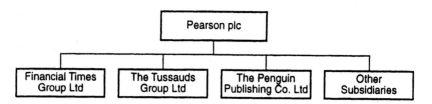

Figure 7.7 A holding company structure

sense and just two main grades of staff. Managers set their own salaries and associates vote on company strategy, decide their own working hours and are responsible for all aspects of production.

Structural elements

Mintzberg (1979) identified six basic elements common to all organizational structures. These are:

- the operating core – the employees who produce the goods or provide the services
- the strategic apex – the management of the organization
- the middle line – as organizations grow, middle-managers are needed
- the techno-structure – analysts such as accountants and statisticians who perform a monitoring role
- the support staff – who provide internal services such as catering, cleaning and legal services
- its ideology – which describes the overarching values, beliefs and aims of the organization.

Mintzberg used this classification of structural elements to analyse how organizations were co-ordinated and how different styles of organization could develop.

Issues in organizational design

Strategic change will generally require structural change. For example, a policy of expansion may require a move towards a divisional structure to co-ordinate the introduction of new products or new markets. A policy of diversification and acquisition of new companies may lead to the establishment of a holding company type structure.

But organizational change may need more than just a change in structural type. For example, the emergence of a strong new competitor/service (e.g. the introduction of the channel tunnel services) may require a fast and adaptable response. In this case organizational responsiveness and flexibility will be a key consideration. Here organizational characteristics are important. Key issues in organizational design include:

- nature of structural groupings
- tall vs. flat structures

- bureaucratic vs. flexible
- centralization vs. decentralization
- co-ordination of structural elements.

Nature of structural groupings

Here the issue is the basis on which the cells in an organizational structure should be grouped. Functional structures have departments such as personnel, finance, research and development differentiated according to different types of work. The benefits of this are that specialists work together and support each other. However, the danger is that employees focus on their job role rather than on service to the customer.

Product or service departments are organized around single products or services and all the activities relating to that product – raw materials, processing and marketing are controlled within that division.

Market departments are organized around specific geographical markets or customer types. The particulars of individual markets thus become the focus of organizational activity. The Air France recovery strategy involved moving to product and market centred groupings, away from functional groupings.

Tall vs. flat structures

A tall structure is one with many levels of management. Benefits derived from tall structures include, first, that the span of control at each level is narrow. This means that each manager supervises perhaps three or four subordinates on the next level and therefore effective supervision of activities can take place. Communication lines are generally clear, as are lines of authority. Tall structures enable specialization of effort and concentration on tasks.

However, in recent years there has been a movement towards flattened structures. Here levels of management are stripped out, leaving fewer steps between the organizational apex and its base and this is one of the features of the new Air France strategy where management layers were reduced from eight to three. One of the prime motives for this is the reduction in costs. Communication lines are shorter leading to a more responsive organization. The management is more in touch with its customers. However, the reduction in levels may make delegation of tasks more difficult since there are fewer subordinates.

A flat organization is not necessarily the same as a lean organization where the aim is to reduce staffing. This may cause a reduction in specialists and reduce an organization's capability to continue to add value to its products.

Bureaucratic vs. flexible

A bureaucratic organization will confine its operations to its organizational structure fairly rigidly. It will be most suitable in stable environments and where procedures and end products or services are standardized. There will be clear supervision of activities.

This may be contrasted with a flexible structure where employees are encouraged to take initiative. Here the structure is indicative rather than rigid and it is therefore open to negotiation and change. Employees are likely to be multi-skilled and their responsibilities may overlap. This type of structure may be necessary for an organization operating in a turbulent environment.

Scandinavian Airline Systems (SAS), under Jan Carlson in the 1980s, moved from a policy of strict adherence to company manuals when Carlson urged staff to 'throw out the manuals and use your heads instead'. A move from the bureaucratic to the flexible was thus heralded and front line staff were given the decision-making power to do what was reasonably appropriate to please the customer.

Centralization vs. decentralization

In a centralized organization, decisions are taken at the apex of the organization in top-down manner. The benefits are that a unified strategy can be more easily directed and a strong corporate identity and image imposed. On the other hand, decentralized organizations encourage decision-making to be made at the lowest possible level. This may be more appropriate for large organizations and where flexibility and responsiveness to changing environments are paramount. Air France's move towards profit centres reflects the philosophy of decentralization.

Co-ordination of structural elements

Mintzberg (1979) concluded that there were three basic ways in which the elements of organizational structure could be co-ordinated.

First, through mutual adjustment where the different elements communicate and adjust their behaviour to reach agreed ends in what is a democratic process. Second, through direct supervision. Here co-ordination is achieved through instruction from the strategic apex – essentially an autocratic process. Finally, co-ordination is possible through standardization. Mintzberg showed that there were several possible targets for standardization. Thus work processes, outputs, skills or norms and beliefs may be standardized in order to co-ordinate the organization's operations.

In the Air France case study it appears that initially standardization of work processes was the main co-ordinating mechanism. Thus there were technical servicing routines for aircraft and routines for personnel practices, all of which tended to concentrate on internal processes and tasks. The new thinking for Air France is to divert the focus towards standardization of outputs and therefore concentrate on service quality. This represents an important change in direction for the company towards more focus on the customer.

Summary

1 The first stage in strategic implementation is the preparation of a detailed strategic planning document.
2 Resource planning is the next key stage. Here the resource demands of the new strategy are identified and questions of resource fit are tackled.
3 A co-ordinating plan is produced to reveal the logistics of the strategy.
4 Finally, organizational structure is reviewed to ensure that it is appropriate to meet the demands of the new strategy.

Review questions

1 Discuss the suitability of using an experimental type of organizational structure, as practised by Semler, for a tourism organization with which you are familiar.
2 Does structure follow strategy or strategy follow structure? Discuss with reference to a named tourism organization.
3 Identify and explain the constituent parts of the organization of Air France according to Mintzberg's six structural elements. Describe the consequences of different ways of co-ordinating these elements.

4 The Air France recovery strategy involved moving to product and market centred groupings, flattening the structure, reducing bureaucracy, decentralization of decision-making and a movement towards standardization of norms. Explain the meaning and purposes of these changes.

5 Explain the implications for human resource planning of a tourism strategy with which you are familiar.

6 Prepare a project plan which demonstrates the logistics of a named tourism strategy.

7 Identify the type of organizational structure which exists for a tourism organization. Is this structure appropriate for the future?

8 Using Figure 7.2 as a template, construct a strategic planning report for a named tourism organization.

8
Managing and monitoring change

Chapter objectives

Case Study Q, on Air France (see Chapter 7) illustrated the difficulties which confront management of change. The challenges for strategic implementation will depend first, on the divergence between the current strategy and the new strategy (i.e. the degree of change proposed) and second, on the ability of the organization to accommodate change (i.e. whether the organization is an adaptive one). These two dimensions are represented in Figure 8.1.

The situation facing Air France can be described in sector D of Figure 8.1. Air France represented an entrenched, bureaucratic organization, unreceptive to change. At the same time the strategic change demanded by the rescue plan was profound. Thus the implementation challenges to managing change for Air France were significant ones.

By studying this chapter students will be able to identify and utilize the remaining techniques of strategic implementation which are:

- management of change
- methods of control
- identification of key factors for effective strategic management.

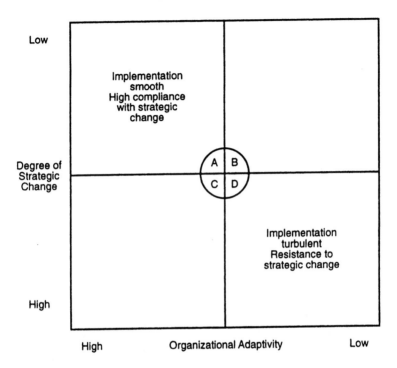

Figure 8.1 Strategic implementation

Management of change

A key challenge for many tourism organizations is that their structures were generally designed to solve yesterday's problems. In other words, organizational structure and culture tend to evolve reactively. So an audit of an organization's capability may well find that it is perfectly structured to deal with the challenges that the organization faced in the past five years, but inappropriately equipped to deal with the future.

To compound this problem organizations may become 'frozen' in a particular state (Lewin 1952), not least because once a particular organizational structure and culture has evolved there is a strong tendency for structural and cultural reproduction. An organization will tend to recruit, induct and reward its staff in line with its established culture and the organization will stay the same.

Lewin's model for creating successful organizational change identified three important stages. First, the unfreezing of current organizational behaviour patterns is necessary in order to make the organization more receptive to change. Second, Lewin identified the importance of movement, which involves the carrying out of change or the reconceptualization of the organization. Finally, Lewin noted the importance of refreezing the organization so as to institutionalize the change.

There is a considerable challenge for management of change, particularly where such change is fundamental in the face of a conservative organization (quadrant D of Figure 8.1). Change in these circumstances is likely to be strongly contested in parts of the organization. The management of strategic change must therefore pay attention to the four Cs of change, which are:

- calculation
- communication
- culture
- compliance.

Calculation

Calculation involves the identification of the likely impacts of a strategy both internally and externally to the organization with a view to discovering where critical blockages may occur. These may inhibit the implementation of change and are known as resisting forces. At the same time it is important to record those factors (driving forces) which may help promote the desired strategy. Force field analysis (Lewin 1935) is a method of examining this. Its aim is to enhance the management of change by generating a tactical approach (Nutt 1989). The steps in force field analysis are:

1 identification of planned change
2 identification of resisting forces
3 identification of driving forces
4 formulation of tactics to reduce or eliminate resisting forces
5 formulation of tactics to encourage driving forces.

Table 8.1 illustrates a force field analysis for Air France's recovery strategy. It can be noted that most of the management of change issues here were internal to the organization.

On the other hand, many tourism strategies involve projects which have a strong impact on their external environment, for example, attractions, hotels developments, whole destination developments and transport developments. Case Study R illustrates issues of calculation surrounding the development of an attraction called 'Movie World' in West London.

Table 8.1 Air France recovery strategy: force field analysis

Strategies: reduce costs/improve services	
Resisting forces	*Driving forces*
● Trade unions	● Survival
● Bureaucratic organization	● Competition
● Job-focused rather than customer-focused workers	● Self-interest
● Defender mentality of senior staff	
Tactics for overcoming resistance	*Tactics for enhancing drivers*
● Bypass trade union and appeal directly to work-force	● Education programme designed to communicate severity of situation to the work-force
● Reorganization of company	● Imitation of winning features of successful competitor airlines
● Create profit centres	● Instigate profit-related pay schemes
● 'Shake up' of senior management	

Case Study R: Movie World

In the planning stages of Movie World (location: West London, planned opening 1999), Warner Brothers (US) and MAI plc (UK) mapped out the force field surrounding the project. A number of potential resisting forces were identified. First, local residents, concerned about noise, traffic congestion and visual pollution. Second, national campaigning groups concerned with environmental protection. Third, those affected by displaced activities (there were sports and leisure facilities pre-existing on the site), and finally the government, concerned by the project impinging on protected countryside ('the green belt').

The Warner Brothers/MAI tactical response to these was to launch a public relations exercise which included leafleting all those in the local impact zone and expounding its 'good neighbour' policy by a series of exhibitions. On the one hand the resistance

Case Study R (*continued*)

factors were played down. For example, it was promised that noise generating parts of the park would be located away from residential areas and sound-proofed. It was claimed that one in three visitors would arrive by public transport and that the majority of cars would arrive and depart outside peak hours, thus minimizing congestion. The visual pollution argument was countered by reference to the low-rise nature of the park and a 2500 tree-planting operation. Similarly, loss of green belt was made to sound less significant at 'just 1.8 per cent'.

On the other hand potential driving factors were played up. Reference was made to 3500 jobs being created nation-wide as a result of the project, with 900 jobs being filled by local people. Additionally, increased local house prices were alluded to by reference to evidence from opening of a Movie World park in Australia. Increased spending on local business and the potential for new hotel and leisure facilities were also noted. Local residents were also promised reduced admission prices.

Communication

Effective communication is at the heart of successful strategic implementation. Even organizations which engage in a systematic process of strategic planning may overlook this vital aspect so that the strategy may remain the property of senior management and its circulation may be intentionally or unintentionally restricted. Such organizations may see strategy formulation as an end in itself and overlook the important process of communicating strategy throughout the organization. Different models of communication of strategy may be located on a continuum which includes:

- democratic
- educative
- autocratic.

Democratic

Democratic communication of strategy occurs where stakeholders of an organization are encouraged at an early stage to participate in the process of strategic formulation. This represents a bottom-up system of communication. A common method utilized here is to establish a series of task groups or working parties which encompass a wide representation of groups and interests. The objective is to improve the quality of decision-making and to ensure wide ownership of strategy that emerges from such a process. Since a large proportion of stakeholders are involved in strategy formulation, communication will be built into the process rather than a separate add-on at the end.

Of course, problems arise with such an approach. It may be difficult to reach agreement, information of a highly technical nature may be mishandled by people who are not experts, co-ordination of activities may be laborious and the process may just be too time consuming. It may also be difficult to escape from the existing cultural perspective.

Educative

Although essentially a top-down model, the educative process encourages a two-way flow of communications. Thus strategy is likely to originate from the boardroom, but understanding and legitimation is sought. This will take place by a series of meetings and briefings where the objectives and purposes of a particular strategy are discussed. Strategy may be amended in the light of feedback, encouraging feelings of participation and empowerment among the wider work-force. Legitimation may be sought through the participation of trade unions.

Autocratic

This may be characterized as 'management by memo' where communication is one way, top-down and the strategy is handed down from the board for implementation. Such a move may be necessary in crisis management where a rapid change in direction is sought, but it may easily alienate those whose job it is to carry out directions. Alienation may arise from resentment at being excluded from decision-making and frustrations arising from an inability to influence. Additionally, strategies implemented in such a way are open to misunderstanding and misinterpretation.

It is possible to interpret the communication systems in the Air France case (Case Study Q) using these typologies. Because of the crisis nature of the Air France situation, democratic communication is ruled out as too slow. It may be suggested that the communications route taken by Bernard Attali was an autocratic one and that the confrontational stance adopted led to strike action. Attali's successor, Christian Blanc, adopted a more educative communications stance. Although the strategy was formulated by senior management, he sought to have it legitimized by a referendum to the entire work-force.

Culture

As noted earlier, organizational culture may be an important factor in inhibiting change, since change will represent a threat to established routines, beliefs and values which may be deeply embedded or frozen within the organization.

The following highlight some cultural problems from the Air France case:

> I am worried because most of you do not have an economic culture.
>
> (M. Blanc, Chairman, speaking to an audience of managers)
>
> . . . you can't alter attitudes just by redrawing the organizational chart.
>
> (M. Dupuy, SMG Consultancy group)
>
> There are many people who are unwilling or unable to change their attitudes.
>
> (M. Dupuy, SMG Consultancy group)

These quotations illustrate some general cultural barriers to change. First, the lack of an economic or commercial or service culture may be identified. This really means a lack of focus on profitability or customers. Instead, employees may be focused on the specifics of their task and see themselves as information technologists or accountants, rather than as contributors to a corporate goal or mission. Second, cultural patterns are less easily changed than more tangible aspects of the organization such as the organizational chart.

It is useful to note that British Airways faced similar cultural barriers to change during its transition from state owned to privatized airline in the 1980s as those faced more recently by Air France. BA's former culture has been described by analysts as bureaucratic and militaristic.

Several changes were made to promote cultural change. First, a new CEO was appointed – Sir Colin Marshall – who had a marketing rather than an Air Force background. Second, BA's mission was redefined from providing transport to providing a service. Third, a training programme – 'Putting People First' – was introduced for all front line staff. Fourth, a number of symbolic changes were made, including new uniforms, new aircraft liveries, new interior designs of aircraft, a new corporate coat of arms incorporating the motto 'We fly to serve' and a new advertising slogan – 'The World's Favourite Airline'. Aircrew were developed into teams to generate an improved team spirit and, finally, a bonus scheme was introduced.

Some of the key factors in promoting cultural change can be summarized from the above example as:

- induction programmes for new staff
- change of symbols
- use of language
- training programmes
- appointment of key personnel
- promotion and dismissal policies
- incentive schemes.

Compliance

Compliance addresses the question of how strategic change can be achieved, perhaps· in the face of opposition. Change may involve deploying political processes, identifying and utilizing sources of power (Mintzberg 1983) and constructing a power base from which to operate. Key issues for achieving compliance include:

- control of resources
- alliances
- rewards and punishments
- charisma
- managing of change skills.

Resources

Acquisition and control of resources is central to the exercise of power and thus a review and reformulation of resource allocation within the organization can be an important way of implementing change.

Resources may thus be withdrawn from areas within the organization where resistance is evident and reallocated to areas where the new strategic policy is supported.

Groups, alliances and networks

The forging of groups, alliances and networks can be important in promoting change. The former may comprise task groups to achieve particular ends. It may also be important to consider alliances with a wider group of stakeholders other than just employees if, for example, shareholder support is needed for a major policy change. Networking involves a more informal web of contacts and supporters who permeate the organization more widely.

Rewards and punishments

Part of the process of gaining support may involve improving the status of those who back the new strategic direction whilst sidelining those in opposition. This may involve adjustments to perks, status, salary and ultimately may be underpinned by a radical hiring and firing policy as in the Air France case study.

Charismatic leadership

Writers such as Peters and Waterman (1982) have emphasized the importance of personality and the power of the charismatic leader. In this view of things the personality traits of managers of change are held to be significant. A charismatic leader is one who inspires others to follow a particular path. Vision, enthusiasm and communications and leadership skills have been identified as key attributes of charismatic leaders.

Skills for managing change

Buchanan and Boddy's (1992) study of the perceived effectiveness of managers of change included the following as crucial competences:

- sensitivity to internal and external environment
- clear expression of goals
- team building skills

- networking skills
- ability to cope with uncertainty surrounding change
- communication skills
- inspirational skills
- negotiation skills
- political skills
- strategic perspective.

Control and evaluation

The strategy process is incomplete without attention to control and evaluation. Control mechanisms are necessary to ensure that the strategy which was outlined and broken down into objectives is delivered according to specification. Evaluation entails assessment of the success of the new strategy.

This brings the discussion neatly back to its starting point. Case Study A, on Disneyland, Paris was based largely on an evaluation that pointed up serious problems in strategy. Disneyland, Paris was not performing, it was not profitable. Thus the strategy process starts all over again. In the Disney case it was not that control mechanisms had failed – the Disneyland, Paris that was constructed was the Disneyland, Paris that had been planned. What they got was what they had ordered. However, evaluation found that what had been ordered was not successful and thus a reformulation of strategy was embarked upon. This is why there is an arrow from implementation back to mission in Figure 7.1. Strategy is a circular process and it is at the evaluation stage that the loop is closed.

Control mechanisms

Control mechanisms to monitor outcomes include:

- management by objectives
- quality assurance
- budgeting.

Management by objectives

The concept of management by objectives has been discussed in Chapter 7 and it is only necessary here to recap that the review of the objectives set for managers may be part of the control mechanism. Appraisal may be used here where an employee's line manager reviews past performance and sets future targets.

Quality assurance

Quality assurance is the name given to the system by which standards are controlled. A common tool of quality assurance is the use of performance indicators. At the level of control, performance indicators in the tourism sector may include items such as

- number of on-time departures
- queuing time for attractions
- customer satisfaction surveys
- number of complaints received
- amount of repeat business.

These items will be particularly important for strategies which have a high value added dimension. Other performance indicators include factors such as occupancy levels. However, there are many aspects of the tourism experience that are difficult to measure, such as atmosphere, excitement, design and aesthetics.

The SERVQUAL questionnaire (Parasuraman *et al.* 1988) was developed to assess customer satisfaction in the service sector. It measures satisfaction against customer expectations, focusing on:

- tangibles, e.g. the appearance of a hotel room, the grooming of resort representatives
- reliability, e.g. do flights depart on time, does the air conditioning work?
- responsiveness, e.g. the promptness of service, helpfulness of employees
- assurance, e.g. the knowledge and professionalism of emplo...
- empathy, e.g. attention to individuals.

SERVQUAL investigations have been carried out in hotels, airlines and ski areas (Fick and Ritchie 1991) and in hotels (Saleh and Ryan 1992).

Benchmarking is a common technique for interpreting performance indicators. A benchmark is a level of acceptable standard. It may be derived from referencing with competitors' services or from an objective analysis of what an appropriate level is deemed to be.

Total Quality Management (TQM) (Oakland 1989) is an attempt to build systems within organizations which guarantee quality standards. They are built around a procedure which sets standards, monitors standards, identifies corrective actions arising from monitoring and implements corrective actions – a sort of quality auto-pilot.

Budgeting

Whilst performance indicators measure the effectiveness of strategy with a qualitative emphasis, budgets measure the efficiency of a strategy using quantitative techniques. They can be used to compare the actual costs of production with planned costs and to ensure that particular activities do not exceed their allocated funds. In this sense budgets offer close control, since projects will not be permitted to exceed their target expenditures without authorization. Budgets are generally allocated to departments which then prepare secondary budgets. So, for example, the marketing budget may be subdivided into market research, advertising, public relations and sales promotions.

Evaluation

Evaluation is then the ultimate test of a strategy – has it been successful? Evaluation must be related back to the mission and aims of the organization. Thus for organizations with mainly profit-centred missions, evaluation will be largely quantitative and may utilize data on:

- return on capital employed
- earnings per share
- dividends paid to shareholders
- turnover
- market share
- profit before tax
- movement in share prices.

Figures such as these may be interpreted according to specific targets that may have been expressed in the organization's mission, e.g. 10% growth in earnings per share, or performance may be related to industry norms. The target for the Rank Organisation plc, for example, is 'to achieve above average growth in normalized earnings per share over the medium term' (Review and Financial Summary 1995).

Financial information is illustrated in Figure 8.2 for Airtours plc, a tour operator with interests in the UK, Scandinavia and Canada. It can

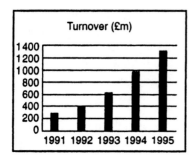
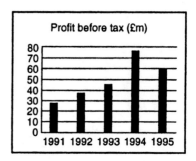
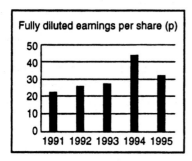
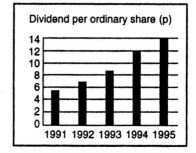

Figure 8.2 Airtours plc – financial evaluation

be seen that the Airtours profit figures show a significant decline of 22 per cent for 1995.

However, care needs to be taken in using such data, for two reasons. First, it is sometimes difficult to determine the performance of a specific strategy in the generality of these kind of global figures. Second, there may be a time lag between a change of strategy and its reflection in changed profitability.

For organizations with non-profit missions, evaluation will utilize different tools. For example, national tourism organizations may use quantitative data such as number of tourist arrivals. However, organizations such as Tourism Concern will resort to more qualitative indicators of their success. These may be based upon case studies which demonstrate the effects of their campaigning.

Finally, all strategies are based on assumptions about how the external environment will change in the future. An important part of evaluation should therefore include the assumptions testing, that is, a regular review that the assumptions underlying a particular strategy still hold.

Effective implementation

Critical success factors

Pettigrew and Whipp's (1992) study of the management of change concluded that there were five critical success factors common in organizations where change had been successfully implemented. These were:

- Sensitivity to the external environment. Successful organizations avoid strategic drift. They monitor the external environment and adapt to it. They are externally oriented.
- Formulation of a strategy for change. Implementation requires change to be addressed as an important issue. The particular way in which change is managed should be sensitive to the particular circumstances of each organization.
- Translation of strategic plans to operational outcomes. This underlines the importance of operationalizing strategy. Important elements include resource plans, setting and monitoring objectives and good communications.
- Effective human resource management. Human resource management needs to be carefully integrated into the strategy process. This is particularly true for tourism organizations where service quality is often vital for success.
- Consistency and coherence of strategic planning. There are a lot of elements to successful strategic management. It is important that these elements are consistent so that there is no conflict between different parts of the strategy. For example, ambitious expansion plans funded at high interest rates would be inconsistent with an external environment which was heading for a period of recession. Consistency also demands not only that strategy and operations move in the same direction, but also that strategy is reinforced by managerial behaviour.

The 7-S framework

Waterman *et al.* (1980) claimed that effective organizational change resulted from a successful relationship between several factors:

- structure
- strategy
- systems
- style
- skills
- staff
- superordinate goals.

In other words, successful change needs more than just an appropriate strategy and company structure. Systems – or how an organization goes about its daily business of routines and procedures – are important. Here the emphasis is on getting the detail right as well as the broad brush of strategy. Style refers to the way the management team projects strategy to the rest of the organization – do they sell the vision? Socialization is an important issue in terms of staff. Waterman *et al.* report that successful companies induct and groom new recruits with great care. They also note that it is important for companies to develop distinctive skills focusing on improving on what they do best. Finally, superordinate goals are explained as the guiding concept – above all else – of the organization. They therefore emerge from strategy and objectives and identify the direction of the organization and give it its drive.

Conclusion

Figure 1.1, which has provided the analytical structure throughout this book, is useful in depicting the strategy process in a logical, organized and coherent way. Thus the first step towards effective strategic management has been taken and a simple overview of the process provided. However, several caveats should be made at this stage.

First, to aid understanding, strategy has been depicted as a logical, linear process where we move neatly from stage to stage. In the real world it is a much more messy business and the arrows in Figure 1.1 in fact often cut across the diagram.

Second, it should be emphasized that the strategy process is a circular one. Note the arrow in Figure 1.1 that links implementation back to mission, showing a continuous process. Strategy should always be under review.

Finally, it is reiterated that this text has essentially taken a classical view of the strategy process. There is considerable debate surrounding reliance on this method. It would therefore be an appropriate moment to review the section in Chapter 1 entitled 'Postscript: Strategy as a complex and contested concept.'

Summary

1 Management of change may in itself be a challenging task, particularly where a traditional organization faces the prospect of fundamental change.
2 Key issues for management of change include:
   (a) calculation and the use of force field analysis to identify aids and blockages to change
   (b) effective communication of the rationale and elements of strategy throughout the organization
   (c) political and tactical methods of achieving compliance with a strategy
   (d) attention to the issue of organizational culture.
3 It is necessary to devise control mechanisms to ensure that a strategy is translated into objectives and key tasks and that the attainment of these objectives is monitored.
4 Strategies need to be evaluated to ensure that they continue to make a strong contribution to achieving the organization's mission and remain appropriate as circumstances change.

Review questions

1 Many airlines are resorting to strategic alliances or horizontal mergers in moves towards more globalization. Choose an airline with which you are familiar and conduct a force field analysis for such a strategy.
2 Compare Pettigrew and Whipp's (1992) five critical success factors with the 7-S Framework of Waterman (1980) as explanations of successful strategic change.
3 Distinguish, with examples from the tourism sector, between methods of control and methods of evaluation of corporate strategy.
4 Discuss the significance of the 4 Cs in the management of change in a tourism organization.
5 Explain what Lewin (1952) meant by the freezing and unfreezing process in achieving strategic change.

Bibliography

Alchian, A. (1950) Uncertainty, evolution and economic theory. *Journal of Political Economy*, **58**, pp. 211–21.

Andrews, K. (1980) *The Concept of Corporate Strategy*, Richard D. Irwin Inc., Homewood, Illinois.

Ansoff, H. (1965) *Corporate Strategy*, Penguin, Harmondsworth.

Athiyaman, A. and Robertson, R. (1995) Strategic planning in large tourism firms: an empirical analysis. *Tourism Management*, **16**(3) pp. 199–205.

Athiyaman, A (1995) The interface of tourism and strategy research: an analysis. *Tourism Management*, **16**(6) pp. 447–53.

Baumol, W. (1959) *Business Behaviour, Value and Growth*, Harcourt, Brace and World, New York.

Becheri, E. (1991) Rimini and Co. – the end of a legend. *Tourism Management*, **12**(3) pp. 229–35.

Bennett, M. and Radburn, M. (1991) Information technology in tourism: the impacts on the industry and the supply of holidays, in *The Tourism Industry – An International Analysis* (eds M. Sinclair and M. Stabler), CAB, Oxford.

Bennett, R. (1996) *Corporate Strategy and Business Planning*, Pitman, London.

Bharadwaj, S. and Varadarajan, R. (1993) Sustainable competitive advantage in service industries: a conceptual model and research propositions. *Journal of Marketing*, October, pp. 83–9.

Bowman, C. (1992) Charting competitive strategy, in *The Challenge of Strategic Management* (eds D. Faulkener and G. Johnson) Kogan Page, London.

British Airways (Annually) *Annual Environmental Report*, British Airways, London.

Buchanan, D. and Boddy, D. (1992) *The Expertise of the Change Agent: Public performance and backstage activity*, Prentice Hall, London.

Buchele, R. (1962) How to evaluate a firm. *California Management Review*, Fall, pp. 5–16.

Burns, P. (1995) Hotel management training in Eastern Europe. *Progress in Tourism and Hospitality Research*, **1**(1) pp. 53–62.

Butler, R. (1980) The concept of the tourist area cycle of evolution: implications for management of resources. *Canadian Geographer*, **24**(1) pp. 5–12.

Chandler, A. (1962) *Strategy and Structure*, MIT Press, Cambridge, Mass.

Child, J. (1977) *Organisation: A Guide to Problems and Practice*, Harper and Row, London.

Cyert, R., and March, J. (1963) *A Behavioural Theory of the Firm*, Prentice Hall, New Jersey.

David, F. (1989) How companies define their mission. *Long Range Planning*, **22**(1) pp. 90–7.

Doswell, R. (1995) *Tourism: Understanding its Development and Management*, Butterworth-Heinemann, Oxford.

Drucker, P. (1968) *The Practice of Management*, Pan Piper, London.

Economist Intelligence Unit (1989) *Developing Strategies for World's Airlines*, EIU, London.

Economist Intelligence Unit (1991) *Competitive Strategies for the International Hotel Industry*, EIU, London.

Elliot, M. (1991) Travel and tourism survey – the pleasure principle. *The Economist*, 23 March.

Endres, G. (1985) Transport: Airlines in sub-Saharan Africa. *EIU Travel and Tourism Analyst*, 5, pp. 4–23.

Faulkner, H. (1995) Toward a strategic approach to tourism development: the Australian experience, in *Global Tourism* (ed. W. Theobald) Butterworth-Heinemann, Oxford.

Ferry, J. (1995) BAA's autopilot. *Management Today*, January, pp. 33–6.

Fick, G. and Ritchie, J. (1991) Measuring service quality in the travel industry. *Journal of Travel Research*, **30**(2) pp. 2–9.

Freeman, R. (1984) *Strategic Management: A stakeholder approach*, Pitman, London.

Frechtling, D. (1995) *Practical Tourism Forecasting*, Butterworth-Heinemann, Oxford.

Friedman, M. (1953) *Essays in Positive Economics*, University of Chicago Press, Illinois.

Gamble, P. (1991) Innovation in Innkeeping. *International Journal of Hospitality Management*, **10**(1) pp. 3–23.

Gannon, J. and Johnson, K. (1995) The global hotel industry: the emergence of continental hotel companies. *Progress in Tourism and Hospitality Research*, **1**(1) pp. 31–42.

Gialloreto, L. (1988) *Strategic Airline Management: The Global War Begins*, Pitman, London.

Gilbert, D. and Kapur, R. (1990) Strategic marketing planning and the hotel industry. *International Journal of Hospitality Management*, **9**(1) pp. 27–43.

Go, F. and Pine, R. (1995) *Globalization Strategy in the Hotel Industry*, Routledge, London, 1995.

Gold, J. and Ward, S. (eds) (1994) *Place Promotion: The Use of Publicity and Marketing to Sell Towns and Regions*, Wiley, Chichester.

Granovetter, M. (1985) Economic action and social structure: the problem of embeddedness. *American Journal of Sociology*, **91**(3), pp. 431–450.

Gratton, C. (1992) Is there life after Euro-Disney? *Leisure Management*, April, pp. 24–7.

Gregory, M. (1994) *Dirty Tricks: British Airways' Secret War Against Virgin Atlantic*, Little Brown, London.

Grover, R. (1991) *The Disney Touch – How a Daring Management Team Revived an Entertainment Empire*, Business One Irwin, Illinois, USA.

Guerin-Calvert, M. and Noll, R. (1991) *Computer Reservation Systems and their Network Linkages to the Airline Industry*, Center for Economic Policy Research Publications, 252.

Hall, R. (1992) The strategic analysis of intangible resources. *Strategic Management Journal*, **13**, pp. 135–44.

Hanlon, J. (1995) *Global Airlines*, Butterworth-Heinemann, Oxford.

Hansen-Sturm, C. (1990) The electronic information revolution. *The Airline Quarterly*, Summer.

Heskett, J., Sasser, W. and Hart, C. (1990) The profitable art of service recovery. *Harvard Business Review*, July–August, pp. 148–56.

Higgs, G. (1995) Short- and long-term business development for travel agents. *Journal of Vacation Marketing*, **1**(2) pp. 181–9.

Hitchins, F. (1991) The influence of technology on UK travel agents. *Travel and Tourism Analyst*, Economist Intelligence Unit, London, **3** pp. 88–105.

Hobson, J. and Williams, A. (1995) Virtual reality: a new horizon for the tourism industry. *Journal of Vacation Marketing*, **1**(2) pp. 125–36.

Hodgson, A. (1987) *The Travel and Tourism Industry, Strategies for the Future*, Butterworth-Heinemann, Oxford.

Hofer, C. and Schendel, D. (1970) *Strategy Formulation: Analytical Concepts*, West Publishing Company, St. Paul, Minnesota.

Holder, J. (1991) Tourism, the world and the Caribbean. *Tourism Management*, **12**(4) pp. 291–300.

Hopper, M. (1990) Rattling SABRE – new ways to compete on information. *Harvard Business Review*, May–June, pp. 118–25.

Humble, J. (1970) *Management by Objectives in Action*, McGraw Hill, New York.

Inskeep, E. (1991) *Tourism Planning*, Van Nostrand Reinhold, New York.

Johnson, G. (1988) Rethinking incrementalism. *Strategic Management Journal*, **9**(1) pp. 75–91.

Johnson, G. and Scholes, K. (1993) *Exploring Corporate Strategy*, Prentice Hall, Hemel Hempstead.

Johnson, P. and Thomas, B. (1991) The comparative analysis of tourist attractions, in *Progress in Tourism, Recreation and Hospitality Management*, (ed. C. Cooper) Belhaven, London, pp. 114–29.

Jordan, J. (1992) Business policy, in *Understanding Business and Finance* (ed. J. Hussey) DPP, London.

Ketelhöhn, W. (1993) *International Business Strategy*, Butterworth-Heinemann, Oxford.

Kinnaird, V. and Hall, D. (eds) (1994) *Tourism: A Gender Analysis*, Wiley, Chichester.

Kotler, P. (1988) *Marketing Management*, Prentice Hall, Hemel Hempstead.

Law, C.M. (1993) *Urban Tourism: Attracting Visitors to Large Cities*, Mansell, London.

Laws, C. (1995) *Tourism Destination Management*, Routledge, London.

Lewin, K. (1935) *A Dynamic Theory of Personality*, McGraw-Hill, New York.

Lewin, K. (1952) *Field Theory in Social Science*, Tavistock, London.

Lickorish, L. and Jefferson, A. (1991) *Marketing Tourism*, Longman, Harlow.

Littlejohn, D. and Beattie, R. (1992) The European hotel industry: corporate structures and expansion strategies. *Tourism Management*, March, pp. 27–33.

Lord, G. and Lord, B. (eds) (1991) *The Manual of Museum Planning*, Museum Enterprises Ltd, HMSO, London.

Martin, J. and Siehl, C. (1983) Organisational culture and counterculture. *Organizational Dynamics*, 12(2) pp. 52–64.

Martin, B. and Mason, S. (1993) The future for attractions – meeting the needs of new consumers. *Tourism Management*, February, pp. 34–40.

McClung, G. (1991) Theme park selection – factors influencing attendance. *Tourism Management*, June, pp. 132–40.

McRae, H. (1994) *The World in 2020*, Harper Collins, London.

Medlik, S. (1993) *Dictionary of Travel, Tourism and Hospitality*, Butterworth-Heinemann, Oxford.

Mendelow, A. (1981) *Proceedings of 2nd International Conference on Information Systems*, Cambridge, Mass.

Middleton, V. (1991) Whither the package tour? *Tourism Management*, 12(3) pp. 185–192.

Miles, R. and Snow, C. (1978) *Organisational Strategy, Structure and Process*, McGraw-Hill, Maidenhead.

Mintzberg, H. (1979) *The Structuring of Organisations*, Prentice Hall, New York.

Mintzberg, H. (1983) *Power In and Around Organisations*, Prentice Hall, New York.

Mintzberg, H. (1987) Five Ps for strategy. *California Management Review*, Fall.

Mintzberg, H., Quinn, J., and Ghoshal, S. (1995) *The Strategy Process*, Prentice Hall, Hemel Hempstead.

Middleton, V. (1994) *Marketing in Travel and Tourism*, Butterworth-Heinemann Oxford.

Mitroff, I. (1983) *Stakeholders of the Organisational Mind*, Jossey Bass, San Francisco.

Nutt, P. (1989) Selecting tactics to implement strategic plans. *Strategic Management Journal*, 10(2) pp. 145–61.

Oakland, J. (1989) *Total Quality Management*, Heinemann, Oxford.

O'Hagen, J., Scott, Y, and Waldron, P. (1986) *The Tourism Industry and the Tourism Policies of the Twelve Member States of the Community; summary of main findings*, Commission of the European Communities, Brussels.

Olsen, M. (1991) *Strategic Management in the Hospitality Industry: A Literature Review*, Belhaven Press, London.

Parasuraman, A., Zeithaml, V. and Berry, L. (1988) SERVQUAL: a multiple-item scale for measuring consumer perceptions of service quality. *Journal of Retailing*, 64(1) pp. 14–40.

Pearce, D. (1992) *Tourist Organisations*, Longman, Harlow.

Peisley, A. (1989) UK tour operators and the European market in the 1990s. *Travel and Tourism Analyst*, Economist Intelligence Unit, London, (5) pp. 56–67.

Peisley, A. (1989) The world cruising industry in the 1990s. *Travel and Tourism Analyst*, Economist Intelligence Unit, London, (6) pp. 5–18.

Pettigrew, A. and Whipp, R. (1992) *Managing Change for Competitive Success*, Basil Blackwell, London.

Peters, T. and Waterman, R. (1982) *In Search of Excellence*, Harper and Row, New York.

Pollard, J. and Rodriguez, R.D. (1993) Tourism and Torremolinos: Recession or reaction to environment? *Tourism Management*, **14**(8) pp. 247–58.

Poon, A. (1993) Tourism, *Technology and Competitive Strategies*, CAB International, Oxford.

Porter, M. (1979) How competitive forces shape strategy. *Harvard Business Review*, March–April.

Porter, M. (1980) *Competitive Strategy: Techniques for Analysing Industries and Competitors*, Free Press, New York.

Porter, M. (1985) *Competitive Advantage*, Free Press, New York.

Quinn, J. (1980) Strategies for Change: Logical Incrementalism, Richard D. Irwin Inc., Homewood, Illinois.

Richards, G. (ed) (1991) *Case Studies in Tourism Management*, University of North London, London.

Richardson, B. and Richardson, R. (1992) *Business Planning*, Pitman, London.

Rogers, H. (1995) Pricing practices in tourist attractions. *Tourism Management*, **16**(3) pp. 217–24.

Rovelstad, J. and Blazer, S. (1983) Research and strategic marketing in tourism: a status report. *Journal of Travel Research*, Fall, pp. 2–7.

Ryan, C. (1995) *Researching Tourist Satisfaction*, Routledge, London.

Saleh, F. and Ryan, C. (1992) Conviviality – a source of satisfaction for hotel guests? An application of the SERVQUAL model, in *Choice and Demand in Tourism*, (eds P. Johnson and B. Thomas) Mansell, London.

Schein, E. (1985) *Organisational Culture and Leadership*, Jossey Bass, San Francisco.

Schneider, S. (1989) Strategy formulation: the impact of national culture. *Organisational Studies*, **10**(2) pp. 149–68.

Schneider, S. and Meyer, A. (1991) Interpreting and responding to strategic issues: the impact of national culture. *Strategic Management Journal*, **12**(4) pp. 307–20.

Semler, R. (1994) *Maverick: The success story behind the world's most unusual workplace*, Arrow Books, London.

Sloan, A. (1963) *My Years with General Motors*, Sidgwick and Jackson, London.

Smith, T. (1995) Why air travel doesn't work. *Fortune*, 3 April, pp. 26–36.

Swarbrooke, J. (1995) *The Development and Management of Visitor Attractions*, Butterworth-Heinemann, Oxford.

Sussmannn, S. and Ng, F. (1995) The expert travel counselling system – the next stage. *Progress in Tourism and Hospitality Research*, **1**(1) pp. 43–51.

Taylor, B. and Harrison, J. (1991) *The Manager's Casebook of Business Strategy*, Butterworth-Heinemann, Oxford.

Taylor, B. and Sparkes, J. (1977) *Corporate Strategy and Planning*, Heinemann, London.

Teare, R. and Olsen, M. (1992) *International Hospitality Management – Corporate Strategy in Practice*, Pitman, London.

Theobald, W. (ed) (1994) *Global Tourism: The Next Decade*, Butterworth-Heinemann, Oxford.

Tourism Concern (1992) *Beyond the Green Horizon*, World Wildlife Fund, Godalming.

Tribe, J. (1995) *The Economics of Leisure and Tourism*, Butterworth-Heinemann, Oxford.

Truitt, L., Teye, V. and Farris, M. (1991) The role of computer reservations systems – international implications for the travel industry. *Tourism Management*, **12**(1) pp. 21–36.

Vernon, R. (1966) International investment and international trade in the product cycle. *Quarterly Journal of Economics*, **80**, pp. 190–207.

Vernon, R. (1979) The product cycle hypothesis in a new international environment. *Oxford Bulletin of Economics and Statistics*, **41**, pp. 255–67.

Vin Linge, J. (1992) How to out-zoo the zoo. *Tourism Management*, March, pp. 115–177.

Waterman, R., Peters, T. and Philips, J. (1980) Structure is not organisation. *Business Horizons*, June.

Webster, M. (1991) *Discussion Papers in Hospitality Management: An Annotated Bibliography of Strategic Management with Reference to the Hospitality Industry*, Leeds Polytechnic, Leeds.

Weiner, M. (1981) *English Culture and the Decline of the Industrial Spirit 1850–1980*, Penguin, Harmondsworth.

Wheatcroft, S. (1990) Towards transnational airlines. *Tourism Management*, **11**(4) pp. 353–8.

Whittington, R. (1993) *What is Strategy – and Does It Matter?*, Routledge, London.

Williams, A. and Hobson, J. (1994) Virtual reality and Surrogate travel, in *Tourism – The State of the Art* (eds Seaton *et al.*) Wiley, Chichester.

Williams, P. and Hobson, J. (1995) Virtual reality and tourism: fact or fantasy? *Tourism Management*, **16**(6) pp. 423–7.

Williamson, O. (1991) Strategizing, economizing and economic organisation. *Strategic Management Journal*, **12**, pp. 75–94.

Witt, S., Brooke, M. and Buckley, P. (1995) *The Management of International Tourism*, Routledge, London.

Witt, S. and Mouthino, L. (1995) *Tourism Marketing and Management Handbook*, Prentice Hall, Hemel Hempstead.

Witt, S. and Witt, C. (1991) *Modelling and Forecasting Demand in Tourism*, Academic Press, London.

World Bank (annually) *World Development Report*, Oxford University Press, Oxford.

World Travel and Tourism Environmental Research Centre (1992) *World Travel and Tourism Environment Review*, CAB International, Oxford.

Index

ROSEMARY CLEMENT-MOORE

the

splendour

falls

CORGI BOOKS

THE SPLENDOUR FALLS
A CORGI BOOK 978 0 552 56135 8

First published in the United States in 2009 by Delacorte Press,
an imprint of Random House Children's Books, a division of
Random House, Inc., New York., as *The Splendor Falls*

Published in Great Britain by Corgi Books,
an imprint of Random House Children's Books
A Random House Group Company

This edition published 2010

1 3 5 7 9 10 8 6 4 2

The Random House Group Limited supports the Forest Stewardship Council
(FSC), the leading international forest certification organization.
All our titles that are printed on Greenpeace-approved FSC-certified
paper carry the FSC logo. Our paper procurement policy can be found
at www.**rbooks**.co.uk/environment.

Set in Mrs Eaves Roman
Book design by Angela Carlino

Corgi Books are published by Random House Children's Books,
61–63 Uxbridge Road, London W5 5SA

www.**kids**at**randomhouse**.co.uk
www.**rbooks**.co.uk

Addresses for companies within The Random House Group Limited
can be found at: www.randomhouse.co.uk/offices.htm

THE RANDOM HOUSE GROUP Limited Reg. No. 954009

A CIP catalogue record for this book is available from the British Library.

Printed in the UK by
CPI Bookmarque, Croydon, CR0 4TD.

To Mom.

For a thousand and one reasons.

Genius is another word for magic, and

the whole point of magic is that it is inexplicable.

— DAME MARGOT FONTEYN, PRIMA BALLERINA

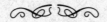

Prologue

For months, I relived the pas de deux in my dreams, in
that multisensory Technicolor of a memory I'd much
rather forget. Nothing ever changed: the backstage
perfume of sweat and hair spray. The heat and glare of
the lights. The delicious coil and spring of my muscles
as I moved through the choreography as if it were a
spontaneous outburst of the joy I felt when I danced.
The glorious triumph over gravity as Pasha lifted me
over his head, and I was untethered, not just from the
stage, but from the earth.

If I could have forced myself to wake up then, it would have been better. Like dying happy. But the dance played out in measured beats, as unchanging as a reel of film.

Pasha set me down, soft as moonlight; the orchestra covered the hollow tap of my pointe shoe on the stage. I balanced on one leg, the other stretched up behind me, prolonging the illusion of flight.

I could never say what went wrong in the next eight bars. The stage was clean, my pointe was solid. It wasn't even a particularly difficult combination. Come down to fourth position, port de bras and *changement* to second position and a quick series of *chaîné* turns.

Right foot, left foot, right . . . then a strange crunching sound that seemed to come from inside my head. Without knowing how I got there, I was facedown on the stage, and the murmurs of the audience were escalating with worry. In my dream – my memory – I tried to get up, but Pasha held me down, lapsing into panicked Russian. I didn't have to understand the language to know that something had gone very wrong.

It's funny how so much can hinge on one missed step.

Not funny ha-ha. Funny that the moment that should have been the pinnacle of my seventeen years on this planet ends up making me famous for the entirely wrong reason.

So I really don't mean funny so much as 'tragically ironic'.

Dancers get injured doing the flashy things, jetés and *échappés*. I mean, who the hell breaks their leg on a turn they teach in the tiny-tots class?

Me, I guess. The month before, I'd gotten a full-page write-up in *Ballet Magazine*. The month after, I was a tragic item in a sidebar to an article on insuring your legs, Betty Grable style, against career-ending injuries.

Sylvie Davis, the youngest-ever principal dancer for American Ballet, suffered a compound tibia and fibula fracture in front of hundreds of horrified audience members during her stunning debut at Lincoln Center.

At least I knew how to make an exit.

Chapter 1

I wanted to hate Alabama, and nothing about my arrival disappointed me.

To be fair, there aren't many places that are easy to fall in love with in ninety-degree heat and eighty-five per cent humidity. The bumpy flight from my connection in Atlanta, on a minuscule plane with doll-sized seats, hadn't helped. And that was before some snafu at the gate forced us to deplane on the tarmac and ride a bus to the terminal.

I'd been out of my walking cast for two weeks. My leg

throbbed like a sadistic metronome as I limped down the concourse, and the toes of my right foot were swollen like fat pink cocktail weenies. Gigi's carrier bag hung from my shoulder, my fingers white-knuckled on the strap. It's bad enough to dread something; it's even worse when the pain of moving forward is more than metaphorical.

I could rest a minute, sit down between the barbecue restaurant and the souvenir shop with the Confederate flag coffee mugs. For that matter, I was inside the security checkpoint. No one could come in and get me without buying a plane ticket. I could just live here until my mother and her new husband got back from their honeymoon and reported me missing.

Granted, that wouldn't really help convince them I no longer needed to see a psychiatrist.

Settling for a brief rather than indefinite delay, I ducked into the bathroom. It was empty, so I put Gigi's bag on the counter while I splashed water on my face and reapplied some lip gloss. Makeup has never been a priority with me – at least not offstage, which means all the time now. But whenever my mother was losing a fight, she always took a moment to freshen her lipstick. Eventually I figured out this was how she bought time to think up an irrefutable argument.

I was merely stalling the rest of my life.

Gigi gave a soft yip of discontent. I unzipped the top of her carrier so that she could stick her head out, then filled her travel bowl from the half-empty Evian bottle in my purse. The dog took a few indifferent laps, then blinked at me. Her subtext seemed pretty clear: What the hell is your problem?

Was it wrong to have a problem with being shipped off like an unwanted parcel to stay with a relative I'd met only once? I vaguely remembered Cousin Paula from Dad's funeral, pressing my mother's hand in gentle sympathy, even though Mother and Dad had been divorced for three years. But as she'd said on the phone, in her Scarlett O'Hara accent, 'Kin is kin,' and she was happy to have me visit.

Maybe I shouldn't be dreading this. These were my father's family. This was my chance to learn where he came from, because Dad had never spoken much about his background. Which raised the possibility that he might have left Alabama to get away from these people.

A thin blonde wheeled her carry-on into the restroom. Gigi pricked her ears forward adorably, but the woman just shot the dog carrier a dirty look before disappearing with a sniff into the handicapped stall. It was as though thinking about my mother had invoked her eviler twin.

I should correct that. My mother is not evil. She's merely self-absorbed. I can be, too.

For sixteen years, our self-interests coincided more often than not. I lived to dance, and she loved having a ballet prodigy for a daughter. So her lack of maternal instinct didn't really affect me until The Accident (it was hard not to think of it in capital letters) ended my skyrocketing career right as it left the atmosphere.

The Accident had also turned me into a child again. I'd been a professional dancer. I'd travelled to Europe and Asia with the company. Nine months of surgery, casts and titanium rods later, I was a seventeen-year-old 'unaccompanied minor' – thanks a lot, Delta Air Lines – pawned off on distant relatives to be babysat.

The infuriating thing was, Mother knew very well how self-sufficient I was, because she'd taken full advantage of it while dating her new husband. I think if it had been up to her, she would have left me on my own while she went off on her two-week honeymoon.

But 'Dr Steve' hadn't considered it an option. I was emotionally fragile, at a crossroads, major cognitive realignment, blah blah blah. God, I hated shrinks.

He wasn't even *my* shrink, just my new stepfather.

So, I couldn't be left alone for two weeks in our Upper West Side apartment with only Gigi, the security staff, the doorman and all the take-out food in Manhattan for company. It would do me good, he said, to get away from the City, the reminders of my old life, and have a change of scenery.

The unspoken thread in this pronounced sentence was that the godforsaken wilderness of the Deep South was the perfect place for me to dry out. A drastic measure, just because I drank myself unconscious at their wedding. Imagine what he would have suggested if he knew about the hallucinations.

❧ ❧

If I hadn't broken my leg, Mother wouldn't have married Dr Steven Blakely. She'd known him casually through one of her arts organizations, and since he was a premier child psychologist, she'd called him after The Accident. Dr Steve had referred me to his colleague one floor down, and asked my mother out to dinner and a show.

They were married while I was still in a walking cast, but Mother insisted that I process down the aisle with the wedding party. That wouldn't have been a big deal if she had gotten married in an intimate little chapel like a normal divorcée of . . . let's just say thirty-nine. But eighteen years ago, she and my dad had eloped; maybe she thought a big wedding would make marriage stick the second time around.

The reception was in the Cotillion Room of the Pierre hotel. The *Pierre*, in May, with three months' notice. Dr Steve had pull. There must be a lot of messed-up kids in Manhattan. No wonder my mother looked so happy.

At least one of us was. After my third or fourth glass of champagne I wasn't any more miserable than usual. Which was actually an improvement over the earlier part of the afternoon. Then my new stepbrother ruined it.

He sauntered up, looking amused and friendly, and said, 'Nice cast.'

John Blakely was in college, a few years older than me. Despite being Dr Steve's son, he seemed almost normal just then, his Ivy League haircut mussed up and the ends of his bow tie hanging loose around his open shirt collar.

'Thank you, Mr Tactful,' I said, giving him the eye.

He shrugged. 'I figured you wouldn't have gotten that colour if you didn't want people to notice it.'

Yes and no. I hated the cast, and I hated that

Mother had made me lurch up the aisle like Igor in a Vera Wang bridesmaid dress. So at my checkup, when I learned that I'd still be hobbling through the Big Day, I'd asked the guys in the cast room for Day-Glo orange. Later, my shrink would have a lot to say about that. My mother sure as hell did.

I admired the way the cast clashed with the pinkish mauve of my silk dress. 'It's not like I can hide it.'

For some reason, John took this as an invitation and pulled out a chair, fortunately not the one where I'd propped my throbbing leg, and sat down. 'So you're hiding yourself in the corner instead?'

Prior to the Big Day, John and I had met twice. Once at the Four Seasons, where my mother and his father announced their intention to get married, as if the choice of restaurant weren't a dead giveaway. And again at the rehearsal dinner. Our conversations so far had consisted of: wedding, wedding, weather, wedding.

'Some people would take that as a hint,' I said, because I wasn't in the mood to broaden our established repertoire.

John blatantly ignored the clues, spoken and not, that I was a pity party of one. 'I just thought we should get to know each other, now that we're related.' He set down his drink – soda and something warm and amber. No one had carded me for the champagne, but I doubted I could ask for real liquor and get away with it. Unfortunately.

'Dad told me you were a dancer.'

My face went clammy, then hot again. *You were a dancer.* He said it so casually, so conversationally, and I wanted to scream, *I was* famous. Ballet Magazine. *Youngest principal dancer ever.*

He kept talking, oblivious. 'Dad says you'll be going to college next year.'

I swallowed my first gut reaction. Then the second. Eventually a civil answer presented itself. 'Your dad thinks it's a good idea.'

From the way his brows drew down, I hadn't hidden my feelings on the subject – of school, or of his father.

'Why not?' he asked. 'You've got your GED, right? It might be too late to apply for this fall, but you could study for the SAT and try for midterm admission.'

My cheeks began to burn. Pale skin hides none of my emotions, and no one had ever accused me of being beautiful when I was angry. 'Did he tell you to talk to me?'

John's surprise seemed genuine. 'No. Why would he do that?'

'Why are you making like a guidance counsellor?' I could hear the venom in my voice, but couldn't seem to control it.

His tan hid plenty, but my eye spotted a guilty flush on his neck. 'I'm just making conversation.'

'Oh my God.' The realization hit me and I slithered down in my chair. 'You're a psychology major, aren't you? I should have known.'

He stared at me. 'How did you . . . ? That's not the point.'

'You're just like him.' I expected a lack of sympathy or imagination from the stepshrink, but not from someone my age. '*His* idea of comfort was to tell me I was lucky this happened while I was still young and could do something else with my life.'

John frowned, like he was searching for the right answer on a quiz. 'Well, I would have said that no matter how old you are, it's not too late to go in a new direction when something doesn't work out.'

His calm ratcheted my anger up another notch. 'It must be easy,' I said, clipping the ends of my words, 'not to be so passionate about anything that you can't change your plan without any trouble.'

Not a flinch or a blink. 'Well, you can't sulk the rest of your life. You've got to find something to do.'

I gaped, stupidly, unable to think of any answer other than 'screw you'. Or bursting into tears, which was *not* going to happen. Shutting my mouth with an audible snap of my teeth, I manoeuvred my fibreglass-swathed limb to the floor and struggled out of my chair. I wanted to surge indignantly to my feet and storm away, but it's hard to *lumber* off in a huff.

John's voice followed me, carrying something that sounded like regret. 'Sylvie, wait.'

The jazz combo was loud enough that I could pretend I didn't hear him. Mother was dancing with Steve, and she looked so happy that guilt topped off my reservoir of misery. I grabbed a glass of champagne from a passing waiter, then realized I would have to run the gauntlet of theatre and dance people near the ballroom entrance, and I couldn't face their hushed, funereal tones as they asked how I was doing.

Rerouting, I ducked out the service entrance and

paused in the hallway between ballrooms to dig in my tiny, spangled bag for the Vicodin I'd slipped into my aspirin bottle, just in case. My leg hurt, but my leg always hurt. At the moment I was only thinking about easing the ache in my heart.

It was a low dose. Half of what I took on the worst days. I downed it with five big gulps of midgrade champagne, set the glass on the service tray and headed for the lobby.

Mistakes are always so clear in retrospect.

John emerged from the door behind me. 'Where are you going?' he asked, taking his new big-brother role much too seriously.

'Away.' I suited actions to words, but moved too quickly, tottering on my one good leg and catching myself on the wall.

John steadied me on the other side. 'How much have you had to drink?'

'Just champagne.' I decided not to mention the Vicodin. It hadn't had time to work yet. And, in my cast, it wasn't as if I needed help staggering.

'I need some air.' It was too close inside, stifling with good cheer. I headed not for the lobby, but for the Fifth Avenue entrance.

John caught up with me as I was looking for a break in traffic. 'What are you doing?' he demanded. Behind him, I saw the doorman staring, like he'd never seen a girl with a broken leg try to cross Fifth Avenue mid-block before.

'I'm going to the park.' I shivered. It was mid-May, and the evening air was still cool.

John's fingers gripped my arm above my elbow. 'You can't wander around Central Park after dark by yourself.'

That my plan seemed perfectly reasonable should have been a sign I was a lot more drunk than I thought I was.

'It's barely dusk.'

'Your leg is in a cast.'

I looked down, not in surprise, exactly. The throb of my leg was constant, blending into the background of my misery. Then something would remind me, *Sylvie, your leg is broken,* and the ache would come flooding back.

Maybe I had reached that point with my emotions, too. I'd ground through the whole day, and now self-pity and passive-aggressiveness weren't enough to distract me any longer. 'I want to go to my dad's bridge.'

Something must have shown in my face. Tightening his jaw in decision, John stuck out his arm and hailed a cab. He had the knack of a native New Yorker, but I think it may have been my Day-Glo orange cast that got results so quickly on a Saturday evening.

❧ ❧

Technically, my father's bridge was called an arch, not a bridge, and it wasn't 'his' to anyone but me. The directions I gave the cabbie were to Greywacke Arch.

The trip was longer than it would have been by foot. By feet, rather, if I'd had two working ones. The driver took the East Drive and I had him stop before reaching the stone arch that bridged the path from the Ramble to the Great Lawn.

It was a struggle just to manoeuvre my cast out the door. I left John to deal with the cab and limped to the side of the drive. The ground fell away steeply to the path below; covering it was the pointed arch, like something from a Moorish temple. The striations of its stone were still visible in the dusky light.

A million familiar city noises covered John's footsteps, but I felt his approach – body heat, a change in the air pressure. Sensing people behind me was a skill I'd developed in dance; it's handy to know who's upstaging you.

'I can only keep the cab waiting for five minutes.'

Kicking off my shoe, I thrust my beaded evening purse into his hands and stepped onto the grass. 'There's forty dollars in there.'

'Not really the point. Where are you going?' He nervously positioned himself between me and the drop-off. 'Let's not risk life and remaining limb, OK? My dad would kill me if he knew I was . . .'

'Knew you're what?' I challenged. '*Enabling* me?'

'Yeah. That.' From the corner of my eye, I saw him slip off his jacket. He settled it, the fabric warm from his body, on my shoulders, defrosting my skin and, unexpectedly, something deeper inside me, too.

'Thanks,' I said softly.

'Don't mention it.' He gestured to the bridge. 'What's the connection? Your dad was a landscaper, right?'

'Landscape architect,' I corrected, automatically,

but the distinction seemed important. 'The arch was originally built a hundred fifty years ago. Restoring it was Dad's first big job.'

I pointed westward, through the trees. 'He worked on the reconstruction of the lawn and Turtle Pond, too.'

'I remember that. Big project.'

'Yeah. This arch is my favourite, though.' The slope to the tunnel was a tangle of lush plantings and tumbled boulders. Like the rest of Central Park, it was an artful illusion of random, natural beauty – exactly like ballet.

'My father would have understood.' The words slipped out on a sigh, surprising me. I hadn't meant to say them out loud. My head was spinning; the whole night seemed to be alive, and moving in strange ways.

'Did he get to see you dance as a soloist before he died?'

'Yes.' A shrink-type question, but I found myself answering anyway. Stupid self-medicated truth serum. 'He was already sick, but I didn't know it.'

I kneaded the toes of my left foot into the grass, with the strange feeling that it connected me to Dad, through this ground that he loved so much. 'He worked until the very end. He said getting his hands in the dirt energized him, like a plant in the earth.'

I was the opposite, a cut flower without roots, no longer attached to the nourishing soil. Melodramatic, yes. But that's how I felt not being able to dance.

John was watching me, but not with a shrink's critical neutrality. Maybe he wasn't completely ruined by the training yet. 'Did you get his green thumb?'

'I don't know. Dad always sent me potted plants instead of bouquets, and I managed to keep those alive.' I didn't quite smile. 'Mother used to get so angry that he wouldn't spring for a couple dozen roses.'

John echoed the humour in my voice. 'I'll bet. That reception alone must have cleaned out a couple of hothouses.'

I might have laughed, if I were the person I used to be. Instead, I pulled the pin from the boutonniere on the lapel of his tuxedo jacket and let the flower drop into my hand. 'When I was a kid, and saw Dad transplant cuttings, it looked like magic. You put this little sprig of green in the ground, and it takes root – keeps growing instead of dying.'

Now I knew it wasn't magic. Some things could be replanted, or even grafted onto something new. Some wouldn't take. What I didn't know was which type I was.

'Back then,' I continued, while I peeled the florist tape from the boutonniere, 'I thought that worked on anything. That it would fix toys, china, dolls . . .'

John sounded amused. 'That could have been grim, if you'd experimented on a house cat or something.'

'No kidding.' He watched, obviously curious, as I lowered myself on one leg, sliding my cast out to the side. I was still impressively limber, and I think the Vicodin was starting to work, making me feel loose in body, and in mind. Because I didn't know why else I was telling him this, or why I was even going through these motions.

'I came up with this sort of spell of my own.' Working my fingers through the webbing of grass roots, into the sod, I made a little hole. 'If there was something important that I wanted to take root, metaphorically speaking, I would plant it. Like this.'

I dropped the boutonniere – a miniature calla lily that echoed the big ones in Mother's bouquet – into the ground.

'That's kind of sweet,' said John. 'I thought you hated my dad.'

With a sigh of reluctant admission, I folded the sod over the lump of the flower. 'I can't hate anyone who seems to be making my mother happy.'

John laughed. 'Now I know you're drunk.'

I chuckled slightly, mostly at my own whimsy. He must be right. I was never whimsical. Not since The Accident.

Still squatting on one leg, I laid both palms on the bump in the grass and pressed it down. A tingle ran up my arms and back down again. I seemed to see – or sense, rather – a wave rippling out from under my hands, like I'd dropped a rock in a pond.

The world tilted, off-kilter for a moment, and I lost my balance, my arms windmilling to catch myself. I fell onto my butt and things righted themselves with a thump. 'Whoa.'

'Nice one, Sylvie.' John bent to pick me up under the arms. 'Way to use that dancer's grace.'

I was too flabbergasted to retort. 'Did you see that?'

'What?' he asked, setting me carefully back on my feet. 'Your magic spell?'

My mouth opened to say 'Yes!' when I realized that

he was being sarcastic. Because magic spells were crazy. And I was just superstitious. And probably drunk.

'I don't feel so good.' My stomach fluttered and twisted, though the dizziness came and went.

'I'm not surprised.'

The cabbie honked his horn. John turned and marched me – figuratively speaking, hobbled as I was by the cast and all – back to the taxi. He had the big-brother thing down. I wasn't sure I liked it, but at that moment, I wasn't sure I didn't.

'My shoe,' I said, when my bare left foot hit the pavement.

He grumbled but made sure I had my feet under me before heading back for it with a curt 'Stay here.'

Of course I didn't. I limped past the taxi, to the other side of the bridge. In the wintertime, I would have been able to see clearly to the Great Lawn – the big swath of level ground where, during the day, dogs would chase Frisbees and kids would play baseball. It was May, so my view was interrupted by the new foliage, but not blocked like it would be in summer. That, plus the moon and the ambient light from the city, left me frowning at the scene.

John came up behind me again. 'Hey. I thought you were going to get in the cab.'

'I was, but . . .' The vista wavered as I stared. 'Are they doing some sort of historical reenactment?'

'What are you talking about?'

I pointed through the trees. 'The village of card-board lean-tos out on the lawn.' I tried to remember the last time I'd been in this area of the park. I'd been lost in self-pity for a while, but this was something even I would have noticed.

John glanced towards the lawn, his brows drawn in confusion. 'You mean, like a Hooverville? The ones built during the Depression?'

That was what I meant, but I didn't understand his confusion. Then I realized, he didn't see it. But the people who moved through the tumbled huts cast shadows in the moonlight. I could see the glimmer of a lantern, hear the crackle of a campfire. The evening chill carried the damp-earth smell of cooking turnips and the mournful whistle of someone trying to cheer himself up after another long day of fruitless searching for work.

I stared at the shades in the twilight, all silhouette and gloom, and the trees around me swayed. No . . . that was me. I was swaying. Was this what being wasted felt like? I was dizzy and confused and somewhat judgement-impaired, but I still felt in control of my faculties. Certainly not so far gone as to be hallucinating in Central Park.

'Sylvie.' John caught me by both shoulders and bent to look into my eyes, blocking my view of the town and the sad people in it. 'Level with me. How much did you have to drink?'

'Just some champagne and . . .' I stopped before mentioning the Vicodin. Or, maybe more important, before confessing that I was seeing images he wasn't, some strange five-senses film reel from one of the Park's major moments. And while this seemed surreal but reasonable to me in my buzzed state, I could see where such a confession could lead to a seventy-two-hour hold for observation at some nice private hospital upstate and away from gossip.

Drunk was better than crazy, and as John's face dipped and swam in front of me, I wasn't faking anything when I answered, 'Maybe more than *some*. I lost track.'

He blew a short strand of hair off his forehead. 'Great.'

Darkness crawled in from the edges of my vision. 'I think I'm going to pass out.' Considering how my brain was whirling, my voice sounded weirdly matter-of-fact. I had to warn him, because he was going to have to catch me. 'Don't tell your dad, OK?'

My knees went limp just as he pulled my arm across his shoulders. 'I won't.'

He'd been so nice to me that I actually believed him. But I'd forgotten: shrinks always stick together.

Chapter 2

A growl brought me back to the present; Gigi had discovered her reflection in the mirror. I heard the toilet flush, and figured I'd better make an exit before Cruella de Vil came out of the stall.

Besides, I'd procrastinated long enough. Cousin Paula might be the type to send airport security to look for me. The public story was that I was visiting my father's family to give Mother and Steve a chance to honeymoon and set up house. But I didn't doubt for a moment that the stepshrink had told Dad's cousin that

I was some kind of teen-starlet substance-abuse cliché, and needed 'special handling' while I 'worked through some things'. Which was Upper West Side speak for 'sobered up'.

I checked my reflection – a matter of habit before going onstage – smoothing back a few pieces of mousy brown hair that had slipped from my bun, checking my teeth for lip gloss. My skin was pale and the fluorescent lighting emphasized the purple shadows under my eyes. Lovely.

My eyes continued downward, over my girly T-shirt and jeans. They were a little loose; I'd kept the weight off, even though I'd never have to worry about lifts again. Just to delay leaving, I moved my sweater from tied around my waist to draped over my shoulders, not because I was cold, but because the pale pink colour made my face look less like the walking dead. It was all about the costuming.

'In the bag, Gigi.' The dog obediently tucked her front paws into the carrier. Feeling rebellious, I let her ride with her head sticking out so she could watch the world go by. At least one of us should be having fun.

By the time I reached baggage claim, the arrivals had thinned out. I cast my eye over the remaining people, looking for Paula. Unfortunately, I wasn't sure I could pick her out of a lineup, let alone a crowd.

I didn't see anyone searching for me, so I headed for the baggage carousel. Unlike Dad's cousin, my fuchsia suitcase was easy to spot. No porters, though. I scanned the area, trying to look like a big tipper, but realized I was on my own.

Switching Gigi to my right shoulder for counter-balance, I grabbed the handle of my suitcase as it came by. The trick was keeping the majority of my weight on my left foot; the orthopaedic surgeon had declared my right leg healed – finally – but its muscles were still weak. I had physical therapy exercises to do while I was here, and a referral to a Montgomery specialist if I had any trouble. I didn't intend to have any trouble that required a specialist. Not for my leg, *or* my head.

I managed to lever the suitcase onto the edge of the carousel, and stood in an uncomfortable arabesque while I tried to figure out how to pull it down without knocking my good leg out from under me. That would be an awkward headline: *Ex-ballerina flattened by actual baggage. Overdose of irony suspected.*

'Careful there.' The masculine voice startled me, but not nearly as much as the arm that wrapped around me, bracing the heavy suitcase. My normal instinct – the one that told me when someone was coming up behind me, the one that told me to scream 'fire' instead of 'rape' if someone grabbed me – all short-circuited with a tangible fizzle so strong that I was surprised I didn't smell smoke.

My inhale of alarm carried in a whiff of herbal soap, but it was the scent of clean air and damp earth that filled my head and took me to a strange place, so I seemed to be simultaneously standing in an airport in Alabama and someplace wild and wet and green. The only constants were the steadying arms around me, and the feeling that my heart was going to beat out of my chest with anticipation, or fear, or both.

It was dizzying, unnerving, like confusing a memory with a dream. For an instant – the nanosecond between information coming in and my brain processing it – I was certain that if I turned round, I would *know* this guy.

My heart squeezed with real fear then, at the thought that reality was going slippery on me. Again. But before panic could do more than flex its claws, the moment ended. The eerie feeling of recognition vanished, leaving just a perfectly normal rush of *Wow, someone smells really nice* in its wake.

A calloused hand covered mine on the suitcase handle. 'I have it. You can let go.'

I couldn't place the accent. Not the expected drawl, but a rounded, liquid slurring of syllables. Vaguely British, but too soft to be Scots or Irish. A tiny echo of remembrance tingled down my neck, but that might have merely been the musical inflection of his voice so close to my ear.

Belatedly, I snatched back my hand and took a discreet step out of the way while he, whoever he was, got the luggage under control. I covered, hopefully, my lapse in composure by checking on Gigi – who had prudently retreated into her carrier during the suitcase wrangle.

I can be very pragmatic about personal space. Doing lifts and holds with a partner, you don't have the luxury of modesty. I'd probably had more guys' hands on my no-touch zones than any other virgin in America. Yet there I was, flustered and blushing, tingles zipping over every point where our bodies had touched.

This, at least, was normal, even if it wasn't exactly normal for me.

Jeez, Sylvie! Stop being such a girl. He could be hideous, or old, or have three eyes. And it wouldn't matter, because he was a random Good Samaritan whom I would never see again.

'Sylvie Davis?'

Or he might be a stalker. A crazed ballet-fan stalker. Stranger things had happened. It figured they would happen to me. It had been that kind of year.

'Hello? Miss?'

Gigi prairie-dogged up from her bag to acknowledge the greeting. I steeled myself and turned, clamping the carrier securely against my side in case I had to run.

A tall young man stood holding my suitcase. Not hideous. Not old. The normal number of eyes, at least where I could see. They were unusual, though, an earthy sort of green that darkened around the edge of the iris. His hair was brown, curling where it touched the top of his ears and the edge of his rugby collar. His face was handsomely chiselled, with the clean, symmetrical lines of classical art. The Romantic period – strong brow, straight nose, firm jaw. Gainsborough, maybe. There was a rustic look to the fall of his hair and in the way his cheeks and nose had been painted warm by the sun.

He didn't look much older than me; I guessed twenty or so, the same age as John the fink. But much more . . . just *more.*

'You *are* Sylvie Davis, yes?' He waved a hand

in front of my face. Gigi lunged playfully, a mile off the mark, but the stranger drew back his hand anyway.

I blinked, and shut my gaping mouth. It was a little harder to get my thoughts back into line.

'Do I know you?' It was a rhetorical question. Momentary weirdness aside, I knew I would have remembered if I'd met him before.

'No.' The word was blunt, but not unfriendly. 'I'm Rhys. Rhys Griffith.' He pronounced it like 'Reese', but with a tiny flip of the r. 'Your cousin Paula sent me in to fetch you.'

I hardly knew Paula, but that didn't seem right. I was 'kin', after all. 'Is there something wrong?'

He smiled, slightly. Apparently I was easier to read than I liked to think. 'She's waiting with the car in the loading zone. Not to worry.'

That was more in keeping with the woman I'd spoken with, albeit briefly, on the phone. It didn't explain this guy, however.

'Is it only the one case?' he asked, while I tried to fix my mental bearings.

'No. There's a smaller one for the dog.' I pointed out Gigi's suitcase on the conveyer belt, and he grabbed it and set it down in front of me, giving my brain a chance to catch up a bit.

'How did you recognize me?' I asked.

He looked me over, teasing, I think. 'Skinny girl, hair wound up tight in a bun, posture like the Queen of England? There's really no mistaking you, Miss Prima Ballerina.'

Now my native suspicions kicked in, and I narrowed my eyes. 'How do I know Paula really sent you?'

'She said you'd be prickly, and likely too stubborn to admit you needed help with your baggage because of your leg.'

I tightened my jaw – stubbornly. 'The whole world knows I broke my leg.'

'Maybe.' He telescoped out the handle on the suitcase with an efficient twist, then raised one expectant black brow. 'But who knew you and your designer-purse dog would be in Birmingham, Alabama, today, princess?'

With that sally, he headed towards the exit, wheeling my big fuchsia suitcase behind him. He moved with an easy gait, comfortable in his own skin. I stared stupidly for a moment, then realized he was leaving with all my clothes.

I pulled out the handle on Gigi's case – it held her collapsible crate, her toys and all her food – and hurried after him, gritting my teeth against the hitch in my step. I didn't always limp, but it had been a long, tiring day. The physical therapist said it was unreasonable for me to expect bone and muscle to rehabilitate overnight. Obviously she didn't know me very well. I was used to expecting unreasonable things from my body.

Fortunately, Rhys wasn't walking very fast. I was able to catch up without too much effort or embarrassment. Gigi, happy to be moving again, gazed around avidly. Airports were full of interesting people – and smells, I suppose, from the canine perspective.

'She's *not* a designer-purse dog,' I said, panting only slightly.

'No?' He glanced down at me, and slowed his steps a little more. I'm tall enough that I can look most guys in the nose, if not the eyes, but my head barely reached his chin. 'What's her name?'

I clenched my teeth and answered. 'Gigi.' He laughed and I bristled defensively. 'It's short for Giselle.'

Actually, she came with the name Gigi, and I'd decided it was short for something less ridiculous. I'd gotten her from a socialite who didn't want her when she – the dog, I mean – turned out to be inconveniently large. That is to say, too big to fit into Prada's new 'it' bag.

'She's a secondhand reject dog, and she's quite vicious. She'll bite you if you're mean to me.'

The vicious dog had propped her front paws on the bag, her ear fluff blowing in the breeze, like she was joyriding from my shoulder in her own mini sports car.

Rhys looked us both up and down. '"Though she be but little, she is fierce."'

Humour broadened his accent, exaggerating the roll of the *r* and the length of the vowels until it was almost unintelligible.

'You're not from around here, are you?'

'What was your clue?' he asked, smiling in profile.

I skirted around a woman with a cell phone and hair like a helmet. 'The accent. And insulting me with a Shakespeare quote.'

He slanted me an unrepentant look. 'Is "fierce" an insult on this side of the Atlantic? My apologies.'

'I meant the "little" part, if you really mean skinny.' He didn't answer, which I took for an affirmative. I switched the hand pulling Gigi's suitcase and shifted the carrier to my other shoulder. 'How do you know Paula?'

'My father and I are staying at your cousin's place while Dad does some work in the area.'

I wrestled with the logistics of that, since *I* was staying there too. 'Is her house particularly large?'

'Large enough.' He glanced at me. 'We won't be getting underfoot, if that's your worry.'

'No.' By which I meant yes, because the other thing in my suitcase besides clothes was books. I intended to park myself on the veranda or under a magnolia tree or whatever they had here and read until it was time to return to civilization. 'Just worried about bathroom space.'

My steps slowed as we reached the exit – a revolving door flanked by two sets of regular ones. Airports were transitional, an extension of the plane that got you there, and a link to the place you came from. Stepping outside and putting my feet on the ground – the real ground, not the tarmac – somehow seemed a bigger commitment than getting on the plane in New York.

Rhys straight-armed the crossbar and held open the door, standing back to let me pass. With Gigi's carrier over my shoulder, I had to edge through sideways. I held my breath, not because the fit was so tight, but to avoid the possibility of another head trip. Imagining things while I was drunk was one thing. Weird déjà vu with a stranger in the airport, on the other hand . . .

I chanced a quick peek up at Rhys and found him studying my face as if there would be a pop quiz later. It was a serious expression, and when my eyes met his, he didn't look away or apologize for staring. He merely raised his brows from their scowl of concentration, and gave me a quick, rueful smile that stopped me in the doorway.

The sounds of the busy airport retreated. Behind him, I could see the steady spin of the revolving door, people coming and going, while I stood on the threshold with Rhys, neither in nor out. The heat and humidity bathed one half of me; the air-conditioning chilled the other. And from the guy sharing the doorway, a different sort of warmth entirely.

'Don't look like that, love.'

The endearment startled me, but he said it like an American guy might say 'dear' or 'honey' – if a guy could manage to say it without sounding patronizing or sexist. Rhys managed to make it merely a friendly word, like buddy or Mac.

'Look like what?' I tried to sound normal, which was a trick, when I hardly remembered what normal was.

'As if you're walking into the lion's den.' He nodded towards the outside, both punctuating his statement and gesturing for me to get on with it. The intimacy of the moment was gone. 'Chin up. I'm sure you'll feel at home in no time.'

I wasn't sure I had a home any more. It wasn't

merely about Mother and me moving in with Steve. The ballet studio had been where I lived. The sweat-soaked air, the squeak of rosined toes on the floor. Our apartment had only been a place to sleep at night, to kill time until I could get back to the studio.

Now I would never dance again, and my whole life had become about killing time, about waiting. But for what, I had no idea.

Chapter 3

I couldn't have described Cousin Paula from the single time I'd met her, but I had no difficulty finding her in the loading zone outside the airport. Not once I'd gotten my sunglasses on and stopped staggering from the heat, anyway.

Rhys wheeled my suitcase towards a white sport-utility wagon. The middle-aged woman standing beside it smiled when she saw me, and came to meet me on the sidewalk. She was medium tall, matronly around the middle, with grey-blonde – I suppose ash-blonde would be more tactful – hair in a ubiquitous Southern style: layered bob, fringy bangs, lots of volume. Big hair. Once again, Alabama did not disappoint.

'Thank heavens,' said Cousin Paula, her drawl thick with relief. 'We were running so late, I was worried we would miss you.'

'Where would I go?' I asked, not meaning to be snide. It was a miserably literal question. I had no?where else to be.

'Well, honey, it doesn't matter. Rhys found you, and you're here.' Smiling, she took my shoulders in her hands. 'We'll be on our way back to Cahaba and get you set to rights in no time.'

I think she meant well. But I didn't need 'setting'. I just needed – well, that was the question of the hour. My mother, the stepshrink, my real shrink, my physical therapist – everyone seemed to know what I needed, except me.

I caught Rhys's eyes on me as he placed the suitcase by the rear of the vehicle, ready to load. The scrutiny reminded me of my manners. 'Thank you, Cousin Paula. It was kind of you to invite me to stay with you.'

That, at least, I could say genuinely, and she seemed pleased, even as she demurred. 'Heavens, child, it's your home, too, for all that your daddy ran off to the big city.'

She motioned towards the car, and started to take my arm, but there was a dog in the way. Gigi gave a friendly yip, and my cousin recoiled with a gasp. 'Good lord.' She stared at the bag, her hand pressed to her heart. 'What in the world is that?'

I glanced down as if I didn't know which 'that' she meant. 'This? My mother's idea of therapy.'

'She didn't mention you were bringing a dog,' said Paula, not quite aghast, but not exactly charmed.

Gesturing to the airport doors, I said, not quite joking, 'Is it a problem? Because I can see if the airline will let me fly back early.'

'No, of course not.' Her tone, though, was doubtful as she eyed the dog. 'But where is she going to sleep? She can't run loose, and the garden fence won't hold her.'

'I have a crate for her.' My small gratitude for Paula's hospitality was fading, replaced with growing trepidation. 'But mostly she goes everywhere with me.'

My cousin's mouth turned down, making long, unhappy dimples. Gigi cocked her head, cranking the cuteness dial all the way up to irresistible.

Rhys cleared his throat. 'If you'll let me take that case, Sylvie . . .'

'Oh, heavens,' said Paula, as if only now realizing we were standing in the loading zone. 'We can talk just as well on the ride to the house. Do you want front or back?'

'Whichever,' I said, letting her choose. She sounded so syrupy sweet on the phone, I hadn't bet on her being such a force of nature. As she slid into the front passenger seat, I noticed that her khaki capris showed a few wrinkles from the drive, but it hadn't erased the creases of careful ironing. This just kept getting better and better.

Wheeling Gigi's suitcase to the open trunk, I eyed

35

the back of my cousin's head and lowered my voice to ask Rhys, 'So, what's with the soccer mom wagon?'

It wasn't the smoothest way to look for some hint as to whether or not Paula had kids. But I didn't think it deserved the coolly sardonic look I got from Rhys. 'Sorry I couldn't manage a limousine, your highness.'

I flushed, and pushed my sunglasses onto my nose, painfully aware that the prominent Dolce & Gabbana logo would seem to prove his point. 'Don't be silly,' I said, matching his tone. 'I would have settled for a Town Car.'

Rhys responded with a sound halfway between a scoff and a laugh as he stowed the last of my luggage, manoeuvring the heavy suitcase easily into the trunk next to the first one. The broad shoulders under his rugby shirt weren't just for show, then. Where his sleeves were pushed up, I could see that his hands and forearms were corded with muscle, crisscrossed with the fading remnants of scratches and cuts.

It had been so long since I'd felt anything other than miserable, it took me a moment to recognize curiosity when I felt it. 'What did you say you were doing in Alabama?'

'I didn't,' he said, shutting me down, but with amusement, finding my perfectly logical question funny for some reason.

I cast my mind back through our conversation, filtered through his digs about my diva dog, and realized it was true; he hadn't said much of anything about himself. That was both frustrating and unnerving. How could I know nothing about him, but feel so familiar with the twitch of humour at the corner of his mouth, as if the expression had irritated and fascinated me for years?

He closed the hatch while I was ruminating, and I found myself staring at a magnetic sign adorning the back of the car. It read: BLUESTONE HILL INN, CAHAWBA, ALABAMA. Under the lettering was a romanticized depiction of an antebellum-style house, overshadowed by a huge, blossoming tree.

'Bluestone Hill?' I asked, trying to tie together the picture, the name, the word 'inn' with the scraps of things Dad had said about his childhood.

Rhys put a hand on the top of the SUV and turned to me, as if I'd asked a stupid question. 'Bluestone Hill. Don't tell me you've forgotten the name of your family estate.'

I ignored that as another gibe at my divaness, because if the Davises were some kind of landed gentry, surely Dad would have mentioned it. 'I mean the "inn" part. Paula runs an inn? Is it a bed-and-breakfast or what?'

'It's a work in progress, actually, but . . .' He broke off and frowned at me, seeming genuinely baffled. 'How did you not know that?'

I shrugged uncomfortably, relaxing my jaw when it wanted to get tight and defensive. His disbelief was valid. Reasonable people took some interest in where they were going. Like I needed the reminder I wasn't reasonable. Confronted with my ignorance, I felt worse than stupid for not asking questions. It seemed a little nuts, and since that night in the Park, that wasn't something I said lightly, even in my head.

'I had other things on my mind,' I said, feigning

carelessness, justifying my ignorance to both of us. 'And my mother made most of the arrangements.'

Glancing at Gigi, who panted placidly in the sticky heat, Rhys acknowledged, 'There does seem to have been some breakdown in communication.'

He smoothly managed the trick of reaching the door before me and opening it. The idea of climbing into another vehicle, so soon after I'd gotten my feet on the ground – or at least the asphalt – twisted another loop into the weary knot in my stomach. I struggled for a moment with how to fold myself into the back seat with any grace or dignity, then gave up and clambered awkwardly in.

'All set?' asked Paula, twisting round to look at me.

I set Gigi's carrier on the seat and tried to find a comfortable position. Alleged divahood aside, a Town Car *would* have had more legroom. I settled for stretching my leg out beside Gigi, and tried not to groan as I slipped off my shoe and wiggled my toes. 'Much better.'

'That's good,' Paula said as Rhys circled to the driver's side. 'I figured if you wanted to, you could go to sleep back there. Travelling always wears me out.'

'I can never sleep in a car.' Or a plane, or a bus. I'd gotten a lot of reading done while on tour with the company.

Gigi wanted to get out of her carrier and into my lap. I needed a better stretch, and a pain pill, but I settled for digging the bottle of Advil from my purse and swallowing three gelcaps with a swig of bottled water.

I waited until Rhys got behind the wheel and buckled his seat belt, then made a stab at needling him in return for that 'princess' business. 'I'm impressed, Cousin Paula. A British chauffeur. That's very high-toned. Your guests at the inn will be very impressed.'

In the rearview mirror, Rhys shot me a narrow-eyed glare, but Paula just laughed. 'If I could afford to offer him a job, I would. As it is, he's been so helpful and tolerant with the work on the house, I hardly think of Rhys or his father as guests at all.'

As the chauffeur in question pulled the car onto the road, I took the opportunity to find out whether there would be crack-of-dawn power-tool wake-up calls. 'How is the work on the inn going?'

Rhys gave a soft snort. He knew that I hadn't known until two minutes ago that there was an inn at all. He didn't mention that fact, and thankfully Paula missed his nonverbal commentary.

'Oh, lord,' she said, as if revving up for a recitation. 'You would not believe the work we've done on the old place. There's still so much left to do; sometimes I don't know where I'll get the strength. This project is half cursed, half blessed, I think.'

'What makes you say that?' I admit that my interest was merely polite. But talking distracted her, and I was able to slip Gigi from her carrier and into my lap, which made us both happier.

Paula shrugged. 'Oh, I suppose we've just met the normal roadblocks. Hundred-year-old plumbing, vintage copper wiring—'

'Installing an extra loo on the first floor,' added

Rhys, his eyes on the road as we approached the entrance ramp to the highway.

'Exactly!' said Paula. She glanced back at me, but didn't seem to notice the dog. Probably because I'd slipped off my sweater and covered Gigi with it. 'But your great-great-great-grandfather – or however many it is – knew what he was doing. The house is solid as a rock. There have been some major expenses, but otherwise things have magically fallen into place. And of course, I'm lucky to have Clara.'

Crap. Was I supposed to know who that was? In the rearview mirror, Rhys looked amused at the hole I'd dug for myself. 'Um . . . so, Clara's been a big help?' I asked vaguely.

'I couldn't ask for a better business partner,' said Paula. 'It helps that she's an amazing cook. She's kept us all fed. And her daughter recruited the Teen Town Council to help with rebuilding the summerhouse. They've been great.'

'The Teen Town Council?' Her tone had definitely capitalized the words, and I repeated it the same way.

Paula waved a hand. 'You'll meet them. Bluestone Hill makes a good meeting place, so they're always around.'

I glanced at Rhys again to see his latest reaction. But he was gazing straight ahead, his hands on the wheel, as if the road required more concentration than a four-lane divided highway warranted.

Paula reached across and patted his shoulder. 'And of course, Rhys and his dad are a godsend. They needed a cheap place to stay and didn't care that we're not even open – goodness, not even ready yet.'

Some tension – maybe I had been imagining it – ran out of him, and he smiled, entirely genuine. 'There's a bed and there's Clara's stellar breakfasts. We can't ask for a better situation.'

'Even when I recruit you to drive me to Birmingham.' She glanced over her shoulder to tell me, 'I don't like to drive so far by myself.'

I wanted to ask more about Rhys and his father's situation, but this last comment distracted me. 'How far a drive is it?'

Rhys looked at his watch. 'Less than two hours. We should be there in time for a late supper.'

'Two *hours*?' Gigi squirmed in my lap, as if she knew what we were talking about. 'We're going to need a rest stop before then.'

Nodding, he changed lanes. 'There's a spot on the way.'

We'd quickly left the suburban homes and strip malls, and were now on the tree-lined interstate. I usually had a very good sense of direction, but I was slow to get my bearings after the tiring trip. I had no idea where we were, except, apparently, a long way from our destination.

'I need to fire my travel agent,' I grumbled.

'Any large airport would be a bit of a drive,' Rhys said.

Paula confirmed this with a chuckle. 'Yes, we're really out in the sticks.'

'And you're opening an inn?' I asked. 'Who do you expect to stay there?'

'Oh heavens. People come from all over to hunt and fish or just enjoy nature. There's antique shopping, we're on the way to Mobile, and Selma's not far away at all.'

I couldn't decide if I was more annoyed or appalled at myself for not asking these questions before I'd left New York. I could have at least looked the place up on a map. 'What's the name of your town again?'

'Well, the Hill is the country, a few miles from a charming little town called Maddox Landing.' Paula spoke with some pride and a lot of tour-guide enthusiasm. 'I expect you'll know everyone's name within a day or two. They're all looking forward to meeting you.'

'Oh God.' I didn't realize I'd groaned aloud until I sensed her bristling in the front seat. No taking it back, I guess. 'Why would they want to do that?'

'Because you're a Davis, of course.' She'd pokered up, her back ramrod straight, giving me a disapproving look over her shoulder. 'It would behoove you to be a little gracious if folks want to welcome you home.'

A quick rush of remorse scorched my ears. I was being ungracious and ungrateful. The fact that this *wasn't* my home seemed like a pointless argument. Especially with someone who used 'behoove' in a sentence without the slightest irony.

I didn't want to look at Rhys, but I couldn't help that any more than my blush. He was watching me again, but not with disapproval or sympathy. Just that same, studying look, as if I were a puzzle he was trying to figure out.

Join the club. *I* didn't even know what was going on with me lately. He would have to stand in line if he had questions.

And I was going to have to figure it out here, in Alabama. Land of my father's birth. Back end of nowhere.

It was so weird to have Paula talk about this being my home, when I'd never been here, never even really discussed it with Dad. I knew he left when he was eighteen. As far as I can remember, he never returned, though he must have kept in touch with Paula, because she'd known about his funeral.

The highway wound around the smoothly tumbled remnants of the Appalachian foothills. In places it dipped down between trees and lush vines that knitted everything together into a comforting canyon. Then it would crest one of the hills and, across the tops of the trees, I could see a panorama of green spread out in a dizzying vista.

I rubbed my hands over my eyes. My body was stiff and aching and a dizzy, disconnected feeling was invading my brain and moving down to my stomach. I'd been travelling since six a.m. Eastern Standard Time – taxi, 747, turboprop commuter plane and now the soccer mom wagon. It all seemed to fall on me at once, an avalanche of exhaustion.

'Next exit,' said Rhys, as if he'd read my mind.

Paula glanced at him. 'You aren't going to wait until Clanton?'

It figured she was a backseat – well, a passenger seat – driver. But Rhys took it in stride. 'I thought the rest stop would be better for her to walk the dog. Lots of grass.'

That was what we needed. If I could just put my feet

43

on the ground, walk around a bit, I'd feel so much better.

Gigi squirmed restlessly as Rhys put on the turn signal and slowed to exit the highway. By the time he pulled into the paved horseshoe in front of a swath of green dotted with picnic tables, my hand was on the door latch, braced for escape.

I grabbed Gigi's leash from her bag and climbed out, not bothering to put on my shoes. I probably should have been worried about glass or other nasty things, but I was mostly interested in feeling the grass under my feet, burrowing my toes down until I reached the cold soil beneath.

Setting Gigi onto a stretch of lawn away from the picnic tables, I did just that, sinking my toes into the grass like I was putting down roots. The queasiness vanished, and a few deep breaths later, my head stopped spinning. Like magic.

I immediately wished I hadn't thought that. It was merely an expression, or it had been until that night in the Park with John. Before I had started second-guessing every whimsical thought that flitted through my imagination.

Really, Sylvie? Magic?

No, not really. I don't think magic exists.

Whew. Then I must not be crazy. Today, at least.

Except then I had to worry about talking to myself. I couldn't win.

From behind me, I heard the car window roll down. 'Sylvie, honey, where on earth are your shoes? Have you lost your mind?'

The question made me laugh. After that, I couldn't pretend I didn't hear her, so I called over my shoulder, 'I'll just be a second, Cousin Paula.'

Gigi, after some searching, found an acceptable spot to christen and I left her to it while I looked around. The rest stop consisted of the paved crescent, the grass we occupied, and the concrete picnic tables, all ringed by a wall of trees. The warm breeze carried a hint of the woods beyond, not really enough to compete with the stink of exhaust from the highway.

A sign warned, ALL PETS MUST BE LEASHED, which was good advice. Done with her pee, my dog trotted persistently around the clearing, nose to the ground, which might mean that she wasn't finished, or might mean she was checking messages from previous canine visitors.

'Don't wander off, Gee.'

She glanced at me – her ears pricked, her fluff standing defiantly out from her head, her plumed tail held saucily over her back – then did exactly what I'd told her not to.

I sighed. This was not going to win us points with Paula.

In addition to being on the big end of the breed standard for a long-haired Chihuahua, Gigi tipped the scales on what dog books euphemistically call an 'independent personality'. As long as I had a treat in my hand, she was reasonably well behaved. But other times she was six and a half pounds of fluffy you-and-what-army.

She pranced purposefully towards a path that led

through the trees, away from the concrete picnic tables, the asphalt circle, and Cousin Paula's soccer mom wagon.

'Gigi! Come back here.' The very expensive trainer that Mom had hired said that I had to be the pack leader, but it was hard to feel like an alpha dog when most days I didn't even feel like getting out of bed.

At my command, Gigi *did* pause – just long enough to pull back her lips in a tongue-lolling smile before she dashed down the path and out of sight.

Paula called to me as I followed Gigi, and I heard the car door open, then close. Ignoring both, I stalked after the dog in my bare feet.

A sign with an arrow indicated we were headed to the 'Indian Mound'. Great. My dog was going to desecrate an ancient burial ground within an hour of our arrival in the state.

My feet weren't as calloused as they once were, but the grass trail was well beaten down. It led to a large clearing, ringed by tall pine trees that cast long shadows in the setting sun. I'm not sure what I expected an Indian Mound to look like, but I was unprepared for the house-sized knoll of grass-covered earth in front of me.

Instead of a dome shape, like a pitcher's mound, it was squared off, with steeply sloped sides going up twenty feet or more, ending in a flat top, like a miniature version of the pyramids I'd seen on a vacation in Cancún.

What a bizarre thing. On the far corner was a placard, possibly explaining the site, but as curious as I was, I was even more interested in collecting my dog, who sat halfway up the slope of the mound, waiting expectantly for me to climb and get her.

With a sigh, I did just that, figuring that if this was some kind of sacred ground, it was better to defile it with my bare feet than with anything Gigi might leave behind. Rather than risk the steep rise with my weak leg, I crawled up on my hands and knees. Gigi started to dance back out of my grasp, but I lunged and caught her. I landed face-first in the grass, but at least I had the laughing dog in my hands.

I knew, as soon as I pushed myself upright, that I had an audience. There was nothing weird or magical about it. Just that there must be some unfair universal law that applied to handsome guys coming along just as you face-plant in the dirt.

Sure enough, when I rolled over, Rhys stood at ground level, holding my shoes and looking very entertained. 'That was by far the most graceful belly flop I've ever seen.'

Nice. Not even the accent made that go down any easier. On the whole, I preferred his calling me princess to his laughing at me.

'Thank you.' I feigned composure, holding Gigi in one hand while I brushed at the grass stains on my T-shirt with the other. 'I've had years of training.'

'I can tell.' He held up my red leather flats. 'Paula sent me.'

'Of course.' I untangled Gigi's leash from where I'd draped it around my neck, and clipped it to her harness. 'My cousin has a real steel-magnolia thing going on, I've noticed.'

Rhys climbed a few steps up the slope, to my

level, his eyes making a sweeping inspection. 'Are you feeling better? You've got some colour back in your cheeks.'

Falling on my face will do that, not to mention that quick but close examination that I felt like the warmth of a spotlight. But I let his assumption stand. 'The fresh air helped.'

Paula would be waiting, but I couldn't make myself hurry back. To my surprise, instead of insisting we go, Rhys lowered himself to sit beside me. Not close. Maybe an arm's length away. It seemed a carefully chosen distance, though, and I wondered if he felt the same zing of awareness that I did.

He certainly gave no clue, so I determined to do the same and distracted myself with a look around the site. The shadows of the trees were lengthening, falling like bars across the clearing. The breeze stirred the branches, so they seemed to move sinuously towards us as we sat on the eerie relic of raised earth.

'What was this place?' I asked, my curiosity genuine. 'Do you know?'

Rhys squinted towards the top of the mound, then around the clearing. 'A mound like this usually means a buried structure of some sort. Unexcavated ruins.'

The authority in his answer surprised me, and it must have shown, because his mouth twisted sheepishly. 'My father is a professor of anthropology at the University of Cardiff. On sabbatical at the moment.'

'Oh really.' In my world, 'on sabbatical' meant that someone was in rehab or on a diet. 'And he picked rural Alabama out of all the places in the world?'

His grudging smile widened a fraction, acknowledging my point, my persistence. 'He's researching a book.'

That reluctant curve of his lip was devastating. My heart tripped all over itself, and I told myself it was merely triumph at having elicited a smile that wasn't at my expense. 'So, you're just here for grins,' I prompted.

He shrugged. 'I'm sort of on a break too. So I'm helping Dad with his research.'

I wondered what 'sort of' on a break meant, and whether that was another way of saying 'out of university but haven't found a job yet'. Not that I was one to throw stones at people who had their lives on hold.

'Are you in the same field?' I asked.

'Not exactly.' He rose to his feet and climbed a few steps higher so he could survey the clearing. 'But I'm getting a grounding in the local history. I can tell you that these mounds baffled early Spanish and French explorers. They considered the natives here too uncivilized to construct anything like this.'

'Of course they did.' Gigi had curled up in my lap, and I ran my fingers through the grass, letting the history draw my imagination down, wondering what lay beneath the surface.

'Is it something like the prehistoric barrows in Britain?' I had the strangest sense, not just of being connected to the earth here, but connected to the past. 'That's what it feels like.'

'*Feels* like?'

His voice sharpened on the question, and, when I

glanced up, the keenness of his look snapped me back to my senses.

'I mean—' What *did* I mean? The words had come out of my subconscious. The one that imagined historical reenactments when I got loaded. 'You know. A *vibe*.' That wasn't too weird, right? 'Some places you just get a sense of them being really old.'

'You mean like Stonehenge.' The curiosity vanished – provided I hadn't imagined it – and he spoke with dismissive condescension. 'Every American says that.'

Good. That meant I wasn't losing it. But also bad, because I didn't appreciate his tone.

'I couldn't see much of Stonehenge through the tourists,' I said coolly. 'I mean all the other stones and heaps of earth we saw on that trip. Dad must have dragged me over half of Britain looking for Iron Age relics. It's like any time your ancestors had a rest stop, they stood a rock up in the ground.'

He tilted his head, either ignoring my snippy tone or simply not thinking he owed me an apology. 'Your dad was interested in standing stones?'

'My dad was interested in everything that anyone ever did to decorate a landscape.' The words were brusque, but I couldn't keep the warmth of memory from my voice, for those weeks spent visiting famous gardens and ancient sites, Dad explaining them with the fervour of a pilgrim.

Rhys gave a considering nod, then went on in a tour-guide sort of voice that amused me. 'Then you know the barrows in Britain are smaller than this. And older. They're burial chambers, from as far back as four or five thousand years.' He glanced up, towards the apex of the structure. 'The people who built these lived here as recently as five hundred years ago.'

'I love how you British think that's recent.'

He turned back to me with a raised brow. 'We *Welsh* think it's recent, and it is – to everyone but Americans.'

My lips curved at that offhand nationalist disdain, even though it should have annoyed me. I mean, *everything* annoyed me lately, yet there I was, sparring with this stranger, feeling a slowly uncurling warmth that I couldn't even name. When I met his gaze, the moment seemed to hang in time, as it had in the door at the airport. Except instead of coming or going, in or out, I was weighing amusement against my usual misery, inexplicable attraction against confusion and cynicism and common sense.

Well, not inexplicable. I liked his strong features and confident bearing. Maybe I was just intrigued by the mystery, because he was so miserly with personal details, and there were so many enigmatic contradictions. He had the body language of an alpha dog, as Gigi's trainer would say, but he was spending a slacker summer working for his dad. He talked like a college guy, but he had the hands of a labourer. There was probably a very boring explanation, and if I knew it, this unsettling . . . whatever it was . . . would go away.

Gigi stretched and yawned in my lap, making me wonder how long we'd been sitting there. 'We should start back,' I said.

Rhys winced. 'I'm surprised Paula hasn't used the

horn.' He descended the ridge, then held out a hand to help me. 'Don't forget your shoes.'

I sighed and put them on. The right one was tight on my still swollen foot, but I'd live until I got back in the SUV. Instead of taking Rhys's waiting hand, I dropped the end of Gigi's leash into it and made my way off the slope by scooting on my rear end. Might as well make the back match the front.

Gigi scampered happily down, and I reclaimed her leash from Rhys. He gestured for me to go ahead of him on the path. It wasn't far, but the vegetation was thick, with dense, broad-leafed vines encroaching on even the cleared areas, creating a wall between this eerie world and the prosaic one where Paula waited in the car.

'So, who's Clara?' I asked, mentally, as well as physically, returning to the road ahead.

Rhys held back a branch, looking amused but answering helpfully. 'Paula's business partner. She handles the cooking. She and her daughter live on the property.'

'And this Teen Town Council?' I ducked under his arm. 'What kind of fifties throwback is that? Are Wally and Beaver members? Do they put on shows in the barn?'

He paused on the path, just before the last bend that would put us in sight of the car. I stopped too, and turned to find him studying me again. 'You truly don't know any of this?'

It was more of a voiced realization than a question, but I pointed out testily, 'I wouldn't be cramming like the five minutes before a pop quiz if I did.'

Gigi waited impatiently at the end of her leash. It was nothing compared to how impatient I expected Paula to be. Still he held me back with a question. 'But . . . it *is* your ancestral home. You have no interest in that?'

I felt a hard jab of anger, because the question forced me to admit with feigned carelessness, 'Dad didn't talk much about his family.'

His brows drew together, and I wondered why this was so incredible. 'Yes, but to come here knowing nothing about Paula, or where you'd be staying—'

'Honestly?' I cut to the chase. 'By the time I realized I wasn't going to be able to get out of coming here, it was too late to ask questions.'

'How is that?' he asked, starting again towards the car.

Falling in beside him, I let my mouth twist just a little, in a rueful smile aimed at myself. 'Because by then they'd closed the door of the plane.'

Chapter 4

I made a liar out of myself by dozing off once we were back on the road. One moment I was watching the Appalachian foothills roll into lush timberland. The next, I found myself slumped over at a very uncomfortable angle, the deceleration of the vehicle sliding me into consciousness.

I'd hoped my nap had gone unnoticed, but I heard Paula say, in a drawl that just barely carried over the noise of the engine, 'Should I wake her up, do you think?'

If I read Paula correctly, this was a rhetorical question. But Rhys answered anyway, his voice almost inaudible. 'Maybe when we turn off the highway.'

The top of Paula's big hair nodded. That was all I could see from my semirecumbent position. Gigi was curled up, not in her bag, but beside me, and my legs were splayed in a very unladylike way.

'Y'all took for ever coming back from the Indian Mound.' My cousin's tone was soft, and not quite idle. At least, it didn't seem that way to me. 'What did y'all talk about?'

I searched my memory, trying to think if I'd said anything weird to Rhys, the way I'd slipped up with John in the Park. Hoping I hadn't said 'déjà vu' out loud.

Rhys paused as if considering his answer, and I braced myself. 'Archaeology, mostly. The site is an odd thing to find in the middle of Alabama.'

'Well, I guess it is.' Her next question came out almost regretfully, as if she was sorry to have to ask. 'But she didn't seem . . . upset to you? It was hard to tell when she bolted out of the car without even her shoes.'

I must have tensed, because Gigi lifted her head. I brushed her with my fingers to keep her quiet as Rhys answered. 'I think she was out of sorts from travelling. Why?'

Paula gave a laugh that almost sounded natural. 'Just don't want to start off on the wrong foot, is all.'

I felt a simmer of anger in my chest. The obvious translation was: 'Just watching for signs my cousin is as messed up as her stepshrink said on the phone.'

Because I didn't put that past Dr Steve. After all, patient confidentiality didn't apply, since I'd never been his patient.

Not that it kept him from interfering in my life.

Gigi looked up with sleepy disdain, and I realized my hands had fisted and the leg she was lying on was tense and hard. Her nap interrupted, she stretched and gave herself a tag-jingling shake.

I seized on this as an excuse to wake up. Cracking an eyelid, I pushed myself upright, rubbing the kink in my neck.

'Where are we?' I didn't have to fake disorientation. Dusk had fallen early, accelerated by the trees that lined the two-lane road.

Rhys answered with a brief glance over his shoulder. 'You slept through Selma. We've just turned off the state highway.'

Paula self-consciously fluffed the back of her hair, which had been squished only slightly by the headrest. 'Did you have a nice nap?'

'Yes, thank you,' I answered, extra polite, hoping she felt guilty for talking about me behind my back.

The road wound through the trees. The only signs of civilization – though I use the word generously – were a trailer up on blocks and, further on, a clapboard house with a sagging roof.

'I thought you said Bluestone Hill was near a town,' I asked as we came to a fork in the road.

'It is.' Rhys gave a nod to the right before turning left. 'Go down this road, and you'll come to Maddox Landing.'

No sign of the town through the forest. An uneasy sense of isolation fluttered behind my breastbone, as if the thread that connected me to my own life, to the rest of the world, was spinning out, growing thinner and more fragile as we drove. The next mile, the next turn, might break it completely.

The trees closed in, their canopies thick with spring growth. Spanish moss hung from the branches, hurrying the dusk. Rhys turned on the headlights, the beams casting a comforting glow. Gigi had adjusted herself into a ball of fur in my lap and I stroked her slowly, soothing myself more than her.

I must have shivered or made a sound, because Rhys reached for the thermostat. 'Are you cold?'

The action was solicitous, automatic. My answer was the same. 'I'm fine.'

'We'll be home in a minute, honey,' said Paula. She kept calling it 'home', which was just bizarre, when my dad had left so long ago and I'd never thought I'd visit.

'Did you grow up here?' I asked Paula as the road curved through the tunnel of trees.

She laughed. 'Practically. Your daddy must have told you about the summers we spent here, playing in the woods, hiking up to swim in the Cahaba River. I wouldn't advise it close to the house, though.'

'Why not?' I asked, in rote curiosity.

'Current's too strong,' answered Paula. 'Though there's an inlet where you can wade. Just watch for snakes.'

I stifled a shudder. 'I might give that a pass.'

The house came into view then, and I forgot about legless vermin as I got my first glimpse of my temporary exile. Rhys drove slowly down a wide gravel drive, which must have once been an impressive sight.

While the picture on the SUV's sign looked like a generic *Gone with the Wind* clone, the actual house had much more personality. It stood in shabby splendour between two hedged gardens. Columns supported a covered porch or possibly a first-floor balcony, and gabled windows hinted at a second-floor attic. The whitewashed sides glowed with the rosy light of the setting sun.

'It's enormous.' I breathed the words, more in horror than reverence. Falling back in the seat, I closed my gaping mouth. 'Dad mentioned spending the summers with family in a country house. I didn't know he meant an *estate.*'

I'd just thought he meant his folks had a trailer home outside the city limits. Fortunately I caught myself before I said that aloud. I'd never met my paternal grandparents, since they'd died before I was born. Dad spoke of his mother fondly and his father rarely, if at all. But an old family mansion? That was a big thing to leave out.

'Home, sweet home,' said Paula, as the car stopped in front of the wide porch steps. I craned my neck to look out the window, taking it all in.

Rhys set the brake with an air of finality. 'Delivered as promised.' He hurried round to give my cousin a gentlemanly hand out of the car, but she was too quick for him and hopped out on her own.

I was slower, still coaxing Gigi back into her carrier. 'Almost there, Gee.' I wasn't sure which of us I was re-assuring. 'Maybe there's a nice garden for you to roll around in.'

She gave a grumbling assent and settled into the bag. Rhys had opened my door by then, so I gave him the carrier, freeing my hands to haul my aching butt out of the SUV. I was so stiff, I expected to hear creaking.

Once out, I turned slowly to get the whole picture. A huge tree, probably centuries old, cast moon shadow over the yard, where the remnants of a red brick wall marked the original borders of cultivated landscape.

'Bluestone Hill.' Paula said it with genteel pride. 'It wasn't always a country house. The first capital of Al-abama was only a few miles away. Folks used to come from the town for grand parties.'

Her words evoked a vivid scene in my mind. Where the drive curved in front of the house, I could picture carriages pulling up and delivering ladies in huge hoop skirts, and gentlemen in top hats and spats. The porch was lit by welcoming lanterns instead of electric lights, and liveried servants stood by the doors.

The scene was so authentic – I seemed to catch a whiff of horse and a snatch of music – that I had to close my eyes, ground myself in reality behind the shutter of my eyelids. I'd always had an active imagination. It came with performing. But since the night of the wedding, I hadn't allowed myself any flights of fancy. It was like keeping weight off a broken toe. I didn't want to test my discrimination of fact versus fantasy too soon.

I wobbled, then opened my eyes and steadied myself with a hand on the car. I hadn't realized Rhys was so close until I heard him ask, in a low voice Paula wouldn't hear, 'Are you all right?'

Of course I wasn't all right. I wouldn't be in Alabama if I was all right. But the moment of disorientation had passed, and slowly my blood was circulating again – to my legs and to my brain – after the long drive. 'I'll live,' I said honestly.

'I'm glad to hear it.' His look was more sympathetic than his words, and he handed me Gigi's carrier so I could slip it over my shoulder. 'You take your vicious purse dog, and I'll grab your luggage.'

'Thanks.'

Once I was sure my legs would hold me up, I circled the car to join Paula. Belatedly, I noticed two other vehicles parked further round the curve, a dark SUV and a big red pickup that gleamed in the porch light.

Paula must have followed my gaze. 'Addie – that's Clara's daughter – and her friends are studying for the end of term,' she explained cheerfully. 'So you'll get to meet them.'

'Can't wait.' That was just what I needed, to start meeting people while I was exhausted and grumpy. Grumpier than usual, I mean.

Paula missed the sarcasm in my drawled words, but Rhys didn't. I caught a hint of a smile as he unloaded my biggest suitcase. Paula had obviously not been paying attention at the airport, because her eyes widened as he set the second case beside the first. 'My. How much stuff did you bring, child? Your clothes can't take up that much room.'

'One bag is Gigi's,' I said, already on the defensive in case she made something of it. Besides, I was going to be in Alabama for a month.

'Of course it is,' she said. 'Rhys, honey, would you be a dear and take Sylvie's case up to the yellow room – it's the one on the opposite side of the stairs from yours. And her dog's things can go in the sunroom for now.'

Letting him play porter wasn't going to make him stop calling me princess. I couldn't do much more, though, than offer to help.

'I can manage the small suitcase.'

He smiled wryly at me, as if on to the fact I was only offering so I wouldn't feel guilty. 'Just go in and see the castle, meet your subjects,' he said.

But he said it without malice, so I took him at his word. Following Paula, I grasped the handrail – which had the sturdy feel of a new addition – and climbed the porch steps, my feet falling in the same traffic-worn place on the bricks as my ancestors'.

'Just keep your puppy in her bag for now,' my cousin said, waiting on the veranda for me. 'Until we figure out what to do with her.'

I got that 'we' meant 'she', but if 'what to do with her' was anything other than 'let her stay with you', we were going to have a problem.

The front door was framed by stained glass on either side and a fan-shaped window above. The lights in the foyer shone through, bright and cheery. I grabbed the door handle, and after a glance at Paula for permission – she nodded almost solemnly – I pushed it open. The warm, humid air rushed in, and cool air rushed out, as if the house were sighing in welcome.

The entry hall stretched up two storeys, panelled in dark, rich wood. Directly in front of me was a staircase, covered in a patterned runner in jewel tones that had become muted with time and wear. I could sense age in the patina of the banister where countless hands had polished it on their way up or down. I didn't have to close my eyes to picture little Confederate children sliding down the oak railing or high-buttoned shoes treading the carpet.

Again, the detail of the sensations put a knot of tension behind my rib cage. I was as relieved as I was startled when Rhys wheeled my suitcases in with an anachronistic bump over the threshold.

He parked the smaller one near a hallway that led further into the house. 'I'll take that to the sunroom after I carry yours upstairs.'

'Thanks,' I said again, including my gratitude for the distraction. It was fervent enough that he glanced at me oddly. To cover, I explained, 'I know it's heavy.'

Smiling slightly, he echoed my earlier reassurance. 'I'll live.'

I watched him start up the stairs, managing the case with impressively little effort. Then I realized I was staring – in a completely normal, noncrazy way, but nevertheless a little inappropriately – and turned my gaze towards Paula.

She stood beside a small desk, checking messages

on a nice, modern phone. Like my bright pink luggage, it looked a bit out of place in the foyer full of old panelling and antique furniture.

'How old is this house?' I asked.

'Honey,' said Paula with a ring of pride, 'this house has been in your family for nearly two hundred years.'

'Seriously?' I cast an eye over the chandelier, dangling like an earring from the high ceiling. Through an arched doorway I could see a formal parlour, looking like a museum of bric-a-brac.

Paula straightened a guest register on the desk. 'The Colonel – that's one of your distinguished ancestors – would be rolling in his grave if he knew I was turning this place into a business. But you can't live on history and a family name, now, can you?'

'I guess not,' I said absently.

My head felt jam-packed – with the trip and the house and Paula and especially Rhys. But the big question elbowing aside all the rest was, how had Dad not mentioned any of this? I tuned out Mother all the time, and I'd obviously ignored everything anyone said about this trip. But I had always listened to Dad. This was kind of a big thing to leave out of descriptions of your childhood.

'You'll have to explore the gardens when it's daylight,' Paula said, seeming oblivious to my distraction. 'See where your dad got his green thumb.'

She gestured to a painting on the wall. I resettled Gigi on my shoulder and went closer. It was a landscape of the house – white, colonnaded, antebellum – set in a very formal geometric garden. Both the painting's style and its perspective were primitive. My eye was drawn to the intricate structure of the gardens at the front and sides of the house, and the orderly rows of a vegetable plot in the back, near outbuildings that might have housed the kitchen and servants. Slaves, I realized, with a guilty twist in my stomach. There was a date on the painting – BLUESTONE HILL, ALABAMA, 1856.

Was this Old South legacy what my dad wanted to distance himself from by moving to New York? Another picture solidified in my head – a scrawny pre-teen, standing in the same place, looking up at the same painting and making the same connection. This time I was torn. I wanted to push away the vision before it got too real, before it passed beyond what were normal imaginings in an evocative old house. But if it linked me to my dad, I wanted to grab it tight. Though not if it meant I was crazy.

I realized Paula was beside me, looking worriedly into my face. 'Are you all right, honey?'

My laugh was, fortunately, more ironic than hysterical. 'People keep asking me that.' I smoothed the strands of hair that had escaped my bun, hiding the shaking of my hands. 'It's a good thing I'm not vain or anything.'

She patted my arm – the one on the far side of Gigi – and said tactfully, 'You look fine, dear. But if you'd like to freshen up before meeting—'

A pair of doors opened behind Paula, interrupting her and startling me. They were set in, so they looked like the rest of the panelling, and I hadn't noticed them until they slid back to frame a sandy-haired young man. He was big and athletic, all-American handsome.

'Hi there!' His welcoming smile hit me like an afternoon sunbeam after a wet and chilly morning.

'Hi,' I answered stupidly.

He turned to include my cousin. 'Sorry we didn't hear you come in, Miss Paula. We had the music on.'

'Hello, Shawn.' Paula didn't sound surprised to see him. In fact, she sounded more genial than she had since she found out I was foisting a canine houseguest on her. The smile seemed to affect her, too. 'Are y'all almost done studying?'

'Not hardly.' There was something old-fashioned in his phrasing, a fifties television nicety that matched his Wheaties-box smile. It struck me as funny, since I'd joked to Rhys about the *Leave It to Beaver*-ness of the Teen Town Council.

Then Shawn's gaze returned to me, taking in the details in a way that wasn't dated at all. His pleasantly appreciative attention tugged at something in my chest, pulling me off balance. A warm bloom of curiosity replaced the first jolt I felt at his appearance. It spread through parts of me that had been cold for a long time.

'So, is this the famous Sylvie Davis?' he asked.

Corny, yes, but with a slight self-awareness that made it charming. I wrinkled my nose and answered, 'Infamous, maybe.'

Holy crap. *I'd wrinkled my nose.* For me, that was borderline flirtatious. I was clearly beyond tired and on to drunk with exhaustion. That would explain a lot.

Paula made the introductions, per Emily Post.

'Sylvie, this is Shawn Maddox. He's a friend of the family and president of the Teen Town Council. I told you about them, didn't I?'

Shawn's smile widened. 'So we're infamous, too. You want to come in and meet the gang?'

Not really. All the handsome charisma in the world couldn't make the pain in my leg go away. I wanted a bath, a bed and a book. But Shawn stepped back from the doorway with a gesture of welcome – despite the fact that it wasn't his house, I noted – and I had no graceful way to decline. I tightened my grip on Gigi's shoulder strap, and entered the cosy den.

There were six or seven young people my age, lounging on couches and on the floor, surrounded by textbooks and cans of soda. The scene was set for a marathon study session, but it was a little too affected, a little too staged. They were carefully *not* staring as I crossed the threshold, but I felt spotlit by their curiosity nevertheless.

'Everyone,' said Shawn, 'this is Sylvie. Sylvie, this is everyone.' Only he didn't actually say 'everyone'. He rattled off a list of names that ran through my brain but didn't stick.

'Hi,' I said, trying to be nice. The coffee table was piled with pizza boxes and greasy paper plates, and my stomach growled. Maybe Paula would think it was Gigi.

But she was too focused on the pile of boxes to notice. 'Who said y'all could order pizza?'

A tall, slim girl, probably about my age, sat in an upholstered chair, her legs thrown over one of the arms. Her skin was creamy brown and her face could have been on any magazine – large, tilted eyes; high cheekbones; lips that women in my mother's circle paid a fortune for.

Her expression, however, bordered on aggressively petulant. 'Don't blow a gasket, Paula. The guys were famished, so Mom said it was OK. She's got sandwiches and stuff in the kitchen for y'all.'

I tried to process that. 'Mom' must be Clara, the business partner in the B&B endeavour. And if *that* was true, then this must be Addie, whom Paula had mentioned in the car.

'Or,' said Shawn, 'Sylvie could eat in here with us. There's still plenty left.'

'That's a fine, hospitable introduction.' Paula set her hands on her hips. 'Cold pizza on the floor of the den.'

'We'll give her a seat on the couch, Miss Paula.' Shawn cajoled her with easy humour, and I could see her sense of propriety unbending under the influence of his smile. 'Don't you worry.'

Gigi had nosed her head out of the bag, audibly sniffing the pizza-scented air. 'Oh my gosh!' A red-haired girl jumped up with a squeal and hurried towards us, climbing over two classmates and their books. 'What an adorable doggie!'

The squeal made my eye twitch, but Gigi accepted the attention as her due. Without asking, Red started petting her, and in a moment another girl had joined us, creating a logjam in the doorway.

'What's her name? Is she a Chihuahua? I've never

seen one with fluffy hair like that. Look at her riding in your purse, just like a little movie star.'

'I don't think a movie star would be caught dead riding in a bag from Petco.'

She missed my sarcasm – too busy petting Gigi – but it got a laugh from Shawn.

An older woman appeared in a second doorway, drying her hands on a dish towel. She was dark-skinned and tall, and the bone structure of her face showed through the padding of middle age – she was definitely related to Armchair Girl. Addie, rather. These people seriously needed name tags.

'I thought all that commotion might signal the Union's arrival,' said the new woman.

That joke was going to get really old, really fast. I didn't say anything, though, because the woman had friendly eyes to go with her matronly figure. 'Welcome to Bluestone Hill, Sylvie. I'm Clara.'

'Nice to meet you,' I answered automatically, my brain slow with fatigue and information overload.

'I'll fix you a sandwich, or we can reheat some pizza.' She smiled kindly. 'Either way, there's cobbler and ice cream for dessert.'

'Oh my gawd,' said one of Gigi's worshippers. 'Clara makes *the* best cobbler anywhere.'

'All right then,' said Cousin Paula as she turned to me, ignoring the two girls still fussing over Gigi. 'You sit in here and get to know everyone for a bit. And for heaven's sake, kids, I hope you're all using napkins and not my rug to wipe your fingers.'

'Gawd, Paula.' Addie rolled her eyes so hard that

her whole head moved. 'None of us was raised in a pigsty.'

'Fine,' Paula answered tartly, fists on her hips again. 'But you're running the sweeper in here tomorrow after school. Now, y'all be nice to Sylvie and make sure she gets something to drink.'

My cousin headed for the inside door. Clara gave me an encouraging smile and followed her out – missing Addie's second eye roll. Left behind, I stood between the sitting area and the door, with Gigi still hanging from my shoulder, along with her admirers.

'Can we take her out?' Red asked.

Setting the bag on the floor, I crouched and unzipped it all the way. 'Don't feed her any pizza, OK?'

'Paula won't like it,' said Addie, from the throne of her armchair. 'She's an absolute freak about her carpets.'

'It'll be OK in here, though,' said Shawn, smiling at me with a hint of conspiracy in his eyes.

I didn't point out that Addie had to vacuum tomorrow anyway. My keen powers of observation told me she didn't need another excuse not to like me. For some reason she was already acting like I had peed in her Cheerios.

In any case, worry over the carpet was moot since Gigi never touched it; the girls took her to the couch and sat with her in their laps, cooing and cuddling her. She looked positively smug, with two such attentive acolytes.

I had a bigger problem. When I'd squatted to release her, the muscles in my right leg had cramped up, and I was stuck in a grand plié, with nothing to grab and inconspicuously haul myself up.

A hand appeared in my peripheral vision. For a startled instant, I thought of Rhys, of the many times he'd already offered me assistance. I would take it now, déjà vu or no. But it wasn't Rhys, of course. He was helpfully stowing my luggage.

It was Shawn. His arm was tanner, more muscular. But equally helpful.

Thinking of Rhys, though, made me hesitate just a moment – for a whole muddle of reasons that didn't really make sense – before I grabbed Shawn's hand. When, after the briefest of bracing pauses, I let him pull me to my feet, there was no shock, no feeling of being hit in the funny bone. Just a warmth that was, oddly enough, as charismatic as his smile.

'Thanks,' I mumbled, grateful for the help, but grumpy and embarrassed that I'd needed it.

Shawn held on until I was steady, my delicate fingers swallowed up in his strong ones. He was taller than Rhys, and definitely broader. Close up I could see his eyes were an interesting shade of blue – dark, with a tinge of green, like sun on salt water.

There was clearly something wrong with me. First idling on the grass at the rest stop with Rhys, and now *this* stranger, holding my hand like I was some swooning Southern belle. And worse, my kind of liking it.

'Glad to help. Here. Have a seat.' Shawn nudged one of the guys slumped in the smaller sofa, who amiably slid to the floor, yielding his spot. No doubt who was the alpha dog in this pack.

I found myself glancing towards the door, for escape, or maybe for rescue. Rhys should have had time to park my suitcases by now. His response when I'd asked him about the Teen Town Council – 'You'll see,' he'd said, unhelpfully – didn't suggest a lot of time spent hanging around with them.

'You want a Coke or something?' Shawn asked, drawing my attention back to him. I liked him well enough – obviously – but the group was overwhelming all at once. Too many names to remember, and being nice was such an effort. I'd never been a social butterfly before The Accident, at least not outside my ballet friends. But I didn't want to alienate the locals, or worse, anger Paula and make my stay here any more wretched than it had to be.

Which I suppose was how I found myself sitting where Shawn had directed me and answering his question. 'Just some water would be great. Thanks.'

With a huge sigh of imposition, Addie rolled her eyes *again* as she pushed herself from her chair and huffed over to a minibar in the corner of the room. 'You'll have to make do with tap water. We don't have any Evian.'

Spurred by irritation, I replied in kind. Seriously, what was her deal? 'As long as it doesn't come out of the creek, that's fine.'

So much for being nice. One of the guys snorted, and Addie shot me a death glare over her shoulder.

I took a moment to look around. The room was more casual than the parlour across the hall, and obviously more used. The furniture was traditional, but not authentic. The mantelled fireplace looked original, but there was also a big-screen TV against one wall, and a neat desk in the corner held a large and clunky computer. That, at least, was an antique. I noticed that, along with the books and binders on the coffee table, some of the kids had brought their own laptops.

'What are you studying?' I asked, because I had to say something.

'Everything,' said one of the boys on the floor. 'Finals are this week for the seniors, and the week after for juniors.'

Shawn sat beside me, which tilted the cushions of the love seat, so I had to tighten my muscles to keep from falling towards him. See? Off balance. 'Kim and Josh and I are seniors. Addie, Caitlin and those guys are juniors.'

I halfheartedly attempted to recall the names he'd rattled off. Gigi's new handmaidens were Caitlin and Kimberly. The other guys were Josh and Aaron and Travis.

'So, what about you?' Caitlin asked, without interrupting her petting. 'Does the school year finish earlier in New York?'

'I finished last year.' I shifted, feeling the weight of their attention heavily. Me, who had never had stage fright.

'How'd you manage that?' asked Josh. 'I mean, I thought you were Addie's age.'

No surprise, I guess, that I'd been a topic of conversation. Paula had hinted as much. So had their avid curiosity from the moment I'd entered.

'I took my GED so that I could be free to travel with the company. The American Ballet Company,' I added at their blank looks.

'Your folks let you do that?' Kimberly asked. 'My mom would have a cow.'

'My mother has always been supportive of my career,' I said. The irony in this understatement was lost on them, making me feel like even more of a stranger. I could only make inside jokes with myself.

Caitlin confided cheerfully, 'Addie got a chance to be a model, but she would have had to miss so much school, her mom wouldn't let her go.'

Addie returned with my glass of water. She held it out to me with two fingers. '*My* mother believes that it's important I get a real education. With a *real* diploma.'

The spark of annoyance flared, fanned by her contemptuous tone. I looked her up and down. She wore a cute little T-shirt and shorts that showed off her lush figure and perfect legs. 'You don't have to rush,' I returned, in the same falsely sweet voice. '*Playboy* doesn't let you model until you're eighteen.'

Kimberly snorted back a laugh. The boys didn't bother to hide theirs. The skin on Addie's sculpted cheekbones darkened in a furious flush, and she shoved the water into my hand before stomping back to her chair. I felt slightly guilty, but only for stooping to her level.

'So, what was it like, dancing with the ballet company?' asked Caitlin. She and Kimberly seemed the warmest, thanks to Gigi's cuteness, I guess. 'Did you

73

have flowers delivered to your dressing room? Get to travel first class?'

'It's not as glamorous as it sounds.' At the pinnacle of my career – that is, the weeks just before my accident – I'd shared a dank basement dressing room with five other girls. And I only flew first class on Mother's dime.

Rather than getting into painful – literal and figurative – explanations, I changed the subject. 'So, this is the Teen Town Council, huh?'

Again, it was Caitlin who explained. 'We're all on it, but this isn't the whole group, since it's not a regular meeting.'

'What does the council do?' I pulled a pizza box towards me and peeked inside. Pepperoni. No way could I do that to myself, no matter how hungry.

'You know how some towns have teen library boards and student councils and stuff?' she said. 'We're all that, sort of rolled into one.'

'That's very efficient.' The strain of being polite put a bit of a sarcastic edge on my tone, but Shawn answered with good humour.

'There's not a big pool to draw from.' He'd noticed my rejection of the pepperoni, and set a different box within reach. 'Since the same people were in every student organization anyway, we just consolidated.'

'Shawn's the president,' said Caitlin, unnecessarily. I'd have had to be blind not to notice who called the shots.

The pizza in the new box was cheese. I didn't especially want it, but grabbed a slice and a napkin to give me something to do with my hands. Across from me, Gigi watched with eager eyes. I'd fed her a quick snack before leaving the rest stop, so her starving puppy-dog face didn't fool me.

'Paula said something about your helping out around here,' I prompted. This was a trick of my mother's, appearing a brilliant conversationalist by keeping people talking about themselves.

'We rebuilt the summerhouse out back,' said Aaron.

'It's just a gazebo, really,' said Shawn. 'And it's a win-win situation, since Miss Paula is nice enough to let the TTC meet there when the weather's nice.'

'Still,' I said, genuinely impressed. 'That's not a small project.'

Shawn shrugged. 'That's what we do. Fund-raisers, odd jobs. We want to support people who want to bring business to the area. Like this inn, when it opens.'

'So, if the inn isn't open yet,' I said, pulling the cheese off my pizza, since the crust wasn't worth the carbs, 'how did Rhys and his dad end up staying here?'

There was a funny sort of pause that made me glance up from my slice, catching the look exchanged between Addie and Shawn. Had my innocent question poked a stick under an interesting rock?

It was Addie who answered, in an almost normal tone of voice. 'Professor Griffith is a friend of the guy in charge of the dig over at Old Cahawba. Dr Young hooked the professor up with Paula, and the Griffiths get to stay here for cheap in exchange for putting up with the construction mess.'

Kimberly leaned forward, telling me in a confidential tone, 'I can't believe Addie is so lucky to have such a hot guy in the house. I thought all English people had pasty skin and bad teeth.'

'I think he's Welsh,' I said, but it didn't seem to matter.

'Oh, my gawd,' said Caitlin, in rapturous tones. 'That accent.'

Addie surprised me with a giggle. 'I showed him how to surf the satellite channels on the TV, and he said, "Cheers, love." '

'I know!' Kimberly squealed, squeezing Gigi like a teddy bear. 'Could you just die?'

'What is it with y'all?' Josh was the guy who'd given up his seat to me. He protested from the floor, his mouth full of pizza. 'What's so hot about the way a foreign guy talks?'

Kimberly threw a wadded napkin at him. 'Ask that after you swallow, you pig.'

'Seriously,' said Aaron. (I hoped I was getting the names right.) 'You showed him how to use the TV remote. It's not like a first date or anything.'

'It's not just the way he talks,' said Addie, scornful again, but at least it wasn't directed at me. 'It's the way he's a *gentleman*.'

Aaron unfolded himself from the floor and helped himself to a soda from the minibar. 'He seems cool enough. But it's not like he hangs with us. When we're here at the Hill, we're usually busy with – you know.'

'With what?' I asked, since they might know, but I certainly didn't. The rest of that sentence could be anything. Like, 'when we're not giving each other pedicures, or performing virgin sacrifices.'

'When we're not doing TTC stuff,' answered Shawn, which didn't exclude any of those things. But it shut Aaron down. Not secretive, exactly; it just put a period on the sentence. But I sensed – let's call it a vibe, since that didn't sound too nuts – that there was a tangled dynamic with this bunch.

Maybe it was just normal girl-boy stuff. I hadn't missed the tension between Shawn and Addie, and I wondered how much of her resentment had to do with his friendliness towards me. Then there was Caitlin, who sat near Travis, but *his* eyes never left an oblivious Kimberly, who, when she wasn't petting Gigi, was playing footsie with Aaron.

I recognized the insular soap-opera drama that happened in a closed group. Between classes and the company, I'd been with the same people eighteen hours a day for the past seven years. People hooked up and broke up, and half the time while they were with someone, they really wished they were with someone else.

'Anyway,' said Kimberly, 'it's sweet that Rhys is helping his dad with his research.'

Travis groaned. 'Can we move on to a new subject, please?'

'Oh my God,' Kimberly snapped. 'How many times did we have to listen to you guys talk about Sylvie? Deal with it.'

I blinked, like I'd been hit by a bucket of cold water she'd meant to throw on someone else. 'Excuse me?'

Shawn cleared his throat and stared at the ceil?ing. Addie rolled her eyes (big surprise). Travis and Aaron exchanged grimaces of chagrin and Caitlin glared at Kimberly, who explained apologetically, 'When we heard you were coming, we Googled you. We've never had anyone famous, or even semifamous, come here.'

'We weren't being creepy,' Aaron assured me, after shooting Kimberly an irritated glare. 'It's just, there was this picture, and you were standing on one toe, with your other leg waaay up here.' He measured a spot by his ear. 'It was kind of impressive.'

'Um, thanks,' I said, vaguely. Dancers didn't take compliments well. Nothing was ever good enough. And now it never would be, because even the *attempt* at a moment of dynamic perfection was out of reach.

Also, if they'd looked me up, then they had to know about The Accident. They had an idea of what I'd once been capable of, and that now I couldn't even get up off the floor without help.

'But,' I went on with a note of irony, 'I'm hardly famous. Or impressive any more.'

Kimberly laughed. 'Oh, honey. You're a Davis. You're automatically famous in Maddox Landing.'

I wanted to ask what she meant, but Caitlin, who still held Gigi in her lap, continued in a cajoling tone, 'And I'll say what these boys are all thinking. You're *still* darned impressive. Lord, what I wouldn't give for a great pair of legs like yours.'

'I don't know about a *pair*,' said Addie, with only a veneer of drollery over the venom in her voice. 'If she had *two* good legs, she'd still be dancing.'

For a heartbeat, icy disbelief kept me numb, certain I'd misheard her. But the awkward silence that dropped like a bomb in the room proved I hadn't, and my ears began to burn.

Shawn tensed angrily beside me, though he didn't speak. It was Caitlin who breathed, 'Jeez, Addie. That was uncool.'

'Please,' she said, waving a dismissive hand. 'I'm just stating a fact. If she hadn't broken her leg, she wouldn't be here, dumped on her relatives.'

'OK. Wow.' Feeling their appalled stares richochet between us, I tried to shake off the daze of the verbal sucker punch. The show must go on. Wiping my fingers precisely and placing my napkin in an empty pizza box, I stood smoothly, with some covert help from the sofa. 'Thanks for this example of Southern hospitality, but I really need to walk my dog, and I can only handle one bitch at a time.'

Addie's face flushed. She opened her mouth to snap back a retort, but Shawn's quiet and clipped words stopped her. 'Cut it out, Adina.' I expected her to tell him where to stick it, but she merely shrugged and threw her legs over the arm of the chair.

He'd gotten up too, and he handed me Gigi's bag. 'Want some help?'

'I can handle this much. Come on, Gigi.' She came running, her little legs prancing, and we headed for the French doors. I didn't know where they led exactly, nor did I care. I just wanted out of there.

'We'll see you around, Sylvie,' said Caitlin, with the deliberate cheerfulness of someone trying to smooth things over. 'Maybe at the Catfish Festival this weekend.'

'Maybe,' I murmured. And maybe I would break my other leg, and be spared that particular joy.

The French doors opened onto a veranda on the side of the house. It was clean but scattered with dilapidated porch furniture. I snapped on Gigi's leash and headed for the steps, wondering how far my leg would take me if I just kept walking.

Chapter 5

The moon had barely risen, but there was enough light from the porch to see where I was going. As satisfying as it would be to storm off into the dark, it would also be self-destructive. Besides, I was too tired and achy to storm anywhere. The best I could do was stagger off in a snit.

Coming down the side stairs, Gigi and I faced the hedged border of what had once been the formal garden, the shape just visible under the excess foliage, like good bone structure in someone who has let himself put on some pounds. Weeds and vines pushed up through the gravel and paving stones of the path, but I braved it anyway.

From the painting in the foyer, I knew this was once a knot garden, but I couldn't see much design in the overgrown shapes of the planting beds. In the centre was some kind of tall topiary, gone shapeless with neglect. Gigi wanted to dive into the circular flower bed around it but I pulled her back, worried about what wildlife might be in the snarled weeds.

I felt a similar pull to investigate, but I resisted it, making instead for the open area between the house and the river. The hedges opened to the southeast, and with Gigi trotting beside me, I stepped out of the garden onto a vista that, even in the starlight, held me transfixed.

From the house, the land rolled softly, in a gently sculpted fall that was too perfect to be natural, to the bright ribbon of the river. It was as if someone had unfurled a bolt of cloth and draped it for artistic effect, with swells and nooks and shadows. It was the contrived nature of an artist in soil – a landscape architect, like Capability Brown, or Frederick Law Olmstead, whom my dad had idolized.

Had this been the beginning of Dad's passion for making art out of nature? I couldn't help but imagine him standing right here, thinking . . . I didn't know what, because he'd never talked about it.

Gigi pulled at her leash, begging to be let loose for a run. I wished I could oblige her; I, too, wanted to run and roll and yell at the universe, but I settled for kicking off my shoes and lowering myself stiffly to the lawn. Then I dug my fingers and toes into the grass, anchoring myself to the ground, to solid reality.

On the slope of lawn leading to the water I saw the silhouette of a small building. The summerhouse, I figured. North of that, the river disappeared behind an area of thick trees. In the dark, the woods were just a swath of deeper blackness, but I could see the tips of the pines against the starlit charcoal sky.

Nothing explained why that made me shiver. It could be the breeze that had come with sunset, carrying the scent of the river.

Or maybe I was just nuts. How many times since reaching the house had I imagined things too well, with so much detail that the line became fuzzy between what was *there* and what wasn't?

It had been a long, tiring day. And here I was in this old house, full of history, trying to connect the father I knew with the teenager Paula remembered. Of *course* I was going to be picturing the past at every turn.

My imagination had always had an outlet in ballet. I created things in my mind's eye, things like transforming swans and dancing candy canes, which I had to make an audience believe that *I* believed were real. I was *full* of creative energy, which, until The Accident, I'd channelled into dance.

Everything had been channelled into dance. Energy, emotion, creativity. For all the months of recovery, most of that had been pushed towards healing – physically, at least. Now it was like a Band-Aid had been ripped off my feelings, and I was one raw nerve.

And then there were the two guys. Rhys and Shawn. Both of them getting under my skin in completely different ways. Before The Accident, I'd dated, as long as it didn't interfere with dance. But what was it about crossing the Mason-Dixon Line that had turned me into this hormone-driven, boy-crazy—

Crap. There was that word again.

I rubbed my hands over my face, the sweet smell of grass and dirt failing to soothe me. Just the stress of worrying that I was cracking up was enough to crack me up.

The ring of my phone startled me, and Gigi barked as I jumped. Prokofiev's *Cinderella* – the stepsister's theme. It was John, the second-to-last person I wanted to talk to while I was thinking about going bonkers. But if I didn't answer, he might tell his dad, who might call Paula, and then they'd *all* be thinking about how I was going bonkers.

So I clicked to answer, and growled, 'Calling to check up on me?'

'Hello, Sylvie.' He took my tone in stride, which stole some of the wind from my sails. In the two weeks since the wedding, I'd seethed and sulked and practically hissed every time I saw him – which was a lot, since our parents were consolidating households before leaving on their honeymoon. Eventually it was too much effort to stay furious, especially at someone who didn't get angry back.

Which was his strategy, of course, as he asked, with exaggerated tranquillity, 'How is Alabama?'

I sighed. 'It's driving me crazy already,' I answered. 'You can report that back to your dad.' Sarcasm made me feel better. I mean, I was only nuts if I thought I wasn't, right? Flexing my feet, I stretched my cramped muscles as well as my figurative claws. 'Mother was too busy packing to check on her only offspring, huh?'

John paused, as if hunting for a tactful answer, then gave up. 'They're getting ready to leave in the morning. How are you?'

'Stiff. Sore. Brain-dead.' Gigi climbed onto my lap, putting her paws on my chest so she could sniff the phone. 'Gigi says hi.'

'If you think I've forgiven her for peeing in my suitcase, you are so wrong.'

'She can't help it. She knew I was mad at you.' I was mad at everyone, all the time.

'*Was* mad? Past tense?'

I sighed and pulled up my knees, trapping Gigi against my chest. She curled up, contentedly licking the buttons on my sweater. 'Half past tense, maybe.' Like I said, angry takes a lot of energy.

'I'm glad.' He sounded genuine, which was the other reason I'd softened to him. That, and if I hadn't, I wouldn't have anyone to talk to but Gigi. 'I take it you got to your cousin's house OK?'

'Yeah. Only get this. It's not a house. It's an antebellum mansion. And it's out in the absolute boonies.'

He sounded amused. 'Not up to your high standards?'

Jerk. 'Like *you've* ever been on a vacation that didn't involve turndown service and five-star dining.'

'That's not true. And it's not the point. Do you think you'll get along with your cousin all right?'

'Maybe.' I lay back, looking up at the stars. 'I don't

know. She talks like that Southern woman on the Food Network. Crap – she even has the same name. Kind of looks like her too.'

'Can she cook?'

'No. Apparently her business partner does the cooking.'

'Business partner?'

'Paula is turning the family homestead into a B&B.'

'Oh really?' I couldn't see him raising his eyebrows, but I pictured it clearly. 'And how do you feel about that?'

I barked out a laugh. It wasn't even ironic. 'I can't believe you just said that. You were born to be a shrink, John.'

His chuckle sounded embarrassed. 'Sorry. I really wasn't trying to – I just mean that you called it the family homestead. It's your ancestral home, too, right?'

'But I don't *own* it. I guess Paula inherited it.'

'Is her father older than your father's father?'

Genealogy made my head hurt. 'Jeez, John, I don't know. Why does it matter? I don't want the place. I didn't even want to come here.'

'Yeah, but it's still your family history.' He sounded very reasonable. 'And as long as you're there, don't you want to find out more about where your father came from?'

'I don't know.' I meant to snap at him, but it came out genuinely uncertain. My gaze turned towards the house; I couldn't see much more than shapes, but in my mind's eye was the painting in the hall and the separate quarters out back.

And there was the curious thing Caitlin had said. Being a Davis made me famous here. What did that mean?

'There's a lot of history,' I said. 'I can't believe Dad never mentioned some of this stuff. He used to spend his summers here, but he never said— It's just sort of a big thing to omit. Even if he never described the house, how could he not mention the gardens and the landscape . . .'

I was talking incoherently, free-associating. Why did that happen with John? He didn't even have a degree yet, and already he had some kind of mojo. He really was born to be a shrink. Or a bartender.

But I stopped before I said the damning thing that had been gnawing at me since I'd first seen Bluestone Hill. The only way I could be this clueless about where Dad came from is if he had deliberately kept it from me. It's one thing to reinvent yourself and leave your upbringing behind. But why keep it secret from your daughter?

If John had asked me just then what I felt about that, my answer would have been pretty profane.

'Do they teach you that in school?' I asked. 'To just let someone ramble until they say something that reveals their psyche?'

He paused. Unlike me, he chose his words carefully. 'Sylvie, believe it or not, when I saw you at the wedding with that Day-Glo cast, my first thought was not, There's a girl who needs psychological help. Though it could have been.'

I gave a derisive snort. Gigi, lying on my stomach,

opened one eye to glare at me for disturbing her sleep. 'Then what *did* you think?'

'There's a girl who desperately needs someone to give a damn about her. And I've never had a sister. This may work out after all.'

I didn't say anything. After feeling nothing but anger for so long, I couldn't sort out the emotions that lodged in an aching knot in my throat. And then John ruined – or saved – the moment by adding, 'Of course, when you passed out on me and I had to drag your drunk butt and your ten pounds of fibreglass cast through the lobby of the Pierre, I had my doubts.'

'You're such a jerk,' I said, and for the first time, I didn't even half mean it.

'I won't apologize for finking on you about drinking the night of the wedding. But I am sorry it got you exiled to Alabama. Though who knows, maybe you're meant to be there.'

I sat up, dislodging Gigi, who slid into my lap with a disgruntled sound. 'What do you mean by that?'

There was a pause long enough for a shrug. 'I don't know. Sometimes things work out. Maybe looking into your dad's past will help you discover something about yourself. I mean, you can't lie around and sulk about your leg for ever.'

'Screw you, John.'

'Sorry, Sylvie. Can't – they frown on that kind of thing between stepsiblings.'

He managed to surprise a laugh out of me. Gigi barked in alarm; she probably didn't even know what that sound was.

There was an echo from the other side of the house. At least, that was what I thought it was at first. An animal sounding off in reply. But then it rose in pitch, like the moaning of the wind. It lasted long enough for me to realize it was coming from the woods, then it faded as quickly as it began.

'That's weird.'

'What?' asked John, reasonably curious.

The noise came again, for all the world like someone crying – a mournful warble, too soft and weak to identify more than that.

'Sylvie?'

'Nothing.' I lightened my tone, shook off the strangeness. I'd had enough of that today, and here, at least, was something I could reasonably dismiss. 'An animal in the woods. I'm not kidding when I say it's a freaking wilderness out here.'

Gigi had climbed off my lap and her nose pointed in the direction of the sound, ready for action with her ears pricked, her fluff aquiver. This was why she had to stay leashed until we knew our way around. Long-haired Chihuahuas have no notion they are bite-sized.

'I'd better go, John. Gigi is way too interested in whatever made that noise. And I guess it's possible someone might be missing me.'

'OK. I'm at the condo for a few more days until I head back to school for the miniterm. Call if you need anything.'

'Sure thing.' I said it carelessly, signing off, and hoped I sounded convincing.

After hanging up, I sat for a moment longer, listening, mirroring the dog in intensity. I did hear a voice, but it was calling my name in a perfunctory and non-chilling tone.

'Sylvie!' Paula's yell carried from the house. 'Sylvie Davis! Do not tell me you went and fell in the river on your very first night here!'

At least my cousin seemed to have a flair for the dramatic, something I could appreciate. I climbed to my feet, slightly better for my stretch but still slow and sore. 'Coming!'

Dusting off the seat of my jeans, I glanced towards the house, and glimpsed a shadow moving across one of the upstairs windows.

I stilled, waiting for some other sign. The idea that someone had been watching disquieted me more than was quite rational. Would anyone have been able to hear me? And what did it matter, except that it was definitely a private, personal conversation. Was I being paranoid?

Well, at least that would be a new symptom.

It could have been someone walking down a hall, not standing at the window at all. Rhys, maybe. Or his father, whom I had yet to meet. Maybe even Shawn – the TTC seemed to have the run of the place. Weird that my mind only supplied male possibilities. Maybe my subconscious had picked up more than my conscious brain had.

When I didn't see anything else, I figured I'd better heed Paula's summons before she came after me. Instead of returning to the house through the hedged garden, I looped around the terraced lawn at the back of the house, where Paula had turned on the flood-lights. She waited on a set of stone steps that faced the river, leading from the back yard to the lawn I'd just left.

'Where did you wander off to?' She stood impatiently, fists on her hips. If I were going to portray her onstage, this would be the posture I would use. 'And what's this about you going off in a huff?'

'I needed to walk the dog.' Gigi danced at the end of her leash, trying to charm Paula. But it seemed she'd finally met someone impervious to her fluffy charisma.

'About the dog,' said Paula, which did not sound promising. 'There is a spot for her crate on the back porch. She can stay there.'

I narrowed my eyes, not liking where this was headed. 'You mean when she's not with me, right?'

'No, I mean overnight.'

'All night?' My voice rose in incredulous anger. 'What about coyotes and things?'

I had put up with a lot that day. Sent off in a cab by my mother, hours on a plane, then the soccer mom wagon. My fragile psyche messed up by a strange place and strange people, and finding out about my dad's secret past as a reluctant son of the South. Separating me from my dog was really too much.

'It's screened in,' said Paula, in an implacable tone. 'Almost like another room.'

'But it's not another room. It's a *porch*. And Gigi has never slept outside in her life. She always sleeps with me.'

'Well, this isn't your New York apartment, and here in the South we treat dogs like dogs, and not like baby dolls.' She dropped her hands, and the discussion, with finality. 'Come and see the place before you pitch a fit. And then you can have some of Clara's cobbler. That's why I came to get you in the first place. We have got to put some meat on your skinny bones.'

I clenched my teeth and didn't point out that dessert wouldn't put meat on my bones so much as fat on my butt. When she turned towards the house, I scooped Gigi up and sulked after her. Paula hadn't said it aloud, but her implication was that Gigi and I were both spoiled. Which might be true, because I was already planning how to get around her on this.

I needed to pick my battles and stay on her good side, even if that meant setting Gigi's stuff up on the porch and eating Clara's fattening cobbler. Afterwards . . . Well, I was still planning that.

Because Gigi was *not* sleeping by herself outside. As the conversation with John had brought home, she was the only creature in the world who would really care if something happened to me, even if it was only because I was the bringer of kibble.

❧ ❦

Even if I had wanted to sleep without Gigi, I wouldn't have been able to. The night was too quiet. Awfully, horribly silent. No traffic, no horns, no sirens. All I could hear was the creak of the house and the thump of my own heartbeat as I lay in bed and waited impatiently until I could sneak downstairs and get my dog.

Paula was, no surprise, an early-to-bed, early-to-rise type. But I wanted to make sure I gave her time to fall into a nice, deep sleep. After I'd settled Gigi in her crate on the porch – which was, as promised, completely screened in, and almost, but not quite, like another room – Paula had given me a rundown of the living arrangements. Her suite – a bedroom and small sitting/office area, converted from the former maids' quarters – was near the kitchen. Clara and her daughter, my nemesis, Addie, lived in an apartment over the garage. According to Paula, one of my great-greats had been very fond of that newfangled invention the automobile, and had the old carriage house rebuilt into a car palace. So 'garage apartment' was nowhere as shabby as it sounded.

I was upstairs, in a small room in the back corner of the house. It hadn't been refurbished yet, and the wallpaper was a faded yellow with a tiny print of pale pink and green flowers. A woven rug warmed the floor, which was spotlessly clean, but scuffed and in need of a polish.

When I'd come up after settling Gigi, I'd found my suitcase waiting for me. I'd stashed my toiletries and undies in the cabinet that served as a closet, then slid the rest of my stuff, still in the case, under the bed. I guess part of me was prepared if Paula kicked Gigi and me out, or I decided to run away, or I got carted off in a jacket with arms that tied in the back.

The brass bed frame was an antique and the mattress

felt like one. There was a tiny writing desk under the window, and a small upholstered chair and footstool in the corner. As I lay in bed, I caught a faint whiff of lilac, which I assumed came from the soap on the Victorian washstand, which also held a basin and a ewer. Very quaint. And practical, since I could wash my face without going down the hall to the bathroom.

When the alarm on the nightstand said it was midnight in Alabama – one a.m. by my internal clock – I figured I'd given everyone enough time to reach REM sleep. Without turning on the light – I'd been lying in the dark in case Paula poked her nose upstairs to check on me – I rolled out of my Gigi-less bed and headed for the door.

The knob was a brass oval, darkened with age; I grasped it and paused, listening for any sounds outside, my heart beating a fast and guilty tattoo. You would think I was up to something a lot worse than sneaking in my dog. Maybe I was overidentifying with some ancestress who had to creep out from under the strict eye of her nursemaid. I had no trouble casting Paula in *that* role.

I brushed off the thought and turned the knob carefully so it wouldn't squeak. Leaving the door open, I headed to the first-floor landing, where the wood floor gleamed in the light coming through the French doors at the end of the hall.

It had cooled off considerably, and I wished I'd put on my slippers. The chill seemed to travel up through the bones of my feet and ankles and settle in the healed fissures of my leg. By the time I reached the carpet runner covering the stairs, I was shivering in my thin pyjamas. The night air eddied through the open centre of the house, brushing the nape of my neck, where wisps of hair had fallen from my scrunchie-knotted ponytail.

The downstairs foyer wasn't much better. Moonlight spilled through the window over the door, a cold, silver glow. I headed quickly towards the back of the house, to the big kitchen where earlier we'd sat down to Clara's blackberry cobbler.

The air felt warmer here. So did the tile floor, which should have been icy compared with the wood planks elsewhere in the house. Maybe it was because the kitchen was a later addition, something to do with ventilation or more-modern insulation. Back in the day, most of the cooking had been done in an outbuilding, to keep the heat away from the main house. Paula had told me the present kitchen had been expanded early in the last century, so that food prep could be done closer to the family's swank house parties. It all sounded very *Great Gatsby*; apparently Prohibition hadn't been much of an impediment to anyone's partying. Not the Davises', anyway.

The downstairs also featured a formal dining room and a small breakfast nook for future guests of the B&B, but I could tell that the kitchen was the heart of the house, and that was obviously Clara's doing. Earlier that night, when I'd come in from settling Gigi on the porch, she'd pointed me, with a queenly gesture worthy of a despot welcoming me to her domain, towards a big trestle table that occupied the space once used to stage fancy-dress dinners.

'Have a seat,' she'd said. At least she seemed a

benevolent despot. 'I know cold pizza is no way to welcome you to Alabama, but I figured you might like to get to know the kids your age.'

Separating me from my dog was no welcome either, but since that wasn't Clara's fault, I didn't unload on her. 'Where is everyone?' I tried to keep the wari?ness out of my voice, since by 'everyone' I meant her witch of a daughter. But there was also no trace of Rhys, or Shawn, and I had mixed feelings about that – disappointment, annoyance at myself for being disappointed, relief that I didn't have to deal with the confused dynamic I felt with Mr Enigmatic or the tug of attraction I felt for Sir Teen Town Council.

Clara had her back to me while she fussed at the counter, so if she reacted to anything in my tone, I didn't see it. 'The gang all had their dessert and went home. You were outside a good while.'

'My stepbrother called to make sure I'd arrived in one piece.' It made a decent explanation, at least. Changing the subject, I ran a hand over the table, which was dark with age and scarred with use. 'This would cost a fortune in an antique store.' Amazing how many reruns of *Antiques Roadshow* you could watch when you were stuck in bed for weeks at a time.

'It's just about the only thing from the original kitchen,' Clara said, setting a china bowl and a spoon in front of me. I'd noticed all the appliances were shiny and new. 'I told Paula if I was going to take charge of the cooking in this little endeavour, no way was I using a cookstove from my grandmother's day.'

I picked up the spoon. The ice cream on top of the cobbler was already melting into a thick white lake around the buttery crumble and glistening purple fruit. This was more calories than I normally ate in an entire day.

Across the table, Clara folded her arms, looking dangerous. 'If you say one word about carbohydrates, Miss Ballerina, I'm going to pinch your head. Now eat.'

Obediently, I lifted a dripping spoonful to my mouth. I expected it to be heavy, cloyingly rich. Instead, I got magic on my tongue. Fresh berries burst against my palate, the tartness sweetened by light, crisp pastry, all bound together with the cream.

'Oh. My. God.' I didn't even care what it did to my thighs, it was that good.

Clara smiled in satisfaction. 'Now, *that's* a proper welcome to your family home.'

My family home. In the dark kitchen, hours later, I let the scene replay, tracing a hand over the old table. My father had eaten at this table, maybe sharing a meal with his cousins while the adults dined in the formal room, with china and linens. The image was so vivid, it was as though I were standing on one side of a window, looking through to someone else's memory.

If I glanced out of the unfocused corner of my eye, I could almost see the servants moving about, preparing dinner. A woman walked past me, laden with a groaning tray, her forearms muscled from the accustomed weight. Details sang in my mind – the black hair curling out from under her cap, the crisply starched ruffles of the apron covering her long calico dress.

The breeze of her passing brushed my skin, and my half-closed eyes flew open. I whirled, and glimpsed the swish of a skirt, the trailing ribbons of an apron, disappearing round the corner, towards the dining room down the hall.

Clara? That didn't make sense. Or maybe it was Paula, but I couldn't believe she wouldn't stop to berate me for being out of bed. Plus, the clothes had been so distinct, and I couldn't picture either of them wearing linen and calico.

I took a single step after the woman, then stopped, as a dizzying wave of horror grabbed my insides and twisted. There was no one there. There *couldn't* be, because I'd been standing in the middle of the kitchen and no one had come in. No one had moved past me but the figures in my imagination.

But I'd felt her. And seen her. Not imagined. *Sensed.*

Forcing myself down the hall was like taking my first steps in physical therapy. An exercise in will. But I had to find the explanation. The drift of curtain or shaft of moonlight that was real and tangible, just transformed by my thoughts, the natural outgrowth of my ruminations.

But there was nothing. The curtains in the dining room were drawn and still. The only illumination was from a night-light in the corner outlet.

Oh crap.

Leaving the room was much easier. I hurried to the kitchen, then out the back door and onto the covered porch, where Gigi was waiting for me in her crate, pawing at the latch impatiently. As soon as I let her out, she jumped into my arms, and I sat down hard on one of the cushioned wicker settees, my trembling legs giving out. Just like my marbles.

The black-humour barrier between me and my fears had come crashing down. This was bad. Unfunny, unvarnished, undeniably awful. What had just happened was different from my earlier imaginings. This wasn't just overly detailed fantasy. I had truly slipped. I'd been convinced the figure in the hall was real, right up to the moment I realized it couldn't be.

It was Central Park all over again. But I was dead sober. Tired, overwrought, totally freaking out, but very, very sober. And I had to face the question, if it wasn't alcohol, and it wasn't Vicodin . . . did that mean it was *me*?

Gigi licked my cheek. I had her cuddled tight to my chest, and she snuggled trustingly against my neck. At least one of us was confident in my ability to take care of us.

It was reassuring in a way that logic could never be. I couldn't crack up, because then who would look after Gigi? Therefore, I would not go crazy. If sheer force of will could keep someone sane, then I was the one to do it. Ballerinas are *made* of willpower.

On the porch, the quiet didn't seem so oppressive. I could hear the wind in the trees and, very faintly, the sound of the river. The night was warmish, but the ceiling fan stirred the air. I grabbed an old quilt from the back of the settee and wrapped it around Gigi and me as we curled up together.

I didn't think I would fall asleep, given the turmoil in my head, and certainly not on the creaky wicker settee. But I couldn't quite face the house and its creaks and sighs. Instead, I stroked Gigi's silky fur and reached for the calm I felt when I dug my feet into the grass. Just like my dad had taught me.

When I opened my eyes again, the moonlight had changed with the passing of who knew how long. I'd worked my way down on the settee, neck at a painful angle, Gigi snuggled against my chest. She was shivering in her sleep, and I realized I was cold too, even with the quilt around us.

I thought – as much as I was thinking anything, because thinking meant remembering why I was there – that the chill had woken me, but then I caught a faint sound, the same mournful keen I'd heard earlier in the evening. It rose in a thin wail, and I lifted my heavy head, then winced at the crick in my neck. Gigi gave a tiny, sleepy growl, but even she was too tired to get excited over it.

The sound faded, and I pushed myself painfully upright, holding Gigi securely in one arm. More than half asleep, I stumbled into the house and down the hall. I limped up the stairs, pulling myself up by the handrail and cursing whatever quirk of ventilation had made the centre of the house so damned cold. Teeth chattering, I found my room, closed the door against the chill and fell into bed, careful not to squish Gigi.

I pulled the covers over us both, and she tucked her head under my chin, already snoring. I wasn't far behind.

The sweet smell of lilacs was strong, and invaded my sleep as I dreamed of searching the woods for something I'd lost, something I was desperate to find.

Chapter 6

I woke to the smell of bacon frying. Or rather, Gigi did. Her wiggling nudged me awake, and I pried open an eyelid as she stuck her twitching nose out from under the covers.

'Ugh. Don't even think about it.'

Struggling against the tangled blankets, I managed to get upright and glance at the window, full of morning light. If someone was cooking, I had obviously missed the opportunity to sneak the dog back down the way we'd come. I would have to improvise.

Something about the daylight made yesterday's strangeness seem small and manageable. Though maybe that was nothing more than the perspective of distance, and when it snuck up on me again, it would be huge and insurmountable.

If it snuck up again. *Think positive, Sylvie.*

I washed my face with the cold water in the pitcher on the washstand. It seemed odd at first, but by the time I'd splashed my face, standing on tiptoe to let the drips fall back into the basin, the motion was oddly natural. I groped blindly for the towel, and found it on the first try.

The soap in the dish jarred me out of the moment. The smell wasn't right somehow. It took a second before I realized what I had been expecting. If the soap smelled of roses, then where was the lilac scent coming from?

I opened the cabinet, looking for shelf liners or potpourri. But Gigi was getting anxious, so I didn't search very hard. I didn't mind the scent, even if it was a little sweet for my taste.

Throwing on a pair of sweats and a camisole, I topped it with an army green hoodie that my mother hated but I loved. Gigi was sniffing one of the rugs, so I scooped her up and tucked her into my sweatshirt, zipping her in. The only real problem with this plan was that I had zero boobs with which to hide her. Hence my neglect to wear a bra.

Too late to worry whether I'd packed my push-up. I poked my head out of my room, and all was quiet, so I closed the door behind me and scurried down the hall.

The landing was warm, the sun streaming through the sheer curtains on the French doors, and with Gigi licking my armpit under my jacket, nothing, not even my own mental state, seemed ominous. I hadn't forgotten about seeing someone standing at the window, though, while I'd been on the phone with John. Curious, I went down the short hall that crossed the main landing, and lifted the thin drape.

The view was spectacular. Forgetting about Gigi wiggling around inside my sweatshirt, and the possibility of getting caught, I unlatched the doors and let myself out onto the balcony.

From this vantage point, in the morning light, it was easier to see the layout of the grounds; the house and gardens were on a cleared area surrounded by uncultivated forest. The river snaked down from the northeast, wide and still in the distance. To the north another, smaller river joined the larger one before it disappeared behind the overgrowth of pine and moss-covered oaks. It reappeared close to the house, where I'd seen it last night, then vanished round a curve on its meandering path to the Gulf of Mexico.

At the railing, I had an overhead view of the back yard, where I'd met Paula after returning from my walk. The yard was enclosed along the north edge, bordered in back by a casually planted cottage garden. It made a cosy spot, with a table for alfresco dining on one side and a small arbour seat on the other.

The northeast side dropped down to the great lawn with a view of the inlet, and the summerhouse on a hill. To the northwest, a trellis-covered path led to a brick building with stairs running up to a second-storey landing. Last night, Paula had gestured that way when she mentioned Clara and Addie's apartment above the garage, and I could see Clara's domestic hand in the flowerpots and window boxes around their door.

My subliminal upstaging sense warned me I wasn't alone. What told me it was Rhys Griffith behind me – maybe some funny-bone-type tingle – I couldn't have said.

I turned to find him leaning against the doorjamb, looking as though he might have been watching me for a while. Apparently my radar was a little slow.

'Is stalking something they do for fun in Cardiff?' I asked, arching my brows.

He wore khakis and a white T-shirt, proving that some things were classics on both sides of the ocean. His dark hair had been finger combed at best. I'd seen guys try way too hard for that attractively rumpled look with much less success. I guess, by definition, 'effortlessly handsome' wasn't something you could work for.

Sauntering over, hands in his pockets, he said, 'Good morning, Vicious. And to your little dog, too.'

I might have blushed if I hadn't been distracted by Gigi, who wiggled so hard in my jacket I thought she'd strangle one or both of us. Despite this, I made a stab at nonchalance. 'I don't suppose there's any point in pretending I have no idea what you're talking about.'

'Nice try. If you want to sneak her out, you'll have to get up earlier.'

It's hard to be arch when you have a puppy's fluffy head sticking out of your shirt, but I tried. 'Yes, well, we divas have only one seven o'clock in our day.'

'I'm sure.' He held out his fingers for Gigi to sniff, then scratched under her ear. His knuckles brushed my collarbone, just briefly, but the echo of his touch seemed to stay on my skin, and my pulse started tap dancing at the base of my neck.

Rhys cleared his throat and stepped back. 'I hope you enjoyed meeting everyone last night.'

Honesty or tact? Which way to go? I settled on ambiguous. 'It wasn't the worst part of my day.' The rueful curve of his mouth said he got what I meant, and I fought the pull of an answering smile. 'I, um, noticed you disappeared.'

His smile broadened, as if my statement had been telling. Which I guess it was. 'I was typing up some notes for my father.'

'Not into pizza with the gang?'

A shrug, and we were back to studied neutrality. 'I'm a stranger here.'

The balcony caught a breeze from the river, and I brushed a strand of hair from my face. 'So am I.'

His brows arched, the way they had when I'd tried to pretend I didn't have Gigi down the front of my sweatshirt. 'Yes, but *you* are a Davis.'

I pursed my lips in frustration. 'Everyone keeps saying that like it means something.'

'Maybe it does,' he said, ratcheting up my irritation with his enigmatic tone.

It occurred to me that maybe I should find out what it did mean. But first I had to get Gigi downstairs. I couldn't do anything until she'd had her morning pee.

As if reading my thoughts – which would add a whole new level of weirdness I couldn't deal with –

Rhys jerked his head towards the corner. 'Come on, then. I'll show you the secret way down.'

He led me to the end of the balcony, where a thick growth of vines hid a spiral iron staircase; I certainly hadn't noticed it in the dark. The stairs had a fine patina of rust, but when Rhys stepped onto them, they seemed sturdy. Still, I hesitated, one hand on the curved railing.

Rhys noticed my uncertainty and paused a few steps below me. 'It's perfectly safe. If it will hold me, it will certainly hold you.'

'Is that another crack about my being skinny?'

'It's an observation of physics,' he said evenly, and offered a hand. 'Give me the dog if you're worried.'

'She's fine.' I, however, was not. I had been down many spiral staircases, but not since I'd broken my leg. The thing about hitting the ground in agonizing pain with your bone jutting out is that it takes a long time to get over the fear it might happen again. If you ever do get over it. I was still waiting.

The twist of the spiral meant stepping on the narrow part of the wedge-shaped stair with my right leg. The traitorous one. It had been incarcerated with rods and splints and casts for months, and after only a few weeks of freedom, it hadn't had time to prove its loyalty.

Gigi, riding like a joey in a pouch, tilted her head as if to ask what the holdup was. I guess dogs had no concept of paralysing fears. Not my dog, anyway.

I stood there so long, Rhys started back up the stairs. 'That's all right, then. We'll go the normal way.'

'No.' I'd had it with my disobedient psyche. It was

just a set of stairs, for God's sake. 'I'm going to do this.'

The solution was one of brains over bravery – I simply turned and went backwards. That put my right leg on the broad end of the tread and, more important, I didn't have to look down.

Midway to safety, Gigi realized we were headed for the grass and started wiggling. I had to give up one handhold to quiet her. Before I could waver, I felt Rhys's hand on my waist, resting there in reassurance. The light yet firm pressure was perfect – no push, no pull, just gentle support to back up his words. 'I've got you.'

Then my feet were on the ground, and I freed Gigi from my jacket and set her on the grass. She ran in frantic, joyful circles around the back garden, flinging up dew with abandon. Even Rhys laughed at her antics, though he shook his head. 'Ridiculous.'

'I know. She grows on you, though.'

'She does, at that.'

I didn't glance his way, because the part of me that inexplicably *liked* this mystery guy – when he wasn't calling me vicious or princess or other inaccurate names – wanted to simply enjoy the moment, feeling like a normal girl, standing beside a boy and wondering if he was enjoying standing next to me. It was an uncomplicated moment in my very complicated life.

'You'd best get in to breakfast,' he said, which settled the enjoying-my-company question.

'Aren't you going to eat?' I made my tone equally neutral, to hide how much the answer mattered.

Rhys looked at me with a teasing smile, even as he started walking backwards down the flagstone path. 'I've already eaten, princess. I'm off to start my day.'

'Oh.' I gave him a closer look, getting past the effect he had on me to the actual clothes he was wearing. The khakis were sturdy, his shoes made for hiking. Well worn, too. 'Where are you going?'

'To work. Strange as that concept might seem.' The cheekiness of that addition made me wonder if all the 'princess' business might be a diversion. When I got defensive, I failed to follow up on unanswered questions. I inhaled to ask – OK, demand – clarification, but Rhys pointed to the hedged garden and said, 'Your designer dog is mucking about in the shrubbery.'

My head snapped to look. Gigi was indeed making a beeline for the overgrown garden we'd passed through the night before. Effectively distracted, I hurried after her through the gap in the hedge.

The low-lying jungle of untamed foliage looked as big a mess in the daylight as it had in the dark. Knot gardens should have formal structure, with paths and planting beds that made intricate geometric shapes, like Celtic knots. But here, grass and weeds obscured the pattern of the gravel and stone paths, and the beds were a jumble of weed-choked herbs.

One path, though, was still fairly clear, delineating the central feature of the garden: the circular flower bed, which was so overgrown I couldn't make out any remnant of an internal pattern. It surrounded the shapeless column of greenery that Gigi and I had noticed on our walk. That was where I found my stubborn dog, bounding into the tangle, barking her breathy little bark.

I grabbed for her, but I would have been too slow even with two good legs. 'Darn it, Gigi!'

Wading into the scraggly, knee-high foliage, I tried not to think about snakes, tried not to picture myself getting tangled up and falling, breaking something new. My steps released the sweet, green aroma of the herbs, and the smell clung to Gigi as I scooped her up. She was soaked with dew, and now so was I.

'Nice job, you stupid dog,' I grumbled, wiping at the flecks of leaves clinging to the front of my hoodie. But it was impossible to stay mad at Gigi when she gave a little 'Ruff!' and grinned, her tongue curled in happiness. I guess for a city dog all this green was a paradise she'd only dreamed of.

I put my hand on the central topiary for balance as I turned, and was surprised when my fingers slid through the foliage and touched a hard, rough surface. The column wasn't a shaped hedge but a stone, almost as tall as me, and covered in thick vines. They were tenacious when I tried to pull them aside, and all I could glimpse through them was dark rock. It didn't seem to be a statue, but just a stone, stood on one end.

Maybe it would make more sense if the garden were in its intended shape. Or maybe there was a piece missing. It was an odd thing to be stuck there, all by itself.

'Sylvie Davis, what *are* you doing?'

I jumped, and Gigi yelped as I clutched her too tightly. Peering around the vine-covered stone, I found Paula frowning at me from the side veranda.

Only her head and shoulders were visible over the hedges that enclosed the knot garden, but I just *knew* her hands were on her hips.

'Walking the dog,' I said, trying to sound as normal as possible.

'In the bushes?'

'She sort of got away from me.' I felt stupid standing in the wet weeds, but brazened it out. 'I wanted to get a look at the garden, since I couldn't see much in the dark last night.'

'Well, you don't have to do it right this minute. Come in and get some breakfast.'

She went into the house, shaking her head, and I let out my breath. She didn't seem more exasperated than usual, so hopefully I hadn't raised some red flag for abnormal behaviour. God knew what the stepshrink had told her to watch out for. I didn't want to think about last night, about how scared I was that I was losing my grip on reality. It was bad enough that *I* was worried I might be going crazy. If Paula suspected something was up with me, things could get miserable. More miserable, I mean. Which was saying something.

I returned through the back yard and carefully climbed the stairs to the screened porch, then tucked Gigi into her crate with a bowl of kibble and fresh water from her bottle. When I went into the kitchen, Paula and Addie sat at the big table, my cousin already engrossed in a newspaper, and my nemesis glaring at me over a glass of orange juice. Clara turned from the stove, frying pan in hand, as I came in.

'Lord, girl! Don't tell me you were out there in your

bare feet. How did you get down without my seeing you?'

I took the same seat I had last night, and fudged a bit. 'I went out the side door in the den and came round to let Gigi out.' Though I was sure the spiral stairs weren't really a secret, I figured I'd keep my knowledge of them on the q.t. for now.

Addie, dressed for school, a large backpack beside her chair, gave my sweats a sneer. 'Nice of you to join us downstairs.'

'I smelled breakfast.' I smelled bait, too, in her words and tone, and refused to rise to it. Instead, I ignored her and turned to Paula. 'What's the deal with the rock in the garden?'

'That's what gives Bluestone Hill its name,' she said, her drawl warming the way it did whenever she talked about the house. 'Though you wouldn't know it, these gardens used to be famous. Your dad came by his green thumb naturally.'

'They seem pretty unique,' I agreed politely, leaving unspoken my doubt that the old-school Davises had done their own gardening. I was more interested in the idea that Bluestone Hill had sparked Dad's interest in landscape architecture.

Clara put a plate of bacon and eggs in front of Addie and a glass of orange juice in front of me. 'How do you want your eggs?' she asked.

I usually just had yogurt or fruit in the morning, but I took the path of least resistance. 'Scrambled.'

Satisfied with my compliance, she returned to the stove and cracked a couple of eggs into a bowl. 'Where are the Griffiths?' I asked, fishing for information by pretending I hadn't already seen Rhys. When Clara glanced at me, brows arched, I added hastily, 'I was looking forward to meeting the professor.'

'Uh-huh,' said Clara in a knowing tone.

Paula, however, apparently read no special interest in my question. 'Places to go, people to see,' she said. 'I think the professor mentioned going down to Mobile, and Rhys went to put on his hiking boots. You must have just missed him on the stairs.'

Addie speared her eggs with her fork. 'Not everyone can lie around in their pyjamas all day.'

I made up my mind to keep ignoring her, since that seemed to annoy her the most, and asked Paula, 'Where did Rhys go in his hiking boots?'

'*Duh,*' said Addie, ignoring my ignoring her. 'Hiking.'

Clara answered more politely as she deftly scrambled my eggs. 'He goes out at the crack of dawn sometimes. I guess he's a morning person. How many pieces of bacon?'

I had to redirect my thoughts at that last question. 'None, thank you.'

Skillet in hand, she turned to glare a warning. 'If this is about calories . . .'

'No,' I assured her. 'I just don't eat meat.'

Clara stared as if I'd said I'd rather have dead baby for breakfast. Addie narrowed her eyes. But most worrisome was the way Paula slowly lowered the newspaper.

Oh boy. I had a sinking feeling in the pit of my

stomach, one that had nothing to do with the menu. 'I'm guessing my mother didn't tell you I'm a vegetarian?'

'You mean,' said Clara, looking distraught, 'you don't eat meat at all?'

'I eat cheese,' I said, trying to help her out. 'And eggs, as long as they're not fried. I don't eat fried food.'

She set the pan on the burner and turned off the flame. 'Girl, no wonder you're so skinny. What *do* you eat?'

Paula had pressed her lips tight together, as if she was annoyed but trying to be polite. Addie didn't even try. 'Come on. You don't expect my mother to change her whole menu because you're a picky eater.'

'Adina!' said Clara. 'Be nice.'

'It's not as if she has allergies, right?'

My cheeks burned with embarrassment. On the one hand, sooner or later, someone at their future inn was going to have dietary restrictions even more rigid than mine. But on the other hand, he or she would be a paying guest, not a relation foisted on them because she had nowhere else to go.

'Just cook what you normally do,' I said, miserable, 'and I'll eat what I can. I'll be fine.'

Paula stood up, folding the newspaper. 'Well, honey, you have to eat,' she said, in the same tone in which she had told me that Gigi couldn't sleep in my room. 'We'll work it out. Clara can tempt just about anyone with her cooking.'

I debated how to take that. Because in Paulaspeak, I'd noticed 'we'll work it out' usually meant 'we'll do what I think is best.' Before I could decide whether it was worth getting angry about, heavy footsteps on the back porch heralded an arrival. Grateful for the distraction, I turned to see Shawn, the leader of the Teen Town Council.

He came in without knocking, charging the air with his presence. 'Heya, Miss Paula, Miss Clara,' he said, and greeted everyone with a casual wave. His smiling gaze rested on me just a little longer than on the others, the warm glow of his attention chasing away my lingering tension.

Paula paused on her way to her room, smiling indulgently back at him, like a teacher at a favourite pupil. 'Good morning, Shawn. Is this your last day of school?'

'One more half-day tomorrow.'

Addie sulked over her eggs. 'I still have finals next week.'

'But then you'll be a senior,' said Clara, in a cajoling voice. 'And you'll rule the campus like Shawn does now.'

The roll of Addie's eyes closed that conversation. Shawn chuckled and pulled out the chair beside mine, straddling it as he sat down, and folding his arms over the back. 'Hey, Sylvie. You disappeared before I could say goodnight yesterday.'

'So I'll say good morning, instead.' The words were almost flirtatious, but I kept my tone reserved, setting my figurative heels against the pull of his charm. It was nice, though, after Addie's glares and Paula's frowns, to have someone smile at me.

'How was your first night in Alabama? Did you sleep OK?'

'Eventually.' I didn't mention I'd spent most of it on the porch, worried I was going bonkers. 'The quiet takes some getting used to.'

'Yeah,' said Addie. 'No police sirens.'

'Just your cat.' I fiddled with my fork. 'You might want to think about getting her fixed. Her wailing gave me the weirdest dreams.'

'What are you talking about?' Addie had a potent are-you-an-idiot stare. I'll bet she practised it a lot.

Clara looked at me oddly as she set down my plate. 'We don't have a cat.'

'Oh.' I reached for my orange juice, trying to keep my expression unconcerned. Just because they didn't have a cat didn't mean there couldn't be some feral feline out in the woods. Or some other reasonable explanation besides the possibility I was now *hearing* things as well as seeing them. 'It must have been the wind.'

'Maybe it was one of the ghosts,' said Shawn, as he reached across the table for a piece of Addie's bacon.

I inhaled sharply, and choked on my juice. Shawn patted me helpfully on the back, looking smug that he'd gotten such a big reaction.

Clara picked up Paula's newspaper with an impatient rustle. 'Shawn Maddox, don't you start that.'

'Aw, come on, Miss Clara.' His voice took on a gee-whiz sort of tone, a little too much to be believed. 'Everyone talks about the ghosts of Bluestone Hill.'

'The what?' I wheezed.

'"Everyone" doesn't have to live here,' Clara chided, hitting his shoulder with the folded paper. 'Don't scare poor Sylvie.'

'I'm not scared.' The thinness of my voice didn't sound very convincing, even to me, so I tried again, speaking sternly to the overactive imagination that kept showing me slide shows of the past. 'There's no such thing as ghosts.'

'Are you sure?' Shawn waggled his eyebrows. 'There are a lot of things in the world that people can't explain.'

Clara clicked her tongue, disapproving. 'You know Paula doesn't like that superstitious talk.'

'She ought to capitalize on it.' Shawn's eyes lit up with enthusiasm and infectious good humour, thawing some of the chill that his suggestion had put around my heart. 'A historic place like this, a ghost might draw tourists. Look at all those ghost-hunter shows on TV. Maybe one would come and do an episode about the Hill.'

Clara rolled her eyes. 'Lord. That would rouse the Colonel, and that's a fact.'

'Who *is* the Colonel?' I asked. Paula had made a similar crack last night, something about the Colonel rolling in his grave.

'Colonel Davis,' said Shawn, relishing my curiosity, like a storyteller with a new audience. 'That's who *supposedly* haunts the house.'

'That's enough of that,' Clara said with finality. 'You don't believe that nonsense and neither do I. Now get off to school.'

Her practical, maternal tone set the morning back on a normal course and returned me to my metaphorical feet. Of course ghosts were nonsense. Of course this place was spurring my imagination. That didn't have to mean that I was losing my ability to tell fantasy from reality.

Addie downed the rest of her juice, rose from her chair and grabbed her backpack, all in the same motion. 'Let's get going, Shawn. I have a review quiz first period.'

She was out the door with scarcely a 'Bye, Mom' over her shoulder. Shawn stood, but didn't hurry off. 'So,' he asked, holding my chair as I rose too, 'what are you going to do on your first day in scenic Alabama?'

'I'm not sure yet,' I answered. 'As little as possible, I think.' Clara had her back to us as she rinsed the dishes, but I suspected she was paying attention to the conversation. Possibly Shawn thought the same thing, because he moved towards the back door, gesturing with a jerk of his head for me to follow him out.

On the porch, Gigi watched us from her crate, tilting her head curiously. 'I get out of school early today and tomorrow,' Shawn said. 'I could show you around the town, or whatever you wanted.'

He stood just on the edge of my personal space, smiling a Tom Sawyer sort of smile, the kind that could get him into, or out of, all sorts of trouble. I had no difficulty imagining that a smile like that could be Becky Thatcher's downfall.

In a way, it was the strength of that pull that made

me hesitate. Liking Shawn was very easy, and it was against my nature to do anything the easy way.

'I'll think about it,' I said, not entirely shutting him down. 'If I feel like getting dressed.'

His grin widened. 'Don't bother on my account.'

He managed to make me blush. Out in the truck, Addie leaned on the horn, and Shawn hurried to join her, letting the screen door bang behind him. The effect of his smile lingered behind him, like the Cheshire cat's slowly disappearing grin.

I let Gigi out of her crate, thinking, strangely enough, about picket fences. Believe it or not, there's a ballet *Tom Sawyer*. It's by a Russian, so I wouldn't use it to write a book report. But my point is that Tom, with his Southern charm and boyish grin, was still a trickster. Maybe I needed to remember that.

Shawn seemed straightforward, but his interest was . . . intense. I'm reasonably attractive, but Shawn was obviously the golden boy around here. Was I a novelty – score with the new girl? And why did he and the Teen Town Council welcome my arrival, while Addie seemed to view it as a personal affront?

Then there was Rhys. I was certainly attracted, but he had no trouble irritating me, too. And what was he working on in the woods? He'd made it sound more than recreational. Or had that been just to tease me about sleeping in?

Two men of mystery. Three if you counted my dad.

I sighed and pulled the scrunchie out of my tangled hair. As if I had any business even thinking about guys when there were big, important things to worry about, like what I was going to do with the rest of my life, and how I was going to keep from going crazy while stuck here.

Crazi*er*, I mean.

Because the thing that shook me up when Shawn mentioned ghosts wasn't the idea that the house was haunted. It was that, just for a second, I hoped it was. If I was grasping at the supernatural for a lifeline where my sanity was concerned, I was a lot farther gone than I had thought.

Chapter 7

Back in the kitchen, I asked Clara how I could learn more about the Davis family history. Thinking about sanity made me think of John, and of what he'd said the night before. While I was here, maybe I *should* find out more about my dad and my family. And the best place to start anything was at the beginning.

Accepting the plates I brought from the table, Clara said absently, 'You could ask your cousin Paula. She'll be happy to tell you anything you want to know.'

I went back for the juice glasses and Paula's mug. 'I

was thinking more about an unbiased source. Like a book or something.'

Clara chuckled. 'I don't expect you'd find anything unbiased here in the house. You could take the car up to Selma, I suppose.'

'I don't have a driver's licence.' I'd never needed one in the city, and I'd been too busy dancing to learn for the fun of it.

'Well, I'll be happy to take you when I go in for groceries. Or you could ask Rhys to drive you, when he comes back from his trekking.'

With a dish towel, I began drying the glasses she set on the drain board. I was hardly the domestic type, but pitching in seemed natural in Clara's homey kitchen. 'So, seriously. Is the guy just a nature nut or what?'

'Seriously,' she echoed, handing me another glass, her brows arched, 'I don't know. It's none of my business. He said something about rock collecting, but I think he was joking. The boy's well past the age for earning Scouting badges.'

'I guess.' I remembered him loading my luggage in the car, and how scratched up his hands were. He was definitely doing *something* out in the brush.

'Anyway,' said Clara as she pulled the stopper and let the sink drain. 'There are some books in the Colonel's study you could start with.'

I stared at her, the towel dangling from my fingers. 'The Colonel's study? The colonel who's supposed to haunt the house?'

With an impatient sound, she took the dishrag and dried her hands. 'Lord, don't you start. Colonel Davis has been dead for a hundred and thirty-odd years. Lots of people have used that room since. Some men cast long shadows, that's all.'

But I noticed she hadn't exactly denied the haunting part.

❧ ❧

I didn't ask for permission to bring Gigi upstairs. Paula had only said she couldn't sleep with me, not that she couldn't come up at all.

Gigi pranced beside me, tags jingling, while I tried to remember Paula's quickly rattled-off orientation to the house. The landing made a U around the stairwell. To the front of the house was a suite that she planned to divide into two bedrooms. To one side was my room, and opposite me, the other guest rooms. I'd already found the French doors to the balcony this morning. Near them, down the same short hallway leading back from the landing, was the study.

At the panelled wood door, I paused, my hand on the knob. Gigi looked up at me, cocking her head in a question.

'It's a test,' I said. 'If I'm crazy, then the power of suggestion will make me see something when I open this door. If there's nothing there, then I am still in control of my senses.'

Unless there really was such a thing as ghosts, in which case, my test proved nothing either way.

Ghosts, Sylvie? Really?

No, not really. But it would explain a lot.

'I could stand here all day at this rate.' And sooner or later someone was going to come by and wonder why I was standing with my face to the door, talking to myself.

Decisively, I turned the knob. The heavy oak swung easily on well-oiled hinges. It stirred the hair that escaped my ponytail, tickling my cheek, but no other sensation came with it. I edged forward and peered in, quickly scanning the room, and found it empty of ghosts or any other apparitions.

The breath I held ran out in relief, and I pried my fingers off the brass doorknob. 'See?' I told Gigi. 'Nothing there. And nothing here.' I tapped my forehead.

She sniffed the air and went in, stiff-legged with curiosity. I followed, distracted for a moment by the floor-to-ceiling shelves that lined the walls, filled with cloth- and leather-bound books. Dust motes danced in the sunlight filtering through the sheer curtains. Heavier drapes framed the windows, faded in streaks, darker in the folds.

It smelled like old paper and furniture polish. The flat surfaces were dust-free, and there were no cobwebs in the corners, though the paint on the ceiling cornices was yellowed with age. All but the edges of the wood floor were covered by a worn Oriental carpet, and a wingback chair and ottoman sat beside the fireplace.

Strangely, I couldn't picture myself curling up to read there. Despite the books and the hearth and the embroidered cushions placed in the chair, this was not an inviting spot.

Gigi seemed to agree with me. She walked in circles, nose to the ground, but didn't look inclined to sit and linger.

Maybe it was the massive desk that dominated the room. The sides were carved simply, the top inlaid with a Greek-key pattern – a beautiful piece of furniture that somehow managed to be unappealing at the same time. Everything about it said it wouldn't be budged. And judging by the pattern of wear on the carpet, it hadn't been moved in a long time. Maybe ever.

I made myself sit in the desk chair. The arms were teak, darker where my hands rested, and the wood creaked softly as I lowered myself into it. The seat and back were leather, but with minimal padding. Uncompromising and uncomfortable, like the man who had sat there.

Come on, Sylvie. Get a grip. How would you know that?

Maybe because the Colonel's stamp was all over the room. He didn't have to haunt in a traditional, chain-rattling sense. Across from the desk was a glass-front case full of antique military regalia: a pair of pistols with ivory handles, a belt buckle and collection of brass buttons, and a big-brimmed cavalry hat with gold cord. A folded flag. Needless to say, it was *not* the Stars and Stripes.

Defiantly, I moved a brass inkwell to the left side of the felt blotter. Take that, Colonel Davis, if you are still hanging around.

Pulling open drawers, I rummaged for treasures of a less military nature, something that would tell me more about my ancestor. Any ancestor. The only antiques I found were a roll of twenty-nine-cent stamps and a telephone book from 1986.

I sighed. 'Whatever you do here, Colonel, it isn't keeping up with correspondence.'

I pushed myself out of the chair and went to the case of memorabilia, taking it in, though not really studying it in detail. Was this what Dad had wanted to leave behind? This glorification of a past that didn't really bear up to scrutiny?

My gaze fell on the wall shelf next to the case. That was sensible filing – the dusty history of the Davises, shelved beside the relics of one man's glorious past. I pulled a book free. Cloth-bound, except for the worn leather on the spine. The pages were unevenly trimmed, so they didn't flip smoothly as I thumbed through the thin volume. The type was old-fashioned, and I checked the publisher and date on the copyright page: University of Alabama Press, 1935.

The Davis Family in Alabama. By William S. Davis, Esq.

Not exactly what I'd meant by unbiased. But Clara *had* warned me.

I poked around and found a few more old books: *Alabama and the War Between the States, Antebellum Houses,* and *Southern Gardens.* All from the last century, all from Southern publishers. Most with the Confederate flag featured prominently on the cover. I guessed the Colonel didn't like any dissenting opinions in his study.

The chair creaked, a distinctive sound, the unmistakable protest of wood. My heart thudded so hard I was surprised it didn't bang against the book I clutched to my chest. When I spun around, I expected to see the dog getting into trouble.

'Gigi?'

I found her by her tiny, electric-motor growl. She'd been beside me already, but now she rose, her neck fluff standing straight up as she stared at the chair behind the desk, empty, yet sighing under an invisible weight.

Chapter 8

$\mathcal{A}$ cold wash of panic froze me in place. I held my breath, waiting to see what would happen. What was the next step in madness? Would I see monsters? Would I snap, start raving about implants in my head and men from Mars?

But nothing happened. I finally had to let out one lungful of air to take another, or I'd pass out. The decision to breathe spurred me past my paralysis, and I scooped up Gigi and fled the study, closing the door firmly behind me.

As if I could close the door on my own broken mind.

I headed for my room, thoughts bouncing around my head like rubber balls, blood zinging through my veins, senses on full alert. Except for the complete inability to focus my thoughts, being crazy felt a lot like the rush of dancing onstage.

Shutting the door carefully, I put Gigi on my bed, numbly marvelling at how quickly she returned to her usual sunny self, exploring the rumpled covers with happy curiosity, when just seconds ago she'd been growling.

She'd been growling. That was important somehow.

Pulling out the chair to the writing desk, I sat down heavily as adrenaline drained the strength out of my legs. Startled to find I was still carrying the Davis family history book from the study, I placed it on the corner of the desk.

Come on, Sylvie. Stop freaking out and focus.

I'm an abstract thinker when it comes to choreography, which is all rhythm and patterns. But my sanity was at stake here; I needed to look at things in a concrete way.

The scent of lilacs wafted out as I opened the centre drawer. I found writing paper – perfumed, I supposed – and a pen, ready for ladylike correspondence. Placing a sheet square on the blotter, I drew a line down the middle to make a two-column list. One side said: *Reasons why I might be crazy.* The other said: *Reasons why I might not be ready for a white coat with sleeves that buckle in back.*

On the *Crazy* side I wrote:

1. There's no such thing as ghosts.

The *Not Crazy* side got this:

1. The fact that I'm making this list.

2. Power of suggestion + creaky, draughty house = over-active imagination.

3. Gigi heard something too.

I hesitated before I added that last one, because it didn't go with the first two. She couldn't have heard my overactive imagination, but she could have reacted to my reaction, in which case it could have gone in either column. But I didn't want *Not Crazy* to be ahead by only one point. Because the point under *Crazy* was pretty unarguable.

Regardless of the score, the act of writing things out had restored some of my equilibrium, like I could grip reality now that I could grip the paper.

A tap on the door made me jump. Gigi's growl was muffled – she'd burrowed under the covers, so I didn't worry about hiding her. The list, however, might as well have been contraband drugs, I was so desperate to get rid of it.

'Sylvie?' Paula's voice came clearly through the door.

'Just a sec.' What I needed was an old-fashioned secret compartment. As soon as the notion entered my head, my hand went unerringly to the bottom of the centre drawer. A tiny latch opened a panel underneath. The paper crumpled as I shoved it in but the compartment clicked firmly closed.

With a quick glance to make sure Gigi was out of sight, I went to let in my cousin. But I moved too fast, coming down hard on my right leg just before I swung open the door.

Paula was dressed in the same crisp khakis and button-down shirt she'd worn at breakfast. She'd already drawn a breath to speak, but when she looked me up and down, she obviously changed whatever she was about to say. 'Good heavens, girl. What is the matter with you?'

'Foot fell asleep,' I said, with a very real grimace. 'Took me a minute to get out of the chair.'

She gave me a doubtful look. 'I'm guessing that's not all that was asleep. I've been calling you for ten minutes. Clara is making lunch.'

'Lunch?' I looked at the clock on the bedside table. 'I guess time got away from me.' At least my mother had taught me a few useful things, like how a little spin-doctoring could save a world of trouble. And I knew what would please Paula, so I pointed to the book on the desk. 'I was reading some family history.'

Her brows winged upward, and she entered without invitation to pick up the book. 'Did you get this from the study?'

'I hope you don't mind.'

'Of course not. I'm happy you're taking an interest.' She laid the book down, then sat at the desk, straightening the pen on the blotter. I kept my eyes resolutely off the drawer.

'Have a seat, Sylvie. Let's have a little chat.'

Crap. Nothing good was going to come of a start like that. What had I done? Had she figured out I'd brought Gigi upstairs – twice? Eyeing the quiet lump under the covers, I sat in the upholstered chair so Paula's back would be to the bed.

'Clara told me you had trouble sleeping last night.' She stared at the wall, just over my shoulder, as if the subject were awkwardly personal. 'Something about a nightmare?'

'Just a dream. Strange place. The wind.' I tried not to sound defensive about the fact that my every quirk was under scrutiny. Maybe this was ironic, since no one was scrutinizing me harder than me. But damn it, I'd just stepped my panic down a notch, and now the knot in my chest was twisting tight again.

'Are you going to report that back to Mother and Dr Steve?' I challenged.

The briefest flash of guilt on Paula's face convinced me I wasn't overreacting. The step-shrink had definitely said something to her. I had to clench my hands on my knees to hold back my anger, which edged out fear by a narrow margin.

Paula shook her head, showing me the magnolia rather than the steel. For now. 'I'm not reporting anything to them,' she said. 'But I do know you've been under a lot of stress. And I just want you to know, you can tell me anything.'

Her earnest gravity forced me to bite back my hot retort. Paula was going on what Mother and Dr Steve had told her. For all I knew he could have warned her I might snap at any time, do a Lizzie Borden number some night. Like my *real* shrink would let me wander free if that were a possibility.

I caught a breath of lilac, which reminded me of my

list and that *Not Crazy* was ahead at the moment. I needed to act like it, or I would be in trouble. If they were watching me, I was going to have to be careful and guard my reactions. Which might be paranoia, and have to go in the *Crazy* column. I unclenched my teeth and choked out, 'Thanks, Cousin Paula. I know you want what's best for me.'

Everyone wanted what was best for me, which was a completely different thing from wanting me to be happy.

She pressed her lips together like she wanted to say more. It was the expression of someone who was choosing her battles, and my sullen tone was apparently a fight she was going to let slide. 'Fine,' she said, as if that settled it. 'Now let's talk about what you're going to do with the rest of your day.'

That was not what I expected her to say. 'Um, I thought I would read my book, then maybe walk to town.'

'Oh, honey, you can't walk to town.'

'But I thought it was close by.'

'Well, yes. About two miles from here.'

Two miles used to be an easy jog. I *could* walk it, but I hadn't tested my leg's limits that far yet. I'd hate to get there and be unable to get back. But I hated feeling trapped more. 'That's not so far.'

Paula slapped her hands on her knees and stood with the purposeful cheer of a cruise director. 'I have a better idea.'

My sigh rang with resignation. 'I thought you might.'

'Why don't you get started painting the front bedrooms?'

I stared at her like she'd suggested I start flying to the moon. 'What?'

'I think it would be good for you to do something active. The whole idea behind your coming here was to give you something to do besides languish around your apartment in that big, anonymous city.'

'You mean, the idea was to use me for free labour?' I struggled to my feet. 'Is that how I'm earning my room and board?'

Paula looked genuinely appalled at the idea. 'Sylvie, this is your family home. We are kin. You don't have to earn anything.' But the steel overtook the magnolia in her voice as she squared her shoulders. 'Which doesn't mean I'm going to let you lie around the house in your pyjamas all day.'

Our voices had roused Gigi, whose lump began writhing under the quilt, emitting little growls. Paula whirled at the sound, just as Gigi popped out from the covers, her fluff standing straight up around her head.

'*What* did I say about that dog?' Paula demanded.

Gigi gave a winsome, playful bark, but my cousin was unmoved. I set my jaw stubbornly. 'You said she couldn't sleep with me at night. You didn't say she had to stay in her crate all the time.'

Paula pressed her hands to her eyes. 'Get dressed and come down for lunch.' She headed for the open door, muttering as she went. 'This is why I never had children of my own.'

I turned to Gigi when she was gone. 'Why does

everyone think I'm so high maintenance? I'd be no trouble to anyone if they had just let me stay in Manhattan.'

If I was enough trouble, would Paula send me back? The thought didn't spark the same hope that it had before I saw Bluestone Hill. Leaving would not be the same as never coming here. I couldn't unlearn my father's background, and I couldn't unask my questions.

❧ ❧

Lunch consisted of a gargantuan salad, as if Clara was trying to make up the lack of carnivorous content in vegetable volume. She and Paula discussed business matters, since I didn't try to make small talk. I felt obliged to sulk, and live up to expectations. Or down, as the case may be.

After I'd finished my salad, I took the Davis history book and the bowl of leftover blackberry cobbler that Clara forced on me – to improve my mood, she said – and went out to the garden with Gigi.

I meant to stay in the back yard, maybe even sit under the arbour, but Gigi headed again to the knot garden at the side of the house. I'd brought an old blanket I'd found on the side porch, one that had obviously done picnic duty before, and I spread it where the invading grass had made a soft spot in the out-of-control garden. Gigi sprawled in the centre of the quilt until I scooted her over so I could stretch out on my stomach, the sun on my back and warm through my clothes.

Despite the overgrown disorder, I felt nature working its usual magic on me. The garden's hedges hid me from the house – unless you were on the balcony up-stairs – and by the time I finished the cobbler and Gigi finished the ice cream, I felt calm for the first time since Shawn Maddox had mentioned the word 'ghost'.

Well, maybe not calm. There was still that lilac piece of paper hidden in my desk. I didn't need to look at it to know how close the score was. But in the garden, that seemed further away. The sun shone, bees flew, grass grew, and the whole thing would keep happening whether I was crazy or not.

Setting aside the bowl, I pulled the book towards me and dove in. Twenty pages later, I decided that slapping up paint would be better than this. Hell, watching paint *dry* would be better than reading William S. Davis, Esq.

I started skimming the text. On one hand, I began to understand why the Davis name was such a big deal here. The family had settled the area and been instrumental in just about everything that happened for two hundred years. But from this book, I didn't get why anyone would be excited about meeting a Davis, living or dead. Old William S. had somehow managed to simultaneously make the family unbelievably grandiose and excruciatingly boring.

Flipping forward, I looked for mention of the Colonel. There was indeed a lengthy chapter on Josiah Davis, and it was as dry as the rest of the book. Blah blah blah Battle of This, Siege of That, yadda yadda yadda Reconstruction . . . But nothing about the man's personality. I had to infer what I could from his study, and the formal portrait in the book.

It was a bad print of an old photograph. One of

those where the subject had to sit still for about fifteen minutes while the image developed. It was hard to see anything other than a man in a high-collared shirt and double-breasted coat sitting ramrod straight in a chair, a young woman with a baby in her arms standing beside him.

I thought she might be his daughter, but the caption underneath said: *Colonel Josiah Davis and his second wife, Mary Maddox Davis, holding their son, Joshua.* She didn't look much older than me. And her expression definitely didn't say it was a love match.

Was Mary Maddox Davis my multiple-great-grandmother? And the maiden name – did that make her Shawn's however-many-great-aunt?

I couldn't tell much from the dark, blurry photograph and the stiff, sober look on her face. She didn't look very nice, though I wouldn't either if I had to marry a man old enough to be my father. I knew girls got married young back then, and a lot of the men her age would have died in the war, limiting her choices. But still. Not a pleasant prospect.

What happened to the Colonel's first wife? I flipped back a few pages and scanned the text. Ah, died in childbirth with her sixth kid. So where were all the offspring? Even allowing for infant mortality, there should be a few to surround dear old dad and their stepmother. Did the sons die in battle? Had the girls all been married off by the time the photo was taken?

I tried to find the answers in the chapter, but the prosaic writing was useless. William S. Davis managed to record every boring detail about the Colonel's charge at the Battle of Chickamanga, and nothing I wanted to know.

To judge by the book, not only had my ancestors been devoid of personality, they apparently bred only boys. There were almost no wives or daughters or sisters mentioned, at least as far as I'd gotten. I rolled over, contemplating the house, and what things would have been like for a Davis daughter in the mansion's heyday, when Bluestone Hill had been full of life and activity.

From where I lay, I couldn't see the satellite dish, or the cars parked by the garage. Lulled by the garden, I indulged my imagination this time, purposefully trying to picture what the place would have looked like in the Colonel's time. Instead of overgrown and weedy, the hedges were neatly trimmed, and the herbs and plantings cut back so that the geometric pattern was clear. I could smell lavender and geranium, crisp and green.

Instead of a quilt, my skirt was spread around me, the hoop carefully collapsed so it wouldn't flip up. My corset stays pressed into my ribs, and I could take only shallow breaths. Not a comfortable position, but I wanted to watch the sun crawl across the sky, marking time while I waited for—

For what? The question nudged me out of a doze, where my creative visualization had gone off-script, undirected. The character I'd created in my head was *waiting* for someone.

My shrink would call this projection. It irritated me, though, that my imagination couldn't supply an identity.

A shadow fell across my face, and I squinted blearily into the sun. Gigi gave a sleepy growl and nestled closer to my side. 'Is it you?' I asked, not sure what, or who, I meant, still caught in the sticky web of dreaming.

'It depends on whom you're expecting.' The accent was lilting and droll. Rhys. Of course.

I rubbed my eyes and sat up. 'Do people really say "whom" where you're from? Outside of the BBC, I mean.'

'Sometimes.' He looked down at me, one eyebrow raised. 'Did you have a nice nap?'

Even with the sun warm on my face, my blush was hot. 'I wasn't sleeping; I was thinking.'

Rhys moved a step over so I didn't have to squint into the light. 'Thinking about what?'

'About my great-great-grandmothers and -aunts, and what it would have been like to live here when this place was new.' Pulling my knees up, I propped my folded arms on top of them. 'Back in the bad old days.'

'Well, it wouldn't have been bad for you, princess.' He wasn't scornful exactly, but his tone was pitched to poke holes in any pretences of hardship I had. 'Being the daughter of the house and all.'

'Yeah. I'd have had it better than most women.' I glared up at him, irritated I had to crane my neck to do so. 'But I'd still have no rights, have to marry who-ever they told me to and have babies until I dropped dead.'

I'm sure he could have countered by pointing out how spoiled I was, or how I took my relative lack of hardship for granted. Instead, after a thoughtful beat, he just said, '*Whom*ever they told you to.'

I laughed, even though I'd been irked a moment before. Rhys looked startled, and my frown snapped back. 'What?'

'Nothing,' he said, sounding bemused. 'You have a nice laugh. Sitting there in your bare feet and your hair all mussed, you don't look like the same girl who got off the plane yesterday.'

'Well, I am.' Uncertainty made me grumpy. I pulled the rubber band from the tangled remnants of my ponytail, and gestured to my jeans and T-shirt. 'This is the real me.'

His gaze went to my feet. 'Do you have something against shoes? That's playing against type, isn't it?'

I tucked my feet under my knees, sitting cross-legged, and scowled for good measure. I'm sure he meant that no self-respecting socialite would be caught dead with feet like mine – calloused, boxy, knobby in the toe joints. Mother had taken me for a pedicure when the cast came off, and the aesthetician had been happy to enumerate the ways in which pointe shoes had given me the feet of an ogre.

'I'm not a *type*.' I would have been angrier, if I didn't suspect he was needling me, as usual.

Gigi got up, stretched and tottered over sleepily to fall into the well of my folded legs. Rhys took the room I'd made on the quilt for an invitation, and lowered himself onto it. I pulled my bare toes in closer, because proximity to Rhys was making them tingle.

He picked up the book I'd set aside. 'What are you reading? Davis on Davis?'

I nodded. 'It works better than Ambien. The author must have had real talent to make so much aggrandizement that boring.' I scrubbed my scalp where the ponytail had pressed in my sleep, and let my hair fall around my shoulders. It felt good, like loosening my bun after long hours of rehearsal or taking off a too-tight pair of jeans. I almost felt like I really had been wearing a corset and hoops for the length of my dream. In my head I could hear the creak of the whalebone stays, the rustle of layers and layers of underwear.

Was the image too vivid? I'd had to wear a hoopskirt once for *The Nutcracker*, so I knew how it felt and the trick to sitting in one. But that was my own memory. Did it need to go on the list?

While I debated, Rhys flipped the pages of the book. Specks of paper lint drifted in the sunlight. 'Did you learn anything, or was that suffering for nothing?'

I curled a strand of Gigi's ear fluff around my fingers as she slept. 'I found out we're cousins.'

'Cousins?'

'Owen Davis came to the United States from Wales in the late seventeen hundreds and claimed this property by the sweat of his brow. William S. makes it sound very noble, but I think it just means that Davis came here without any money.'

'He wouldn't be the first person to come to America fleeing something,' said Rhys casually. 'Religious persecution, potato famine. Debt. Prison.'

'What about you?' The question popped out, startling me.

'Me?' he asked. It startled him, too, apparently.

'Yes, you.' I wasn't sure where it had come from, but the shuttering of his expression confirmed the lucky guess. 'What are you running away from?'

His eyes – very green, very direct – met mine in a challenge. 'What makes you think I'm running away from anything?'

I didn't back down, but ran an assessing glance over him. He was work-dirty: knees of his khakis grimy, tails of his shirt streaked where he'd wiped his hands. 'You're, what, twenty? Twenty-one? Handsome, not fashion-impaired – despite grubbing around in the dirt for some reason. Not *too* socially maladjusted. You seriously have nothing better to do with your summer than follow your dad around and type his notes?'

He rose to his feet in one fluid move, the better to look down at me. 'You don't know me, princess. Some people have reasons for doing things, and don't just go wherever they're told or drift whichever way they're pushed.'

My teeth clenched. Point to him, but it was a low blow. Since I couldn't parry that, I pursued the opening he'd given me. 'So you do have a reason for being here.'

His mouth opened, worked for a moment trying to block the thrust of my question, then closed as he narrowed his eyes at me. 'Yes. I'm helping my father with his research. But I'm also working on something of my own.'

What was so hard about that? I nodded to the dirt on his khakis. 'Does it have to do with your rock hunting?'

Again, I'd managed to knock his feet out from under him. 'How did you know about that?'

My eyebrows shot up in surprise. 'Clara thought

you were joking. What are you doing, working on a merit badge?'

He pressed his lips together in offended dignity. 'As it happens, I'm a geologist.' Then the starch ran out of him, and he admitted, 'Or I will be, when I go back to finish at university.'

'You mean you really are looking for rocks?' I felt stupid sitting on the ground while he was standing, but I knew I'd look as graceful as a three-legged foal if I tried to get up, so I stayed where I was.

There was a pause while he seemed to edit his answer. 'I'm also doing some volunteer work at a dig at Old Cahawba.'

'Old Cahawba? What's that?'

'The archaeological park up the river.' His brows drew down in a perplexed V. 'How do you not know any of this?'

'Why should I? I've never been here before.'

'But this is your' – he searched for the appropriate word – 'your legacy.'

'Oh for heaven's sake.' Aggravation wouldn't let me keep still. I didn't care how it looked. I moved Gigi out of my lap and climbed to my feet. 'I had to look my family up in a *book*. I'm hardly the lost heir returned to claim a birthright. For one thing, it's not mine, it's Paula's.'

Rhys caught my hand when I wobbled, an instinctive move, I think. But he didn't let go. He grasped my fingers and looked hard into my eyes, as if trying to read my thoughts.

'You're serious,' he said with a note of discovery, a

statement of whatever he saw in my gaze. 'You didn't know *anything* about Bluestone Hill when you came here.'

'Have we not established that I have an all-day pass for the clueless bus?' My utter frustration almost made me miss the emphasis he put on 'anything', as though there was something I should know but didn't. 'What is it I'm supposed to have known?'

He let my hand go and straightened. 'I thought . . . Well, never mind what I thought.'

I glared at him. 'What? That I'd come to finagle my way in here? Somehow take the property from Paula? My dad left me well provided for. An antique mansion in the middle of nowhere isn't a huge temptation.'

I heard how the words sounded as soon as they left my mouth, and wished I could snatch them back. But life was like a live performance: There were no retakes. Dad left me money, but I didn't know or care about the details. All I'd cared about was that it kept me in toe shoes. The money was all in a trust I'd never planned to touch because I was going to be a famous ballerina.

And now Rhys was looking down his nose at me like I'd crawled out from under one of his rocks. 'Thanks for clearing that up,' he said coldly. 'I think I have your measure now.'

'No, you don't,' I said hotly, and it wasn't about the money or my snooty words. 'Nobody here does. *I* don't even know what kind of person I am any more.'

I picked up Gigi and turned, the grass cool under my bare feet, but not enough to cool my emotions. I hadn't gone five steps when Rhys called my name.

'What?' I snapped, turning back.

He looked at me as if he would have said something else. An explanation or apology would be nice. But he just tightened his jaw and held out the Davis family history to me. 'Here's your book.'

'Thanks so much,' I ground through my teeth, and headed for the house.

❧ ❧

I went in through the side porch to the den, not wanting to go upstairs and have to decide what, if anything, of this afternoon's events I needed to add to the crazy list. Flopping on the couch, I grabbed the remote and clicked on the television, just for the modern inanity of it. Gigi jumped up beside me and regally crossed her paws as if she were claiming her rightful place.

That was the undertone of Rhys's comments. He seemed to expect me to view Bluestone Hill as my rightful place. Which was stupid. No matter how seamlessly I'd slipped into the role of my imaginary ancestress while I was in the garden, I was not here to reclaim anything. I wasn't even here by *choice*.

I flipped channels without really paying attention, and finally settled on a mindless syndicated sitcom.

A movement in the foyer made me jerk guiltily forwards, hiding Gigi from view. When no one descended to tell me to get the dog off the furniture, I called tentatively, 'Paula?'

There was no answer. It could have been something

as simple as a shadow from the upstairs landing, but I got up anyway, leaving Gigi snoozing on the couch. Poking my head out the den door, I peered up the stairs. Had Rhys come in through the back and gone up to his room?

My eye caught someone whisking round a corner in the parlour, and I followed, determined to satisfy my curiosity. But by the time I crossed the foyer, all I saw was a flutter of apron strings at the second door. My heart recognized similarities before my head, and accelerated with an unformed fear. But I wove through the antiques and knickknacks to the dining-room door, and – placing a hand on the frame – braced myself before looking in.

'Clara?' I called softly. 'Paula?'

Again, the room felt as if someone had just left it. And maybe they had. But I couldn't get the image of long skirts and starched cotton caps out of my head. It was an impression, not even an glimpse, but so close to what I'd imagined last night. Maids would have walked these halls every hour of every day, wearing the same thing, and—

'Chasing more ghosts?'

The caustic voice made me jump and whirl, strangling a shout of alarm, but not quite quick enough. Addie looked at me with arch enquiry, and no small amount of satisfaction.

Annoyance chased away any lingering unease. 'Just exploring.' My tone was unapologetic, maybe even a bit challenging. 'What are you doing home? I thought you had school.'

She didn't like the reminder that I was past all that. 'Did you lose track of time while you were catching up on your soap operas?' she asked. 'School is out.'

Now I noticed Caitlin and a girl I didn't know petting and giggling over Gigi in the den. My dog was still on the sofa, receiving their worship as her due. I hadn't heard a car arrive, but the TV was still on, and I'd been pretty intent on following . . . nothing, it seemed.

'Hey, Sylvie,' said Caitlin, as I crossed the foyer to the den. 'This is Melissa. She's on the TTC too.'

I exchanged greetings, but Addie wasn't bothering with niceties. She looked pointedly at my dog, the remote still in my hand and the pillow I'd thrown onto the coffee table so I could prop up my leg. Then she dropped her book bag where I'd been sitting, a territorial display that I didn't miss. 'We usually study in here after school.'

For all my protestations that this wasn't my home, that it was Paula's house and I wanted no claim to it, Addie's implied order that I vacate *my spot* sent a surge of possessiveness through me. I met her eye and held my ground, just long enough to make sure she knew I was doing her a favour by moving.

When I saw the realization flicker in her eyes, I clicked off the TV and tossed the remote on the cushions. 'Knock yourself out.'

Calling for Gigi, I headed up the stairs to my room.

Chapter 9

In my room, I contemplated the secret drawer in the desk, wondering how I'd found the latch so easily before, yet couldn't seem to manage it now. I was just about to see if I could crawl under the desk to look from below, when Paula knocked on the door. Her rap was distinctive.

I flipped open the Davis book, and called for her to come in. Gigi, lying in the reading chair, pricked her ears forward, but didn't bother to try more charm than that. She had Paula figured out. Or maybe she saw the frown my cousin shot her before she got down to business.

'Addie and the girls are going to get something to eat at a hamburger place out on the highway. They asked if you'd like to come with them.'

Somehow, I had trouble picturing this invitation, even with my overactive imagination. It made me a little snarky, especially as I was still sore over the earlier implication that I was being vegetarian just to be difficult. 'Come along and watch them eat hamburgers, you mean?'

Paula got that tight-lipped 'pick your battles' expression. 'I'm sure they have salads and things. Most places do. I think you should go. You can't sulk in here all day and all night.'

I'd been 'sulking' in the garden and in the den, too, but I didn't point that out. 'If I go, will you let Gigi spend the night inside?'

She sighed and set her hands on her hips. 'No. But I won't complain about her staying with you as long as you're awake.'

I agreed. It wouldn't stop me from sneaking Gigi in after dark, but it would save me some grief the rest of the time.

And seriously, when your day includes making a list to see if you're crazy or not, there's not much further downhill things could go.

❧ ❧

I predicted the outing would be excruciating, and was pleasantly surprised that it was only intermittently unpleasant. Joe's Big Burger, located halfway to Selma on the state highway, was a popular place, and I had no trouble finding something to eat, as long as I wanted a wedge of iceberg lettuce or a grilled cheese sandwich. Addie, Caitlin and Melissa discussed people I didn't know, parties I hadn't been to and things I'd never heard of. Which suited me fine, because it meant I didn't have to talk about myself.

When they asked me about life in New York, I answered a few questions, then turned the conversational burden back to them. 'So, what do you guys do for fun around here?' I asked, figuring everyone liked to talk about their pastimes. 'Besides build summerhouses and plot world domination through catfish.'

Caitlin and Melissa laughed. 'We keep busy,' said Melissa. 'There's football in the fall, and basketball in the spring. School dances are fun.'

'And like you mentioned, there *is* the Catfish Festival coming up,' said Caitlin. 'You're coming to that, right?'

'I'll have to check my social calendar,' I drawled, and they laughed again – not Addie, of course, but the other two – missing the edge to my remark. Just as well. They seemed like nice girls.

'So if you live in Maddox Landing,' I said, 'then what is Cahaba? Another town?'

'Oh, Cahaba was the first capital of Alabama.' Melissa dragged a fry through her ketchup. 'Now it's a ghost town on the other side of your house.'

'A ghost town?' I deliberately didn't look at Addie, though after Shawn's jokes at breakfast and Addie finding me hunting shadows that afternoon, I wondered if I'd been set up.

But Melissa meant it colloquially. 'It doesn't exist any more. There's a couple of old buildings, and they've made a historic park there. Old Cahawba. With a *w*.'

I looked at Addie for clarification. 'But the sign on the wagon says Bluestone Hill Inn, Cahawba.'

She'd defrosted somewhat during dinner, as long as the conversation was about her and her friends, and not about me. Now she answered almost nicely. 'They can say whatever they want, since it's not in Maddox Landing, either.'

'Don't mention Old Cahawba to Shawn,' warned Caitlin. 'His dad is trying to develop some land on the other side of the park and the state is being kind of a bear about it.'

'I'll keep that in mind.' I made one of those connections that makes you feel a little slow in retrospect. 'So, Shawn's family . . . Maddox Landing is named after them? They must go way back.'

I'd finished my sandwich – as much as I was going to eat of it, anyway – and it was a good thing, since Addie's icicle stare would have congealed the melted cheese in a hurry. 'The Maddox and Davis families go way back together.'

The other two girls held in giggles. But not very well. 'Oh my gosh, Sylvie.' Caitlin's eyes brimmed with matchmaking fire. 'Shawn was *totally* talking about you today too.'

Crap. They'd clearly taken my interest the wrong way. Well, maybe the right way, but a whole lot further.

'I only ask because I saw the Maddox name in a book I was reading about my own family history. I was wondering if we were cousins.'

Melissa grinned broadly, taking my clarification as confirmation instead of denial. 'Don't worry. If you are, it's far enough back not to matter.'

'It's never mattered much anyway,' drawled Addie. 'Y'all's families are as inbred as a redneck joke.'

'Don't listen to her,' said Caitlin. 'That's just a Southern cliché.'

That didn't make me feel better. I'd seen some real-life clichés since I'd arrived. I slid a covertly curious glance at Addie. Was this assumption I was going after Shawn the root of her dislike? Her digs were at my sense of entitlement. Maybe she thought *I* thought I was entitled to Shawn.

'I don't want to poach on anyone's territory,' I said, just to see what would happen. Addie rolled her eyes and the other two girls laughed, and this time, I didn't get why. 'What's so funny?'

'Nothing,' said Addie, with a repressive look at Melissa and Caitlin, and their in-joke giggles. 'Let's get out of here. *Some* of us have things to do tomorrow.'

❧ ❧

The house was quiet when Caitlin dropped Addie and me back at Bluestone Hill. Paula had left lights burning on the front porch and in the foyer. In the kitchen, too, I saw, as the car pulled in front of the garage to let us out.

My hand on the door latch, I turned to the other three girls in the car. 'Thanks for inviting me to dinner,' I said, twisting to include Melissa and Addie in the back seat. 'I'll tell Gigi you said hi, Caitlin. It was nice meeting you, Melissa.'

She waved. 'You, too. I guess I'll see you Thursday night.'

I cast back through the conversation at dinner, trying to find a reference to an event. 'What's Thursday night?'

'The circle.' The 'of course' was unspoken.

'She means the Teen Town Council circle,' said Caitlin smoothly, though I hadn't missed the poke Addie had given Melissa in the ribs. 'That's what we call our closed meetings.'

'Which only Shawn can invite anyone to,' Addie said pointedly.

Melissa glared back at Addie. 'Sorry. I assumed he had.'

'Why?' I asked, curious at the underlying dynamic.

Caitlin smiled, her drawl widening too. 'Because you're a Davis, of course.'

But I was only here for a month, and had no desire to get involved in junior politics. Not that I had a chance to point that out, since Addie was already climbing out of the car. I got out too, slowed by my stiff leg, then waved as Caitlin pulled from the driveway.

Addie didn't wait for me, heading straight for the stairs to her apartment. I wondered, thanks to the subtext in the car, if maybe she wasn't as territorial about Shawn as about this inner circle. I could explain to her that I wasn't interested in infringing on her position as alpha bitch of this pack. Though maybe I should put it in more tactful terms.

It would have to wait, though. By the time I reached the sidewalk that connected the apartment stairs with the back door of the house, Addie was already on her landing, letting herself in. And she didn't even say goodnight.

❧ ❧

Gigi gave a yodelling bark of welcome as I came in the screen door to the back porch. I shushed her, in case Paula had gone to her own room to watch TV or go to sleep; there had been no light on in the den, and I didn't see anyone in the kitchen. I hoped I could let Gigi out for her last walk of the night, then slip upstairs and be done with sneaking around.

When I opened her crate, she bounded out with a playful growl, then went straight for the screen door. I grabbed a scooper bag and let us both out, easing the door so it didn't bang closed. Gigi made a full-tilt circuit of the back yard; then, while I was carefully making my way down the rail-less stairs, she shot off down the terrace steps to the great lawn.

'Dammit, Gigi!'

The worst thing I could do was run after her. Fortunately, at the end of the long day, the best I could manage was a hobble. She paused to pee, allowing me to keep her in sight. Then, reaching the open area that stretched between the house and the woods on the left, and the inlet on the right, she headed purposefully for the trees.

Snakes, coyotes, bobcats – I could barely see Gigi at the edge of the brush, but in my mind I could picture any one of those things snatching her up and making a meal out of her. Desperate to stop her, I reached down beneath the panic for the alpha-dog voice I'd never managed before.

'Gigi, stay!'

She planted her feet. It was too dark and too far to tell, but I imagined she was quite surprised. I certainly was.

'Come, Gigi.'

Maybe I was connecting with the Davis in me, some piece of the Colonel passed down. I didn't have to *like* my ancestry to draw on it, I suppose. Gigi trotted back to me, and as tempting as it was, I didn't scold her. I just scooped her up for a cuddle of relief.

Then I heard what she was after. The same wailing noise from the night before. Only here it was clear, distinct, and I realized it wasn't a cat in heat. It sounded like a baby's cry.

A *baby*? Seriously? I couldn't chalk this up to the old house and the power of suggestion. What sick part of my psyche could have dreamed *this* up?

The air was clammy against my skin; I didn't know if it was the cold sweat of fear for my sanity, or a sudden damp wind off the river, but a shiver ran through me, and I clutched Gigi closer to my chest.

She squirmed to peer over my shoulder at the house. Her low growl vibrated against my cheek, spread through me like a second shudder. The hair on my arms rose, my spine tingling with the awareness of someone watching me.

I knew the feeling too well to mistake the sure electricity of an audience. But this was different – the stinging rush of cold horror at being *caught*. The heavy weight of dread sat on my heart like a stone.

Despite my fear, I couldn't make myself turn slowly; I whirled, like jumping in a frigid pool. My gaze went unerringly up, to the first-floor balcony, and the French doors there. Like the shadows before, the figure was a wisp of distinction that fled before my eye could focus on it.

But Gigi had seen it too.

Which meant the watcher was real enough. Only my reaction was nuts. The thought was enough to spur me forward with purpose, leaving my fear behind me, as I headed for the house as quickly as my limping determination would carry me.

❧ ❧

The stairwell was cold, and the landing even colder. The hall leading to the French doors was empty and the sheer curtains hung in still folds. To my right, the soft glow of the bedside lamp marked my room. To the left was the brighter yellow strip of light shining from under the door that mirrored mine.

With Gigi still tucked securely against my side, I marched to it and knocked – at the last moment remembering to keep quiet so I didn't alert Paula. I counted seconds, reaching five-one-thousand before it opened. Rhys stood backlit in the doorway, obviously surprised. 'Sylvie?'

The prickling jolt of awareness, the way my skin seemed to measure the distance to his, only escalated the tension. Desperation to find just one answer to *something* put a rash edge to my demand. 'Was it you?'

His surprise turned to confusion. 'What?'

I wrestled my voice down in volume and pitch. 'Were you looking out the back window just now?'

'No,' he said slowly, perhaps cautiously, 'I've been in here working since after dinner.'

My questions shot out like an interrogation. 'Is your dad home yet?'

Rhys paused in very deliberate irritation, leaning a hand on the doorframe with a forbidding frown. 'What are you on about? Dad came home and went to bed.'

'It's only nine-thirty,' I said.

'Well, some of us were up at dawn.' He glanced behind me, towards the junction of the hallways, and there was a flicker of concern in his eyes. 'You said you saw someone at the window?'

I inhaled to answer, then my better sense – what was left of it – and self-preservation trapped the words in my throat. What was I doing? It was logical that Rhys might have looked out the window – I had called to Gigi rather forcefully. But if it *hadn't* been him, it was not smart to lay all my crazy cards on the table. I'd been so frantic for an explanation—

'Sylvie?' Paula called from the ground floor, softly

so as not to wake any sleepers. 'Did I hear you come in?'

With Rhys still frowning down at me, I changed gears and tried to salvage the situation. 'Yeah,' I called back in the same muted tone. 'I'm back, safe and sound.'

Well, physically sound, anyway.

Gigi wiggled in my grasp, eager to say hi. I grabbed her tags to keep them from jingling.

'Did you have a good time?' Paula asked, still a dis-embodied voice from below.

Was she going to insist on a briefing? I couldn't keep shouting down my answers in a stage whisper; that would be weird. And I couldn't carry Gigi to the railing with me, or the jig would be up. If I set her down, there was a good chance she would run to greet Paula herself.

I'd only wrestled with the dilemma for a moment before Rhys took the little dog from my arms and jerked his head towards the landing in silent instruc-tion. Nodding my distracted gratitude, I went to the balustrade, leaning over so Paula could set eyes on me and relieve her mind.

'Everyone was very nice,' I said, only lying a little bit.

Paula smiled in satisfaction. 'Didn't I say you'd be glad you went?'

'Yes you did.' I managed to keep my voice free of sarcasm, letting her interpret my ambivalent agree-ment as she wished.

'Well, goodnight then, honey. Don't stay up late reading.'

'I won't. Goodnight, Cousin Paula.' Returning to Rhys, I reached for Gigi – who was happily chewing on one of his fingers, which was not allowed – but he retreated through his doorway, and I had no choice but to follow if I wanted my dog.

The room was very similar to mine, though the colour scheme was more masculine – dark wood and faded reds and blues. Even the writing desk looked like the twin of mine, except stained dark brown instead of painted white.

Unlike my room, however, his was distinctly lived-in. There was a pile of books and papers on the writing desk, along with a laptop computer and assorted electronics, and a few clothes thrown over a chair. Rhys gestured for me to close the door. I did, and he set Gigi on the floor, where she went to investigate a kicked-off jumble of shoes. Rhys's feet were bare.

'You didn't answer me,' he said, sitting on the bed. 'What makes you think someone was watching you from the window?'

I shrugged, as casually as I could. 'Gigi growled up at it. I guess it could have been a shadow on the glass or something.'

He contemplated me seriously for a moment, maybe considering what I'd said versus what I hadn't. Then he shifted, crossing his ankle over his knee. 'Let me ask it this way instead. What made you think *I* would be watching you?'

'I don't know,' I said in frustration. It was the only thing that made even a little bit of sense. 'You were the one being all weird this afternoon. You obviously think I'm up to something.'

Denial rushed to his face, but he caught himself before he'd done more than open his mouth in indignation. He closed it, and seemed to chew on his next words for a long time. 'I don't know *what* to think about you, Sylvie.'

'Well, I don't know what to think about you either.' The height of understatement. The energy between us just then was not soothing or comfortable. It was charged, even in the way he said my name. I folded my arms, as if I could block out this push and pull on my emotions, and fired back inanely, 'For all I know, *you* may be up to something.'

I was only reflecting back the ridiculousness of the argument – a sort of 'I know you are, but what am I?' – but as soon as I said it, I thought about the way his expression had shuttered when I'd suggested he might be running away from something, like my own immigrant ancestors.

And the way it had closed off now. 'What would I be up to?' he asked too casually.

His reaction spurred me on. I threw out suggestions, just to see what he would say. 'I don't know. Maybe there's oil under the land. Maybe buried pirate treasure.'

That seemed to amuse him. 'I don't know anything about buried pirate treasure. If I did, though, I would definitely be looking for it.'

I narrowed my eyes, irritated but speculative. 'You admitted this afternoon that you have some secret project.'

He exhaled incredulously, not quite a laugh. 'I did not. I said I'm helping my father on *his* project and working on something of my own. *Not* searching for pirate treasure.'

'Maybe your dad is just a cover story.' I let my imagination expand to include the nonsensical. Not that pirate treasure was exactly reasonable. I put my hands on my hips, copying Paula's take-no-arguments stance. 'I haven't even seen him yet. Maybe he doesn't really exist.'

Rhys smiled slightly. 'Get up at a decent hour tomorrow, and you'll meet him.'

'Seven-thirty *is* decent. It's not like I have anywhere to be.'

'That's right.' He leaned back on his hands, tone turned mocking. 'The lady of leisure.'

'That's not—' And then I stopped, because he was doing it again. Whenever I pried into his business, he started goading me with accusations of divahood.

'That's not what?' he asked when I snapped my mouth closed and dropped my hands from my hips.

'Not important.' I waved a hand, made my tone as airy as possible and saw his eyes narrow, just a fraction. Gigi had curled up on the rug, and I stepped around her as I sauntered oh-so-casually to the writing desk, and the bunch of books by the computer. 'I mean, your dad must exist, since Clara and Paula aren't delusional. And you have all these books.'

He stood up as I ran my finger down the spines of the stack, reading titles aloud in the same offhand tone. '*North American Geology. Native Americans of the Southeast* – that must be how you knew about the mound builders.'

'You've become quite the girl detective in the twenty-four hours you've been here,' Rhys remarked, moving to join me at the desk. Pointedly, he reached across me and closed the laptop and the spiral notebook beside it.

Ignoring the comment, I picked up the last book, which showed its age in its tattered fabric cover. '*Notable Gardens of the South.*'

'That last one isn't mine,' he said. 'I found it here.'

I opened it to a marked page and saw a very old photograph of Bluestone Hill taken from a distance. When I looked up at him pointedly, he shrugged. 'Naturally I wanted to know more about this place.'

Holding the page with my finger, I flipped to the front to check the copyright date. It was a nineteen-sixties reprint of a turn-of-the-century book. 'Did you find this in the study?'

'No, actually. In this room.' He paused, then flipped a few pages, the book still in my hands. His fingers brushed mine, and I chided my heart for its erratic reaction. I was still . . . not angry, exactly. Perturbed – that was the thing. He perturbed and intrigued me more than a mere acquaintance should.

His words, though, evicted all that from my mind. 'Someone wrote in the margins,' he said. 'Maybe one of your relatives.'

My racing heart gave a funny stumble as the book fell open to a page of text, a photo of the knot garden and a woodcut print of the house's landscape. But my eye fixed on the pencilled notes along the side.

I sat down, landing in the chair only by accident, as my knees stopped working. 'This is my dad's writing.'

'Are you sure?'

'Yeah.' I traced the faint graphite lines. At first touch, they tickled my fingers, as if the letters were raised. They should have been. Raised or etched . . . something to denote the impact that script had on me. 'Maybe he wrote it when he was my age.' My voice sounded oddly fragile. 'Paula says they spent every summer here.'

'I wondered about that.' Rhys leaned back against the desk, strikingly casual compared with my awe at this find. 'When you mentioned that your father was interested in stone circles and monuments, I wondered if the monolith in your family's garden might have inspired him.'

'Maybe so.' I could see in the illustration that the rock was bare of foliage, just standing in the middle of the garden.

'You can take that with you, if you like.'

The offer shook me out of my fog. My eyebrows climbed and I shot him a look. 'You think? Since it's sort of mine, anyway.'

Rhys gave me the same sardonic stare, of the same mild intensity. 'So . . . you only get possessive about things here when it's something you want. It's Paula's house, but it's your book.'

'It *is* Paula's house.' We had come full circle to our last conversation. 'And I really don't have designs on it.'

'So you said.' He didn't sound censorious, though maybe a little droll. 'You have plenty of money.'

'That came out all wrong this afternoon.' My tone was half confession, half apology. 'I don't care about money.' I smoothed my hand absently over Dad's book, the picture of the garden and the rock, and the ghost of his thoughts on the page. 'All I want in the world is to be able to dance again.'

I felt a small shock at the words. I never spoke them aloud. It was too foolish to wish for, too selfish and ungrateful, when I was lucky to be able to walk. But the wish was always there, the seed of all my misery. Blurting it out was like pulling the ugly white roots of my anger and bitchiness into the light for this guy, who should be a stranger but didn't *feel* like one, to see.

'It's late,' I said, even though it wasn't really. Unable to look at Rhys, I slid out of the chair and went to pick up Gigi, who made a drowsy protest.

'Sylvie.' His voice, pitched low, caught me as I turned towards the door. I paused as he straightened from the desk, crossing the small distance. After the slightest hesitation, he touched my arm, and I forced my gaze up to his, just so I wouldn't have to call myself a coward.

The moment *slipped* somehow, with the sensation of a train that starts too abruptly, before you've braced yourself. Rhys's grip tightened, and I realized I'd actually swayed on my feet.

'I'm sorry,' he said.

'For what?' The question was breathless with the sudden sprinting of my pulse. It was the déjà vu again, the feeling that we could be talking about any incident, at any point in history, and not just the short time since we'd met.

'That this happened to you.' The vagueness of his answer stretched the moment longer. 'Having to re-think your whole life isn't easy.'

His guarded compassion made me wonder what he knew about needing to change plans. My brow fur-rowed, a tacit encouragement to explain. Instead, he withdrew, taking a step backwards and shoving his hands into the pockets of his jeans.

The surrealness vanished, with the gentle bump of returning to my feet after a long, inverted lift. I took a breath and let it out, collecting myself, searching for something to fill the silence. 'Well, thanks for the book. Sorry I accused you of being a creepy spy.'

Crap. I was pretty sure I winced visibly as soon as the words were out. I'd traded insane for inane. But Rhys seemed distracted too, maybe even a little relieved at the shift back to where we'd started this bizarre in-terlude.

'No problem.' He opened the door, but instead of stepping aside to allow me to pass, he went out first, looking up and down the hall. 'What was it you saw, ex-actly?'

So much for the hope he'd let the reminder pass. 'I saw a shadow on the glass of the French door to the balcony.'

He ventured to the landing, where he could see straight down the hall to the door. 'Nothing there now.'

'No.' There was indirect light from his room and

from mine at the other end. The temperature was cool, but not any more than the air-conditioned comfort of the rest of the house.

'You'll be all right?' He turned to me, then answered his own question with a hint of a smile. 'Of course you will. You've got your vicious little dog to protect you.'

Since my vicious little dog was snoring softly in the crook of my arm, the observation was not terribly comforting. I watched Rhys for signs he was humouring me, but he seemed to take me seriously – that I'd seen something, even if it wasn't him or his father.

'We'll be fine,' I said, though I wasn't sure of it at all.

He studied me a moment longer – but with no hint whether he bought my assurance. Whatever he was thinking, he merely said, 'Sleep tight, Sylvie,' and moved towards his door.

'You too,' I whispered, and went to my own room.

Once inside, with the door safely shut, I put the garden book on the desk and the dog on the bed and changed into my pyjamas, moving automatically through my nighttime routine, distracted by my thoughts.

When I'd washed my face and brushed my teeth, I stood in front of the desk, contemplating the secret drawer, and the paper inside. Where would I put any of this on the list? My conviction that the shadow had been someone watching me, and the out-of-proportion anxiety about it. The cold on the landing, and the inexplicable moment with Rhys—

Who was I fooling? Rhys would fill a page by himself.

Back to the watcher at the window. Maybe, like the creak of the chair in the study, there had been a tangible thing – a reflection, the drift of the curtain inside – that Gigi and I both saw. But that didn't explain my emotional reaction, and why I was so full of dread at the thought of discovery, when I hadn't been doing anything wrong.

I left the list where it was and grabbed the garden book, then climbed into bed with my vicious guard dog. Flipping the pages to the chapter on Bluestone Hill, I again traced the faded pencil of Dad's notes. I didn't try to decipher them in the soft lamplight. It was enough to let this evidence of his being here, of our occupying the same space in different times, connect me to his memory. Our travels together, his passion for growing things, for making art out of nature.

What would my father have thought of Rhys? I'd never had the chance to introduce Dad to a guy I was interested in. Though 'interested in' was an inaccurately mild way of describing what I felt. What happened tonight wasn't just attraction, or romantic tingles, or even déjà vu. When we connected like that, I was convinced – the way I was convinced I'd seen an aproned woman in the kitchen, the way I was sure someone had been watching me from the window – that Rhys and I were more to each other than we were. It would explain why – *sometimes* – I was so comfortable with him, why his smile seemed familiar, why his scent tripped my switch. And also why he could get under my skin with such ease.

If this were not a completely insane idea, I would have wondered if that was why Rhys seemed confused by me, too, as if he kept expecting me to react differently to things.

But that *was* crazy, and by now I was pretty sure that column would exceed the Not Crazy one by a mile. And that meant it was time to curl up with Gigi and try to get to sleep.

I set Dad's book down, but only as far away as the bedside table, and only after running my hand over it once again. Then Gigi, jealous I was petting the book more than her, wiggled under my arm and curled up under my chin.

Chapter 10

I'd meant to set the alarm – there was a vintage windup clock on the nightstand – but fell asleep so quickly that I forgot. I woke early anyway, thanks to the dog licking my face, telling me she was ready for a walk.

I got up on autopilot, splashed some water on my face, wondered sleepily why I had rose soap when it should be lilac.

The thought snapped me awake. I expected lilac as I moved through my routine at the washbasin. Which couldn't be *my* routine, because I'd only been here two mornings.

Gigi whined and danced on the corner of the bed, and I was grateful for the distraction. I threw on my jeans from the night before, a clean T-shirt and my hoodie against the morning chill, then picked up the dog. With the briefest peek out the door, I slipped down the hall. At the juncture I slowed, and then turned deliberately towards the French doors. The sun glowed on the sheer curtains and the air was warm.

I sighed, unsure what I was expecting, and went down the stairs, through the den and out the side doors. From there it was easier to go through the knot garden and avoid being seen from the kitchen windows on the way to the back yard.

I yawned while Gigi finished her business, then I cleaned up after her. *This* was my morning routine. Nothing rose-scented about it.

The worn wooden steps squeaked as I climbed to the screened porch. Through the kitchen door I saw Rhys at the table, and I felt that aggravating spark again – excitement, recognition, expectation. I collected myself, focused my energy on not letting anyone see anything odd in my demeanour. The Sylvie-is-not-crazy show must go on.

While I was distracted, Gigi pranced past me as if she owned the place. 'Lord, girl!' Clara called from the sink, where she was running water into a pot. 'Keep that dog out of here while I'm cooking.'

Annoyance flared and I tried to temper it with a reasonable argument. 'Can I just keep her away from the food? She's little and low to the ground.'

'The health inspector would love that.'

With a chagrinned start, I realized there was

another man at the table with Rhys, an older man who gave me a friendly smile as he stirred sugar into a mug of tea and said, 'You're not open yet, Clara, and I don't mind. My wife had so many dogs, I was forever picking hair out of my soup.'

'That's not the best argument for a dog in the kitchen, Dad.' Rhys spoke dryly into his own mug before taking a sip. He'd glanced rather inscrutably at me when I came in, as if he, like me, was trying to figure out what ground we were on today.

The older man was obviously Rhys's father. Besides the identical accent – and the fact that he'd called him 'Dad' – he also had the same facial structure – the cheekbones, the jaw, the arched brow – and the same wavy hair, though the professor's was white at the temples and scattered with silver.

He bent in his chair, clapping his hands to call Gigi. 'Come here, little one. Aren't you a darling thing.'

She bounded over and wasted no time charming the man with all her coy puppy tricks. I followed more slowly, and since Rhys didn't make the introduction, ventured, 'You must be Professor Griffith.'

'Indeed I am.' He smiled, and I pictured classrooms packed with infatuated coeds. 'And you must be Sylvie Davis. We finally meet.'

'You see,' said Rhys, with a tinge of humour. 'He does exist.'

My eyes snapped to him, my insides knotting in panic. His brows climbed at my reaction, and I realized he'd been teasing me. And he looked like he regretted it, so maybe he wouldn't say anything else about our late-night chat or my imagining stalkers at the window.

I escaped his gaze and busied myself washing my hands, glancing at the kettle on the stove. 'Is there still hot water?'

Clara set down another mug and pointed to a tin of assorted tea bags on the table. 'I guess Paula is the only coffee drinker. What will you have, Sylvie? Scrambled, poached or boiled?' I noticed 'none' was not an option. 'White or wheat toast?'

'Scrambled. And, um, wheat.' It was easier to agree than to argue about carbs. I picked a black tea, poured hot water over it, and sat in my usual spot.

As the professor played with Gigi, Rhys not-quite ignored me by straightening his spoon and napkin. I wondered if he also felt awkward and uncertain, as if we'd been up to more than talking last night. To distract myself, I tried to picture him in his family home, and wondered why his dad had talked about his mom in the past tense.

'What was your dog's name?' I asked.

'How's that?' Rhys's brows twisted in confusion. I supposed it was a non sequitur. I was way out of practice with small talk.

'One of those many dogs must have been yours. What was its name?'

He finished futzing with his cutlery and said sheepishly, 'Bendy Gaid Fran.'

'What?' I knew kids named dogs stupid things – I mean, Gigi, for heaven's sake – but Bendy Gaid Fran?

'Bendigeidfran,' said Professor Griffith. 'He was a hero of Welsh myth.'

I slid an 'I see' glance Rhys's way. 'A heroic hero, or one of those ambiguous types who kills people indiscriminately and then has to make up for it for twelve lifetimes?'

The professor laughed. 'I see you're familiar with Celtic archetypes.'

Shrugging, I pulled the tea bag from my mug. 'People draw on some weird legends for ballet. It's not all sugarplums and dancing candy canes.'

'They're really only strange to our modern sensibilities,' he said. 'The original tales of *The Arabian Nights,* for example—'

'Dad!' Rhys cut him off. 'That's not really breakfast conversation. And if you get started now, we'll be here all day, and unlike the princess here, we have things to do.'

So, we were back to that. I made a face at him, but didn't let it sidetrack me.

His father grimaced in chagrin. 'Sorry,' he said to me. 'I'm used to lecturing.'

'That's fine.' I looked at Gigi, who lolled on her back in the professor's lap, letting him rub her belly. 'Rhys said you teach anthropology?'

'Indeed I do, during the normal course of the year. I'm on sabbatical at the moment, doing some research.' He sipped his tea while absently petting the dog with his free hand, barely breaking his speech. 'Tomorrow, for instance, I am going to a state park where there are archaeological artifacts I am excited to see, in case they support a hypothesis I'm devel?op-ing.'

Clara set two plates on the table, one for me, and one for Rhys. He had Canadian-style bacon with his eggs. The toast was on an actual toast rack, and there was butter and orange marmalade. The Griffiths might not be official guests, since the inn wasn't officially open, but Clara was making them feel at home.

'Archaeological?' I asked, picking up my fork. 'Like the Native American mounds we saw on our way here? Is that what you're writing your book about?'

'No. Though they are fascinating, aren't they? Up near Tuscaloosa there is a whole city of them. The similarities to the flat-topped pyramids of Mesoamerica seems to be coincidental, but—'

'Dad . . .' Rhys warned.

'I know, Rhys. But she did ask. And we can't go anywhere until you eat.'

I glanced at Rhys. 'You're going too? More rock hunting?'

'Not exactly,' he said, cutting into his bacon with a frustrating lack of concern for my curiosity.

Professor Griffith reached for a piece of toast, and Gigi pricked her ears hopefully. 'I do hope Rhys's knowledge will be useful, though. We'll be examining ruins of a prehistoric fortification that uses construction techniques that were unknown to the Native Americans of the period to which the structure dates. They were, however, common techniques in Wales in the corresponding century.'

I stared at him blankly. 'You think there's some link

between the prehistoric culture here and the one in Wales?'

Clara came to the table, delivering more toast. 'Don't keep her from eating with your stories, Professor.'

He pointed to my plate with his corner of toast, indicating I should eat while he talked. Obediently I dug in. 'I'm on the trail of a – well, it's almost more of a folktale. There's a story that a Welsh prince came to the New World in the tenth century to establish a colony. Some people think he landed, as the Vikings did, in the northeast. But others believe he landed in Mobile Bay and sailed up the Alabama River.'

My fork paused on its way to my mouth. 'Seriously? I didn't think there were any Europeans in North America until the sixteen hundreds. Well, Leif Eriksson, but that was up in Canada, not way down here.'

The professor smiled in approval. I guess I had managed to learn something besides pirouettes. 'The Spanish landed in Mobile Bay in the fifteenth century, so why not a longboat a few hundred years earlier?'

I considered this as I grabbed a piece of toast. 'Then wouldn't this be – I don't know – Bendy Gaid Fran Land?'

Rhys shot me a glare, but his dad, who was enjoying telling his tale to fresh ears, just smiled tolerantly. 'The colony was a doomed enterprise, obviously. The settlers may have all died, or they may have been absorbed into the local people. French and Spanish explorers, when they finally did get to the region, told tales of fair-haired natives, and isolated tribes that – reportedly – spoke Welsh.'

'Seriously?' I chewed my toast and swallowed, fascinated by the story, curious about what parts might be real, and what was just legend. 'That's so wild.'

'Yes, but there's no solid proof,' said Rhys in a wet-blanket tone, 'so at the moment, it's just a story.'

'True,' his father agreed equably. Then to me he said, 'The most tangible link is the bluestone monolith in the middle of your garden.'

'The rock covered with vines?' I felt a spark of excitement, as if one small puzzle piece had just fitted into another, even though I had no idea what the big picture was. 'Paula said it was what gave the house its name. Bluestone is the type of rock?'

'Yes.' The professor's eyes lit with answering enthusiasm.

Rhys sighed, and corrected in a staid academic tone that didn't hide his exasperation with his father, 'British bluestone is correctly called Preseli dolerite, if you wish to be specific. Which you should, Dad.'

Professor Griffith waved that off, as if he had heard it often, which I bet he had. 'The point is, that particular type is found only in the Preseli Hills. And Stonehenge, of course.'

I sat forward, my breakfast forgotten. 'I remember this. Dad told me how whoever built Stonehenge had to get the bluestone all the way from a mountain range in Wales.'

'That's it,' said the professor. 'One of my goals is to find records that indicate whether your rock was here before the house was built, or if your ancestor brought it.'

'Paula doesn't know?' The William S. Davis book hadn't said. Or at least I hadn't run across any mention of the stone before my eyes had crossed with boredom.

Professor Griffith shook his head. 'She only knows it's been a curious feature of the gardens since anyone can remember. It's why I'm starting my research here. That, and it's just up the Alabama River from Mobile. Imagine how lucky I felt when a friend told me that Ms Davis was opening this place as an inn.'

I worked out the timing in my head. 'So you'd heard of Bluestone Hill before you knew of it as a place to stay.'

'Of course. It would be too coincidental otherwise, wouldn't it?' The professor smiled. 'Rhys read about it. Ran across mention of the house and the stone on the Internet while studying. Wasn't that it, Rhys?'

Rhys got up and took his plate to the sink as he replied. 'I don't remember, Dad.'

The vague answer felt evasive. So did the move to the sink, which put his back to us both. He definitely seemed to be hiding something.

But before I could question him, I heard a pickup pull up in front of the garage. And whether it was logic or something else, I knew exactly who it would be. Clara confirmed my instinct when she looked at the clock in surprise. 'Shawn's early. He must be eager for his last day of school.'

'Or something,' murmured Rhys, under the sound of running water. Did he mean me? I caught

Professor Griffith sort of smiling into his mug of tea, which hinted at yes.

How did Rhys know Shawn had been paying me attention? I didn't think he'd seen us together. Had he been listening to Teen Town Council gossip?

Shawn came in noisily, bounding up the porch steps, letting the screen door slam behind him. I braced myself instinctively, the way you brace yourself before a wave at the beach – determined not to let it bowl you over, yet with some enjoyment for the sensation of the water washing over you. But when he flashed me a smile, I was helpless not to smile back, just a little bit.

Even that made me feel fickle, at best. I glanced at Rhys, who was giving his studied attention to drying his dish.

'Morning, all,' Shawn said, very much the bon vivant, then greeted the elders by name, like a well-?mannered Southern boy. 'Prof, Miss Clara.'

The professor nodded, intent on sneaking Gigi a crust of bread, and Clara smiled at him on her way to the fridge. Rhys didn't respond at all, unless you counted the stiff set of his shoulders and the fact that he didn't even turn round.

'Have a seat, Shawn,' said Clara. 'Addie's not down yet.'

'That's fine.' He took the seat nearest me at the table, the one Rhys had vacated. 'I'll sit here and see how our visitor is enjoying Alabama.'

'Hi, Shawn.' He had the charisma turned up to full this morning. But the cynical observation didn't stop the slow flush of warmth as he grinned at me. 'Last day of school?'

'Yep.' He leaned his elbows on the table. 'I've got the afternoon free, if you want to take me up on that tour guide offer.'

Returning to his co-opted spot, Rhys reached past Shawn and picked up his half-full mug. 'Excuse me,' he said, pointedly polite. 'I'll just get this out of your way.'

'Oh, I'm sorry, man.' Shawn sat back in the chair, obviously not sorry at all. 'Was that your cup of tea?'

His tone turned 'cup of tea' into something dainty. Rhys responded with an understated 'Yes,' and left *Your point?* unspoken. On the surface, they could have been two guys giving each other a hard time. But there were oceans of subtext in the exchange. The only thing I could see for certain was their clear and established dislike for each other.

Clara set a glass of OJ in front of Shawn, dispelling the testosterone moment, and frowned at my plate. 'Those eggs aren't going to do you any good if you don't eat them.' I obediently pushed the remains around with my fork. 'Help yourself to some toast, Shawn,' she said. 'I'll go hurry up Addie.'

Rhys downed the rest of his tea and put the mug in the sink. 'I'm off. Dad, I'll see you later. Don't talk Sylvie to death.'

'Yes, General.' The professor had an absentminded academic thing going on and seemed content to let his son manage him.

'More treasure hunting?' I ribbed him without

thinking, noting he was wearing his hiking boots and sturdy clothes again. After all, he'd started the morning with that comment about his father's existence proved. But Rhys stiffened, and glared at me in a quickly checked warning.

What had I said? Was it because Shawn was here? My joke had definitely upped the tension another notch, which was the exact opposite of my intention.

Shawn raised his brows, and turned in his chair to look at Rhys. 'Are you searching for buried treasure, Griffith? Funny, you don't look like a pirate.'

The muscle in Rhys's jaw clenched and released. 'I'm off to Old Cahawba. I'm helping with the archaeological excavation there. They need to get it done before some land developer runs roughshod over the place.'

He spoke to me, but that last part was aimed at Shawn. The girls last night had said Cahawba was a sore spot with the Maddoxes and their new development.

Shawn smiled, but I noticed a little tightening around his eyes. 'Good thing that state land is protected from *evil* folks who want to build stuff that will bring more business to the area. Including more traffic to the park.'

Before Rhys could reply, Addie came banging in the back door, nearly running him down. 'Sorry,' she murmured, then flung herself into a seat and pointed to Shawn's orange juice. 'Are you going to drink that?'

'Help yourself,' he said.

I glanced towards the door, but Rhys had departed. I wrestled with mixed feelings of disappointment and frustration, and turned to Shawn for answers instead. 'I take it you're the evil land developer?'

'My dad is.' He grabbed a piece of toast and the butter dish, seeming completely at ease now that Rhys had gone. 'Maddox Point is going to bring more people to the area. It'll be great for the town, which will be great for everyone. And the park, too, if they wouldn't freak out about it.'

'Where is it going to be?' I asked.

'Upriver from here.' He flashed that engaging smile, his blue eyes bright. 'I'll show you around if you want. As I may have mentioned, I'm free this afternoon.'

'Not today.' It came out more curt than I intended. I was curious about Old Cahawba. It kept cropping up, first in the Davis book, then again at dinner. But it struck me as wrong to accept Shawn's invitation right after he'd argued – well, exchanged veiled barbs – with Rhys. It seemed like I would be choosing sides somehow.

All the same, I softened my refusal. 'I'm sure you have better things to do on your first afternoon of freedom. Don't you want to celebrate with your friends?'

He gave an exaggerated frown, rubbing his square jaw. 'Let's see. Hang out with a bunch of guys I've known my whole life, or spend time with the cute girl from out of town. Not really a contest.'

There was a cheeky self-awareness in his quick smile, and that, more than the heavy-handed compliment, made me blush. Or maybe it wasn't a blush but the warmth of his attention. I only vaguely heard Professor Griffith chuckle behind his newspaper, barely noticed the roll of Addie's eyes and Clara's poorly hidden smile as she set a plate of bacon and hastily scrambled eggs in front of her daughter.

I was shaken to discover how hard it was to tell him no. In a way, that strengthened my resolve. 'I've got some things I want to do today. Some other time.'

'Suit yourself.' He didn't seem offended, just stuffed the rest of his toast in his mouth and asked conversationally, 'So, have you seen any more ghosts?'

I blinked, hoping my rush of panic didn't show in my face. 'Any *more* ghosts?' Crap. What had I given away yesterday? 'I haven't seen any at all.'

Addie pointed out between bites, 'You said you heard a cat, when it couldn't be a cat.'

It figured she would pick this point to stop ignoring me. 'But I never said I thought it was a ghost.' I cast back through my memory, which was possibly as flawed as my perception. But I was certain I'd been careful what I'd said. Paranoia will do that.

'What are y'all talking about?' asked Clara as she came to the table and picked up on the atmosphere.

'About how there's no such thing as ghosts,' I said firmly.

'Actually' – Professor Griffith had been reading the paper, Gigi still in his lap, but he lowered it as the conversation got interesting, and reached for tea, as casually as if we were talking about the weather – 'it *is* interesting how the idea of lingering spirits is something that crosses so many cultural divisions.'

'Professor, don't *you* start,' chided Clara.

Round the corner, I heard the door to Paula's bedroom open and close. Clara looked a warning at me. 'Sylvie . . .'

'I know, I know. Paula doesn't like superstitious talk.'

'No. Get the dog out of here.' She dried her hands on a dish towel, then flung it over her shoulder. 'And Addie, you eat up. You and Shawn have to scoot off to school.'

The professor handed me the dog and we exchanged guilty – though not really – smiles. Shawn stood up as well, while Addie wolfed down her eggs. 'I'll walk you out,' he said, and gestured me ahead of him onto the porch.

Once there, I gave Gigi some breakfast, so she was happy to hang out in her crate for a while. As accustomed as I was to an audience, I was still very aware of Shawn watching me fill the dog's water bowl. 'So, Sylvie,' he asked amiably, leaning a shoulder against one of the posts supporting the porch roof. 'Is the English guy the reason you have other things to do this afternoon?'

I shot a tart look up at him from my crouch by Gigi's crate. I might have been more tolerant of his feeling out the competition, except for the animosity I'd seen between him and Rhys. It made my answer a little prickly. 'No. Incredible as it sounds, I actually have other things to do.'

Shawn laughed, taking the pushy out of his persistence. 'You don't sugarcoat things, do you?'

I arched a brow. 'Not the second time I have to say them.'

Raising his hands in surrender, he said, 'I get it. But let me pick you up this way, at least.' With a disarming smile, he took both my hands and pulled me effortlessly to my feet. His fingers tightened as I swayed, finding my balance, and the warmth of his skin spread to mine, up my arms, over my shoulders, soothing any irritation at his presumption.

To my surprise, I found myself rethinking my plans for the afternoon. Then Addie came banging out of the kitchen door. 'Come on, Shawn. You can flirt with Sylvie later.'

As she stalked off to his truck, Shawn's smile softened with sheepish regret, and his thumbs trailed the backs of my hands as he let me go. 'Duty calls. See you later, maybe.'

I made a noncommittal sound, but he was already hurrying away. Probably a good thing.

Crap. Was I really this fickle?

The energy I felt with Shawn was completely different than with Rhys. Shawn's charisma was like a high-wattage lightbulb. It pulled at me like a splash of sunshine on the carpet pulls a cat on a cold day. I wanted to bask in that warmth.

Rhys's effect on me was like a magnetic field. Invisible, inconspicuous, indisputable. The thing about magnets was they could draw or repulse, depending on which end you got. And I never knew which it was going to be.

While I tried to compare apples and oranges, and

Gigi crunched her kibble, Professor Griffith stepped through the door Addie had left open, carrying his mug. In his button-down shirt and cardigan he made a comfortably frumpy picture, especially as he sipped his tea, looking after Shawn's departing red pickup. 'That young man is full of charm.'

'Yeah.' Now that he was gone, I was a little embarrassed at how completely I'd been bowled over by tidal wave Shawn. 'Clearly there's no love lost between him and Rhys, though.'

The professor smiled ruefully. 'As an anthropologist, I could comment on the sociobiology behind young males and perceived territory.'

I frowned at his word choice. 'I hope you don't mean me.'

'Not entirely,' he said, missing the point of my protest. 'They've been at odds since they laid eyes on each other. Rhys only said that Shawn reminded him of someone.'

Someone he didn't like, obviously. I glanced cautiously towards the kitchen, where I could see Paula and Clara chatting. I wanted to ask Professor Griffith about what he'd said about lingering spirits, but I worried it would give something away. Though, even if I'd never seen anything strange, I would be naturally curious. I figured as long as I kept my interest casual, I wouldn't raise the crazy flag.

'So, Professor Griffith,' I began, oh so idly, 'about what you said in there, about different cultures having ghost stories . . .'

'Ah yes.' He perched on the arm of the wicker

settee, looking pleased at the opportunity to continue his lecture, and apparently finding nothing odd in my bringing it up again. 'The idea of some tangible psychic impression on a physical location is quite common.'

I sat on the cushioned chair, taking the weight off my leg. 'What do you mean, "psychic impression"?'

He finished his sip of tea and answered in the same academic tone. 'Some people think of ghosts in the traditional restless-spirit way. Souls who can't move on because of unfinished business.'

'Like Hamlet's ghost,' I said. A fitting reference, since some people think Hamlet was just imagining his father's spirit as a precursor to going bananas.

But Professor Griffith nodded. 'Yes. But another theory to explain people's experiences is that people or events might leave a stamp on a place. Perhaps it's a big thing that happened once – like the scene of a past murder that always feels cold. Or something routine that happened for years – like reports of sentries who still walk castle battlements.'

'So, hypothetically speaking' – I kept my tone light – 'have you ever thought you'd seen a ghost?'

He shrugged affably. 'Hasn't everyone had some inexplicable experience? A feeling of being watched; a glimpse of something in the corner of one's eye, gone as soon as you turn?'

My heart gave a jolt of recognition, which I tried to keep out of my face. 'But no one has ever proved anything.'

'That depends on your level of proof,' said the

professor. 'Ghost hunters point to all kinds of things as evidence. Blurry streaks on photos, static on recordings, changes in temperature or electrical fields—'

'Changes in temperature?' The question shot out, spurred by my memory of the chill out on the lawn, and the lingering cold at the top of the stairs.

But the professor merely nodded, still taking my interest as academic. 'Temperature changes are a measurable event that paranormal investigators look for. But most reported experiences are subjective. How do you record a *feeling*?'

I chewed my lip, choosing my words carefully. 'Seriously, Professor. Do *you* believe any of this stuff? Isn't it kind of crazy?'

He chuckled, so I must have hit the right note. 'I do not discount people's experiences. Though I would look for a natural explanation before a paranormal one.' Smiling, he gave a 'what the hell' shrug. 'However, I allow that just because something hasn't been proven to my satisfaction doesn't mean that it *couldn't* exist.'

In other words, yes and no. The professor was well educated, and seemed reasonable and functional. 'Open-minded but critical' sounded like a good approach. I didn't want to believe in ghosts, but I didn't want to believe I was nuts, either.

Gigi was done eating, and came trotting out of her open crate, expecting praise for finishing her breakfast. It was a timely interruption. Bending to give the dog due worship hid my face while I processed what had been said.

The professor finished his tea and stood. 'I'd best

get on with my day. If I'm not done with my next chapter when Rhys gets back, he'll know it was because I was lecturing again.'

I glanced up, with a tentative smile. 'I wouldn't want you to get into trouble. But I appreciate you chatting with me.'

'Any time. Those ghost-hunter shows are a guilty pleasure of mine – as a cultural anthropologist, I'm interested in the folklore aspect.' He grimaced sheepishly. 'And as you've probably noticed, I do love to share my obsessions.'

I picked up Gigi, then realized I had an opening to pry about more than supernatural theories. It didn't seem quite fair – not least because Professor Griffith was such a nice guy – but I felt at such a disadvantage, I could reconcile a little cheating.

'You're pretty lucky, though,' I said, striking as casual a tone as I could, 'that Rhys took a break from school to help with your research.'

The professor nodded, but his answer was coloured with regret. 'I *am* lucky, though I wish he hadn't put his own thesis on hold to do it. Still, I can understand his wanting to take a break after what happened.'

My conscience stabbed at me, because that was too easy. But not so much that I didn't ask the obvious question. 'What happened?'

He hesitated, then gave an almost invisible shrug. 'He doesn't like to talk about it, but I don't know why – there's nothing shameful in it. He was on an externship between terms, in the mountains, when an abandoned slate mine collapsed.'

'Oh my God.' I had a vivid image of the groan of

earth, and suffocating darkness. The stuff of real nightmares. Rhys had said something last night, about having to redirect your whole way of thinking. Had the poignancy in his voice been related to this? 'Was anyone hurt?'

'It wasn't as bad as it could have been, considering. But some of Rhys's fellow interns were injured. His friend was in a coma for some time. He's having to learn to walk again.'

The guilt knife twisted, but not because of my prying. No wonder Rhys had no patience with me. I couldn't dance professionally, but I could walk. The limp wasn't even bad unless I was tired. It was a wonder he spoke to me at all.

Professor Griffith sighed, and reached out to pet Gigi's soft ears. 'Rhys feels somehow responsible. I haven't figured out why. But he wouldn't appreciate my talking about it.'

'I'll keep it to myself,' I vowed, and meant it.

As he reentered the kitchen, I went to the screen door, planning to go out and round to the main stairs, to avoid incurring Paula's puppy-in-the-kitchen wrath. I did linger a moment, watching as the professor greeted the women at the breakfast table, just to make sure he didn't report back to them that I'd been asking suspicious questions about ghosts.

Whatever he said, it didn't make them turn my way, and I was glad my instincts had been right. I liked Rhys's dad, in a refreshingly uncomplicated way.

Which didn't mean I could let down my guard.

Chapter 11

Paula looked up in surprise as I came into the kitchen with my sneakers on, ready for a trek. 'Going somewhere?'

'I thought I'd go to Old Cahawba.' I'd meant to spend time with Dad's book, but my thoughts were too muddled for me to enjoy it. I felt a need to move, to channel my spinning brain into physical action.

She stared at me with a growing frown of concern. 'Are you sure, honey? That's a mighty long walk, and you're not exactly able-bodied.'

If I hadn't been sure before, I was after that. 'I'll be fine,' I said, hardly gritting my teeth at all.

Clara said more kindly, 'Of course you will. You have your cell phone so you can call if you need us?'

I hadn't thought about the phone since talking to John the night I'd arrived, but I slid my hand into my jeans pocket and found I'd grabbed it automatically. 'I'm good.'

After another sigh from Paula and an admonition to be back for lunch, I snapped on Gigi's leash and we set out down the great lawn towards the woods. The plume of her tail rode at a jaunty angle, and she showed no qualms at diving into nature.

At the forest's edge I paused, because the route would take us in the direction of the wailing sound I'd heard three times now. Open-minded or not, I wasn't keen to invite inexplicable experiences. But Gigi didn't seem interested in anything but the trail.

Trekking through the dappled shade wasn't much like striding down the streets of Manhattan. The looming pines and thick oaks made a sort of rustic palace, with a carpet of pine needles and tapestries of Spanish moss. To my right was the faint music of the river. Paula had warned me it ran too fast for safe swimming, but to the ear it was lazy and comforting.

We came to a fence, but there was a stile that made it easy to go over – if you weren't encumbered by a wiggling dog and a fear of falling. I managed not to drop either of us and, with an unfamiliar feeling of pleasure, I continued down the path, idly imagining who had taken it before me. The trees showed no hint of an old road. This would be a shortcut for servants going into town, or for the boys of the house to run to meet their playmates. The girls would be forced to go by carriage, to preserve their dresses and dignity.

I wondered if the girl who'd lived in my room, back when the floral wallpaper and dainty furniture were new, had found that as annoying as I would have. Maybe it was sleeping on the antique mattress or using her washbasin and cupboard. Maybe it was Paula's strictures, like those of an overzealous governess. In any case, like yesterday in the garden, I found myself wondering how I would feel in her shoes.

The path finally met a dirt road. I was either on park property or trespassing on someone's land. I hadn't bothered consulting a map. I knew from the Davis book that the old capital was at the junction of the rivers I'd seen from the balcony, and had headed in that direction.

Gigi and I continued along the road – both of us slowing down a bit – until we reached the decaying remains of a two-storey, columned box of a mansion that looked a little like it could be Bluestone Hill's aged and shrunken poor relation. There was a sign on the split-rail fence in front of the house that indicated I had indeed reached Old Cahawba Archaeological Park.

According to the plaque, this had been the house of a prominent family during the town's heyday. After the population largely decamped for Selma during the Reconstruction, the house was bought by one of the former slaves, who'd lived there until his death in the early nineteen hundreds.

It seemed like it would be weird to go back to a place where you were owned. But maybe it was awesome. I hoped the man filled the house with children and went to bed every night with a smile of smug contentment.

My musings seemed to blur my vision, and I grasped the fence, its wood smooth with age. For a moment I could see the ruin of the place, and on top of it, like a projection slide, was a freshly painted house with a manicured yard. When I blinked, it was gone, and I was again looking at a sagging roof and falling-down porch.

I rubbed my hand over my eyes. Maybe this hadn't been such a great idea. I was tired, but didn't want to acknowledge that Paula had been right. My leg was weak, and it had been a long walk. I'd been exhausted the night I arrived at Bluestone Hill, too. Maybe it was fatigue that allowed these impressions to sneak up on me, weave into my consciousness and seem too real.

Gigi pulled at her leash, eager to investigate the dilapidated place. I shuddered at the thought of rats, and walked on, tugging her along with me.

There weren't many standing houses or even ruins; here or there was the rubble of foundation, the spar of a support beam, but mostly empty flat plots of land. 'Ghost town' seemed very appropriate. The trees looked like they grew around invisible shapes, the ground flattened under unseen weight. Here was proof that the impact of something on its environment could outlast its physical form.

But that was a house, not a person. Still, it made me consider what the professor had said, about impressions of the past. Was it possible that servants passing from kitchen to dining room, all day every day for at least a hundred years, could wear a pattern in the atmosphere of the house like wearing a path in a carpet?

My mental rambles were taking me to a dangerous place, one where I was making impossible things sound reasonable. Fortunately, I was distracted by the fact that my physical ramble had reached an asphalt road.

A street sign – definitely not a hundred and fifty years old – indicated I was at the corner of Capital and Oak, in the Old Cahawba Historical Site.

I turned onto Capital and headed towards the gleam of sunlight on the river. The trees opened up into a broad avenue, and I imagined it – deliberately this time – as a bustling street full of horses and buggies and men in tall hats.

Envisioning the place full of people made it less lonely; Gigi and I seemed to have the park to ourselves. I hadn't felt odd in the woods or the side road. But walking the thoroughfare seemed peculiar, as if I was identifying a little too closely with my great-great-whatever, who would have shocked everyone if she'd walked the main street alone.

The street ended – *finally* – in a traffic circle, with a crumbling stone column in the centre. I picked my way across the grass surrounding the monument, and while Gigi sniffed the base, I read the inscription carved on the side:

CAHABA FIRST STATE CAPITAL
1818–1826

According to William S. Davis, Esq., my great-times-six-grandfather had been a mover and a shaker in Cahawba/Cahaba. It seemed no one could decide whether there was a *w* or not. I looked back down the empty avenue, then turned in a slow circle, my eyes following a pitted dirt road that made a horseshoe around what must have once been the centre of town.

It was eerie, really, how a town substantial enough to be the capital could have disappeared so completely. Maybe that was the source of my unease as Gigi and I started walking across the flat, tree-dotted space between the monument and the river bluff. Across the field was a brick column, a forlorn remnant of some industrial space. This must have been the commercial district – at the end of the main street, near the river – the interstate of the eighteen hundreds.

The ground was slightly uneven, but that wasn't what made me pause as I reached the centre of the horseshoe road. It was cooler than the shade could account for. More than cool. Chilly. The humid morning had turned clammy, as if the sun were obscured by more than the towering oaks with their draping of moss.

Great. The power of suggestion was not my friend. The professor had mentioned cold and now my imagination ran away with me in every draughty, shady place. *Get it together, Sylvie.*

I pushed forward just to prove that I wasn't affected, that I didn't believe this was anything other than a breeze from the river. Gigi had to pick up her feet as we trekked through grass and pine needles. She didn't look happy about it.

As I got closer I realized that the brick remnant wasn't a column, but a chimney. Stubbornness gave way to curiosity – a chimney without a house? – and I would have gone on, but Gigi sat down and refused to move. At the end of the leash, I stopped too, listening to Gigi's electric-motor growl, and the sudden sound of my heartbeat in my own ears.

The soft, subliminal rush of the river disappeared, and the sunshine seemed to dim, as if we'd stepped through a curtain. The chill I'd tried to ignore rushed in, moving with the currents of air to stroke my skin like fingers. The cold crawled up my legs and spread through my body, and I shuddered with a despairing ache.

Sorrow and hopelessness pressed in on me like a funeral crowd. I gasped, and my stomach cramped at a fetid smell. In that instant, I did believe I was mad, because no one in their right mind would imagine such thorough wretchedness.

Then came a completely pedestrian sound – the honk of a car horn. Gigi barked and ran for the dirt horseshoe road. The six-pound jolt was minor, but enough to shake me back into motion. The gripping strangeness fell away as I stumbled after the dog into the welcome sunshine.

There were picnic tables by the river bluff, on the other side of the dirt road. Numb and bewildered, but fully myself again, I walked to one, limping hard, and sat down. Gigi leaped into my lap. With a trembling hand, I wiped a line of sweat from my lip, and looked at the spot I'd just crossed.

What the hell was that? The moment had the intensity of a plunge into an icy, dark well, but there was nothing to mark it. No evocative old ruin, no shadow at a window, no military relics in an old man's study. Where could it have come from but my own mind?

There was no denying – though my returning reason floundered desperately in the attempt – that the echoes could have come from my psyche. The days when the pills were too tempting, when I could barely make myself get out of bed. The days when I didn't. There weren't many; I didn't like to admit there were any. I wanted to believe I'd never been that weak. But the cold had flooded me with those memories. I would swear I had felt grasping hands dragging me back to that painful, bleak time.

But what had prompted it? Yes, my leg hurt, but what else was new. Since coming to Alabama, I'd felt more connected to the world than I had in a long time. I didn't feel back to normal, because without dance I didn't know what normal was. But I didn't feel crazy. Even in those moments when there was no other explanation for what I was sensing.

Gigi gave a warning bark, and I heard the sound of an engine a moment later. A pickup truck bounced towards us, around the bend of the dirt road.

The disorienting fear of the past few moments solidified into something more specific. I was alone out here. Alone and at the mercy of faulty senses. My pulse trip-hammered in my neck as I scooped up Gigi and stood.

'Hey there, little lady.' The truck stopped beside us

and a twinkling-eyed Santa Claus of a man hung a sun-burned elbow out the window as he greeted me. He didn't look much like an axe murderer, and I was relieved to see the logo of the park stitched on the front of his polo shirt. 'You doing OK?'

'Yes,' I said warily. Did I look like I was about to do a header into the river? Anxiety and confusion sat on me like elephants on a circus trainer, but the cold and despair were gone.

Santa seemed to find my suspicion amusing. 'You're limping quite a bit, and I was worried you might have twisted your ankle on the grass. It can be uneven after the spring rains.'

'Oh!' Relief drained some of the tension from my shoulders. 'No. I just— It's an old injury. And I've been walking a while. I didn't realize this place was so big.'

'Lordy! Where did you walk from?'

'Bluestone Hill.' I gestured vaguely in the direction I'd come. The man's practical warmth had pushed my worry into a corner, where I could ignore it until later. 'I'm—'

A grin split his white beard. 'I know exactly who you are, Miss Davis.' He reached across the wheel to stick his right hand out the window. I shook it automatically. 'I'm Jim Young. I'm friends with Paula and Clara. And with your fellow houseguests.'

'The Griffiths?' I felt a satisfying click of comprehension. This was the mutual friend, then.

Mr Young chuckled. 'Don't I look like a world-travelling archaeologist-turned-folklorist in my retirement?'

'You look like Kriss Kringle.' The observation slipped out, surprising me. I didn't joke with strangers. Or anyone, really.

He laughed loudly, and didn't seem offended. 'Are you looking for Rhys? He's over by the dig.' He made a vague and unhelpful gesture.

I shook my head. 'I'm trying to find out more about my family's history. Which today, I guess, means finding out more about this place.'

Delight lit his jolly face. 'My dear girl, you have made my day.' He put the truck back in gear and gestured for me to step back. 'Let me move off the road.'

There was no way to avoid his joining me. If I'd wanted a tour guide, I could have taken Shawn up on his offer. But I'd wanted to explore alone. The wildness of the place made me want to poke into its corners and lift its figurative carpets.

Or it had, until the awful moment under the trees. Suddenly the distraction of company seemed a good thing.

When Mr Young rejoined us, Gigi sniffed excitedly at his trouser legs and he bent to pet her. 'So, what do you want to know?'

'What happened to the town?' It was good to focus on practical questions. And this way, I could find out some facts without having to go back to William the Boring.

He chuckled. 'Which time? A lot has happened here.' He gestured for me to follow him to the gap in the trees at the river bluff. I stopped a few feet back: the bank was steep, and the water was a long way down. Paula's warning against swimming made a lot of sense.

'The Native Americans had a community here first,' said Mr Young, deciding to start at the beginning, I guess. 'Though it was gone by the time Cahaba was settled. It's a natural place for a settlement, of course, since it's the juncture of two rivers. Which means easy transportation and irrigation, and the land is very fertile.'

He pointed to where a smaller river joined the wide swath of the Alabama coming from the north. Maybe it was Dad's influence, but I found it interesting how the lay of the land affected civilization, before we started changing the terrain to suit us. However, that wasn't what I'd asked. 'And this became the capital?' I prompted.

My attempt at subtlety failed, judging by Mr Young's grin. 'Cahaba, at its peak, was a thriving community, and the home to three thousand people. Vine Street was lined with stores and businesses. There was a fancy hall for dances, a female academy, two churches, and, of course, the state house.'

My gaze ran over the empty roads he indicated, and I pictured them lined with buggies, the way New York streets are lined with cars. The contrast between my serene and rustic walk and the bustling city he described was disconcerting. 'What happened to all of it?'

'Things go in cycles, don't they? That's the funny thing about Cahaba. Things were booming, and then there was a yellow fever epidemic, then a flood, and finally the state voted to move the capital to Tuscaloosa.'

'Well, who could blame them,' I said. 'If disaster struck twice.' That would be the river's fault; the asset was also a liability. I prodded him to get to the point. 'So a flood wiped out the town?'

'Oh no.' He was clearly enjoying the story too much to let me rush him. 'It was a setback, but the pendulum swung back the other way. Cahaba was a major shipping point for the cotton plantations in the area. Which, of course, you know, as a Davis. Steamboats ran up and down the river, carried the crops out to Mobile, then on to textile plants in the North and in Europe.'

'Then what?' I didn't bother to hide my impatience, but there wasn't much bite to it. Not in the face of Mr Young's humour. 'Was there another flood?'

He grimaced ruefully. 'Among other things – like the war. The railroad was torn up, its iron used for a more strategic line. That was the beginning of the end, in a way. In 1866, when the county seat moved to Selma, a lot of families did, too. Lock, stock and barrel.'

'But not the Davises,' I said, rather unnecessarily, trying to fit the story together. 'What about the Maddoxes? Were they here from the beginning too?'

'Oh yes. Bluestone Hill weathered everything better than the town. The Maddox family established the new town downriver. In fact, they gave an incentive to families to move their houses there instead of Selma.'

'The whole house?' The image – buildings taken apart like Lincoln Logs and put back together again – was startling. 'That's why there are so few structures here?'

He nodded. 'Even after the war, with all the manufacturing in the North, it was difficult and expensive to get building materials down here. So what wasn't moved wholesale was cannibalized.' He grinned with enthusiasm. 'But it left the underground stuff for us diggers to find.'

We'd walked as we talked, and now we were coming up on the spot where the chimney stood eerily alone under the trees. It gave no sense of warmth, only the impression of bitter cold.

'What was this place?' I asked, nodding to the brick relic. 'Where the chimney was?'

'That was the Cahaba Federal Prison.' He cleared his throat delicately. 'For prisoners of war. Union soldiers.'

I fought a shiver, even at a distance. The complete logic of it was a shock of confirmation. A Civil War prison would give anyone the horrors. But how could I have known that, even subconsciously? Had I read it in the Davis book? Would that explain my certainty that something *bad* had happened here, something that re-verberated through my psyche?

'Did it flood, too?' I asked.

'Among other things.' Mr Young's Santa Claus face turned grim. 'The conditions were very bad by the end of the war. Overcrowded, disease-ridden. Prison mortality was bad on both sides, but I can't pass this place without thinking this was a low mark in human nature.'

I looked at him fully, curious at his phrasing. Did he feel something too? Like me, he'd stopped walking rather than go any nearer.

Gigi pawed at my leg, asking to be picked up. I

obliged, cuddling her close. Was this the kind of haunting Professor Griffith had talked about? I still rejected the idea of ghosts, but there was – seemed to be – the imprint of something horrible here, like a stain that wouldn't come out in the wash.

'Enough about that,' said Mr Young, determinedly steering us back into the metaphorical sunlight. Less figuratively, he took my arm and turned us both away from the prison's spectre, guiding me over the uneven ground, towards his truck. 'What else can I show you while we're here, Miss Sylvie?'

Maybe it was asking for trouble, all things considered. But I wanted – needed – to know more about the past, and the people in it. 'I'd like to see the cemetery, actually.'

He grinned like Christmas had come early. 'You are truly a girl after my own heart.'

※ ※

I could see how Mr Young and Professor Griffith were friends. They had the same love of imparting their knowledge. In Mr Young's case, it was the history of Cahaba, and the cemetery was the perfect place for it.

I'd been nervous when he'd pulled the truck up by the cemetery fence. Whether the moment by the river was the suggestive environment working with my overwrought emotions, or something I didn't want to speculate, this was a *graveyard*.

But the morning was warm and the only shadows

were the ones from the spreading oaks. It felt more peaceful than lonely, despite the way the age- and weather-darkened monuments were left abandoned, broken and tumbled.

Gigi flopped onto a pillow of shaded grass, her tongue hanging out. I didn't blame her. My legs were tired and aching, and they were a lot longer than hers. But there was still something I was after, so I looped her leash around a branch and left her to nap while I followed Mr Young around the cemetery.

'Where are the Davises?' I asked.

'Oh, you won't find them here. The Davis family is buried in Saint Mary's churchyard.' He waved vaguely towards Bluestone Hill. 'It's past your place, on down the river just a bit, before you get to Maddox Landing.'

Maybe I was cranky because my leg hurt – I hadn't walked so far since The Accident, and most of it on unpaved ground – but he could have mentioned that earlier.

Oblivious to my frown, he went on enthusiastically. 'There are a couple of Maddox graves, though. You might be interested in those, since your families are so connected.'

I wondered what he meant by that. Addie had said something similar, if 'connected' was Mr Young's tactful way of saying 'inbred'.

He started across the grounds, waving for me to follow. I had to pick my way carefully over molehills and around fallen stones. I rejoined Mr Young at a sturdy but rusted fence. An ornamental pear tree shaded a plot containing three large monuments and several smaller ones, all eroded and darkened by the elements, but pristine compared with some of the others in the cemetery.

'The tree and the marble would have been brought here from elsewhere,' said Mr Young. 'Someone wanted dear old dad to be comfortable.'

'And had the money to make sure of it,' I mused, squinting at the inscription: MATTHEW MADDOX, PATRIARCH AND STATESMAN. 1785–1860. 'Wow, he was really old.'

Mr Young gave me a disapproving look. 'That's the same age as me, little missy.'

I grimaced. 'I meant for the time.'

'Well, that's true enough.' He nodded to the ornate monument, the fanciest in the cemetery. 'Mr Maddox was on the state legislature, the lone dissenting vote against moving the capital. His son went up to Tuscaloosa, though. The Maddoxes have always been politicians.' Mr Young smiled at some private joke. I sort of knew what he meant, though. Shawn had that good old boy charm and I'd seen hints of his leadership in the way he handled the Teen Town Council.

I noticed something else as I looked over the other stones in the plot. 'There are some Davises here. They're just all married to Maddoxes.'

Mr Young nodded, starting towards the cemetery gate. 'That's what dynasties do – secure alliances with marriages.'

'What kind of alliances?' I caught up to him easily.

'Business, of course. Your family grew the cotton; the Maddox family shipped it. The Davises owned the ironworks across the river, which made the parts to build Maddox steamboats.'

'Huh.' I collected Gigi from under her bush, and she grumbled until I picked her up and carried her. It sounded like the Davises and Maddoxes had been in bed together in a lot of ways.

The topic of business brought me back to the barbs that Rhys and Shawn had traded that morning. 'What about this latest venture of the Maddoxes? Rhys seems to think it might threaten the park and the archaeological work you're doing.'

Dismissing that with a wave, Mr Young opened the gate and waited for me to pass through. 'I'm just a history nut and a digger. I don't like talking about the modern stuff. The land is listed with the National Registry of Historic Places, which gives it some protection. If Mr Maddox wants to get his hands on it – which I'm sure he does – he'd have a hell of a time.'

'After so many floods, why would anyone want to build on this site?'

'Well, you could use it for hunting and recreation for all the people who are going to buy the overpriced homes in your little planned community upriver.'

'Oh.' I felt an odd surge of protectiveness at the thought of ATVs tearing through the woods, pickups four-wheeling where the Union soldiers had been imprisoned. Not to mention innocent wildlife getting picked off.

Mr Young smiled at my expression, which must have been easy to read. 'I think you're all right, Sylvie Davis. Now, you want to go see the dig? We've got half of the old church excavated, and you might like to meet some of the college interns.'

'I'd love to.' Rhys might see it as sticking my nose in his business again, though that didn't bother me much. But as I glanced at my watch, I discovered a different problem.

'Oh, I can't. Paula will kill me if I'm not back for lunch.' I was surprised at how disappointed I was not to see a hole in the ground. 'It's already noon and I still have to walk back.'

'Well, don't despair. How 'bout I give you a ride?' He looked at Gigi, lounging in my arms. 'I didn't want to damage your pride by offering you a ride home, but your little dog is done for.'

He tactfully avoided mentioning that I was pretty obviously done for too. I knew it showed in my step and probably in my face. I didn't even bother to hide my relief. 'Mr Young, you're a lifesaver. Gigi thanks you and so do I.'

Chuckling, he held the truck door for me, then climbed behind the wheel. 'Just come back and see me sometime, and we're even.'

We headed down the dirt road that had brought me there. It led through a gate in the fence I'd climbed, then made a turn where I would have walked straight through the woods to the back of the house. 'Gigi and I will have to work on our stamina before we trek out here again.'

'Just keep an eye on her,' he said with a grin. 'She wouldn't be more than a mouthful for the gators.'

'Gators?' And I'd just been worried about bobcats.

'Yep. You'd better stay on the roads and paths yourself. There are some old, open foundations here and there. And the drop to the river is steep in places. We had a man, upriver from here, doing some surveying. He fell and ended up in traction.'

'That's awful!' I knew about traction. Picturing the sheer bluff at the headland, I felt a rush of sympathetic vertigo. 'Is he OK?'

'Probably will be eventually. But you be careful. Wouldn't do for you to go breaking your other leg.'

As much as I whined and worried about my current situation, I did admit that things could be worse, and that would do it.

Chapter 12

Paula's comment when she saw that I'd hitched a ride home didn't actually contain the words 'I told you so,' but it might as well have. I gritted my teeth on a retort, but fortunately Clara, chopping vegetables at the counter, laughed and broke the tension. 'Paula, ease up. I'm sure Dr Young enjoyed having a captive audience.'

I grimaced at my mistake. 'I've been calling him Mr Young all day.'

'If you listened to his stories,' said Clara, 'he'll forgive you.'

With a shrug, Paula unbent. 'That's undoubtedly true. Now go upstairs and wash up, and don't even think about taking that dog with you while she's filthy from walking in the woods.'

Annoyance flared again, and it would have been satisfying to stomp to the porch, if I could. As I closed her crate, Gigi looked at me reproachfully, and I apologized with a treat.

I should have been grateful to Paula for her dislike of dogs. Irritation was – well, maybe *comfortable* wasn't the right word, but familiar. And it gave me the spur I needed to get my sore, exhausted butt up the stairs.

A typical day for me used to be four hours of dance before lunch and at least six hours of rehearsal after, often with a performance in the evening. Now a couple of hours of walking made me feel like I'd hopped all the way to Atlanta and back.

Plus, as I washed my hands and arms and splashed water over my face, I saw that I had a slight sunburn on my nose, so I was probably going to get skin cancer as well as freckles.

And wrinkles, added my mother's voice in my head.

I went to my bedroom to grab Dad's garden book so I wouldn't have to come back upstairs for it. But I paused on the open threshold, one hand on the knob. It smelled as if someone had delivered an entire bouquet of lilacs while I was gone.

Maybe Clara or Paula had dusted with some kind of scented cleaner. But I knew the smell of fresh versus perfume, and this was definitely fresh. Even in the small space, I couldn't localize the source. Each way I turned, I caught an elusive whiff.

It wasn't unpleasant, but it was odd, and I'd had enough odd for the day. I resolutely leaned over the desk and opened the window a crack, then grabbed Dad's book and went downstairs for lunch.

❧ ❧

Clara served an amazing tomato-and-spinach quiche for lunch – delicious, but my cholesterol was going to be sky-high if I didn't make her see the joy of tofu soon. After excusing myself from the table, I went to the porch and brushed the fragments of leaves and pine needles from Gigi's soft fringes of fur. When she was lovely again, we went out to the knot garden, where she promptly dived into one of the herb beds and started rolling around.

I sighed. At least it smelled like tansy, which, according to my dad, repelled insects. Funny how many things he told me had lodged in my brain, popping up when I needed them.

Spreading my old, faithful quilt on the ground, I sat and pulled off my shoes, then picked up *Notable Gardens of the South* and held it a moment, savouring the anticipation of deciphering Dad's handwritten notes. After suitable reverence, I flipped to the short chapter on Bluestone Hill.

There was a very grainy black-and-white photograph of the knot garden that showed the properly trimmed hedges, paths and planting beds. There was the stone, looming in the central circle, the path around that and the herb beds at each corner. Inside each, I could just make out some vague Celtic knot design, but not with enough detail to satisfy my curiosity.

The author wrote that he included the garden in the book because of the contrast between its formal layout and the rustic simplicity of the standing stone, where a statue or topiary would have been more traditional.

Almost in answer to that, beside the photo, Dad had lightly pencilled in a diagram of the garden and written: *Stone. Circle? Stone circle? Stonehenge?*

Had he realized the stone's origin? There was nothing about it in the text of the book, and the Internet hadn't existed then. I wasn't seeing the association. But then I realized I was looking at a column of green, and not what Dad had seen at all.

Setting the book aside, I struggled to my feet and waded into the central bed, past where Gigi was snoozing, belly up, in the unkempt greenery. The crush of leaves was cool under my bare feet and the woody stems prickled my soles. Reaching the stone, I grabbed two handfuls of the covering vine and pulled, trying to part the broad leaves like a curtain.

It didn't want to budge. The stuff was tough as rope, and clung to the rock like a lamprey on a shark. I changed my grip and tugged harder, tightening my teeth in determination.

Was the monolith at his family home why Dad found the standing stones in Britain so fascinating? And why hadn't he taken the opportunity to tell me about this one while we were there? Again I felt a guilty stab of anger at Dad for keeping so many secrets. I gave a vicious yank at the vine, and the trailing stems slid through my fists, scoring my palms.

I yelped in surprise and pain, and stared at the red welts blossoming on my skin. Crap, that hurt.

It all hurt. Dad's secrets; the weight of worry over the weirdness in my head and my heart; the aimless, adrift life raft of my existence. Cradling my burning palms, I surveyed the garden in frustration, overwhelmed by the overgrowth and unable to make heads or tails of the internal pattern. Whatever had been here was lost.

Resignation heavy on my shoulders, I sank to the ground beside Gigi, digging my fingers and toes through the leaves and stems of the plants, down into the earth. It stung the welts on my hands and cleared my head. Damn it, I hadn't gotten to be the youngest soloist in the American Ballet Company by giving up when I felt overwhelmed. Hell, I wouldn't be alive if I gave up when things were hard. I just had to figure this out – *all* of it – the way I learned everything else: step-by-step.

With renewed resolve, I climbed to my feet and stepped out of the circle of plants to fetch the book, picking it up gingerly. It slipped through my fingers and hit the ground. My heart dropped with it when I saw some pages flutter out. If the Colonel didn't haunt me for ruining his book, Paula would kill me.

But when I retrieved the pages, and the book, I saw they'd slipped from the back, not from the binding. They looked like plain old paper. Fragile excitement fluttered against my ribs as I hoped, and then confirmed, that the sheets were covered with my dad's handwriting. They'd been hidden among the end pages, like a note from the past.

On one page, he'd diagrammed the garden, in much more detail than I could make out from the photos in the book. Back when he was here, the pattern would have had twenty-five fewer years of neglect.

The second page was a list of plants, flowers and herbs that corresponded with the drawing. I could recognize about half of them easily, more with help from a book or the Internet.

Gigi raised her head suddenly, the jingle of her tags alerting me that someone was coming. Instinctively, I tucked Dad's pages into the back of the book and closed it. They were too special to share just yet.

Rhys came through the gap in the hedges. He didn't look surprised to see me, though maybe a little bemused at the way I was standing like a dope in the middle of the weeds, clutching *Notable Gardens of the South* to my chest like it was a holy relic.

'What are you doing?' he asked, eyeing me with suspicion.

'Who says I'm doing anything?'

'You have a guilty look on your face.'

I wasn't feeling guilty so much as secretive, but I guess they amounted to the same thing. 'I dropped the book, and I thought you were Paula.'

'I see.' Rhys looked amused, if not totally convinced. Gigi had run to greet him, and he squatted to scratch her ears. 'I heard you went over to Cahawba today. Why didn't you visit the dig?'

His equable tone surprised me. 'You wouldn't have minded?' Tucking the book securely under my arm, I crossed the path to join him.

'Why would I?' He paused in petting Gigi to look up at me curiously, seeming genuine. For now.

'Because you're so touchy about your secret projects. You get all prickly when I mention them, and you start calling me princess in that infuriating way.'

A flicker in his eyes said I'd scored a hit, at least in regard to his favourite diversionary tactic. With a rueful expression, he stood. 'Everyone knows I'm volunteering at the archaeological park. That's not a secret.'

I cocked my head, like Gigi did when she was figuring out how to finagle a treat. 'But the rock hunt?ing is?'

He grimaced, and his eyes slid away from mine, towards the stone and the vines I'd been molesting. 'Let's just say that's an investigation I want to keep quiet.'

'Oh!' The startled sound burst out as the pieces clicked together. I couldn't believe I hadn't thought of it before. 'I know what it is! You're looking for more bluestone.'

His gaze snapped back to mine, equally startled, but not nearly as pleased with my intuitive leap. 'What?'

'The Preseli dolerite, or whatever its name is. If you found some just out' – I waved a nonspecific hand towards the woods – 'lying around somewhere, it would solve the mystery of where my rock came from.'

He lifted his brows at my word choice. '*Your* rock?'

'The Davis rock. Whatever.'

There was a pause while he formed his answer. I'd noticed that if I could take him by surprise, I usually discovered more than if he had time to think. 'Finding the same sort of dolerite here in North America,' he said, 'would be a significant discovery. It would negate *one* of my dad's Wales and Alabama connections, though.'

'Oh.' I considered that for a moment. 'I think I see. You don't want anyone else to scoop you on the find, if there's anything *to* find, and you don't want your dad to know you're trying to disprove his theory.'

'I'm not *trying* to disprove his theory. But still . . .' He lifted his hands in a 'what can I do' sort of gesture.

'OK,' I said, feeling something ridiculously like a smile pulling at my mouth. A *giddy* smile. I'd solved another Rhys mystery, and it wasn't anything bad or, more important, anything *weird*. It wasn't even tragic, like the accident that I wasn't supposed to know about. 'I'll keep that on the down low.'

With one of his rare smiles, he put out his hand to shake on it. Automatically I put mine in his, heady relief making me forget about déjà vu and Rhys's magnetism. My only sensation was the sting of his warm palm against mine.

I must have winced. In abrupt concern, Rhys turned my hand upwards, examining the welts, like rope burns, the vine had made. 'What did you do?'

'Nothing,' I said, making light of my fit of pique at the plants. Not that I'm much of a poker player, either. 'Grabbed the wrong thing and it slipped through my fingers.'

'You should get that cleaned up.' His thumb traced the edge of the score, and I shivered at the faint scrape of his finger on the delicate lines on my palm, and the care he took with my hand.

'I was just headed in, actually.' Though I made no move to pull away. He didn't release me, either.

'Listen, Sylvie,' he said, holding my gaze as surely as he held my fingers. 'I was thinking about last night.'

Wariness unravelled the moment. I suppose it was too much to hope that he wanted to discuss the scandalous fact of my being in his room in the middle of the night. 'What about it?'

'Just that maybe you should leave off wandering around outside after dark.'

'Do you think—' I broke off, because I wasn't sure what to ask. Did he think the house was haunted? That there was something more pedestrian and earthly going on? Both ideas alarmed me, and neither would sound very rational. And I had to, even with Rhys, sound rational.

He seemed to consider his answer a little too long, looking as if he regretted saying anything in the first place. 'I just think you should be careful where you go and who you go with. That's the same in the city and the country.'

I finally pulled my hand from his, disappointed in his avoidance after we'd been – I'd thought – so candid. It stung almost as much as my cuts and made me cranky. 'If you're going to warn me about something, it might be more helpful if you actually, you know, *warn* me.'

His eyes narrowed. 'What if I said, be careful whom you trust.'

I jabbed my fists on my hips, but the sting of my palms wasn't enough to turn me from the headlong rush of frustration. 'Why don't you tell me anything until I drag it out of you? Like your rock hunting. Or your—' I caught myself before I broke my promise to his father. 'Or why you're on a break from school. Is it such a big secret?'

He stiffened defensively, and parried my question with a thrust of his own. 'You're not exactly forthcoming yourself, princess. So I guess we're even.'

'Oh, we are *so* not even,' I fired back. 'What *I'm* not saying is nothing compared with what I suspect *you're* not saying.'

His mouth dropped open wordlessly – I guess trying to find a reply to that convoluted argument – and finally he just shook his head. 'That doesn't even make any sense.'

Of course it didn't. 'Since I got off the plane, nothing has made any sense. Least of all *you*, Rhys Griffith. Come on, Gigi.' For the second day in a row, I left him standing in the garden. Though I suspect the majesty of my departure was undermined by the Chihuahua prancing at my heels.

🌿 🌿

I went into the house my usual way, through the den's side door, and stopped guiltily when I saw Paula at the desk, head bent over some paperwork. She looked up at the jingle of Gigi's dog tags, and frowned.

'I brushed her out and wiped her paws.' I defended her preemptively, my held-over frustration with Rhys boiling back up. 'She's even had herbal flea treatment.'

Closing her eyes with a shudder at the mere mention of fleas, Paula said, 'Fine. Just . . . not on the furniture.' She didn't wait on my agreement before adding, 'I told Clara we'd be happy with sandwiches tonight. The Griffiths take care of themselves for dinner, and Addie is studying with friends.'

'That sounds great.' I saw Gigi heading for the love seat, and picked her up, not wanting to push Paula any further. 'I'm OK with leftovers or whatever. She doesn't need to cook every meal. At least, not for me.'

My cousin smiled wryly. 'Food is Clara's passion. The cooking part of this business didn't just fall to her. It was her idea.' Paula sighed and shifted her papers. 'Provided we ever open. For real guests, I mean.'

The steel was definitely absent from her magnolia voice. I had no idea what went into starting an inn, even if you didn't have major renovations. Paula seemed overwhelmed, maybe even as swamped as I'd felt in the garden.

I edged to the arm of the sofa, and half sat. 'I was thinking about what I might do to stay busy.' Her brows climbed, but she couldn't have been more surprised than I was. I didn't realize I'd been thinking about it at all, but it made perfect sense. 'I want to work in the knot garden, get it cleaned up.'

She laid her pen on the desk. 'Are you sure, honey? That's hard work.'

I could point out that she'd said a productive occupation would be good for my mental health. Or that I knew how hard it was, since it had been my dad's job. Or that I wasn't an idiot. But I was trying to make nice, so I only said, 'I'm not planning on attacking it with electric hedge clippers or anything. I just want to do some weeding, see if I can uncover the old pattern.'

I saw her weighing the pros and cons, and added, a little slyly, 'It *is* a historical feature of the house. It might be nice if people could actually *see* the bluestone of Bluestone Hill Inn.'

Her tart look said my wiles hadn't gone unnoticed, but after a moment she gave in. 'All right. I think there are some clippers and some gardening gloves somewhere. But start tomorrow. You've already done a lot today, walking to Cahawba.'

With an unexpected flush of triumph, I thanked her and turned towards the foyer, Gigi still in my arms. At the threshold, though, I paused and pivoted back with a question. 'Paula. I was wondering about my room. Who did it belong to?'

She looked up again from the desk, frowning in confusion. 'You mean, originally? How on earth would I know that, honey? Is there something wrong with it?'

'No, it's great,' I reassured her. 'Well, the mattress *has* seen better days.'

That got a wry nod of acknowledgement. 'It's been that way since I slept on it. Every summer when your dad and I would visit.' Her face softened, as it did when she talked about those halcyon days. 'The room always smelled of lilac soap. I tried to find some for you, but had to make do with rose.'

'Lilac?' I parroted in shock. Paula looked at me strangely, and I schooled my expression to mild interest, while my mind spun in circles. 'Is that why you put lilac potpourri in there?'

Her frown deepened. 'What do you mean?'

Oh crap. Way to advertise your olfactory hallucinations, Sylvie.

I kept that out of my airy tone, though, as I tried to cover my slip. 'Nothing. It must be the new detergent I used before I packed. I'm not used to Dr Steve's stuff.'

With a wave, I ducked out before she could call me on this somewhat improbable lie. My relief, though, lasted only until I reached my bedroom door. I opened it with trepidation, worried what I would sense, expecting the smell to rush out and attack me. But there was nothing unusual about the air in the room. Rose soap on the washstand, my own dusting powder on the shelf. Warm breeze through the barely opened window.

Placing the garden book and Dad's pages on the desk, I sank into the reading chair with Gigi in my lap. Either the phantom flowers were, for lack of a better word, *real,* because Paula had smelled them too, or I was somehow picking up a past scent that wasn't there now.

Both ideas were impossible. But it was getting harder to ignore all the impossible things that kept happening to me.

'God, what a day.'

Gigi whined softly, picking up on my distress. I drew a long breath, then let it out, centring myself the way I did before a performance. 'Here are my options, Gee,' I said, stroking her fur to soothe us both.

'Either I'm crazy, in which case there's nothing I can do about it, except try to keep people from finding out. Or there's something . . . supernatural going on here, in which case I can investigate it and try to regain control over my senses.'

There. I'd said 'supernatural' out loud. And nothing snapped in my head. If anything, I felt better having decided to stay open-minded to the possibility that not everything that was true had yet to be proven.

Gigi barked and pawed at my right hand, and I nodded. 'I agree. Anything that gives me an illusion of control gets my vote, too.'

Chapter 13

I might have worried that my new open-mindedness would show on my face, but dinner passed without incident. And without Welshmen; the Griffiths had gone out. Slightly disappointed, I figured it was for the best. My reactions to Rhys were always odd, and maybe opening the figurative door on the whole ghost idea was enough to handle for one evening.

After eating my sandwich, I soaked in a hot bath, walked Gigi, and retired for the evening. Then, ten minutes after Paula's bedtime, I snuck back down to get my dog and bring her upstairs. At least my cousin's regimented schedule was good for something.

Settling Gigi on the bed, I sat at the desk and opened *Notable Gardens of the South,* pulling Dad's handwritten pages from the back. I'd barely glanced at them in the garden, and though I'd made my plan before dinner, I'd delayed more careful study for when the house was asleep, savouring my anticipation of this private father/daughter moment.

The diagrams were neatly drawn. I'd need to refer to them outside, but I didn't want to get the originals dirty, so I traced Dad's plot of the planting beds onto a fresh sheet of paper from the drawer. The thin, ladylike stationery was perfect for that, but I taped it afterwards to a sturdier piece of printer paper I'd scored from Paula's desk.

As I'd guessed from the photograph in the book, the corner beds were a Celtic knot, but the pattern in the central circle was more interesting. It was more like a maze – Dad had even written *Labyrinth* on the side – but designed so that the pattern made pie pieces. Or, if you looked at it in negative, the spokes of a wheel.

There was a key, with a corresponding list of plants. I copied those, checking off the ones I recognized and marking the ones I wouldn't know from a weed. Then I sat back and rubbed the crick in my neck, stunned at how long I'd worked.

I could stop for the night, but momentum had its foot on my backside, propelling me forwards. Still, I needed a book on plants. And if I wanted instant gratification, there was only one logical place to look. The study.

I didn't want to give into my dread of an empty room. That seemed to be giving too much importance to a far-fetched possibility. So with a mix of resolve and resignation, I squared my shoulders and looked at Gigi, who was happily gnawing a rawhide bone in the middle of the bed. 'Are you up for braving the Colonel's study, Gee? Because I'm not going without you.'

She sat up at her name and gave a brave yip, as if she'd understood me. Now I had to go, or have her think I was a coward.

The hallway was all clear when I opened the door. The stairwell was dark, the foyer chandelier turned off, so I guessed everyone was in for the night. I left my door open for light, and padded in my bare feet to the landing, Gigi trotting beside me. At the corner I paused, then turned into the back hall, where there was nothing but moonlight at the window.

I gave my first sigh of relief, but I still had to open the study door. I did it quickly, not allowing myself time to be scared, and found nothing to be afraid of after all.

Of course not, you dope. Scolding myself made me feel only half as silly for the double-time beat of my pulse.

Switching on the light – hooray for modern conveniences – I glanced at Gigi, who only seemed interested in exploring the corners for dust bunnies. I got to business, browsing titles for an encyclopaedia of plants. If the gardens had always been a big part of the manor's reputation, surely there had to be something like that. The Davises, as I was coming to understand them, would want to keep that point of pride up.

I didn't hurry, exactly. But I was anxious to get in, find a book and get out. There was no logic behind it. But it seemed there was no logic behind half the things I felt in the house.

Finally I located a shelf of DIY books from the seventies, including something called *Antebellum Architecture,* and *Laura Ashley's Guide to Style.* I guess that would explain the Victorian striped wallpaper in the bathroom.

And then, *The American Horticultural Society's A to Z Guide to North American Plants.* Success.

I pulled it from the shelf just as Gigi began to growl. My gaze snapped to the desk chair, wondering what she saw, but Gigi dashed for the exit. Book in hand, I barely managed to grab her. Momentum carried me out of the study, and I found myself at the French doors, where she must have been headed. The glass panes looked out on the woods, and I could hear – just barely – the familiar, tremulous wail.

It was so faint that I might not have noticed it if Gigi hadn't alerted me. But she had, and as I stood listening, a movement in the moonlit clearing in front of the woods sent my heart thumping against my ribs.

Clutching Gigi tight with one hand, I pressed the other to the window and my nose to the pane. It was a girl-shaped something – Addie? No. I glimpsed long hair, and longer skirts. Even if she was wearing odd clothes, it was harder to change the way one moved. Then my breath clouded the cold glass, and I couldn't see anything else.

I jerked back, because the glass *was* cold, and getting colder. Pulse hammering, I stared at the outline of my hand on the windowpane as the growing chill chased away the imprint. Frigid eddies brushed my bare arms, my toes, my face. My breath made thin curls of mist as I exhaled in shallow fear. I was standing in the watcher's place.

Had I created this moment out of expectation and suggestion? Or if I stood there long enough, what would I see? The watcher? The Colonel?

Part of me wanted to confront it, but the larger part, the smarter part, knew my fragile brain might break whichever way it went, ghost or madness.

The smarter part seemed to be in control of my legs. Holding Gigi tight, I backed away.

Right into a tall, warm body. His arms came around me automatically, keeping me from falling as I spun round, off balance with fear. My scream never got past the knife-sharp inhale of panic as Rhys's hard whisper reached through the ringing in my ears. 'Sylvie, it's me. It's all right.'

'Oh my God,' I breathed, pressed against him, my face buried in his T-shirt. He felt warm and real and so *right* that I couldn't move away. 'You nearly scared me to death.'

His hands moved to my shoulders, as if to pry me off, but he stopped in surprise. 'Your skin is like ice.'

He rubbed my arms to chase away the cold. There was a casual intimacy to his touch that made me shiver, nothing to do with the supernatural. 'You feel that too? The chill?'

'Yeah.' He looked over my head, towards the window. 'That's a wicked draught. Come on.'

Rhys pulled me towards my room, closing the door

before he steered me to sit in the upholstered chair. For once it felt good to be handled. It felt good to be handled by *him;* the brush of his skin and the way his scent filled my head evoked tempting ways to chase away ghosts, literal or figurative. At least for a little while.

Crap. I really was freaking out. Not because I was tempted to close the short distance between us as he leaned close to wrap the quilt from the bed around Gigi and me. But because I thought he might not object.

Gigi licked my face, her tongue warm on my skin. I curled my fingers into her fur, hiding the shaking of my hands. From the night I'd arrived, I'd been glimpsing the past of the house – servants in halls and guests arriving in carriages. The figure in the window. But *not* seeing anything had freaked me out exponentially worse, because I could *feel* it, incipient and awful.

Rhys sat in the desk chair and leaned forward, elbows on his knees, staying close. 'What was all that about?'

I had to get a hold of myself, be analytical. Or at least coherent. 'Did you see anything by the window?' I asked.

He shook his head. 'No. Did you?' His tone was neutral, though serious, as if we were comparing notes.

'No.' It was the truth, though I would have lied to keep from sounding nuts. 'But you felt the cold, right?'

Slowly, he nodded. 'I felt a draught. And I felt how

chilled you were. Will you tell me what happened? What has you so upset?'

No matter what I admitted to myself, there was no way I could say aloud, not to him, not to anyone, that I was experiencing these things. That I was moving through a morning routine that wasn't mine, and smelling flowers that weren't there. That an empty spot in the park plunged me into an icy well of despair. That I felt such bone-deep horror at the inexplicable chill and the building pressure in the air . . . It touched too close to my psyche, to the part of me rocked off my already shaky foundation.

So I shook my head, answering his question – *Will you tell me?* – even as I lied. 'Creaky, draughty old house and an overactive imagination, I guess.'

Rhys sat back with a sigh, running a hand over his hair. He sounded almost disappointed. 'All right. I don't guess I've given you reason to trust me.'

No. I barely knew him. But here I was, sitting in my pyjamas, in a bedroom – *again* – talking about extraordinary things. 'I don't know why you're always around when I get spooked.'

'Probably because it keeps happening right outside my door,' he said wryly.

'I'll try and have my next meltdown somewhere else.'

It was a darker joke than he could know, but Rhys smiled, grudgingly, then ran his hands over the knees of his jeans before speaking again. 'Listen, Dad and I are leaving before the break of dawn tomorrow—'

'For good?' My voice rose in way more distress than I meant to show.

'No, no,' he assured me, as if it weren't odd that a girl he barely knew was upset by his departure. 'A field trip to the northeast corner of the state. I think Dad mentioned it.'

'Oh, yeah. Ancient fortress.' The discussion – had it only been this morning? – seemed distant from the weirdness in the hallway. Which was welcome, as it grounded me in the real world, and I took the opportunity to break the tension by needling him a little. 'Isn't it kind of Anglocentric to think Native Americans couldn't build forts as well as the Welsh?'

'I would be Celt-centric, to think that,' he corrected me with some humour, allowing himself to be distracted for a moment. 'But we don't. Different isn't the same as better. But that's beside the point.' He took a breath, getting serious again. 'I want to try and be back tomorrow night, but you've seen how my dad is. If he finds a kindred spirit, we'll be there until next week.'

'Not that I won't miss these scintillating late-night visits, Rhys' – and I would, for several reasons I didn't examine too closely, but which might have to do with how his knee bumped mine when he shifted in his chair – 'but what does this have to do with me?'

Again, he drew a breath, like he was bracing himself. I knew dancers who did that before a difficult step or jump. Eventually they broke the habit, or they passed out. 'I want you to promise you won't go wandering about after dark.'

'Oh for heaven's sake.' I shrugged off the quilt, because I'd definitely warmed up. 'This again?'

'Just tomorrow.' He raised his hands as if warding off my anger. Or possibly just my raised voice.

'Why tomorrow?' I demanded more softly, resorting to sarcasm to try to get some answers. 'Is the moon full? Do the vampires and werewolves prowl for young maidens?'

He looked at me askance. 'You really do have a lurid imagination.'

I made an exasperated sound and stood up, plopping Gigi on the bed, where she watched with interest as I paced the tiny room. The thing was, I didn't *want* to go outside after dark. But he was hiding something and it was pissing me off.

'Give me a good reason why,' I challenged, 'and I'll think about it.'

Rhys stood up too, and the room suddenly seemed that much smaller as he looked down at me from an intimately close distance, his green eyes appearing very dark in the indirect light of the lamp. I had to check the instinct to step back, because my senses were again *full* of him, and I was trying to stay focused.

'Because,' he said distinctly, as if I weren't very bright, 'even if you arrived in Alabama as ignorant as a newly hatched chick, you must see by now that there are, as my dad would say, strange dealings afoot.'

His candour surprised me, and I was too pleased that he'd acknowledged that much to be irked by his tone. 'When you say "strange dealings" . . .'

A smile turned up the corner of his mouth. 'Well, I don't mean werewolves or vampires. Or pirate treasure,' he added, when I drew a breath.

I wanted to keep it light, but I was getting worried. 'Seriously, Rhys, if someone is doing something illegal—'

There was a flash of hurt in his eyes, quickly covered by anger. 'If someone was doing something illegal, I would go to the police.'

The way he fired back made my ears burn, as if I'd accused him unfairly. But I didn't back down. 'Then why are you being so cagey? Maybe *you* don't trust *me*.'

His quickly shuttered expression spoke volumes. The flush ran out of my cheeks, and hurt jabbed me in the heart.

'I keep forgetting we just met,' I said softly.

'I know.' His admission surprised me, and eased some of the irrational pang. The confession seemed to take him a bit off guard too, and he stuck his hands in his pockets, like he didn't know what to do with them.

'Look, Sylvie,' he said, 'you're not telling me everything either.'

I started to deny it, then, after a pause, decided on a measure of honesty. 'Maybe not. But that's personal.'

'So is my problem.' Again he caught my gaze and held it. 'And I can't tell you more than that just yet.'

It was the 'yet' that convinced me to let it go, for now. 'All right,' I said. 'I'll stay inside. Anything else?'

He smiled a little sheepishly. 'Just be careful whom you trust.'

It didn't take a huge leap to guess who – *whom* – he meant. 'Are you saying don't trust Shawn?' That wasn't a surprise, given their animosity. But I was a little disappointed in Rhys for getting in digs when his opponent wasn't there to defend himself.

'I am saying,' Rhys clarified carefully, 'he's a very charming guy.'

'And you don't like that,' I prompted. Which made me a hypocrite, since a moment ago I had been annoyed he was running Shawn down. But I wanted his thoughts on *something*.

He shrugged, not as casually, I think, as he intended. 'I think charm is overrated.'

That made me laugh, and it wasn't even bitter or sarcastic. 'You *would* say that, Mr Sunshine.'

He drew himself up, so offended that I laughed again, and covered my mouth before the sound made Gigi bark. Slowly, Rhys acknowledged my point with a smile that chased away my irritation and left only the pull of attraction.

We stood that way for a long, ridiculous moment, until my out-of-practice grin faded, and there was nothing left to say but goodbye. But the longer he didn't say it, the more I didn't want him to.

I certainly couldn't. My tongue had tied itself in knots. Maybe because I was suddenly very aware that we were in my bedroom, and I was wearing my camisole and pink pyjama pants with bright yellow ducks. Which hadn't seemed like such a big deal until we shared that smile.

'Are you all right now?' he asked, and I hoped he was asking because he didn't want to go either. Maybe it was wishful thinking that it wasn't just me remembering that moment he'd held me securely against him, the way his hands had rubbed the chill from my skin. Wondering how it would feel if he touched my arm for no reason but that he wanted to. If he brushed back my hair and traced the line of my neck.

It would be magic. I knew it like I knew my own name. And that was as crazy as any other thought that had entered my brain since I'd arrived in Cahaba. Maybe it was a good thing he was leaving for at least a day.

I remembered he'd asked me a question, and figured out how to make my tongue work again. 'I'm fine. Right as rain.'

Great. Babbling clichés was always impressive.

Rhys smiled, like he knew me well enough to follow my thoughts. 'I'll see you tomorrow night.'

I opened the door for him, offering more inanities. 'Safe journey. Remember – drive on the right side of the road.'

He didn't dignify that with a laugh, just a wry 'Got it. Right side.' But his hand brushed my arm as he left, a seemingly unconscious gesture of farewell that had no less – maybe even more – impact for how natural it was.

Shutting the door, I turned to find Gigi looking at me, cocking her head in confusion at this uncharacteristic flush of giddy girliness. 'I know. It's my *arm*, for God's sake.'

Get a grip, Sylvie. There are strange dealings afoot.

I liked that phrase. It encompassed a lot. Natural, unnatural . . . But it didn't settle my mind as I tried to get to sleep.

Chapter 14

At breakfast the next morning, Clara introduced me to hominy grits. I finally discovered why God put cheese and butter on the earth.

Not even the delicious treat – which I gathered wasn't everyday fare – was enough to cheer up Addie, however. She stirred the grits in her bowl and said in her most peevish voice, 'These are loaded with fat, Mom. Why don't I just paint them on my thighs.'

'That would be an interesting fashion choice,' I said. Pretty mildly, I thought, but she pinned me with a glare like an icicle.

'Why are you even hanging around here? Shawn's not picking me up today – he's done with classes.'

'Yeah.' I drew the word out sardonically. 'Because I'm definitely building my day around a guy I've met three times.' Although I let a guy I'd only known for three days into my room. So maybe I shouldn't have been so quick to get on my high horse.

I left Addie to her sulk, and collected Gigi from her crate, where she'd been eating her own breakfast. As Paula had predicted, I found some basic gardening tools on the porch, including gloves. My hands had healed remarkably quickly – they'd stung in the bath last night, but I was surprised this morning that the skin was just a little pink, no blisters or scabs at all. Still, I'd learned my lesson: respect the greenery.

In the knot garden, I dove into weeding with an enthusiasm that lasted a solid thirty minutes. I'd only *thought* I grasped the difficulty of the project. Or maybe I'd thought, because I was my father's daughter, my knees wouldn't hurt and my leg wouldn't ache.

But it wasn't as if I had to be done tomorrow. I slowed down a bit, enjoying the soft earth and the quiet calm of the plants. Whatever else was going on at Bluestone Hill, I loved the feeling that I shared this spot with Dad, him in his time, and me in mine.

Paula came out after I'd been at it about an hour. I could see her checking over my work, which, I had to admit, didn't look that impressive. 'Well, bless your heart, just look at that. I didn't even remember there was a bench there.'

That was how overgrown the place was. The first thing I'd done was rather haphazardly yank greenery out from around the wrought-iron bench, and tether Gigi to it. Otherwise she would have wanted to help me weed, and she couldn't distinguish the difference between a dandelion and a daffodil.

Sadly, I wasn't sure I was much better. I'd had to refer a few times to the horticultural society's A to Z guide to plants. I'd found it in front of my door that morning. Rhys must have put it there, since I was pretty sure I'd dropped it in the hall.

Paula picked her way over the uneven path. She wore a salmon-coloured sweater set and a flowing floral skirt. Not exactly paint-the-front-bedroom clothes. 'You look very nice,' I said, curious what had prompted this costume change. 'That colour suits you.'

She looked pleased with the compliment, though she made a this-old-thing face as she smoothed the front of her sweater. 'Thank you. I have an appointment in Selma and will probably be gone for lunch.'

'Is "appointment" the Southern way of saying "hot date"?' I asked, fishing for details with an attempt at humour.

Her sideways look was the most droll I'd seen her. 'No. It's a meeting about money. Refurbishment is expensive.'

'Oh.' I felt a little awkward, since I hadn't thought about finances. Looking at the grand old Southern house and the acres of land, I assumed there was grand old Southern money to go with it. I tried not to visibly wince when I remembered telling Rhys that I had no designs on the place because Dad had left me well off. But he had.

'If you're going back inside,' I said, glossing over my own awkwardness, 'would you tell Clara not to trouble herself to make lunch if you're not going to be here? I'll just heat up some of yesterday's quiche.'

'I'll do my best to convince her.'

'Seriously. She feeds me like I'm an underweight turkey in September.' Clara's food was like Dad's allowance – wonderful to have, but more than I needed.

Paula made her exasperated face, her mouth tightening in annoyance. 'Well, Sylvie, honey, that's how we take care of people down here in the South. Don't be ungrateful.'

'I'm not!' I protested, irritated that the one time I wasn't being snarky, I still caught flak for it. Gigi barked, echoing my objection.

Paula dropped her hands from her hips. 'Suit yourself. I'll see you this afternoon.' Skirting the pile of discarded weeds, she added, 'I'm sure there's a trash bag somewhere, so you can clean up when you're done.'

Fortunately, she turned to exit the garden, so she missed the roll of my eyes. Then I looked at the magnitude of growth in the garden and realized I *was* going to have to see about starting a compost pile somewhere.

I worked until midmorning, then took a break, stretching my back and flexing my fingers. I was definitely going to need better clippers and – I examined a new blister on my thumb – new gloves, too. After grabbing a drink from the kitchen and leaving Gigi with a bowl of water on the porch, I figured the best place to look for that kind of thing was in the garage. I headed there via the back yard, and entered through the door underneath the stairs to Clara and Addie's apartment.

It took me a minute to find the light switch. Growing up in Manhattan, I didn't have a lot of familiarity with family garages, so I wasn't sure where to start looking for gardening tools. This one was packed with *stuff*. Maybe not the accumulated detritus of the full two hundred years of Bluestone Hill's existence, but definitely the past thirty or so.

I poked around two lawn mowers – one gas-powered, and one push mower, as seen in fifties movies – and came up with a trowel, another hand spade and a not-quite-half-rusted pair of gardening clippers. No wonder the hedges were in such bad shape.

And then I found a real treasure. A bicycle. It looked about the same vintage as the push mower, but the tyres (incredibly) still had air, and it seemed in pretty good shape. It made me ridiculously happy. Not because I loved to ride bikes, or had fond childhood memories of learning, but because I was no longer trapped. I might not be able to go far, but I could certainly go farther than on foot. And that meant I could go to town.

It was sort of sad that I was already looking forward to a trip to Maddox Landing like it was a trip to Paris.

Chapter 15

A sign in front of a historic train depot said MADDOX LANDING VISITORS' CENTRE, and I gratefully turned my bicycle – almost as old as the train station – into the parking lot. Riding the stationary bike in physical therapy wasn't quite the same thing as pedalling two miles down a narrow country road. For one thing, in therapy I hadn't had a dog riding in a basket attached to the handlebars.

Gigi was strapped in – the harness a bit makeshift, but secure – and was having a great time. My backside, on the other hand, was not. I hadn't accounted for the jarring of potholes, or the stress of riding on the grass shoulder when a car came barrelling down the road. There was also the problem of lack of padding, both in the bike's seat and my own. My butt hurt almost as much as my leg.

The train station, just off the state highway, was so quaint it was almost kitschy, especially compared with the rural dilapidation I'd glimpsed on my bike ride – more trailers and old houses, cars on blocks, mechanical parts littering yards like redneck lawn statuary. In town, however, the only thing that differentiated an old house from a new one was vinyl siding versus wood, and the commercial buildings all conformed to a sort of redbrick, small-town, Main Street charm.

The train-depot-slash-visitors'-centre was a narrow building, with platforms on both sides where once, I imagined, people had waited for the train to take them to civilization. I unfastened Gigi's harness from the basket, clipped her to her leash and left the bike propped up against the depot platform, figuring that if anyone stole it, at least I'd have an excuse to call for a ride. This time I'd made sure my phone was charged and ready. Just in case.

The window in the door looked suspiciously dark, and sure enough, when I pulled the handle, it didn't move. Only then did I read the sign that said OPEN TUESDAY, THURSDAY AND SATURDAY, 9–5.

I stared at the words with a sort of fatalistic frustration, then glanced down at my dog. 'It figures. I guess visitors are only welcome every other day?'

Gigi sneezed her opinion. While she checked the canine messaging system on the ground, I investigated the notices posted on the glassed-in corkboard beside the door. Some were ads for local businesses and nearby attractions (like Old Cahawba), but most were postings for upcoming events, like the County High School graduation, to be held in the school auditorium on Saturday, and the impending Catfish Festival.

My excuse for coming to town was that I needed some tofu or soy milk to convince Clara I was getting enough protein. But I also wanted to find out more about my family, about the Davises and about Maddox Landing. Visiting Cahawba had helped, but now I needed some perspective newer than the eighteen hundreds.

So I found the lack of welcome at the visitors' centre inauspicious, and I tried to form a plan as I returned to the bicycle and tucked Gigi into her basket. My best bet – for my grocery-shopping cover story, and for getting more information on the town – would be downtown. There were only two blocks of it, so surely some opportunity would present itself.

I hadn't gone far, walking my bike along the shoulder, when a shiny red pickup slowed next to me. The truck looked familiar, and I definitely recognized the guy driving – his comfortably confident slouch behind the wheel, the way the curve of his easy smile made an answering one fight to turn up the corners of my own mouth. Even today, when I was hot and tired, and the ring of Rhys's words echoed in my head. *Charm is overrated.*

'Hey, Sylvie,' said Shawn Maddox. He'd rolled down the passenger window and leaned across the seat as he drove, one hand on the steering wheel. 'Don't tell me you rode that piece of crap all the way from Bluestone Hill.'

Even with the wink in his voice, it was kind of an annoying question. 'Of course not,' I said dryly. 'Gigi pedalled part of the way.'

The dog barked at her name, and Shawn laughed. 'You should have called me. I said I'd show you the town.'

'I don't need to see the *whole* town,' I answered, unbending a little. 'Just the grocery store. Maybe a gardening store, if you've got one.'

The truck crept along, keeping pace with me, tyres crunching on the asphalt. 'We've got a hardware store, if that will work, and I can run you by the Piggly Wiggly.'

I stopped to face him incredulously, the bike leaning against my hip. 'The *Piggly Wiggly*? You're making that up.'

The pickup stopped as well, causing the even bigger truck behind him to pull around with an angry rev of the engine.

'Why would I do that?'

'To tease the Yankee.' I pushed my hair back from my face. I'd twisted it into a loose bun that wasn't standing up to the heat or my exertion, and long strands clung damply to my forehead and neck. The AC from the truck wafted through the window, enticing me as much as – more than, really – Shawn's flirtation.

He put a hand on his chest as if I'd wounded him. 'I wouldn't tease you. You're kin.'

I rolled my eyes. That word was dated enough when Paula said it. From someone my age, it sounded like he should be in a movie. One with a lot of banjos in it. Taking the handlebars again, I resumed walking. 'Everyone is kin down here.'

Another car, travelling in the opposite direction, honked at Shawn as he crept the truck along. He gave a friendly wave, proving my point. Then back to me: 'Throw that old bike in the back and hop in. I'll run you to the store, then treat you to a piece of pie at the Daisy Café.'

Good grief, people down here loved their dessert. 'I have Gigi with me. They might not let us in.'

'We'll work it out,' Shawn cajoled, as another truck pulled around him, blowing the horn. 'Come on. Best pie in the county.'

I sighed. It wasn't the pie that sold me but the fact that I might wander around all day looking for this Piggly Wiggly place. And really, an air-conditioned ride trumped worry of what Rhys would think. After all, I'd been aware of the pitfalls of charm before he had said anything. I could enjoy Shawn's company at face value. I was a big girl.

'OK,' I said, pretending he'd worn me down.

With a grin, Shawn pulled onto the shoulder, while I unfastened Gigi and took her from the basket. With one hand full, and the heavy bike leaning against my hip, I was trying to figure out what to deal with first when I heard Shawn's door slam. He reached around me to steady the bike, putting me in the circle of his arms. The action sent a pinprick rush of surprise over my already heated skin, and it melted together into something ridiculously tempting.

'The kickstand is your friend,' he said in my ear, humour keeping that comment from being *too* insufferable.

I turned my head, getting a delicious close-up view of his blue eyes and the dimple beside his mouth. But even as I stood there, snuggly trapped between him and the bicycle, the warmth of him seeping into my bones and making even my aches disappear, I couldn't help feeling there was something calculated about the clinch. It was another movie moment, only this time accompanied by harps and violins.

Another car honked at it drove by, and someone yelled out the window, 'Hey, Shawn! Way to go!' It re-inforced the feeling that I was being *presumed* about, and I was grateful for the excuse to duck primly out from under his arm.

He didn't seem to think anything of my retreat, and lifted the cycle with impressive ease. 'Hop in while I stow this, and we'll get going.'

I delayed just a moment, watching the play of his muscles under his T-shirt as he very carefully set the rust-spotted and dented bike in the bed of the truck, preserving his paint job. A little caustically, I wondered what he would have done if, as he'd suggested, I had just 'thrown' the bike in the back.

Setting Gigi on the seat first, I climbed into the cab, which was a trick, considering how high it was off the ground. Shawn got behind the wheel and gave Gigi

– who sat in my lap with her front paws on the dashboard, tongue hanging with a grin – a wordless look before he put the pickup into gear. 'What are we after at the store?'

'We're after tofu. Or soy milk.'

He laughed, easing onto the road without looking for traffic. 'Now you're pulling *my* leg. Teasing the good ol' boy.'

'Not this time,' I said, struggling again against his charm. I noticed his accent got thicker when he talked about being a country guy. 'I know Clara's just taking good care of me, but if I have to eat another egg, I'm going to hatch chicks.'

He chuckled, and turned onto a side street. 'Well, no promises. We're thorough carnivores here.'

'I'll take my chances.' I stared out the window at the faded awnings over the Main Street stores, the crumbling brick patched with greying mortar. And the sad thing was, this town was in much better repair than half the ones we'd driven through on our way from the airport.

'When Maddox Point is finished, it'll be different,' said Shawn. 'More people shopping in town means a better selection in the stores.'

'Maddox Point is your dad's development, right?' Addie and the girls had mentioned this at dinner the other night. I was just confirming it to lead into more questions.

'Yep.' He pulled up to a windowed storefront. The Piggly Wiggly. After all that, he'd only driven me a couple of blocks.

'Can I leave Gigi with you while I run in?' I asked.

'Sure thing.' He said it in the same tone that he might say, 'Sure, I'll hold your purse in the middle of this crowded store.' But he reached for Gigi all the same, taking her carefully into his hands. 'I'll take good care of the little munchkin.'

Since she looked OK with this plan – confident, no doubt, that he was another would-be worshipper – I left them in the truck – windows rolled down, of course – and headed inside.

One look at the small, dimly lit store and I almost gave up without trying. As it happened, though, they did have a package of tofu and a carton of soy milk – the nonrefrigerated kind, with the shelf life of tinned goods – but they wanted New York prices for them. No wonder both were covered in a layer of dust.

I also picked up a jar of peanut butter, trying not to think about trans fats, and checked out. When I emerged, blinking in the sunshine, I saw that Shawn was now standing by his truck, using my dog to pick up women.

OK, maybe not. But as Shawn held Gigi like a football in one arm, an older woman wearing a smart pantsuit cooed and scratched the dog's ears. She had to be about my mother's age. Which didn't mean there wasn't some cougar-type flirtation going on.

Or maybe I imagined the vibe, because neither looked disappointed at the interruption. The woman held out her hand as Shawn started to introduce me. 'I know who this is,' she said warmly. 'I'm so glad you've come back home to Bluestone Hill, Sylvie.'

I shook her hand automatically, though I was

flummoxed as to why she was greeting me like I was returning gentry. I mean, I got the Davis thing, but 'back home'?

'I'm just here for a few weeks,' I explained politely, correcting any false impression I was there to stay, a second-generation prodigal returned to the nest.

'Oh, I know.' She glanced at my leg – hidden by my jeans – and her mouth turned down in a sympathetic frown. 'The accident. I'm glad to see you're getting around all right, though.'

It made sense that if the Teen Town Council had discussed the details of my visit, the adults would, too. But it was still disconcerting, and a little annoying.

Shawn smoothly filled in the blanks in the introduction, almost as if he could tell I was struggling for something nice to say. 'Sylvie, this is Ms Brewster. She's on the real town council.'

She waved a demurring hand. 'Shawn and the kids have done so much for Maddox Landing. One of the biggest problems in these small towns is that the youngsters are only marking time until they can run off to the big city. No investment in the future of their home. But Shawn has really motivated our little group into a force to be reckoned with when it comes to getting things done for the good of the town.'

'Aw shucks, Miz Brewster.' He ducked his head, and scuffed his toe on the pavement, playing up the good ol' boy thing with a twinkle in his eye. 'You make me blush.'

Seriously? Even with the laughter behind the act, it was an eye-roll-worthy performance. I realized he was putting off the compliment – sort of – with that bit of soft soap, but 'Miz' Brewster seemed utterly taken, and giggled. *Giggled.* 'Honestly, Shawn. You're such a card.'

A card? Was that fifties-sitcom speak for 'full of it'?

Still chuckling indulgently at Shawn's country schoolboy shtick, Ms Brewster turned to me – I quickly wiped the disbelief off my face – and indicated my plastic bag. 'Did you find what you needed, sweetie?'

'More or less.' Rather less than more, but there didn't seem much point in complaining.

With a sigh, she looked at the storefront. Faded poster-board signs taped to the inside of the windows advertised specials on Christmas cookies. They ought to have been dirt cheap, since it was the first of June.

'We're hoping to bring in a new grocery chain. It would be good to get a few nice items without having to drive into Selma.'

'I'm sure it would,' I said tactfully. For speciality foods, you'd be out of luck unless Velveeta was your idea of a gourmet cheese.

'Maybe when the new development gets going. Right, Shawn?'

He nodded. 'That's what Dad is hoping, Ms Brewster.'

Hearing this premise two times, and so close together, gave it the ring of a party platform. Dr Young had said yesterday that the Maddoxes were politicians from way back. Maybe it was his observation, as much as Rhys's comment, that had me viewing Shawn's flattering attentions more cynically today.

Ms Brewster smiled brightly, first at me, then at

Shawn, then back at me. 'So. Are we going to see you two at the Catfish Festival?'

Shawn grinned back, looking completely at his ease with an elbow propped on the shiny red hood of his truck, still holding my dog. 'You know I wouldn't miss it.'

Her eyes twinkled knowingly. 'And are you going to bring our famous ballerina guest with you?'

'I'll try and convince her,' he said, sliding his gaze towards me, as if judging my reaction to this sledge-hammer matchmaking.

'Excellent!' She beamed at us, seeming oblivious to the knit of my brows. 'I'll see y'all there!'

I stared after her as she headed down the cracked sidewalk in her sensible pumps. What was that about? I seriously doubted Shawn needed help getting his own dates.

Sort of proving my point, he smoothly gave Gigi over with one hand and opened the truck door for me with the other. 'Ready for some lunch?'

'I'm not really that hungry,' I said, unsure of how I felt about being seen with him if everyone was going to assume we were an *item*.

He hooked his arm over the top of the door. 'Just some chocolate pie, then.'

'Clara will be expecting me.' Which wasn't quite true either. She would be, eventually, but not necessarily for lunch.

'I'll call her.' Tilting his head, he turned on the Tom Sawyer charm. 'You don't really have a choice. I have your bike hostage.'

Pursing my lips, I swung my grocery bag onto the

seat so I could climb in with Gigi. 'Some good old country boy you are.'

'I'm smarter than I look,' he said with a wink.

※ ❧

The Daisy Café was on Main Street – one street over from the Piggly Wiggly. There were a couple of tables outside, under an appropriate yellow-and-white striped awning, but Shawn handed me Gigi's carrier bag – which I'd brought in case I needed it – and said, 'Go ahead. No one will notice.'

I arched my brows. 'No one will notice the airholes in my tote bag?' She was used to going everywhere with me, and the bag did look like a large and not entirely unfashionable purse. But I had a feeling – more than a hunch by this point – that a Maddox and a Davis out together wasn't going to fly under the radar.

'It'll be fine,' he assured me, with the blithe tone of someone who's used to getting away with everything. Again, not really much of a leap to see that happening.

Slipping Gigi a rawhide chew and zipping her up, I let Shawn give me a hand down from the truck and hold the door for me as we entered the Daisy Café.

It had a certain chrome and vinyl charm, complete with black-and-white checked tiles on the floor and waitresses in little scalloped aprons. The lady behind the counter greeted Shawn with a wave, then came over when she saw me with him.

'You must be Sylvie Davis.' She had long, cold

hands, and pressed my fingers between hers. 'I'm Daisy, and it's a delight to meet y'all.'

I hadn't realized that 'y'all' could be singular. She grinned up at Shawn, pink lipstick on her teeth, a knowing look in her eyes. 'I should have known you wouldn't let any grass grow under your feet, Shawn Maddox.'

That was twice – three times, if you counted the honking car out on the state highway – that people had assumed we were together, or he was *courting* me. Suddenly I remembered the giggling girls at dinner, when I'd said I didn't want to poach, if someone had dibs on Shawn. Obviously, *I* had dibs on Shawn. Or vice versa, which was probably more accurate, and definitely more irritating.

I noticed he didn't correct her. But then, denial would only fuel the fire. 'You got a booth free, Daisy?'

'Sure thing.'

She didn't even glance at my tote bag as she led us to a booth with red vinyl seats. I guess I was the only one who could hear the little smacking sounds of Gigi ravaging her rawhide bone. Placing the bag on the seat, I slid in, doing my best to hide it from view.

Shawn sat across from me, and as soon as Daisy left, I ambushed him with the question I was exploding to ask. 'Is there some custom in Alabama that says that accepting a ride from a guy means you're going steady?'

His smile turned sheepish. 'It's because you're a Davis and I'm a Maddox. Our families go way back. There's sort of an assumption.'

'Yeah. I'm picking up on that.' People had told me

– the TTC girls, and even Dr Young at the cemetery – but of course I didn't think it applied in the twenty-first century. 'So it's a dynastic thing?' I asked, wanting Shawn's reaction.

He had the sense to look embarrassed. 'More of a superstition, believe it or not.'

'A superstition,' I repeated in disbelief. Except that the evidence was obvious in the looks we were getting, the discussions behind menus and even a couple of cell-phone calls. Being a soloist with the ballet hadn't exactly prepared me for this kind of celebrity.

His shoulder lifted in a sheepish shrug. 'It's good luck when a Davis and a Maddox get together.'

I sat back, trying to look amused, but feeling a thread of unease weaving through my scepticism. Dancers are notoriously superstitious. So why the idea that two people hooking up could bring good luck was any more unbelievable than lingering spirits, I couldn't say. Maybe because I felt like my free will was at stake.

'I figure it this way,' he continued amiably. 'When the two big families get together it's usually for business, and business is good for the town.' His easy explanation took some of the stiffness out of my shoulders. 'Plus, you're a knockout,' he added, with that self-aware cockiness that amused and annoyed me in equal parts. 'And as you've heard, I don't let any grass grow under my feet.'

I gave a snort, not giving in to his flirtation. 'You can flatter yourself, but leave me out of it.'

'Come on. Long legs, gorgeous hair, big brown eyes . . .'

Fortunately, our waitress arrived. It was Kimberly from the Teen Town Council study group – she must have been a graduating senior too, since she wasn't in school. She squealed when she saw me sitting across from Shawn, and welcomed me like an old friend.

'Hey, darlin'! How are you likin' your digs at the Hill?'

At the sound of her voice, Gigi gave a muffled yip of greeting. I froze, but no one seemed to have heard it over the music from the jukebox. 'They're great,' I said vaguely, paying more attention to Gigi than the question.

Shawn gave me a slight smile, and I realized he must have heard Gigi or guessed from my expression what had happened. Kimberly, though, was busy sidelining me with her next question.

'Have you seen any ghosts yet?'

'*What?*'

Without any chance to brace myself, my wheeze of shock had given me away. Kimberly's eyes widened, her mouth opening in a gasp of excited horror. 'Did you really? Oh my gawd, I would just die.'

'What is it with you people and ghosts?' I snapped, a little too vehemently. 'I never said I saw a ghost.'

Shawn grinned, like it was a big joke. 'Oh, come on. Your *face* said it.' He leaned forward, elbows on the table. 'Was it the Colonel?'

My heart tripled its rhythm, but I denied the question emphatically. 'No.' I got that 'the Hill' was the local sensation. It was like visitors to New York asking if we ever saw any celebrities. Shawn and Kimberly didn't – couldn't – realize this subject had ramifications for me. That no matter what I had or hadn't seen – which was still debatable in my mind – I couldn't talk about ghosts or I'd set off warning bells for my handler, Paula.

'That would be crazy,' I said. The words made me a hypocrite, but it was better than a trip to a shrink. 'There are no such things as ghosts.'

Kimberly gave me a disapproving eye. 'Don't go saying that down here. Half the people in this diner, including that banker on his lunch break, have their doors painted blue to keep the haints out.'

'What's a haint?' I didn't know the word, but her reasonable tone quieted some of my nerves.

'Evil spirit.' She said it matter-of-factly, as if anyone should know that, then elaborated. 'Well, a ghost, but you can never be too careful. My grandmother used to swear the dead were always angry when they came round, ready to make trouble. She had her door painted, a bottle tree in the front yard, and a mirror on the front porch to catch the devil.'

I looked from her solemn face to Shawn, who had stopped smirking and was watching my reaction, which I *hoped* was casually curious. I took the chance that mere discussion wouldn't brand me as nuts, and dug for more information. 'You guys take this pretty seriously down here. Do you have a particular infestation of the dead, or what?'

'Ooo, don't even joke about that.' Kimberly gave a

shudder, the beads in her hair clicking together. Raising her order pad, she poised the pen over it and changed the subject abruptly. 'What are you having for lunch?'

I reeled for a moment, still contemplating how naturally she'd talked about 'haints' and how useless my 'open-minded but critical' plan would be if I freaked out and got defensive at the mere mention – possibly even joking – of ghosts. I hadn't looked at the menu, but Shawn ordered for both of us. Of course he did.

'Sylvie would probably like the avocado BLT without the *B*.' He glanced at me for approval, and I nodded, not really caring what I ate, even for the sake of feminism. 'And a piece of chocolate cream pie. I'll have the meat loaf and a slice of the same.'

Glancing at the chalkboard over the counter, I asserted a little independence. 'I'll have the lemon chess pie, actually.' The sandwich sounded good – and I'd noticed he'd avoided egg salad, so points to him for paying attention.

'You want a Coke or anything?'

'Not unless someone wants to rush me to the hospital in a sugar coma,' I said, returning somewhat to my sarcastic self.

'You got it.' Kimberly grinned. 'The pie, I mean, not the coma.'

She bounced off and I turned to Shawn with a glare. 'Seriously. I never said I saw ghosts. You're the one who keeps bringing it up.'

He shrugged. 'You heard Kim. It's not crazy to believe in ghosts.'

'No. Just to see them.'

'Touchy, touchy.'

I clamped my teeth on a retort as Kimberly brought back two glasses of iced tea (unsweetened, since I'd asked her to hold the sugar coma) and a basket of dinner rolls. Somehow, I managed to wait until she was gone to ask, 'Has anyone actually *seen* the Colonel's ghost?'

He shrugged. 'It's one of those things everyone knows about, but no one will fess up to themselves. Friend of a cousin of a classmate. You know.'

I picked apart a buttery roll, trying my best to act casual. We were, after all, talking hypothetically and without Paula to interrupt us. 'What does he supposedly do?'

'Hangs around in the study, cleaning his pistol. Some people have heard him whistling "Dixie."'

That last bit made me suspect he was pulling my leg. And it was stupid to be disappointed that the stories hadn't meshed with my own experiences. Plus, I was worried too much interest would come off as odd, no matter what Kimberly said.

So I sipped my tea and changed the subject. 'I understand that Colonel Davis married a Maddox. Doesn't that make it kind of gross that people assume we are, or will be, dating?'

Shawn laughed. 'Mary Maddox was my great-great-whatever-aunt. Five generations back. That makes us kissing cousins, as we say down here.'

'A family tree that doesn't branch, is what we say up north.'

Another grin. 'See, that's why I like you. You say what you're thinking. Southern girls always say what they think you want them to be thinking.'

I arched my brows. 'And Southern boys always make sweeping and sexist generalizations?'

He grimaced guiltily, and it looked genuine. 'Yeah. We are prone to those.'

From what I'd seen, the town thought the sun shone out of Shawn's butt. So maybe girls down here *were* in the habit of telling him what he wanted to hear.

Our food arrived quickly, but Kimberly was too busy to talk. Just as well, since my purse was audibly sniffing Shawn's meat loaf from across the table. The lunch rush had just started, but the tables were a lot more full than when we'd arrived, with a lot of attention directed our way. Just how seriously did people take this 'good luck' superstition? As seriously as they took haints?

I picked up my sandwich and tried to ignore the feeling I was eating in a fishbowl. I wanted to know more about the bone of contention between Shawn and Rhys, and I wanted Shawn to do most of the talking, so I said, 'Tell me about Maddox Point.'

He looked pleased by my question. 'It's out on the Cahaba River. A place for city folk who want to enjoy the country, but don't want to feel like they're living in the sticks.'

'So you're bringing the suburbs out here?'

'Well, the lots will be bigger, and wooded. Some houses will have views of the Cahaba, but everyone will have access. There'll be a marina for putting in boats, docks for fishing, a dredged area for swimming. Plus a clubhouse with a pool, if river water isn't your thing.'

'So it's sort of like a really country country club.'

He chuckled, and acknowledged the slight humour in my description with a tilt of his head. 'Yeah, there will be tennis courts, and maybe a golf course eventually.'

I took a big bite of sandwich to give myself time to think. That sounded like a lot of real estate. Maybe the folks at the archaeological park had good reason to worry about encroachment. Swallowing in a gulp, I asked, 'Where is this in relation to Old Cahawba and Bluestone Hill?'

Grabbing a plastic bottle, Shawn drew a curved line of ketchup horizontally across the table, then placed a sugar packet next to it, to his left. 'That's the Cahaba River and the future Maddox Point.' He drew a more or less vertical line, which joined with the first and continued down, then added two more packets of sweetener, one for the park and one for the Hill, explaining, 'The old town – the yellow packet – is here at the junction of the rivers, and your place – the blue – is further down from that.'

The packets made a triangle, with Old Cahawba at the apex. 'And where is *this* town?' I asked, meaning Maddox Landing.

He put another sugar packet downriver from Bluestone Hill. Now Maddox Landing and Maddox Point made a triangle with Old Cahawba, with Bluestone Hill in the middle. I didn't know if there was any significance, but the pattern was distinct.

'Aren't you worried about the Cahaba Curse?' I asked, since he was being so informative.

He gave a confused laugh. 'The what?'

I gestured with the hand not holding the sandwich. 'Floods, yellow fever – I know you're not building *on* the old town, but you are right near it.'

'Oh. You've been talking to Dr Young.' He didn't exactly sound upset about it, more notably neutral. Pointing to the yellow packet, he said, 'See how the town is in that curve of the Cahaba? It's surrounded on almost three sides by the rivers. That's why they kept getting hit by floods. As for yellow fever, I hear they have a vaccine for that now.' He grinned. 'But it's not required to visit Alabama. It's not a third-world country, no matter what y'all may think up in New York.'

'Point taken.' I pulled a little piece of crust off my bread and slid it into my bag to reward Gigi for being quiet and good. My eyes, and my brain, stayed on the makeshift map. 'Did your family originally own Maddox Landing, too?'

Pushing aside his empty plate – and I do mean empty – Shawn picked up his fork and took a bite of pie. He didn't seem to think there was anything odd about all my questions. 'When folks started deserting Cahawba after the war – you know about that, right? – some wanted to stay in the area but get away from the flooding and the bad associations. So my however-many-great-grandfather donated land for a new city hall here.'

'That was very generous,' I said, noticing he'd left out what Dr Young had told me, about the Maddox of the day offering incentives for people to move to his new town. Then I took a bite of my own pie and, for a moment, I lost track of my line of questioning. 'Oh my God, this is good.'

Shawn grinned. 'I told you. You want to try a bit of mine?'

I shook my head, not wanting to spoil the tart, creamy goodness with chocolate. 'Maybe next time.'

His smile widened, spread up to warm his eyes, making the blue seem darker. 'I'm glad you're agreeable to a next time.'

Crap. I couldn't help my blush. It was just so *hard* to keep my guard up around him. It wasn't just that he was gorgeous and charming, the town golden boy and the big man on campus. It was all those things, plus something I recognized very well from ballet: he had stage presence.

Of course I was attracted to him. It was logical. I realized that with an odd sort of detachment, even while my stomach fluttered in reaction to his smile. It was completely unlike the way I felt around Rhys, which was totally illogical and inexplicable. The weird thing was, I didn't know which, if either, reaction was more honest.

'Anyway,' Shawn continued, and I had to remind myself what we were talking about, 'Great-granddad needed a town here to support his business interests. It was a win-win situation.'

There were echoes of that theme in Maddox Point. Shawn kept saying how good it would be for the area. I had to admit, it would probably be good for Paula, too.

Just because it rang like a party line didn't mean it wasn't true. So I knew I should just tell that little voice in my head – which sounded a lot like Rhys at the moment – to shut up.

Shawn polished off the last crumb of his pie. 'I'll take you to see the site sometime, if you like. It's not much more than a bunch of forested acreage and a big sign by the road right now, but that will change.'

'So you haven't started building?'

'Not yet.' Shawn waved to Kimberly to bring the check. 'Have to get the right approvals and all. Doesn't help that the guy the state sent out to survey by the river busted up his leg before he could finish his report.'

I winced in deep sympathy for the man, but the mention also rang a more recent bell. 'Did he fall by the river embankment? Dr Young told me about that.'

'Yeah, that was him.' He looked at me curiously, almost a little warily. 'What else did Dr Young say?'

With a wry smile that I hoped hid any evasion – I didn't need to tell Shawn we'd talked about his family, past and present – I replied, 'To watch out for alligators.'

Shawn laughed, drawing the attention of the eavesdroppers in the restaurant. I could feel their speculation ratchet up another notch. 'Now, that is good advice.'

I had to agree, because sometime during lunch I'd decided I needed to watch my step with Shawn. If my performer instincts recognized Shawn's charm as stage presence, didn't that mean that some part of me was thinking he was putting on at least a little bit of an act?

Shawn didn't ask if I wanted him to drive me back to the house: he just assumed he would, and it was one time I was happy to let him presume. I did attempt to pay for my own lunch, but when he insisted it was his treat, I realized that arguing would attract more attention than simply giving in. As it was, between the people who stopped by the table while we waited for the check and the change, and those who greeted us on our way out, I was sure by tomorrow morning the whole county would know that Shawn Maddox had taken Sylvie Davis on a date.

At Bluestone Hill, he pulled into the front drive, hauled my bike out of the truck and leaned it against a big fluted pot, pausing to look at it sadly. 'If it was a horse, you'd have to shoot it.'

I privately agreed, but his scorn for the poor thing made me perversely attached to it. 'It got me where I was going. More or less. Gigi and I are grateful for the ride back, though.'

When I'd set her down, Gigi had run to the grass for a quick pit stop, then pranced to the house and up the steps so she was closer to eye level. The better to watch Shawn as he asked, 'So, about this Catfish Festival. Would you like to go?'

I suspected I wasn't going to be able to get out of it. It felt like a fait accompli, and only sheer stubbornness made me ask, 'Is this a Maddox asking a Davis? Or Shawn asking Sylvie?'

He shrugged amiably. 'We can't help who we are and what it means around here.'

That wasn't exactly an answer. But given my feeling of inevitability, maybe it didn't really matter. 'I'll think about it,' I said.

'Is it because of the cousin thing?' he asked earnestly. 'Because really it's like fourth cousins twice removed.'

That rated a half-smile. 'It's more the catfish thing. I don't eat them.' I turned, and Gigi trotted beside me as I walked along the porch, heading for the back door.

Shawn accompanied us at more of a stroll, but he stopped when he saw the garden where I'd been working. 'Hey, you're clearing out around the big rock.'

'Yeah.' He jumped off the porch and went through the hedges. Gigi barked and ran after him, and I followed, too, surprised Shawn was so interested. I was proud of my start, but there was still an overwhelming amount of ground to cover.

I joined him at the central planting bed, not sure why I needed to explain, 'It was something to do. Paula's big into the whole "idle hands are the tools of the devil", I think.'

'Are you going to uncover the rock?' he asked, nodding to the vine-covered stone in the middle. 'I always wondered what this garden was supposed to look like.'

'Yeah,' I said, answering his question. 'I need some better clippers, though. That vine is insane. Is it kudzu?'

'The vine that ate the South,' Shawn confirmed. 'I'm surprised it hasn't blanketed this whole garden. You may have a tough time getting rid of it.' He glanced down at me with a smile of approval. 'This is a good sign.'

'The kudzu?' I asked doubtfully. My dad had told me it was originally imported and planted to prevent soil erosion, but it grew out of control and turned into an invasive nuisance, an example of what happened when you introduced something and upset the natural balance of an ecosystem.

Shawn laughed. 'No, that you're working on the garden. You know, digging into the old family place.'

He winked, acknowledging the pun. But the statement shook me, resonating with my childhood fascination with how cut plants would put down roots, what I'd told John seemed magical to me. Dad had taken pains to cut himself off from his family tree and transplant himself halfway across the country. Was I now grafting myself into the very place he'd left?

I couldn't ignore the question that wrapped around my mind like the kudzu around the rock. What if there was a good reason that Dad had left here in the first place?

Chapter 16

After Shawn went home, I let Gigi run around for a few more minutes before we headed for the back door. Paula was in the kitchen with Clara, so I left the dog on the porch to play with one of her toys.

'How was your meeting?' I asked, making conversation.

'Just fine.' She sat at the table, still wearing her going-to-town clothes, a big glass of iced tea in front of her. 'How was your lunch?' she returned with pointed curiosity.

'Oh my God.' I fell into my usual chair, stunned – but also not – that the news had made the rounds so quickly. 'You mean it didn't even take an hour for it to get back here?'

Clara, not bothering to hide her amusement, joined us, settling down with her own glass of tea. 'Rhonda Maxwell from Paula's bridge club called from her cell phone before you'd even ordered your meal. Did you like the lemon chess pie?'

I covered my eyes and groaned, not really exaggerating my consternation. 'It's like I've gone through a time warp to the fifties, but with better telecommunication.'

Paula actually laughed; her meeting must have gone very well. 'That Shawn Maddox. He doesn't move slow.'

'I don't get it.' I wished I could enjoy the moment, that I could be a normal girl being teased about her social life by her relatives – in Clara's case, an honorary one – and not be unnerved by this outdated matchmaking.

'Well, honey,' said Paula, misinterpreting my confusion, 'not to put too fine a point on it, you're a novelty. You'd be getting plenty of interest even if you were uglier than a coonhound. But you're not.'

'Plus, I'm a Davis.' Sobering, I sat up in the chair, getting to the crux of my unease. Gossip was one thing. But this level of excitement about my social life made the townspeople's expectations more than irritating. 'How much of this is because it's supposed to be good luck when our families get together?'

Paula took my question seriously, maybe picking up on my disquiet. 'I know it seems strange to you. It's just that the Davis and Maddox families have a long history together. In business, and otherwise.'

'I get that a hundred years ago people sealed deals with marriages and dowries and stuff. But seriously, this is the twenty-first century.' I couldn't explain my sense of outrage. Maybe I was again identifying with the Colonel's hypothetical daughter, the duty she'd have to marry for money, or business reasons, or class. Adding 'luck' to the list of reasons didn't seem quite fair.

'It's just a silly superstition, honey.' Paula patted my hand. 'Don't let it bother you.'

The patronizing hand pat annoyed me and made my reply sharp. 'Did it seem silly to you when *you* were young?'

Paula's eyes narrowed and her lips pursed. 'Before I was as ancient as I am now, you mean?'

Clara chuckled, defusing the moment, and rose from the table. 'I'll leave you to this family discussion. Addie will be home from school soon and I want to make sure she studies before her council meeting.'

I looked up, momentarily distracted. 'Is that tonight?' It seemed ages since the conversation in Caitlin's car.

She shook her head as she went to the door. 'I swear sometimes it feels like every night.'

Turning back to Paula, I began a new question. 'About when you were here when you were young—'

'For heaven's sake, Sylvie! No one tried to set me

up.' She got up and took her glass to the sink, dismissing the question, and me.

My tone turned chilly. 'I was going to ask about my dad, actually.'

Contrite, she returned to the table, resting her hands on the back of her chair. 'Go ahead.'

'Do you know if anything happened the last summer he was here?' For all we didn't get along, I didn't want to purposefully hurt my cousin's feelings. She talked about the past like it was something ideal, and I imagined it would sting to know Dad had never mentioned his family history. 'I just mean . . . It seems strange he never came back to visit.'

Paula gave the question some thought. 'I don't know, honey. I was a year or two older, and stopped coming before he did. When you grow up, you don't have the luxury of summers off.'

'I don't suppose Shawn has an aunt about Dad's age.' I was half joking. But only half.

Paula didn't smile. 'I just figured he became too busy to visit. I only came back once or twice until I inherited the place.'

'From your parents?' I asked, trying to sort out the family tree.

'From my grandfather. Your dad's great-uncle. I'm the only child of his oldest son. Though, of course, primogeniture doesn't really matter, since there's no one else.' Her gaze lost focus as memory reeled her in. 'Granddad Davis was old as the hills when he finally passed away. He'd been in a home for the last ten years, so the place was empty . . .' She trailed off and looked at me. 'No wonder people see you as a good omen! Young blood, back in the old family manor.'

'Somehow this conversation has failed to reassure me,' I said sceptically.

She smiled, seeming almost sympathetic. 'We are very set in our ways down here. Even – no, *especially* – when it comes to socialization.'

I had a sudden, horrible thought. 'I'm not going to have to do a cotillion or anything like that, am I?'

'Of course not,' Paula said, with no apparent irony. 'Debutante season has already passed.'

My stricken expression made her snort. 'Honestly, Sylvie. It won't do you harm to get a bit involved here. Of course people are going to be all in your business. You're the last of your line.'

'So?' In the back of my mind I'd realized this, but something about that phrasing made me uneasy, which made me grumpy. Grumpier than usual, I mean.

'So . . .' Paula drew out the word, her subtext very I-can't-believe-you-haven't-figured-this-out-for-yourself. 'I have no children. I hope it will be a long time from now, but you'll eventually inherit Bluestone Hill.'

'Not if you sell it.' Her look of absolute horror told me what she thought of that suggestion.

'And you,' she continued, as if I hadn't voiced the idea, 'will have the money to really fix it up, if you want.'

My forehead knit in confusion. 'What do you mean?'

'Well, your father's trust.' She registered my blank

look and explained, matter-of-factly, 'That's the way things split up. His side got the ironworks – which has since gone public, and the funds put into a trust. My side got the house and all the land.'

My stomach twisted. Had I been living on the Colonel's money all this time? 'I thought my allowance came from what Dad invested from his business. And the life insurance.'

'I don't know about that. I suppose it does, because you won't have access to the Davis trust until you're eighteen. That's the age your dad used the money to move away and go to school.'

I sat back, flummoxed. 'I just thought it was all Dad's money. And not—' I made a ballooning gesture, encompassing the weight of a family legacy.

'It's all your dad's money, honey,' Paula said pragmatically. 'You should really find out more about your business affairs. You're almost eighteen, for heaven's sake. Not a child.'

You wouldn't know that from the way she treated me, but my irritation took a back seat to my resurgent anger and confusion. Dad had – well, not hidden this, exactly, since I would have found out in a few months, even if I hadn't come down here. But he'd certainly kept it separate and secret.

I pushed that thought away, and concentrated on what I could discover about him here. Reading his mind was not an option, so I could only follow his past actions.

The thought spurred me, and I got up – then had to take hold of the back of my chair to stretch the bike-riding muscles that had stiffened into knots.

Paula frowned, borderline sympathetic. 'Why don't you go put your feet up. You've had two hard days, walking to Old Cahawba, then biking to town. I can't believe you did that.'

'I'm supposed to exercise my leg,' I said, irked more at my own body than at her, 'or it won't get stronger.'

'Yes,' she said dryly, 'but there's such a thing as moderation.'

'So I've heard.' I headed for the back door, trying not to limp and prove her point. As I let Gigi into the kitchen, it occurred to me that my cousin hadn't answered my half-joking question. 'Hey, Paula? *Does* Shawn have an aunt my dad's age?'

She'd been on the way back to the sink, but she paused, answering with a smile of remembrance. 'No, but he has a second cousin who used to play with us when we were little. Rainbow Maddox.'

'*Rainbow?*'

Paula's smile turned wry. 'Her parents weren't from around here.'

'It sounds like her parents weren't from this planet.' At her 'be nice' expression, I asked, 'Whatever happened to her?'

'Heavens, Sylvie, how should I know? Went back to California with her folks, I guess.' With a purposeful air of dismissal, she finished rinsing out her glass. 'It's just a silly superstition. Don't be so paranoid.'

The word put an end to my questions. I couldn't afford to have her think I was paranoid any more than I could let her think I was delusional.

Was I? I gnawed on the question. There was no

reason that my nagging unease with this matchmaking had any connection to Dad and his time here. Except that the idea – and despite Shawn's logical explanation about business deals and local dynasties, it was *archaic* at the very least – would, by its nature, go back generations.

Everything here seemed to go back generations. Maybe that was why the notion of ghosts didn't seem as crazy as it should. If there was any place where the habits of long-dead people and the impact of past events might echo into the present, it was at Bluestone Hill.

❧ ❧

I climbed the stairs stiffly, carrying Gigi in one hand and leaning heavily on the banister with the other. At my door, the lilac scent welcomed me back. It was the one peculiarity of Bluestone Hill that didn't alarm me.

Setting Gigi on the bed, I grabbed the back of the desk chair, bending over to stretch my hips and legs. The position put me at eye level with the drawer, and the Crazy/Not Crazy list inside. Was there any point in digging it out now?

I sat down, my fingers slipping unerringly to the secret latch. The compartment popped open easily, and I pulled out my crumpled list. There was something underneath it, and I caught my breath when I realized what it was – a dusty leather book with the ruffle-edged pages of a handwritten journal.

Gigi raised her head, ears pricked, nose twitching. The same alert curiosity rushed over me, my hands tingling as I carefully pulled the book from the compartment. The pages were yellowed with age. I gently ran my finger over the edges and dislodged something, which fluttered to the carpet.

The pressed flower was flat and papery, but the now-familiar fragrance filled the room as if I'd found a whole spray of fresh blooms. Lilacs.

With Christmas-morning excitement I carefully opened the book. There was no inscription in the front, no name. The ink was faded, and the handwriting spiky and uneven. Not exactly the neat script young ladies were supposed to practise.

March 1863. Marnie and I took blankets and medicine to the prison in town. Those poor souls — is that what we would want for our men and boys? When I think of my own brothers, off fighting with our father in Virginia . . .

The book confirmed my instinctive certainty. Lilac Girl was the Colonel's daughter.

Chapter 17

I spent the afternoon reading the journal, though deciphering might be a better description. By the time Paula called me down for dinner, I was bleary-eyed and pretzel-necked from hunching over the desk to get the best light on the page. I wanted to read the book in order, but it was slow going, between the handwriting, the author's use of initials and shorthand for the things and people common to her but mysteries to me, and the fact that I had to be so careful with the fragile paper.

The entries were a combination of her ruminations

and a diary of events and domestic activities. She seemed so young, but she had a tremendous amount of responsibility. Her mother was dead, and all the men were off fighting. Plus, I'd seen *Gone with the Wind* and Sherman's march to the sea, so I knew there was danger, even for those at home. But I couldn't forget the old photograph in the Davis history book. No daughter in evidence. What had happened to her? I was as anxious for Lilac Girl as if she were a personal friend.

I returned the journal to its hiding place before I went down to dinner. Eventually, I would have to tell Paula about it. The little bit I'd read so far might have value to a historian. She might get some money for it, to help with the house's upkeep. But for now, my roommate was my secret.

Once Gigi was in her crate with her own dinner, I went to the kitchen. Paula was pouring iced tea into four glasses. Addie had just finished setting the table. I didn't understand the dagger-sharp look she threw me until I remembered that I hadn't actually spent the entire afternoon a hundred and fifty years in the past. I'd had lunch with Shawn Maddox, and obviously news of my date had reached the high school campus.

'Have a seat,' Clara told me. 'I'm dishing up now.'

Things were looking up on the food front. Clara had made a spicy dish of red beans and rice, with a cucumber salad to counteract the heat. 'This is fantastic,' I said, barely waiting until she and Paula sat before digging in.

Addie, however, poked at her bowl and said, 'I can't eat this, Mom. It's nothing but carbs.'

Clara didn't improve things by nodding at me as she buttered a piece of corn bread. 'Sylvie's not worried about that.'

Addie shot me another glare. 'She's so skinny, she can eat whatever she wants. Bowls of carbs. Eggs every day. Pie at the Daisy Café.'

Since I realized that the food was not really the issue, I shouldn't have baited her. But I took a big bite of the savoury rice and said, 'The pie was delicious, too.'

She narrowed her eyes dangerously. I expected another frontal attack, but instead, she came at me sideways. 'So. Kimberly says you've seen the Colonel's ghost.'

My stomach dropped with a sickening twist. Clara and Paula, who'd been ignoring Addie's sniping, stopped eating to stare at me in surprise and dismay. They couldn't possibly have been more surprised and dismayed than I was.

'I never said I saw the Colonel's ghost.' Frantically I cast my mind back over the conversation, trying to make certain. 'Because I *haven't*.'

Which was the truth. I hadn't *seen* anything definitive.

Paula's face pinched in concern. 'Did Shawn rattle you with ghost stories? He's always been fascinated with the tales, but that's all they are, honey.'

My hand fisted on my spoon. Her patronizing tone was infuriating, but I was already furious at Addie, and at Kimberly, so it was hard to tell the difference.

Clara reached across the table to squeeze my hand. 'Don't let them harass you, girl. These old houses will play tricks on you. And the woods aren't any better.

When the wind starts blowing the moss around, I'd swear my old granny was coming to get me.'

'I'm not rattled!' But my voice climbed in panic. I *was* unnerved, just not for the reasons they assumed.

Addie looked like a cat with canary feathers in its mouth, and I couldn't figure out what she was trying to accomplish, other than to make my life miserable. 'Kimberly said y'all had a whole conversation about spirits and stuff.'

'Look,' I said, getting myself under control. I wasn't going to convince anyone of my sanity by raving. 'Kimberly brought up the ghost thing. And yeah, Shawn did before that. I never said *I* saw anything.'

Did I? The worst thing was, I couldn't be certain. Whatever her intentions, Addie had managed to make me doubt myself. Maybe I *was* nuts if I was saying things and then forgetting them.

'Maybe you blacked out the conversation,' said Addie, as if she'd read my thoughts. 'I hear that can happen when you're drying out.'

'*What?*' I stared at her blankly, my brain completely shut down in outrage and disbelief.

'Addie!' snapped her mother. 'That's enough.'

My nemesis just shrugged. 'Everyone knows that's why she's here.'

'*Everyone* knows no such thing,' said Clara. 'And neither do you, young lady.'

I turned to Paula and demanded, 'Why would people think that?' Because the only way they could have gotten that idea was if a certain someone blabbed what the stepshrink had told her.

'No one thinks that, Sylvie,' Paula said impatiently, but I wasn't listening.

Pushing back from the table, I stood as calmly as I could, worried any quick movement would break my control over my feelings and I would scream at Paula, or pull Addie's hair, or start to cry. 'I've lost my appetite.'

No one tried to stop me. On the porch, Gigi stood in her crate, her front paws up on one of the metal crossbars, waiting for me, as if she sensed that I was upset. I let her out, fitted her harness and snapped on the leash, taking no chances of her running off in the dark. I moved by rote, because I was choking on emotion.

I headed for the garden, trying to outrun the fury that kept catching me. A few hours of distraction this afternoon, and now I was angry again. At Paula, at Addie, at Rhys. Not to mention Mother, the stepshrink and John. I was mad at the world, and most of all, I was mad at myself.

I *hated* that I'd circled back to where I'd started, wondering if I was crazy, wondering if anything would ever be right again. Other people dealt with tragedy without coming apart at the seams – or so my shrink told me. Why was *I* seeing ghosts and forgetting conversations and imagining connections with the previous occupant of my room?

Kicking off my shoes, I let the gravel of the path roughly massage my feet. I surveyed my work, willed my accomplishments to soothe me. I had gotten a startling amount done, clearing a tiny, pie-shaped segment of the central circle. Once I'd gotten some of the weeds pulled out, I was surprised at how many of the plants on Dad's list were still alive, just choked and pathetic.

My hands itched to get back in the dirt. Looking at it wasn't enough. Securing Gigi's leash to the bench, I knelt in the planting bed, burrowing with my toes as if anchoring myself and digging my fingers down to the roots of the weeds.

I didn't bother with gloves, and I didn't need light. By now I could go by feel, the texture of the plant, the shape of the leaves. More than that, it was something that I identified through my skin. I didn't think about whether this was strange or unnatural. I just worked the earth, and freed my mind from the awful knots of anger and fear.

The more I thought about it, what Addie implied didn't make sense. No one in town treated me as if I was unhinged. According to Kimberly, most of them believed in ghosts. Or at least the possibility of them. And if they thought I was an alcoholic, it didn't stop them from treating me like returning royalty. As long as their prince accepted me, I was golden, even if I did have bats in my belfry.

And speaking of Shawn . . . It kept coming back to him. Maybe it was unfair to blame Kimberly for blathering about ghosts to Addie, when she obviously believed in them. But it was Shawn who kept bringing them up. Shawn who was the big fish in this small pond, who ran the Teen Town Council, whose charm and influence were off the chart.

Who was courting me, the last Davis, and apparently heir to not only a lot of money but Bluestone Hill itself. In my head, I saw the triangle of sweetener packets on the table. If the properties were game pieces, they would trap Old Cahawba and give the player a lock on the corner where the rivers met – a lot of rustic paradise for hunting and ATV trails.

There's an old movie, *Gaslight,* where Ingrid Bergman plays an heiress, and this guy marries her and then makes her think she's going crazy. It has something to do with getting her house or her fortune.

Could someone be gaslighting me? I knew from performing, there were plenty of stage tricks you could use: scrim curtains, a TV screen reflected in a pane of glass, a costume and a well-placed mirror. Even fog machines were easy to get.

It might make sense – if I could think of how anyone would benefit from making me think I was nuts. I already had plenty of doubts, without anyone's help.

Sitting back on my heels, I wondered if I could feel this clearheaded and still be crazy. The world seemed to be trying to convince me my own senses were faulty, and Rhys had warned me to be careful whom I trusted. If I couldn't believe my own instincts, what did I have left to rely on?

❧ ❧

I woke, facedown on my bed, William S. Davis's book digging into my side. With a groan, I pulled it out from under me and flopped back down. It was a good thing,

I guess, that I'd taken a break from reading the journal; the ancient pages would have been ruined if I'd fallen asleep on top of them.

Squinting at the bedside clock, I saw it was half-past indecently late, and other than the sharp corner of the Davis family history, I couldn't figure out what had woken me.

Had the Griffiths come in? When I'd returned to the kitchen to wash my hands, Paula had told me – after complaining about my getting dirty all over again – that the professor had called to say they would be rolling in very late, if they made it back that night at all.

'Will you be all right upstairs by yourself?' she asked, in the tone people use when they're concerned, but trying not to *sound* concerned.

'Why wouldn't I?' I challenged, some of my hard-won calm slipping away. 'I'm sure you've hidden all the liquor, so I can't get into too much trouble.'

'Sylvie—' she started in an annoyed voice, then stopped and blew out a breath. 'Addie wouldn't be able to get to you if you weren't so prickly.'

There were so many arguments I could make to that, but half of them would just prove her point, so I let it go. But I noticed she hadn't denied my accusation.

I listened for the sound of someone coming up the stairs, but heard nothing. So, whatever had woken me, it was not the Griffiths returning.

Gigi stood on the edge of the bed, her little body stiff, her hackles raised as she stared at the window. I turned off the lamp, so the room was lit only by the moonlight, then went to see what had disturbed her.

Peering out, I scanned the lawn, the woods, the river, all painted in a silver glow. The moon was three-?quarters full, and I sort of wished I hadn't joked with Rhys about werewolves.

I leaned across the desk to slide open the window. There was a strange electricity in the air, like a static charge. Gigi growled softly, and I thought about how dogs were supposed to be able to sense earthquakes and natural disasters right before they happened. The night had the kind of pent-up energy that ran through me when I was backstage waiting to go on, the stored potential of bunched muscle preparing for a leap or a turn.

It didn't make sense. But neither did my inordinate fear of the watcher, and I'd accepted that. Whatever the cause, the *feeling* was real.

A shadow moved swiftly and stealthily across the lawn. Unlike before, the girl wasn't wearing a long skirt, but jeans. She glanced towards the house, and I ducked down, but not before I recognized Addie.

What was she doing out? And where was she coming from? I listened for a car engine, or the crunch of tyres on the gravel, indicating she'd been dropped off. But she hadn't come from the front of the house. She'd come through the back garden, from the southeast. There was nothing in that direction, except for the river and the summerhouse.

Was she just now leaving the Teen Town Council meeting? It was a school night, and this was *way* past curfew.

The way she'd looked up at the house – had she seen

the watcher? Or had she merely glimpsed my light going out? I risked a peek over the windowsill, but there was no sign of her. Of course, the balcony blocked my view of the back yard. Cautiously I levered myself up on the desk, then craned out the window. I could just see the corner of the summerhouse and what *could* have been a glimmer of light. Or it might have been the moon reflecting on the river behind it.

I'd promised Rhys I wouldn't go wandering around in the dark, but curiosity steamed like a kettle inside me. The weird charge in the air made it impossible to stay still.

Gigi jumped down from the bed and scratched eagerly at the door. That settled it. My dog had to pee. I *had* to go outside, even if it was just to the yard.

I grabbed her extra leash from a hook on the cabinet and clipped it to her collar. Pausing briefly, I grasped the doorknob, feeling for cold the way they teach you to feel for heat in a fire. The brass felt only cool, so I poked my head into the dark hallway.

Nothing. If there was a chill, it was slight enough to be my imagination or maybe the air-conditioning. I picked Gigi up and hurried anyway, avoiding the French doors, taking the main stairs down. With the dog held tightly against my chest, I crept to the kitchen and out through the porch.

The night was reassuringly warm, which was a good thing, since I wasn't wearing a jacket, just a camisole and pj's. These had psychedelic daisies on them. During my months of convalescence, I'd built up an impressive collection of pyjama pants. Though with my nocturnal ramblings with Gigi, I was going through them fast.

Walking the dog wasn't only an excuse. She got quickly to business in the back yard, while I crept towards the hedgerow that obscured my view of the summerhouse. I wasn't halfway there, however, when a light snapped on in the kitchen.

Crap. Forget sneaking the dog in; Paula would have plenty to say about my being out in the middle of the night. I tucked Gigi into the crook of my arm and made for the spiral staircase, avoiding the kitchen windows on my way.

The steps were cold and damp under my bare feet, and the iron grating bit into my toes. I held onto the vine-covered railing, reaching the top just as a breeze began to blow. It rustled the leaves and drifted my hair around my shoulders. The coiled-spring feeling in the air intensified, like a clock wound until the key wouldn't turn any more.

When the sound came from the woods, I was already expecting it. The wailing cry was unutterably sad. It burrowed into my chest and made a painful knot of heart-deep sorrow. It twisted parts of me that I didn't even know could ache. The piteous noise reached through my rising fear and tore a gasp of sympathy from my throat.

I still clutched Gigi against me, and her growl vibrated against my ribs. Setting her down, I went to the balustrade and peered out into the woods.

Through the trees, I could see a figure moving. She ran through the woods, the branches catching at her long skirts, tangling her loose hair. Her headlong rush would carry her straight to the river, where the ground dropped steeply to the rushing water below. There was no time to wonder how I could see her so well in the shadows, how I could sense what she meant to do, as if some string connected our hearts. It was strange, and terrible, and terrifying.

'No!' I shouted it across the night. 'Don't jump!'

But she did, flinging herself from the embankment, and disappearing into the water.

I had to call the police, the sheriff, whoever was responsible. Through the pulse pounding in my ears I heard Gigi barking frantically, but my head was so *full* of this girl and her flight that all I could think about was helping her.

I whirled and ran to the French doors. My fingers closed on the handles, registered the burning cold of the metal. I snatched them back, cradled them against my chest to warm them. Only then did I look in through the glass.

A grey man in military dress, thick sideburns and moustache stood looking out at me, watching through hollow blackness where his eyes should have been.

Chapter 18

My scream was loud enough to wake the dead. Those that weren't already walking.

It also woke the household, including Clara and Addie in their apartment over the garage. Gigi's barking helped with that, I imagine.

When the doors in front of me flew open, I screamed again, but it was Paula, not an empty-eyed spectre, who rushed out.

'Sylvie!' She grabbed my arms and shook me until my eyes focused on her fully; then her hands slid down to mine, chafing them briskly. 'Oh my God. Your fingers are freezing. What happened? Are you all right?'

I stopped shrieking and started babbling. The logic parts of my brain were completely overrun by panic. 'There was a woman, and a man at the window. The watcher. We have to call nine-one-one for the woman in the river.'

'What's going on?' I heard Clara yelling from her first-floor landing across the lawn.

Paula stared at me, uncomprehending. 'What on earth is wrong with you!'

I realized the words had spilled out in an unintelligible rush. And Gigi was still barking, covering up anything sensible that did come out. 'I saw . . . I thought I saw . . . There was a woman in the woods. And a man at the window.'

'Honey, are you sure?'

'I—' The words seized up in my throat. I looked into her eyes and saw overwhelming concern, but there was an underlying thread of 'Oh my God, how am I going to explain this breakdown to her mother' that cut through my blind panic.

I *knew* what I'd just experienced was real, and not in my imagination. But that was meaningless. I knew I wasn't a drug addict or a drunk, either, but I'd still had to endure the humiliation of Mother and the step-shrink searching my room for booze or drugs, even though I'd voluntarily handed over my postsurgical Vicodin. No way was I giving anyone ammunition to do that ever again.

'No,' I said, wrestling back control over myself.

'I'm not sure. I was getting Gigi – sorry, Paula – and the glass, it can look like something is there.' I raised a trembling hand – I didn't have to fake that – to rub my brow and hide my face as I lied. 'It must have been all that talk today.'

Paula's jaw set. 'That Adina. I'm going to have a *stern* talk with that girl.'

'It's not her fault.' I took a noble tone, but I was more worried about retribution from Addie if Paula read her the riot act. 'Shawn started it, then there was all that talk about haints and bottle trees at lunch—'

'What's going on? Is everyone all right?' Clara called again.

'We're fine,' Paula shouted back. 'Just a nightmare.' Then she looked at me, a warning in her eye. 'She doesn't need to know how much Addie upset you.'

'Yes, ma'am. I don't want to upset Clara.'

Her expression gentled, which was a relative thing with Paula, but still. I was almost touched. 'Are you going to be all right?'

That was highly debatable. I picked up Gigi, who'd finally stopped barking, and she licked my face with anxious puppy kisses as if to ask the same question.

'I'll be OK. I'll be better if Gigi sleeps with me.'

Paula's eyes narrowed. 'Now I'm beginning to think this is an elaborate ruse to get that dog in your room overnight.'

I was fine with that, actually, glad for any excuse for my behaviour. So I said, 'Would I do that?' in a purposely too-innocent way.

'Humph. Just for tonight.'

She walked into the house, and I followed her closely through the hall, certain that no ghost would dare appear to practical Paula. She walked me all the way to my door, then gave me one last worried look before she left.

I shut the door, set Gigi on the bed and went to close the window. The night seemed resoundingly normal now. No sounds. No cold. No tightly wound tension in the air. It was as if I *had* imagined everything. In that way, the quick return to normalcy was scarier than any ghost.

Almost.

I didn't think I'd sleep, but when I crawled under the covers, Gigi curled into the curve of my neck, and her even breathing coaxed me into slumber.

I dreamed of dancing, and of falling, and of the sweet smell of lilac.

❧ ❧

Despite everything, the morning found me surprisingly optimistic. Maybe it was the reassuring daylight. Or it might have had something to do with Rhys coming back. Compelling or exasperating, at least he was a distraction from my *seriously* weird problems.

As I threw on my clothes, I strengthened my resolve to keep an open mind. It was counterproductive to wear the same circle of worry through my mind, and I knew I'd get a lot more done if I just formed a working theory based on an assumption of sanity, then went from there. I was proud of how logical that sounded.

'Here's what we have to work with today,' I said to Gigi as she watched me pull on my jeans. I needed to think aloud, even if my only sounding board had four legs and a tail. At least I could trust her to keep my secrets. 'There seem to be three things. The sound in the woods. The girl, who might be connected to the sound. And the watcher.'

I suppressed a shudder, even though the sun streamed in the east-facing window, setting fire to the fine particles of dust in the air. I suppose I could start calling him the Colonel now.

'Next,' I told Gigi, tugging on a T-shirt, and pretending I was as brave and logical as I sounded. 'They're getting worse.'

I managed to say it without too much of a quiver in my stomach. Gigi cocked her head, and I sat on the bed, running a hand over her silky fur. The thing about the Colonel was, if ghosts were just impressions of the past, the leftover psychic fingerprints of the routine of daily living, then the apparition at the window wasn't so much a thumbprint as a deep, gouging scar. I'd always felt menaced by the watching presence, but last night, face to face—

My stomach did turn over then, and as if sensing it, Gigi climbed into my lap and I cuddled her close.

Seeing the Colonel face to face had been like plunging from the high dive into a frigid pool. Hitting a wall of icy malevolence.

I had to keep my thoughts moving forward, or fear would paralyse me. 'So, what was different last night, Gee? The full moon? Being outside? The TTC?'

It had always struck me as strange that they met in the summerhouse. Which made it odd that I hadn't made it out there yet. Time to change that.

Despite the fact that Gigi was authorized to be upstairs, I didn't want to deal with Paula just yet. It would have been easier to go down the spiral staircase, but I wasn't brave enough to go through the French doors, even though there was no sign of anything weird in the hall. Instead, I took my usual route through the den.

Instead of going to the summerhouse directly, Gigi and I walked straight down the sloping lawn and into the trees. It was cool under the canopy of leaves, but only because the sun hadn't reached in to drive away the morning damp. Gigi made sniffing forays through the pine needles, but never went too far before coming back to me.

We reached the river at the point where I'd seen the girl disappear. Looking back towards the house, I wondered how I'd managed to see her with such clarity. Then I shook myself. Duh. Ghost. Normal rules may not apply.

Bracing a hand on one of the trees that clung to the edge of the embankment, I peered over. It was a steep, treacherous drop, and the Alabama River ran by at a swift clip. But there was no sign of an actual fall. No disturbed earth, no broken branches, no marks in the mud.

A wave of vertigo tightened my grip on the rough bark of the pine tree. Time made one of those sideways slips in my head, and I couldn't tell if I was falling now, or remembering the fall onstage, or somehow remembering *her* fall, empathizing too closely with a girl who possibly never even existed.

'Who are you?' I whispered. That had to be my next move, finding out. 'And what are you running from?'

Gigi barked, bringing me back to the present. I forced myself to retreat a step and turned downriver, the dog trotting amiably beside me, unaffected by my momentary fugue.

The path took me downhill, the embankment shortening until eventually the land and water met on the same level. We'd reached the clearing of the inlet – a V-shaped slope that climbed steeply back up to the summerhouse. Set between the house and the water, it would have an excellent view and catch the breeze.

A raised octagon with a pointed roof, the summerhouse had a latticed half wall with screens above it. It was more of a gazebo really, but the tightly woven screens gave the walls a sort of opacity. Even during the daytime, anyone inside would be a shadow at best.

Gigi sniffed the perimeter, ending her patrol at the wooden steps to the entrance. They seemed in good shape, and there was even a handrail. The whole structure was freshly painted and looked a lot better than I would have thought, considering a bunch of teens worked on it.

The screen door opened noiselessly, and a strip of insulation inside the frame made sure that it wouldn't bang closed. The purposefulness of the silence seemed eerily secretive. I found myself walking quietly, half holding my breath as I came in. The click of Gigi's nails on the floor was loud, like a pair of high heels in the hush of an empty church.

Trying to shake the feeling, I let Gigi explore, which she did, nose to the ground. There was a wood table, its paint peeling off, that would get a good price from a chichi antiques barn. So would the chairs scattered around the room. Two wicker ones were set with a battered steamer truck between them like a coffee table. The furniture was old but clean, and the place didn't feel deserted.

There was a faint smell of – herbs? Potpourri? Citronella candle? Maybe a mix of all those things. Several used matches lay on the corner of the trunk, and a lot of wax drippings pooled on the table.

I tried to open the trunk, but it was locked. More secrets. Why did the Teen Town Council meet in the summerhouse when there was a perfectly nice den in the house? And why was Addie out here so late? Did the meeting go into the wee hours, or had she lingered here, maybe with someone else? Shawn?

After an initial stab of outrage – he had a lot of nerve buying me pie – the idea didn't entirely hold up. I believed Addie and Shawn might be thick as thieves, but it didn't feel like they were *involved* in that way.

The summerhouse didn't look like make-out central, despite the candle smell and the matches. And I didn't smell pot or tobacco smoke. So what were they doing? Playing Scrabble?

This was occupying way too much of my mental energy. What could this possibly have to do with anything? With my dad, the weirdness in town, the whole

Davis/Maddox thing, and last – but so very not least – with the things I was seeing and feeling.

I opened the screen door and looked towards the house. The rosy morning light blurred the shabbiness of the dingy whitewash and saggy trim like a soft-focus camera lens. The overgrown hedges, the moss-draped oaks, the vines crawling up the side columns – all made it seem like the house had been grown rather than built.

The gap in the hedges was aligned so that I had a clear view of the kudzu-covered stone in the garden. An invisible string tied between the rock and the centre of the summerhouse could be pulled straight and taut, like one of those tin-can telephones in old movies.

More disconnected mysteries, like puzzle pieces jumbled in a box. The wailing in the woods and the watcher in the window. The candles and secrecy here in the summerhouse and the monolithic keystone of the garden. Rhys's secret agenda and his rock hunting, and the antipathy between him and Shawn.

'Gigi, sometimes I think the ghosts are the least weird thing going on here.'

She growled, and I turned to see her plumed tail sticking out from under one of the built-in benches that ringed the half walls. She emerged backwards, pulling out something oblong, grey and fuzzy.

My stomach turned. 'Oh my God. That had better not be a rat.'

Gigi bore it proudly towards me in her teeth, shaking it with a tiny growl, making sure it was dead. Thankfully, as she got closer, I saw it had never been alive; at least, I didn't see any tail or feet.

I got her to drop the thing and, picking it up between two fingers, I examined what appeared to be a bundle of dried twigs or herbs. A tentative sniff said a mix of both. I smelled some kind of fragrant wood and a pungent green. How weird. The bundle was tied with a piece of cotton string, and it appeared to be charred at one end. When I touched it, my fingers came away black, as if I'd drawn on them with charcoal.

Incense? Maybe Addie *was* hooking up in the gazebo, and setting the mood.

Gigi's ears swivelled towards the house, and she ran to the screen door, barking an alert. I slipped the charred bundle into the pocket of my jacket, as if I had something to hide, and wiped the traces off my fingers before going to the door.

But no one was coming. Gigi was barking at Caitlin's compact car as it pulled round on the drive, heading towards the county road and on to the high school. I glimpsed Addie in the passenger seat, waving her hands as she told an animated, and apparently very humorous, story. Somehow, I was sure it had to do with my screaming bloody murder in the middle of the night.

Nice. I sighed and pushed the door open for Gigi, then carefully manoeuvred down the steps and climbed the sloping lawn towards the house. At least I could now eat breakfast without Miss Malice ruining my appetite.

❧ ❧

Clara and Paula were deep in conversation, and they started guiltily when I came in. Obviously I was everyone's major topic of conversation this morning. I *knew*

Paula felt guilty, because she didn't say anything when Gigi trotted in alongside me.

That is, she didn't say anything about the *dog*. 'Where did you come from?' she demanded.

'I had to take the dog out for her morning business,' I said. Honest, if incomplete.

Her gaze dropped to my muddy tennis shoes, and the balance of guilt shifted back to normal. 'You didn't go out to the river, did you?'

'Uh.' I was so used to lying when sneaking Gigi in and out of the house that you'd think I would have been prepared with something better than a blank stare now.

'Oh, Sylvie.' Her exasperated lament had a worried edge to it. 'Did you have to?'

Clara intervened on my behalf. I had started thinking of them as a pair of aunts, the familial version of good cop, bad cop. 'Paula, she's fine. Look at her. She looks a lot healthier than when she got here.'

Paula frowned at me, but apparently this was a convincing argument. Still, she wasn't completely swayed. 'Can you blame me for being concerned?'

'Lord,' said Clara, pushing herself up from the table. 'This big ol' house has a history that's enough to give a girl the horrors. When I first came here, *I* used to have nightmares about the Colonel coming to get me. Why do you think I'm happy in an outbuilding, like my ancestors? I don't want anything to do with yours.'

This was an interesting piece of news. Intrigued – not to mention hungry – I took my normal seat at the table. Gigi stretched her front paws up to my knee, asking to be picked up, and while Paula's attention was on pouring herself a fresh cup of coffee, I slipped the dog into my lap, hidden by the table.

'What kind of nightmares?' I asked Clara as she returned to the table with a glass of orange juice for me.

She gave me a 'don't be naïve' look and pointed to her dark-skinned face. 'What kind of nightmares do you think?'

'Oh, of course.' My ears burned with the realization I'd said something stupid and possibly offensive. 'I'm sorry.'

I was apologizing for a lot with those two words. Clara seemed to get that, and smiled slightly. 'The past is a fact we can't change. I live in the present.'

'But . . .' I looked from one woman to the other, seeing an opening for some prying. 'It's like you said, Clara. The house really is full of history. The past seems so close. Hasn't your imagination ever run away with you, Paula?'

She blinked, her hesitation covered by Clara's laugh. 'The Colonel wouldn't dare haunt Paula.'

It was the smallest chink, but I pursued that momentary delay in answering. 'Maybe when you were a kid?'

This time, Clara noticed the hesitation too, and stared at her friend. 'You did. I can see it in your face.'

Paula huffed, irritated that we had cornered her. She resisted for another stubborn moment, taking a long sip of coffee, then said, 'When I was a little younger than Sylvie, I had a sleepover. We were "camping out" ' – her tone supplied the quote marks – 'in the summerhouse. And Rainbow Maddox—'

'Rainbow?' echoed Clara.

Paula ignored her. 'We were doing silly girl stuff. Telling fortunes, ghost stories. I think there was a Ouija board involved. We were trying to scare ourselves, so it's no wonder . . .' She paused as if regretting starting the story.

'Go on,' said Clara.

Paula blew out a breath and half rolled her eyes. 'Rainbow heard something outside, and when we went to look she swore she saw someone at the upstairs window, watching us. That it was the Colonel, and he was going to get us for doing magic in his summerhouse. Everyone screamed and hid in their sleeping bags, pulled them up over their heads.' She chuckled. 'It was the hit of the party, really.'

While I stared at her, trying not to look as gobsmacked as I felt, Clara said, amused, 'I'm so glad to know you were once capable of being silly.'

I leaned forward, figuratively holding my breath. Something she'd said clicked, and I had to phrase my question carefully, to keep the mood light and the emphasis off my nighttime adventures.

'Do you think,' I ventured casually, 'this is where the rumour that the house is haunted came from? Kimberly and the others really seem to believe in ghosts, and you said yourself Shawn is fascinated. Those would be their mothers, wouldn't they? The girls at your slumber party.'

Paula blinked in surprise. 'I never thought about that.'

Should I press my luck and point out how this meant

I wasn't nuts? That she could stop worrying about me? Or would it just remind her about last night? Her story didn't explain the girl at the river, after all.

While I debated, Clara got up from the table and asked, 'What do you want for breakfast?'

'Is there cereal? I should have gotten some when I was— Oh, crud.' I edited my usual curse word. 'I left the soy milk I bought yesterday in Shawn's truck.'

'Uh-huh,' said Clara knowingly. 'I guess you'll have to call him to bring it over.'

Or not. I didn't think he needed encouragement. Even forgetting that Addie had been out late with *someone* last night, if my gut said things like 'stage presence' and 'Tom Sawyer trickster', I needed to pay attention. Which was easier to do when Shawn wasn't around.

My noncommittal 'Humph,' which both women seemed to find amusing, put an end to the conversation, or at least that part of it. As Clara and Paula exchanged a few words about groceries, I ventured into the inner sanctum of the kitchen and found regular milk and some bran flakes, carried them back to the table and poured myself a generous bowl. And then, suddenly, Clara left, as if she and Paula had made some agreement while I was crunching and couldn't hear, and I was alone with my cousin.

'Listen, Sylvie.' She leaned her elbows on the table.

I set down my spoon warily. Nothing good was going to follow that gently concerned overture. The phone rang, and I grasped at the diversion. 'Do you need to answer that?'

'Clara can get it in the den.' She cleared her throat

and continued. 'Your stepfather gave me the name of a colleague of his in Birmingham, who will see you at a moment's notice. Maybe I should call and make you an appointment.'

'What? No! Paula—' My protest was incoherent, the emphatic slash of my hand endangering my cereal bowl. 'I don't need a shrink. Weren't we just talking about how rumour and the history of the house can make even *your* imagination run wild?'

She didn't look pleased with the reminder. 'Imagination, yes. Screaming night terrors, no.'

My heart pounded in my throat. A junior shrink had gotten me into this mess, his confiding manner making me say too much. The stepshrink had told Mother I couldn't stay by myself, and she'd believed him over me. My own, real shrink was no help at all when I'd begged – well, demanded – that he tell Mother I was fine. He'd just said his usual crapola about mourning and moving on. The psychiatrists who *knew* me didn't believe I wasn't drunk or depressed or deranged. What the hell would an actual stranger do to me?

'Paula, please,' I said, knowing that giving into irrational raving was not going to convince her I didn't need professional help. 'I'm fine. If it happens again' – by which I meant, if I got caught in a situation I couldn't bluff my way out of – 'I'll talk to . . . I don't know. Anyone but a shrink.'

For a long moment, she studied my earnest expression. 'What about Reverend Watkins at our church? Will you talk to him?'

I sat back in my chair, struck by the possible

providence of this suggestion. 'Which church?' I bit my tongue to keep from blurting out: *The one where the Colonel is buried?* I didn't want to say anything to make her rethink the shrink issue.

Paula stood up, as if the matter was settled. 'It's between here and Maddox Landing. You may have even seen the steeple from the road. It's been the family church for generations.'

'So . . .' I pretended to be reluctant about the idea. 'I could even ride my bike over there.'

She was so relieved, her spine relaxed a millimetre or so. 'I'll be happy to drive you, honey.'

It wasn't difficult to manufacture a pained expression. 'Please. Leave me at least the illusion of independence.'

'Fine,' she said, getting the last word. 'I'll call the reverend and tell him you'll be out sometime today.'

I was eating my bran flakes, grumbling silently about being outmanoeuvred, when Clara came in from the front of the house. Something in her step made me look up, and I swallowed hard at her worried expression.

'What's wrong?' Paula asked. I remembered the phone ringing, and my heart plummeted.

Clara lifted her hands in a calming gesture. 'Everyone is all right. Professor Griffith just called; they were in a minor accident on the way home last night.'

'Are they OK?' I asked, half rising out of my chair, oblivious to the fact that she'd just said so. There were different levels of 'all right'.

She nodded. 'He and Rhys are fine. Bumps and

bruises. But it was late, and they had to have the rental car towed; they're working on getting another one. He didn't want us to worry if they didn't arrive back until this afternoon or evening.'

Paula leaned a hand on the counter, one hand on her chest. 'Well, thank God for that. I've grown rather fond of those fellows.'

'You're not the only one,' said Clara, and I thought she was talking about herself until she said, her voice warm with sympathy, 'Sit down, honey, before you fall down. They're both fine.'

I didn't feel like I was going to fall down. I felt like I was going to throw up. I'd known Rhys less than a week, not nearly long enough to justify the wrenching knot in my chest at the thought of something dire happening to him.

'I'm OK,' I said. 'I'm just going to go, um, change my jeans and work in the garden for a bit.'

Calling for Gigi, I headed to the front of the house. I didn't care about my jeans; as the dog jumped onto the love seat, I grabbed the home phone and checked the caller ID. My cell phone was still in my pocket from the day before, and it even had a charge. I entered the number – a US one, probably a throwaway phone for their stay – into my cell, then grabbed Gigi and went out the side door to my garden.

Impatiently I unlaced my sneakers while the phone rang. I'd just gotten them off and was kneading the grass between my toes when Rhys answered.

'Hello?' I recognized his voice with no trouble, even though the accent was the same as his dad's.

'Are you really OK?' I asked without preamble.

There was a funny sort of exhale on the end. Realization, relief, recognition – I couldn't tell, except that his tone warmed a little. 'Yeah. We're both all right. The car's a goner, though. Dad's doing the paperwork now.'

'How are you all right if the car's totalled?'

'Air bags, love. Fantastic invention.'

Gigi was sitting in the flower bed, getting dirty. My knees weak, I joined her, lowering myself into a soft, green patch. 'Where are you? What happened?'

'Gasden. It was the closest city.' There was a pause, then he lowered his voice. 'I swerved to avoid a deer. At least I think it was a deer. And I, ah, may have corrected in the wrong direction.'

'Oh my God.' His humour was reassuring. 'I *told* you. Right side of the road. I don't even have a licence and I know that.'

'Yes, well.' His voice dropped further, giving a feeling of intimacy to the conversation. 'I'm not twenty-four, or however old the rental place likes you to be, so I wasn't driving, if you know what I mean.'

'You rebel. Out joyriding with your old man.'

'An old man who is waving me over now. I've got to ring off.'

'Sure, of course.' I suddenly felt embarrassed for calling, giving in to the impulse to reassure myself.

'I'll see you shortly.' He paused, as if he was going to say something else. But he merely finished with, 'Cheers, Sylvie,' and hung up.

I lowered the phone to my crossed legs and looked

at Gigi. 'I just wanted to make sure he and his father were all right,' I told her. She stared back with half-closed lids that asked, very clearly, who I thought I was fooling.

❧ ❧

Saint Mary's Methodist Episcopal Church was almost as old as Bluestone Hill. It had a gabled roof and a tall steeple, which, as Paula had predicted, I could see from the road. The brick foundation looked meticulously preserved, and the wood siding had a new coat of white paint. Set in a clearing, surrounded by majestic trees and a cloudless sky the colour of a Tiffany's box, it was as pretty as a postcard.

Paula had put her foot down when she found out I planned to bring Gigi. We almost fought about it – again – but I backed down when I remembered I could be on my way to a shrink instead of pedalling voluntarily to a place I wanted to go anyway.

I parked my bike against a tree next to the iron fence that surrounded the churchyard. Though I supposed it would be better manners to go in and meet the reverend first, I was drawn irresistibly to the northeast side of the clearing.

The Alabama River glinted through the trees, moving more slowly here than up by the Hill. I followed a tidy path to a fenced graveyard, the stones a patchwork of white and grey and age-darkened brown. On the graveyard's outer edge, the markers were arranged in a modern, orderly fashion. Closer in, the headstones were grouped, often with another iron fence around them, or a tree that someone had planted long ago to shade the dead.

It was a peaceful place. There was a gentle serenity to the way the sun dappled the ground, like a patterned quilt draped over those who slept.

'Hello!'

The greeting startled me, especially after my fanciful thoughts. I whirled, one hand going to my heart. I was going to be old before my time at the rate I was racking up shocks.

'Sorry.' A man in a clerical collar stood on the path behind me, raising his hands in the universal gesture of 'don't freak out' and smiling sheepishly. 'I suppose a graveyard isn't the best place to sneak up on someone.'

'Um, no.'

I'd expected the reverend at a historic church to be similarly antique, but this man was maybe in his early thirties. Tall and thin, he had light brown skin and features that pointed to a mix of races, and his eyes were kind and friendly. I guess that was a plus in his profession.

'I'm Reverend Watkins,' he said, unnecessarily. 'If you're Sylvie, your cousin called and told me to keep an eye out for your arrival.'

'That was nice of her.' I thought I managed to say this without sarcasm, but the glint in his eye said maybe I'd missed the mark.

'Are you looking for your family's plot?' he asked, surprising me. Not that it was a major intuitive leap, but I'd expected he'd want to talk about my *feelings* first.

At my startled silence, he pointed further down the path. 'The Davises are over here, in the oldest part of the cemetery.'

He pressed the latch on the gate and gestured me ahead of him. I paused for a moment, not worried about ghosts, for once, but struck by the deep sense of purpose to this place. Not every sanctuary or temple impressed me as being so . . . hallowed. This one did, through the soles of my shoes.

'How old is the church?' I asked as he closed the gate behind us.

'Old. Some of the family plots date back to the eighteen twenties, when the church was built.' He walked casually, with his hands in his pockets. And he still hadn't asked how I was feeling. 'But during some restoration in the seventies – the nineteen seventies – there was archaeological evidence that this might have been a Native American site as well.'

'You mean a burial ground?' I asked, intrigued by the possibility.

'That would be quite a coincidence, wouldn't it.' He shrugged with a wry half-smile. 'Probably just an extension of the settlement at Cahawba – much like this was an outgrowth of the ex-capital. But I like to imagine there's something special about this place.'

We'd stopped under one of the spreading oaks, and I smiled at a memory. 'Funny. My dad used to say that some spots were meant to be sacred. Which was why successive civilizations would sometimes build one temple on top of another, without even knowing what was there before.'

Dad had designed more than one beautiful cemetery, which was why I'd found it odd that he'd wanted to be cremated and not interred. But looking at one of the raised marble mausoleums, I had to think it would have made Dad sad to be in the earth but not part of it.

'Were you and your father much alike?' The reverend's tone was conversational, not the funeral-soft way most people asked about the dearly departed.

I made a so-so gesture with my hand. 'Mother said we had the same temperament. I guess that explains why they got divorced.'

Reverend Watkins chuckled, as if in spite of himself, then said kindly, 'You've lost a lot in two years.'

'I'm impressed,' I said, letting him know that I recognized a leading statement when I heard it. 'That was a very smooth segue.'

His grimace was rueful. 'Not so smooth you didn't catch it.'

'I'm very shrink-savvy.' I liked that he owned up to it right away, though. Points to him for being candid. 'Did Paula tell you about the nightmare?'

'Yes.' He nodded, folding his arms, as if settling in for a chat. 'Except, I gather you weren't actually asleep?'

I chose my words carefully, not wanting to lie in a churchyard. 'I'd *been* asleep. I'd gone down to let my dog out for a pee, then came back up. I could have been only half conscious, moving on autopilot. Haven't you ever been dreaming on your feet?'

He acknowledged that with a nod. 'Paula's just worried about you, that's all.'

'Well, I've got a lot on my mind.' Like wondering if something was up at Maddox Landing, and why people kept bringing up ghosts, and what the TTC – or maybe just Addie – was doing in the summerhouse so late. But that wasn't what he was asking in his roundabout way.

'Maybe my half-sleeping brain dreamed up a girl jumping into the river,' I said, then lifted my hand in an oath. 'But whatever the reason, I promise it is *not* because I'm contemplating doing the same thing.'

After studying me for a long moment, the reverend nodded. 'All right. You've satisfied me and kept your word to your cousin. I'll let you get on with what you really came for.' Smiling slightly, he nodded to a fenced rectangle of ground. 'Colonel Davis is over there.'

He'd taken me by surprise again. 'Either you are psychic' – scary thought – 'or I am *really* transparent.'

With a soft chuckle, the reverend stepped off the path, heading for the plot. 'Sylvie, everyone who grew up in this town – which is about ninety-five per cent of the current population – at least half believes the Colonel haunts that house. *I* can't believe you didn't come to see his grave sooner.'

I laughed, briefly but honestly. 'I thought it would be at Old Cahawba, so I went there first.'

We reached the spot where a huge oak tree shaded generations of my ancestors. The men had a lot of military titles: Major Jack, Captain Samuel and even a lowly lieutenant. He died in 1969 at the age of twenty-one. He hadn't had a chance to rise to the ranks of his predecessors.

There were a lot of children. No immunizations in 1856. Lots of women dying and being buried with their infants. Motherhood was a dangerous occupation.

'It's so weird,' I said, a little numbly, 'to go from no roots – that I knew of – to all this.'

Circling the plot, I read more names, saving the big monument on the corner for last. COLONEL JOSIAH DAVIS, CSA 1821–75. The Confederate army was ten years gone by the time he died, but he'd had it etched in stone beside his name.

The inscription below was odd: I WATCH, AND WAIT, FOR THY RETURN IN SPLENDOUR.

A frisson ran down my back, as if that word – *watch* – had touched a nerve. I'd been certain, from the beginning, that the figure at the window was watching for something.

'What does that mean?' I asked the reverend. 'Is it scripture?'

'Not really. It could be a reference to the Second Coming, when Christ will return to earth in glory and gather the faithful. Which I'm sure Colonel Davis considered himself.' We shared a smile at my ancestor's expense. 'But local lore,' Reverend Watkins continued, 'passed down from those who knew him, says it's probably a more secular reference.'

'Oh. "The South shall rise again"? That kind of thing?'

'Precisely.'

'I hope he's not still holding his breath on that one.'

The reverend laughed. 'Oh, there are plenty of living people who are still holding their breath on that.'

'How can they?' I asked. 'All things considered.'

'Well, as we're taught here in the South, the War Between the States wasn't about slavery, it was about states' rights. But that's an ugly history lesson for such a beautiful day.'

'I suppose it is.' I read over the nearest gravestones, still searching. I'd wanted to see the Colonel's marker, to satisfy my curiosity. But my other purpose was to find the information I couldn't seem to locate in the house.

'I see Mary Maddox Davis, his second wife,' I said. 'And this must be the son from that marriage. But where is his first wife? And the children from that marriage?'

'You do realize that was before my time,' the reverend said with a straight face. 'But they say his first wife specified in her will that she wanted to be sent back to South Carolina, where she was from.'

'That was unusual, wasn't it?'

He confirmed that with a nod. 'Wives are virtually always buried in their husband's family plot.'

'Is that why there are no daughters here?' I pointed to the section with the Colonel's children. 'I see sons that must have died in the war. But except for one infant, there're no girls.'

An uncomfortable expression passed over the reverend's face. 'There is one. But it's not with the others.'

He pointed, sighting along the Colonel's grand marker, which was canted, not at a nice forty-five degrees, appropriate for the corner spot, but at an odd angle, as if he, in death, had turned to look at something.

I walked forward from the monument. Trying to stay a straight course through the gravestones was tricky, and there was a point where the ground abruptly dipped and came back up, as if there had been a thin trench there. And just beyond that, there was a small, plain stone, covered with dark stains from the elements.

HANNAH DEIRDRE DAVIS
BORN DECEMBER 21, 1852
DIED JUNE 20, 1870

There were lilacs growing over her grave.

My heart gave a pang, as if I'd just learned of a old friend's death. Which was absurd – I'd known Lilac Girl was long gone. But it was different seeing her grave, knowing from the dates that it was *her* thoughts I'd been reading, her path I'd imagined down the streets of Cahawba.

Reverend Watkins had followed me from the Davis plot, and I turned to him, emotion making me abrupt. 'Why is she way over here?'

'You see that?' He gestured to the spot where I'd almost tripped, where the shallow trench was all but hidden by the grass. 'There used to be a line of shrubs marking the edge of the churchyard. The edge of hallowed ground, to use an outdated term. When the cemetery started filling up, the hedges came down, so it could expand.'

My heart slowly sank with an awful suspicion. 'So, Hannah was originally buried outside the cemetery?'

After a brief pause, during which he seemed to debate what he was going to share with me, the reverend nodded. 'Apparently she committed suicide.'

'"Apparently"?' He was watching me for a reaction, so I tried not to give him one. 'She must have, if they wouldn't bury her on holy ground. That's the punishment, right?'

'That would be a reason, yes.'

'How did she do it?' I asked, even though, in the pit of my stomach, I already knew the answer.

Watching my face, the reverend told me. 'She threw herself into the river and drowned.'

Chapter 19

Reverend Watkins looked suddenly alarmed, and he took me firmly by the arm, as if he thought I might pass out. Which, to be honest, I felt like I might.

'Are you all right, Sylvie?'

'Yeah,' I said, not even convincing myself.

'Let's go sit down.' He directed me to a bench under one of the trees. He didn't speak or prompt me, just waited for me to say something.

'Was that some kind of test?' I demanded, anger surging hot under my skin now that the cold of shock had passed. 'I saw – *dreamed* about a girl jumping in the river, and you wanted to see how I'd react to Hannah's grave?'

'No. Not at all.' The reverend sounded genuinely contrite. 'I didn't think about the similarity until it was too late to change the subject. And once you'd figured out she committed suicide, I couldn't very well lie about it.'

I chewed on the quandary this posed, wavering in my resolution that my psyche wasn't making this up. Could I have heard this rumoured about somewhere? I was sure Shawn and Kimberly hadn't said anything about a girl in the woods.

The reverend was watching me warily, and I slid a guarded look towards him. 'If I ask you a question, will you promise not to read anything into it?'

'I promise I'll try.'

'Do you believe in ghosts?'

He didn't seem surprised; I suppose it wasn't exactly a non sequitur, given our earlier discussion. 'I believe our souls go on to some other plane. Heaven, I hope. Would *you* want to stick around here?'

'Not really.' But the Colonel might, waiting for the South to rise again. Looking between the two markers, the grand column of the Colonel's and the small, worn stone of his daughter's, I asked, 'What made her do it, do you think?'

It wasn't *quite* rhetorical, but I was surprised he had an answer. 'The story goes that she had a suitor that her father didn't approve of. The Colonel refused to let them marry, and the guy left town. When Hannah realized he wasn't coming back, she threw herself off the embankment. The reverend here at the time tried to smooth things over for the girl, suggesting that it had been an accident. But it didn't fly, at least not with the Colonel. And you see where he had her buried.'

My heart ached for Hannah, and for the cold lack of sympathy from her one family member. I could do the maths. All her brothers must have been gone by then, killed in the war. 'What a hateful bastard.'

Watkins didn't correct me, though he said sympathetically, 'The reverend kept excellent diaries; he implied that Colonel Davis was never quite right in the head after he came back from the war.'

'Whatever happened to her sweetheart?' I asked. Did Hannah love him so much that life wasn't worth living? Did he betray her? There was more story here. It was a far, faint resonance, like a bell rung on a distant hill.

'No one knows. He was never heard from again.' Reverend Watkins let that sit a moment, then checked his watch. 'I have an appointment to give the convocation this evening at the high school graduation. But I hate leaving this on such a sad note, especially when I've really enjoyed talking to you, Sylvie.'

Attempting to shake off my disquiet, I arched an eyebrow. 'Discussing my family's sordid history, you mean?'

'Every family has skeletons in the closet.' His smile took on a teasing slant. 'And what about you? Are you feeling more peaceful of mind and spirit?'

My own tone turned droll. 'I'm feeling like Paula might give me some peace now, if that counts.'

Chuckling, he rose and gave me a hand up. 'It counts for something.'

I glanced back towards Hannah's grave. 'Who planted the lilacs for her, I wonder. Did the reverend say?'

Watkins followed my gaze. 'I don't recall. I'll find Reverend Holzphaffel's journals and see if he mentions them. I read his diaries when I first came here, to get a sense of the history of the place, then put them in a safe place.' He gave me a wry look as we took the flagstone path towards the front of the church. 'He didn't mince words in his opinions of people.'

I bet that would be a lot more interesting than William S. Davis's book. As he opened the cemetery gate for me, I said honestly, 'Thank you for your time, Reverend Watkins.'

'Whenever you want to talk – about the present or the past' – he grinned – 'just stop by. I'm almost always here.' We'd reached my bike and he asked, 'Are you all right to ride back? I noticed you were limping a little bit back there.'

'Just on the uneven ground.' I looked down automatically. 'After two days of bicycling, I'm surprised it's not worse.'

'Well, I'm glad it's not.' Reverend Watkins held out his hand. I put mine in his to shake it, but he held my fingers in a strong, sure grip. Looking me in the eye, he said, 'God bless you, Sylvie.'

The words startled me a bit. They were strange to hear when I hadn't sneezed. But they had meaning for him, and that gave them a sort of power. 'Thank you,

Reverend,' I said, a little formally in return, then smiled. 'I probably need all the help I can get.'

❧ ❧

The ride back to Bluestone Hill passed in a haze. Despite my assurances to the reverend, by the time I reached the turnoff to the house, I *was* tired and sore – and strangely disheartened. The shock of learning about Hannah's suicide was settling in and wearing me down.

I should have seen that if my roommate and the Colonel's daughter were the same person, odds were she was also the third ghost, the woman at the river. Or maybe that was only obvious in retrospect. After all, the house had been standing for almost two hundred years.

What I couldn't reconcile, what kept sticking in my throat as I swallowed the story, was how disappointed I was in her. I was sad *for* her, of course, outraged and horrified at the judgemental Colonel. But to kill herself because she'd been dumped – as awful as that must have been in her day – didn't seem like something the resourceful girl I'd met in her journal would do. Maybe it was irrational, but I felt almost angry with her. I'd thought a Davis would be stronger than that. By taking her own life, she'd let the Colonel win.

Or maybe I was projecting. Some days – when the pain of my healing bones, the surgeries and the apparatus on my leg had been almost as unbearable as the knowledge I'd never dance again – the only thing that kept me going was knowing I couldn't let the pain win.

Pedalling on the gravel was too much for me, so I got off the bike to push it the rest of the way. I went straight to the garden, let the bicycle drop in the grass outside the hedge and kicked off my shoes. My first afternoon here I'd lain in the grass, imagining myself in the hoopskirt and corset of the daughter of the house. Imagining I was Hannah.

Had she waited here in the garden for her sweetheart? I looked towards the first floor of the house. You'd have to be standing at the corner of the balcony to see down into the hedges. She could have sat with her guy on the iron bench, out of sight of the Colonel, had he stepped out of his study and stood at the French doors.

I needed to change my clothes and dig for a while. Channel my disquiet into activity. With that thought in mind, I walked on autopilot into the back yard and climbed the steps to the porch. Gigi yawned and stretched in her crate, tail wagging as I came to let her out. I'd just bent over, hand on the latch, when I heard Addie's voice from outside the screened walls.

'I can't believe you want to *ruin my life* this way.'

At first I thought she was talking to me somehow, and a furious 'What now?' jumped to my lips. But as I straightened, I saw that the door to Clara and Addie's apartment was open.

Her mother's answer was unintelligible, but Addie was upset, and her voice carried easily. 'Do you have any idea what a big deal this is? That they called on the last day of the school year? It's a *sign*, Mom.'

Clara came to the landing outside their door, shaking out a dust rag. With Gigi watching me curiously, I dropped behind the wicker settee. 'But it's not just a summertime commitment, Adina,' Clara said. 'It would interfere with your senior year. You may not think you want to go to college, but I don't want anything to limit your choices.'

'I can go to college later,' Addie whined. 'When I'm *thirty* and too old to model any more.'

Even the snap of Clara's dust rag sounded irritated. 'Does nothing in that sentence seem wrong to you, Adina Jackson? A career where you can only work for ten years?'

'That's why I have to start now, while I'm young.'

Ironically, I was on Addie's side of this argu?ment. There were prima ballerinas who danced for thirty years, but realistically, ballet was so hard on the body that it was practical to start young so you had as much performing time as possible. Even if you moved on to choreographing or directing a company, the prestige jobs went to those who'd built up the most performance cred during their active dancing career.

'One year isn't going to make that big a difference, Addie,' said Clara. 'Why don't you look into modelling classes in Selma or Montgomery? I'll drive you to anything, as long as you keep your grades up.' Her voice started to fade like she was going back inside. 'And on that subject – about these meetings. I was all for the TTC at first, but this spring you've been out too late and too often.'

'Mom! You can't take everything away from me—'

I strained to hear Clara's words. 'Out in the summerhouse until all hours . . .'

Crap. Her voice disappeared and the door slammed shut, just as they were getting around to something interesting. I was surprised to hear Clara speaking anything other than one hundred per cent in favour of the TTC. Everyone else did.

While I was down on the floor anyway, I let Gigi out of her crate. She bounded out, growling playfully, thinking I was on my hands and knees for her amusement.

This was a sad commentary on my situation. I'd become an eavesdropper on other people's lives – in the present, and the past.

Chapter 20

I spent the afternoon in the garden. Since the vines that covered the rock were too tough to tackle until I got a better pair of clippers, I worked on the planting bed, moving on to the next wedge-shaped piece of the centre circle.

My copy of Dad's diagram was on the bench, weighted down by a rock; I wouldn't have found the labyrinthine pattern in the mess of plants and weeds without it. I wasn't sure I would be able to duplicate it even with his notes, but I figured the only way to start was to clear out the weeds to see what was left.

Hard at work and lost in my thoughts, I didn't really notice that a car had arrived until Gigi uncurled from her favourite bed of greenery, looking eagerly towards the house, her tail waving.

I kept working, because it was silly that the same sort of hopeful excitement was bubbling up in me, too. I was not a puppy looking for belly rubs, and I was not a sheltered, innocent, 1860s Hannah Davis. I was a modern and sophisticated Manhattanite. I was *not* going to squeal, even internally, with the hope that Rhys Griffith had missed me like I'd missed him. He might not even come out to see me.

But a few minutes later, he did. I felt his step into the garden through my fingers in the earth, and Gigi, with one bark of welcome, bounded over to see him. I confined myself to sitting back on my heels and rubbing some of the dirt from my hands.

'You've been busy,' he said ambiguously. I assumed he meant in the garden, but I'd done a lot of other things in the past two days, like meet half of Maddox Landing. Not to mention my dead relatives.

Brushing the hair out of my face with the back of my hand, I climbed to my feet, irrationally disappointed with this tame and vague beginning. 'It gives me something to— Holy crap.'

As I stared, Rhys raised his brows – and then winced. The bridge of his nose was swollen, with a cut across the top. He had bruises under both eyes, but it was worse on the left, where the whole top of his cheekbone, curving up to the big knot over his eyebrow, was mottled purple.

'You said you were fine!' Wiping my hands on my jeans, I crossed through the plants to get to him, barely registering the crush of herbs under my bare feet.

'I said bumps and bruises,' he responded flatly, then gestured to the garden. 'What's all this? Lowly work for a princess.'

'Did you really think I was going to sit around all day and eat bonbons?' The retort was automatic, and I didn't let him distract me. 'You talked like it was a fender bender.'

His expression softened slightly in admission. 'It was a bit more than that.'

We stood close, and the smell of turned earth and bruised greenery was insufficient to soothe my shock and worry. The livid purple around his eyes made them look startlingly green. I reached up on impulse and, when he didn't draw away, very gently touched the goose egg on his brow. He winced slightly, then sighed, his shoulders relaxing, as if my cool fingers on the fevered swelling were a relief.

'Is your dad really OK?' I asked, trying to quiet the anxiety that crawled inside of me as I realized the air bag probably saved his life.

'Dad's got barely a mark on him,' Rhys said gently, as if he were comforting me, instead of the other way around. He was all right; it was over. But if my concern eased a fraction, it was only to a lingering disquiet.

I was suddenly aware of how close we were, and the intimacy of standing in the hedges, hidden from view, stroking his face as if I knew him a lot better than I did.

Heat rushed to my cheeks, replacing the cold of alarm, and I drew back my hand. My withdrawal seemed to make Rhys aware of all the same things. He dropped his gaze and cleared his throat.

'Dad's inside, talking to Paula about the trip,' he said. 'Clara's got the kettle on, and I smelled baking when we came in.'

'OK,' I said, awkwardness making my voice too high. 'Let me grab my stuff.'

Gigi had run off with one of the gloves, and while I was finding it, Rhys got to the drawing on the bench before me.

'What's this?' he asked.

'It was in the book.' I had to stifle the urge to snatch the paper up and hide it. My secret connection with Dad. Instead, I tried to lessen its importance with a casual tone.

Turning back to me, he started to lift a brow, then obviously thought better of it. 'I read that book. This wasn't in it.'

There wasn't any point in lying, I suppose. 'It was in the back. That's a tracing of a drawing my dad must have made when he was here.'

Rhys touched his forehead with a careful frown, still gazing at the diagram. Scanning the work I'd done, he brought his eyes up to mine again, guarded. 'Do you even know what you're doing here?'

Irritated, I plucked my paper from his fingers. 'No. Of course not. I'm just making this up as I go along.'

The muscle in his jaw twitched, as if he had been

hoping for a different answer. 'I know you must want to reconnect with your father, but this isn't the way to do it.'

Bitter anger rushed to my tongue. 'How is that any of your business?' And how could he say such a thing? He *had* a dad. He should have known how important this was. I was amazed at how quickly my emotions could swing from 'Oh my God, I'm so glad you're not dead' to 'I might have to kill you myself for that remark.'

Raising his hands defensively, he said, 'I just don't want you to get in over your head.'

'What are you?' I demanded. 'The gardening police? What difference does it make?'

He blinked, then narrowed his eyes. 'What are you talking about?' he asked.

'Gardening. What are *you* talking about?'

'Something else entirely.' He busied himself, very obviously, with collecting the gloves Gigi had scattered over the garden, while the perpetrator rested in the shade under the bench.

'Rhys,' I said, in as close to an alpha-dog voice as I could manage, 'what the hell is going on?'

I meant with him, but I could have shouted the question to the universe, demanding answers in a much broader sense. Why did everything I discovered today, every conversation I had – or overheard – only lead me to more questions?

'Why don't you tell me?' he snapped back. 'We stopped to eat in town, and everyone is talking about you and Shawn.'

'Oh my God.' I pressed the heels of my hands to my forehead, leaving gritty streaks on my face. 'I am not making a play for Shawn Maddox!'

That came out way louder than I meant it to. Gigi barked from under the bench, and I closed the distance to Rhys so I could lower my voice. 'I can't believe we are arguing because I had lunch with Alabama's answer to Tom Sawyer.'

He set his jaw, almost masking his surprise, but not hiding his flush at all. 'Why can't you believe that?'

'Because . . .' Wind cut from my sails, I floundered to finish that thought. 'Because it's stupid. I just *met* Shawn.'

With a small, wry smile that made me a liar somehow, Rhys took a step into my personal space. 'That doesn't mean anything. You and *I* just met.'

True, yet the connection between us heated the air, made my heart stumble a little. 'That's different.' I just hoped he didn't ask me how, because I didn't have an answer.

'You rang me up to see if I was all right.'

'To see if you and *your dad* were OK.'

'So . . . you cared.'

Part of me squirmed with glee that he was standing so close, with that smile, and speaking in that low voice and smooth accent. And a much tinier, more cynical part of me speculated that he'd changed his method of diverting my questions.

'So,' I said, my voice annoyingly breathless, 'the thing about getting in over my head. That was about Shawn and me?' It actually made sense. Getting involved with a Maddox would certainly seem to be a way of connecting with my Davis heritage, given our families' intertwined history. And since even I had misgivings, there was reason to warn me.

A flicker in Rhys's eye said he wasn't happy about my dogged pursuit of the matter. But he answered, 'It's about Shawn, who is not everything he seems.'

I nodded. 'Yeah, I figured that out on my own, actually.'

'Good.' There was a flattering satisfaction in that one word. 'You'll give him a wide berth, then?'

'No.' That would make it hard to find out what he and the Teen Town Council were doing in the summerhouse. 'But I'll be on my guard.'

He took a frustrated step back, raising his hand to rub his forehead, then cursing when he touched the bruises. 'Sylvie,' he said through the grimace of pain, 'you don't know what you're dealing with.'

'Then tell me!'

'I can't.' He lowered his hand, and his voice. 'Why don't you tell me what *you* know?'

Like what? That I thought the house was haunted? That I was being set up with Shawn because of some old tradition? It all sounded paranoid and delusional, and the threat of Paula calling the shrink loomed large and terrifying.

'I can't,' I echoed, wondering if that sounded as miserable as I felt.

'Then it's a stalemate,' said Rhys, his expression grim but resigned.

'For now,' I murmured. Because as much as I was

drawn to him, I couldn't forget that Rhys was one of the many mysteries at Bluestone Hill.

❧ ❧

I was determined to get through the night without budging from my room. I'd taken Gigi for her last walk while the house was still awake, and then sneaked her upstairs to stay. To make sure nothing disturbed us, I'd found my MP3 player and put Brahms on an endless loop to cover any sound. Then Gigi and I curled under the covers where no cold could get us.

The only thing I'd ever sensed behind my door was the lilac smell, and I'd never felt any threat from that – from Hannah, I corrected, accepting that there was at least an echo of my ancestress here in the room we shared. Though I supposed she couldn't really be my foremother if she'd killed herself when she was my age.

I couldn't imagine ending it all because some guy left me. But I was thinking like a twenty-first-century young woman with a world of options – except dance.

Had she felt about *him* the way I did about ballet? Letting the music seep away my present, I imagined Hannah lying in bed, maybe even on the same lumpy mattress, praying for guidance. If her family had money, she could hope for a good marriage, maybe even to someone she picked for herself. If she couldn't, or wouldn't, marry, then she had her choice of crap jobs – governess or paid companion if she was lucky. And God help her if she got pregnant.

My gasp was loud enough to wake Gigi, who

growled softly and went back to sleep. But I sat up, pulling the earphones from my ears and swinging my legs off the bed.

Oh. My. God. Hannah had been pregnant. I knew it the way I knew she loved lilacs and that she had lain in the garden – *my* garden, the same spot where I liked to lie – waiting for *him*.

Pregnant, with a guy like the Colonel for a dad, one who hated her boyfriend. A guy whom she loved and trusted enough to give herself to, in an era where girls didn't do that sort of thing. A guy who abandoned her to that fate.

I went to the desk and opened the secret drawer. Pulling out the journal, I set it on the blotter, and gathered my courage, like I was preparing to open a dreaded letter. I already knew the news, but reading it would somehow make it fresh. Closer to me.

Opening the book from the back, I paged carefully through the empty sheets at the end, the unwritten days. When I came to the last entry, I sat and read.

> *It is harder than I thought it would be. I think the day is coming quickly, and I look forward to it, grateful for escape.*
>
> *I do not know where I shall end up. But at least I will no longer be alone.*

Chapter 21

For the first time since my arrival at Bluestone Hill, I slept through the night without incident – once I'd finally gone to sleep. I'd lain awake for a long while, thinking about Hannah's last entry and how she seemed more hopeful than frightened. It made me want to not believe in ghosts again, just so I could think that Hannah was at peace.

Retiring early did mean that Gigi was in a big hurry to get downstairs. I wasted no time taking the dog out the side door and to the back yard for her morning frolic. I was putting down her breakfast on the porch when the screen door opened, and Rhys came in.

I straightened quickly, and he froze, his hand on the door as if he might flee. We'd all eaten dinner together – except for Addie, who went with her friends to the convocation for the graduating seniors – but it was different now without the buffer of the adults.

He was dressed for the day, in cargo pants, a T-shirt and a denim shirt over that. I tugged at my own T-shirt, which matched the cartoon dogs on my pj's. I also hadn't combed my hair or brushed my teeth. It was Saturday morning, for crying out loud.

'Were you outside?' I asked. 'I didn't see you.'

He let the door close, deciding, I guess, to stay. 'I was in your garden, looking at how much you'd gotten done in two days. Very impressive for a ballet princess.'

So, we were back to that. The gibe didn't distract me, but the sight of his face did. 'You look better than I thought you would.'

He could almost raise that brow without wincing. 'Thanks. I heal quickly.' Gesturing to the kitchen door he said, 'Coming in?'

I left Gigi on the porch with her kibble and a squeaky toy. The kitchen was full of cheerful activity. Clara hummed at the stove, the kettle was on the boil, and at the table, the professor was telling Paula about his trip.

'Biscuits and gravy, Sylvie?' Clara asked as I washed my hands.

I eyed the saucepan on the stove. 'Sausage gravy?'

She held up a box, reading from the back. 'Texturized vegetable protein sausage gravy.'

'You're kidding!' From her pleased face, she wasn't. I laughed, surprised and touched by the trouble she'd gone to. 'You had to find a way to feed me something Southern. You are awesome, Clara.'

Clara, looking embarrassed but pleased, bustled me towards the table. 'It might not even be any good.'

Professor Griffith paused in his conversation with Paula to interject. 'Don't be modest, Clara. I doubt anything less than tasty has ever come out of your kitchen.'

She conceded this with a small tilt of her head. 'In any case, Sylvie, you should thank the professor and Rhys. They picked you up a care package on their way home.'

The tone of my surprise changed. I was still grateful, but suddenly self-conscious. I couldn't remember the last time someone had bought me something just because. Flowers at the hospital didn't count. And Mother bought me things she wanted to see me in, not things I would pick out for myself.

'Thank you,' I said to the spot just above the professor's head. I didn't trust myself to look him, or Rhys, in the eye.

'It was nothing, love,' Professor Griffith said amiably, then amended, 'Well, it was one wrecked car, but at least it was a rental.'

His joke broke my bubble of awkwardness, and I returned his smile. 'I'm very glad you weren't hurt.' Finally glancing at Rhys, I corrected, 'Seriously hurt, I mean.'

He met my eye with a sheepish smile of his own. 'Like Dad said. It was nothing.'

The kettle started to whistle, and I was grateful for the distraction. 'Sit down,' said Clara. 'I'll bring you a plate.'

Obediently I went to my place, conscious of Rhys at my elbow. Paula looked almost relaxed in a tracksuit and sneakers. We were only missing one person. 'Is Addie sleeping in?'

Setting a plate in front of me, Clara said, 'She spent the night with Caitlin in town. They're doing some set up for the festival and then going to graduation.'

'Ah.' I kept my voice neutral, glad she was having a good time so I didn't have to feel guilty for being happy she wasn't around. No Addie not only meant no sulks and arguments, but also that I could put off TTC mysteries until after breakfast. Glancing at the professor, I said, 'You didn't say last night – was your trip productive?'

He tilted his head in a 'sort of' gesture. 'Cultural anthropology isn't always about finding empirical evidence of an event. The course of the story is academically valid too.'

I chewed a mouthful of fluffy biscuit and spicy faux gravy and attempted to decipher that statement. Rhys translated. 'He means, how a legend arises and where it spreads is sometimes as important as proving an actual event occurred. Like Prince Madoc's expedition here.'

The name startled me, but I had to swallow before I could ask, 'Prince Maddox?'

'Madoc,' the professor corrected, with a slightly different pronunciation. 'That's the name of the Welsh prince who, according to legend, brought a band of settlers to the New World.' Seeing my confusion, he explained, 'I was taken with the similarity of the name too. Madoc, Maddox Landing. But all my research points to its being coincidence.'

'Except for the bluestone in the garden,' I said, glancing up to find Rhys watching me.

'Yes. Fascinating, isn't it,' said the professor, relishing his mystery. I wish I felt the same about mine.

Gigi's bark interrupted the conversation, heralding an arrival at the back door. Rhys's quickly shuttered expression told me who it was, even before Shawn called out a hello. Speak of the devil and he'll appear – and enter without knocking.

Maybe that wasn't an entirely fair way to describe Shawn Maddox, but he was certainly at the heart of too much for me not to be wary of him. His high-wattage warmth filled the room, and I could still feel the tug of attraction, but now doubt kept me grounded. That, and the awkward awareness of Rhys bristling at his end of the table. It charged the air, and though no one else seemed to notice, I instinctively braced myself against the tension between them. Between the three of us.

Shawn was oblivious, or at least putting on a good show of it. Gigi had followed him in, and danced around his sneakers, pulling at his pants legs with her teeth. 'Sylvie,' said Paula, with a sigh, 'control your dog.'

'I'll get her.' Seriously, you would think Gigi was

a two-hundred-pound slobbering Saint Bernard, the way my cousin acted.

Shawn grinned at me as I bent to unfasten Gigi from his jeans. 'Good morning, gorgeous.'

'Oh, don't even,' I said, to all of it. His overt flattery, my uncombed tangle of hair, the whole café fiasco, not to mention Rhys *sitting right there*.

I carried Gigi outside and put her in her crate so she wouldn't offend Paula while I concentrated on the dynamics of dealing with Shawn. I could hear through the door as he greeted everyone. 'Hey, Miz Paula, Miz Clara, Prof.' Then a low whistle. 'That is some shiner you've got, English.'

Crap. That nickname was *not* going to go over well.

I slipped in behind Shawn and saw that Rhys wasn't bothering to hide the annoyance in his narrowed eyes. 'It's Welsh, actually.'

Shawn gave a contrite wince. 'Sorry. I thought Wales was part of England.'

'It's part of Britain.' Rhys left 'you moron' unspoken, but just barely.

'Think of it like this,' the professor said more smoothly. 'Calling us English is like calling you a Yankee.'

'Actually,' said Paula, looking at him over her reading glasses, 'it's like calling you a carpetbagger.'

'Oh.' Shawn flashed a repentant grimace. 'My apologies, then.'

My cousin nodded her approval, and I clamped my jaw to keep it from dropping. Was she kidding? Paula was letting him off the hook with that grin and the good ol' country boy act? Regardless of his grasp of geography, Shawn would have to be an idiot not to have figured out by now that that nickname would needle Rhys. And Shawn was no idiot.

He turned to me, and I quickly schooled my expression. 'Speaking of carpetbaggers,' he said, still smiling, 'here's our own import from the North.'

'Nice.' I folded my arms, shielding myself from that uncanny charm. 'You're insulting everyone's origins today.'

Bumping my elbow with his own, he cajoled, 'I'm just joshing with you guys. Rhys gets that, right?'

'Sure,' said Rhys tightly. 'I get *exactly* what you mean.'

I was amazed none of the adults seemed to pick up on the undercurrents. Or maybe they did, and attributed it to something natural and not the dynamics baffling me.

Shawn took Rhys at face value – or pretended to – and turned back to me. 'Anyway. Don't be mad, because I come bearing gifts.'

In the confusion with Gigi, I hadn't noticed he'd carried in a canvas tote. As he held it out to me, I was surprised to see it was full of gardening tools – all of them new, with matching green and yellow handles.

'For working in your garden,' he said, unnecessarily. 'Here's hoping you put down some roots.'

The wording gave me pause. On one level, it was a cheesy pun, but on another, it was a reference to the tendrils of the past that kept drawing me in deeper, to Bluestone Hill and everything around it.

My emotions were hopelessly tangled. I was delighted with the tools, because now I could finish cutting back the nest of vines around my rock without giving myself carpal tunnel syndrome. But even without Rhys's warning, I had to wonder what Shawn was up to. And putting all *that* aside, I was confused why the gift didn't warm me from the inside out like a box of fake sausage had. I didn't think it was because the way to my heart was through my stomach.

'Isn't that nice,' observed Paula, with the cheery note of a matchmaker. 'You can put those to good use, Sylvie.'

'Yes, I can.' I smiled a little stiffly at Shawn, aware of our audience. 'Thank you.'

'And it's not even Christmas,' said Clara, chuckling.

I covered my discomposure by looking through the pockets of the tote, trying to be genuinely grateful, despite my misgivings. 'This is just what I need. And it was sweet of you to drive all the way out here just to give them to me.'

'No problem.' Shawn stuck his hands in his pockets and shrugged. 'I was running out to the Point before the graduation ceremony this afternoon.'

With all the other drama, I'd forgotten it was graduation weekend. 'I should say congratulations.'

'Thanks.' He smiled, as if my sentiments had been much warmer than they were. 'Party tonight, by the way. If you want to come.'

'I wouldn't want to crash it.'

'Oh, everyone in school will be there.' He looked at Clara. 'Addie's coming, right?'

She sat down at the table with her mug of tea. 'I doubt I could keep her away.'

I knew I should go and learn more about Shawn and the TTC. Be sly and ask questions. But the thought of being on my guard all night, watching what I said and how it was taken, dealing with their expectations, seemed huge to me. It had nothing to do with Rhys's eyes on me, or his inscrutable disapproval. Nothing at all.

'We'll see,' I finally said, using one of Paula's favourite phrases.

Shawn obviously knew my cousin well enough to interpret, and he chuckled, not sounding put off. 'I guess I'll just have to content myself with tomorrow, then.'

I searched my mental calendar and came up blank. 'What's tomorrow?'

'The Catfish Festival.' The 'of course' was implied by his tone.

I stifled a groan. I felt the same way about the festival as I did about the graduation party, multiplied by the population of the town. If I'd planned ahead, I might have had an excuse. But with Paula smiling encouragingly and Clara grinning – and Rhys just *watching* – all I could think of to say was 'Can't wait,' in a tone that implied anything but anticipation, letting them assume my reluctance was a joke.

'Great.' Shawn grinned, buying it easily. Because we *Yankees* are so droll, I guess. Reaching for the bag I held, he asked, 'Now, where can I put these for you?'

'Oh, I'll take them.'

I gripped the handles, but had to relinquish them or get into a tug-of-war. 'Just show me where,' he insisted amiably.

My irritation must have shown, and at Paula's disapproving look, I lightened my tone. 'By the door would be great. Thanks.'

He carried them to the porch and I followed, to be polite, though it didn't seem very sporting of him to give a girl a gift and remind her of a date right in front of his rival. Provided that Shawn even admitted he had a rival for my attentions. It was clear by now that he took a lot for granted.

'So, what time tomorrow?' he asked.

'Paula declared we're going to church, so after that.'

He smiled, completely at ease. No, definitely not admitting any competition from anyone. 'I'll see you there.'

When he was gone, I collected Gigi from her crate and went into the kitchen, disappointed to see both Griffiths had left. Clara and Paula were still there, conferring over the remains of breakfast.

'Where'd they go?' I asked.

Paula didn't look up from the list she was writing. 'The professor went upstairs to answer some e-mail, and Rhys said he was going to Old Cahawba.'

Clara gave me an amused look. 'Are you starting a boy harem, Sylvie? You city girls.' She shook her head with a tutting noise.

'I'm not . . . Oh my God.' I ran my hands over my face. As if my psyche weren't boiling over with complications without adding romance to the pot. 'I'm just . . . *not.*'

'You shouldn't let that stop you from going to the party tonight,' said Paula. 'It'll be fun for you to get out.'

'Don't push her if she doesn't want to go.' Clara must have picked up on my reluctance. 'The kids will probably all end up here or at the summerhouse anyway.'

The mention of the summerhouse prodded me to voice the question I'd been turning over since I'd explored the place. 'Does the teen council always meet out there? Isn't that kind of an odd spot?'

Clara obviously didn't think so, from her shrug. 'It gives them some privacy.'

My brows drew together in confusion. This was counter to her tone with Addie yesterday. Not that I could say that, since I'd been eavesdropping when I heard it. 'Aren't you worried they could be drinking or smoking pot or something?'

Clara laughed and rose from the table. 'Not these kids. They've got too much going for them.'

With a blithe lack of concern, she carried her glass to the sink. I stared in disbelief. *Surely* she checked up on them. Was there a parent on the planet who really believed that even a good kid wouldn't get a bad idea? Even *my* mother lectured me about drugs and premarital sex, and she knew I wouldn't do anything to risk my dancing career. It was like the entire TTC was under the umbrella of Shawn Maddox's get-out-of-jail-free grin.

That was why I had to keep my guard up around him, to keep fighting his charm. Maybe he and the TTC were as Mayberry and squeaky clean as they seemed, painting fences and saving puppies and helping old ladies across the street. But something made me think not. And I'd vowed to trust my instincts, no matter how strange things seemed.

Chapter 22

Regardless of my confusion and suspicion about Shawn, I was grateful for his gift, because with a decent pair of clippers, I could finally uncover the standing stone. I was anxious to attack the tenacious foliage around it and get a good look at the mystery rock.

It was slow going. Years of growth meant thick layers of tough green vine, interwoven and clinging like a net. I clipped and pulled and clipped some more, until my arms ached and I fully believed the stuff was growing as fast as I cut it.

By the time Professor Griffith visited me, I was glad for the distraction. As usual, he greeted Gigi first, bending to scratch her belly as she rolled in the tangled bed of herbs, soaking her fur and releasing the fresh, green perfume.

'Good grief, Gigi,' I said. 'Do you have no morals at all?'

Professor Griffith smiled at me over his shoulder, in his open, friendly way. His easy manner made him a good balance for his more complicated son.

'We were just enjoying the morning.' He stood and nodded to the tall rock, which, as its name implied, looked blue-grey under a light coat of dew. At least, the sliver I'd uncovered did. 'Rhys said you were clearing the stone, but he didn't mention you'd done such an amazing amount of work on the planting bed, too.'

I shrugged, embarrassed at the compliment. 'Thank you.'

He gazed around, squinting in the sun. 'I thought this whole garden was done for. Such a shame. But look.' He gestured to the bed where Gigi lay, and to the few buds of colour beginning to show. 'These are already doing better now that they're not choked with weeds. I believe that you have a green thumb, my dear.'

'I get it from my father.' My reply was simple, but I felt a happy glow inside at the thought. 'They said he could grow anything.'

Snipping another tangle of vine, I uncovered more of the rock. Flecks of mineral – quartz, I guess – glittered in the dark stone. I ran my finger down its rough surface. 'This is really the same kind of stone as at Stonehenge?'

'According to Rhys.' He said it with a bit of pride in his son, the geologist. 'This type of dolerite is the same as the world's most famous standing stones. Is it warm?'

I glanced over my shoulder, wondering which of us was supposed to be the crazy one. 'Warm? It's a rock, and the sun hasn't been up long enough to dry the dew.'

The professor laughed. 'Bluestone is supposed to be warm to the touch. At least, relative to other stones. Something about it having electromagnetic properties or some such thing. Rhys would hate my even mentioning it. It's not *scientific*.'

'But you study folklore, right? Why would he get bent at your mentioning it?' I asked.

'He's very serious about geology. He hates it when the New Agey folks start spouting "pseudoscience" about his precious rocks.' Professor Griffith looked heavenward with a fond sort of exasperation. 'Don't even get him wound up about crystals.'

'I'll avoid the subject,' I said, so seriously that the professor laughed again.

I bent to pick up Gigi, who had curled at the base of the stone, completely relaxed. She flopped over bonelessly to lie on her back in my arms, like a baby. 'The electromagnetism works on my dog, anyway. She loves to hang out here.'

He steadied me with a hand on my elbow as I stepped out of the planting bed. 'Well, if you'll forgive a little more pseudoscience, there might be a reason for that.'

'I won't tell Rhys.'

'Oh, he knows this one, too. Standing stones are thought to mark places that have certain properties. The mystics say it's earth energy. The pseudoscientists call it a magnetic field. You may have heard of ley lines?'

I shook my head, and he went on, clearly happy to have a fresh ear for his lecture. 'Some people think there is a grid or web that connects centres of earth energy. Usually there are springs or wells along the points, as well as ancient sites, like barrows and standing stones. Also, churches and other, more modern sacred spots too.'

The mention of churches struck me, because I'd just been talking about that the day before, with Reverend Watkins.

'So, this energy . . . Is it like feng shui? Supposedly, I mean.' I tacked that last part on to make sure he knew I was asking a hypothetical question. Open-minded but critical.

'Not really. That's an Eastern practice of manipulating the energy flow – more of an air element in concept.'

He'd taken a seat on the bench, which was everyone's favourite spot. I sat on the ground, slipped off my shoes and wiggled my toes into the grass.

'My dad used to talk about how the geography of a place could have good energy flow or bad. When we travelled together, he pointed out how both ancient temples and cathedrals are often built near springs.'

'Right. Some people would say it's because springs and wells are sites where these energy lines connect.'

The idea excited me somehow, maybe because it dovetailed with Dad's opinions. But I made myself play devil's advocate and present the pragmatic argument. 'Though if you're going to build a place where people congregate, it makes sense to have a water source.'

Professor Griffith laughed. 'Yes, but practical reasons don't necessarily rule out intangible ones.'

I grinned and ducked my head, forming my next question carefully. 'Listen, Professor. I wanted to ask you about something you said the other morning. Purely hypothetical.'

He smiled as if he understood, though somehow I doubted he really did. 'All right. Hypothetical.'

'You said something about cold spots?'

He nodded. 'Temperature changes are something that paranormal investigators – ghost hunters – try and quantify. Temperature, humidity, even the electromagnetic charge in a room.'

I jumped on that idea, like Gigi jumped on her favourite squeaky toy. 'Electromagnetism? Like my standing-stone spot?'

The professor grimaced ruefully. 'Yes, in theory, but that's pseudoscience, remember. It's conjecture at best. Don't get me in trouble with Rhys.'

I ran my hand through my plants. Professor Griffith was right: they were already thriving now that the weeds weren't choking them and taking all their water.

'So Rhys doesn't believe in any of this stuff? The special stone, the connection to Wales, any of it?'

'Oh, he believes what can be proven. Like if your stone really comes from the Preseli Hills.'

I turned my head to look at the small section of rock I'd uncovered. 'What would it mean if it does?'

He chuckled. 'In a practical sense? Or an existential one?'

'I don't know.' I shot him a shrewd glance. 'And I'm betting you don't either.'

His amusement broadened. '"Meaning" is an ambiguous word. It would mean that we're all connected. But it would also mean nothing significant, since we don't know when it was placed here or with what intent.'

While I digested that, the professor stood, dusting off his hands. Glancing at all the work I still had ahead of me, he said, 'I do wonder if whoever created this garden knew the stone's alleged connection with ley lines and stone circles.'

I startled at his words. My father had made the connection, at least to the stone circle; he'd written it right in the book for me to find. But other than the obvious – the standing stone, its mysterious possible origin – I didn't see the link. 'Why do you say that, Professor?'

'Some of these plants. Meadowsweet, vervain, mint.' He pinched off a leaf and rubbed it to release the scent. 'Rue and sage. All you need is some mistletoe and holly, and you have a druid arsenal.'

With a click into focus, I saw what he was getting at. 'So druid types would use these in their ceremonies?' I asked, still not certain where this fitted in the puzzle of Bluestone Hill.

'Yes, seems so. For healing, power and protection.' Then he smiled, because of course this was all hypothetical. 'Don't tell Rhys I said that, either. All that New Agey stuff, you know.'

'Sure thing, Professor.' I spoke the words absently, my mind busy pulling apart this idea to try to get at the meaning in the middle. Hang around with artistic people long enough, and you'll run across every kind of belief. I knew plenty of crystal-wearing, incense-burning types. I might have felt stupid for not seeing it before, except that to me this was just aesthetically pleasing greenery.

He wandered off, whistling, while I sat in the middle of my herbs, trying to figure out what was ringing the bell of my memory. When Gigi stirred in my lap, growling softly in her sleep, I had it.

Sliding the dog to the ground, I got up just enough to reach my jacket, which I'd thrown over the back of the bench when the day had warmed up. Digging in the pocket, I wrapped my fingers around the singed bundle of plants that Gigi had found in the summerhouse.

There was a dancer with the touring company who refused to move into a new dressing room until he'd cleansed it by burning sage leaves. On the sly, of course, because of the fire hazard.

The leaves and twigs in the bundle I'd found in the summerhouse were bound tightly, and so dry that they crumbled off in my hand. Rubbing the flakes in my palm, I thought I smelled chicory, and there was something that looked like a kernel of wheat.

What the hell were they doing in the summer-house? And what, if anything, did they have to do with the echoes of the past manifesting at Bluestone Hill?

❧ ❧

I worked in the garden until it was too late for anyone to pester me about going to the graduation party. By then I was exhausted, and all I wanted was to get clean. The bathroom, just down the hall from me, was a shabby Victorian palace. The wallpaper was a faded rose, and the slipper chair in the corner, where Gigi liked to curl up while I bathed, was covered in worn gold jacquard. But the godsend after spending all day weeding was the enormous antique claw-foot tub.

I ran the water as hot as I could stand it, then sank in up to my earlobes and soaked until it was almost cool. When I was done, I let Gigi paddle a lap around the tub. I had no idea a Chihuahua could love to swim, but this one did. Her little legs churned underwater while her fluffy head glided along on top – there was a metaphor there for my current situation. Something about deep water, and trying to keep my head above the surface.

After putting on fresh pyjamas – my last pair – and wrapping my hair in a towel, I dried Gigi, too. Then I checked the hall for lurking cousins and carried my dog to my room.

Music drifted faintly through the slightly open window. It startled me at first, but I doubted that any of my ghosts had listened to much electric guitar in their day.

I guessed – and a peek out the window confirmed it – that the graduation party had, as Shawn predicted, moved to the Hill.

I closed the window and put on my earphones, hoping to repeat last night's uninterrupted sleep.

❧ ❧

Gigi woke me with a soft bark. She stood on my chest, tail stiff behind her, a ridge of fur standing up on her back. When she growled, it wasn't her playful, electric-motor noise. It was as deep and throaty a warning as I'd ever heard from her.

'Quiet, Gigi.'

She stopped growling, but her body stayed rigid with purpose. Then I heard what had set her off. The high, thin wail was so quiet, it wouldn't have woken me – if not for the dog.

Setting Gigi on the bed, I struggled out from the covers and went to the window. I had to lean awkwardly over the desk to open it. It stuck a little in the humidity, but I managed. Without the glass in the way, the keen seemed to swell and build, mournful and wretched.

I knew what to look for next: a moving shadow where there should be none. It took me a moment to find her from this angle; I'd never seen her from my – our – room. But there she was, a female figure hurrying through the trees.

A fierce compulsion seized me. I *had* to follow her. I had to see her up close, like I had the Colonel, and

350

eliminate the possibility it was a trick. It seemed too convenient on the heels of the party in the summer-house. In my head, I heard Addie and Shawn, confusing me by twisting my words, my conversations. Just because I believed in echoes of the past didn't mean there wasn't something here in the present working against me.

Forgetting my resolve not to budge from my room, I thrust my feet into my sneakers and grabbed my hoodie, throwing it on over my pj's. I told Gigi to stay on the bed, and she wasn't happy about it. Flinging open the door, I took just a few steps down the hall and felt the cold reaching out to stop me.

It was worse than before. Like the pitiful wail outside, the cold flooded over me, a cruel and icy surge. I told myself it was just an echo, that nothing could hurt me, but there was such a *presence,* I couldn't push past the wall of my own fear. I fell back into my room and closed the door, knowing no one could fake that.

But I wasn't done yet. With Gigi bouncing at my heels, I climbed up on the desk, confirming with a glance that my window was above the balcony, though not with easy access. A good thing I was still limber.

I went out feetfirst, sliding in a backbend while I held onto the frame for support. My feet touched the balcony without a sound, and I hurried to the spiral staircase. For just an instant I hesitated, my phobia rising up and tangling with the anxiety of what I was doing: racing into the night after a ghost. Then I grabbed the rail and went down backwards, with quick but trembling steps.

Cutting through the corner of the back garden, I slipped through the hedges and made for the woods in a halting run. I'd lost track of the figure as I'd been coming out of the house, and the trees were a maze. The thick cover of pine needles hid any kind of path, or any footprints.

Sudden, disorienting panic gripped me. It was like being turned upside down underwater. I could barely tell which way was up, let alone which way I'd been going or which way to the house. The hanging moss curtained the stars, and my heart pounded too hard with fear for me to hear the river.

Come on, Sylvie. You never get lost.

I reined in my instinct to run in a random direction like a spooked animal. I was smarter than that. I just needed to catch my breath, settle down and get my bearings.

My calming breath brought the faint, startling scent of lilac. I turned in a slow circle, but couldn't catch the direction. My searching gaze, though, fastened on a pale, cold glow through the trees.

The glow wrapped around the girl like a halo. My panic had faded, but my heart still drummed against my ribs as I stood frozen, fear mixing with fascination. I was so close, I could see the detail of her calico dress. The neck, high and wide, was framed in crisp white, as were the cuffs of her long sleeves. Her skirt had a hooped petticoat underneath that swayed like a bell as it caught on the trees and brush.

Her hair was soft brown, like mine, and her skin was pale, almost luminous. I stood unmoving, my hand pressed to my chest, awed by the anguish on her otherworldly face. The depths of despair in her hollow eyes chilled my racing heart, and I shivered in sorrow and unease.

I shook myself again when I realized she was moving away from me, and quickly. I broke into a run after her, or as near to one as I could manage on the uneven ground. There was no path at all, and I didn't see how she could move so smoothly, while I had to weave between trees, the roots catching at my feet and the branches tearing at my hair. It was all I could do to keep her in sight.

Then she vanished. And so did the ground.

I'd stepped out into open air, nothing beneath me but the swollen river, rushing twenty-five feet below.

Chapter 23

The momentum of my headlong dash carried me forward, even as I registered what was happening. I'd reached the embankment and stepped off the edge. My arms windmilled, searching for a handhold, as my one foot still on the ground slipped in the crumbling mud. I flailed, grabbed a fist of Spanish moss and kept falling.

My fingers scraped against rough bark and I clutched desperately at the trunk of a fir tree, leaving a layer of skin behind.

I was going to die. My life didn't flash before my eyes, but I *did* think I heard Gigi barking.

Then a hand closed on my wrist. The jerking stop wrenched my arm and slammed me against the tangled tree roots jutting from the riverbank. It jolted a howl of pain out of me, but no complaint.

'Hold on,' said Rhys from above me. 'I've got you.'

Twisting my neck, I could just glimpse the hand that grasped the tree while the other clutched my wrist. I was facing out, deadweight, hanging like a fish on a line, and the mechanics were against him.

'Can you turn round?'

Strain drew his voice taut. My own was thin with terror. 'I'll fall.'

The way my wrist was turned, I couldn't even grasp his arm. From here, the slide down the embankment would slow my descent, but I'd probably break more than just my leg. And that was before I even hit the river.

The familiar phobia rose up, clawed its way through my chest to squeeze my heart, making it impossible to breathe. I relived the endless moment of The Accident, feeling my toe come down and my leg snap, the grind of the bone against the stage as I collapsed, the glare of the lights and the panicked murmur of the crowd, babbling like the water rushing below.

'Sylvie.' Rhys's voice was calm and deep with certainty. It called me out of my panic and anchored me to *this* moment. 'Turn round and look at me. I won't let you fall.'

Forcing myself to breathe, I did as he said, twisting so that I faced the embankment. My wrist slipped in his fingers, and a terrified whimper slipped out before I could clench my teeth on it.

'I've got you.' He tightened his grip. Now I could close my own hand around his arm, strengthening the hold. 'Up you go.'

He pulled, using the tree as leverage. I hadn't realized how far he'd had to lean out to grab me. He inched backwards, drawing me with him, and I scrabbled at the dirt for a toehold. Finally he could let go of the tree and hold out his other hand. 'Grab on, Sylvie. Almost there, love.'

I reached out to clasp his hand, and with a grunt of effort he dragged me onto solid ground. The pine needles were thick and soft, and I lay in them gratefully, the scent of wet earth filling my head.

And then there was a tiny dog tongue licking my face. Gigi. I hadn't imagined her barking. I was relieved to know that not all the whining had come from me.

Rhys nudged the dog out of the way and leaned over me, feeling my shoulder, my arm, making sure everything was in the right place. 'Are you all right? Did I break you?'

'I'm bent,' I said, still dazed, not least by his rather proprietory touch. 'But not broken.'

He rubbed his face with his hands, leaving it streaked with dirt. 'What were you *thinking*?'

'I wasn't.' I moved Gigi from my chest to my lap, and struggled to sit up. 'God, that was stupid.'

Only then did I notice how hard he was breathing, the sheen of sweat on his face. He must have run like the devil.

'Where did you come from?' I asked.

'From the house, after I heard your dog barking to wake the dead—' At my stricken look, he broke off. 'What?'

'Did you see her?' My fingers tightened on Gigi's fur and she licked my hand in reassurance.

After an almost imperceptible pause, he said, 'I didn't see anything, but I was intent on keeping Vicious in sight.'

I began to shiver in the warm night air. It wasn't a ghostly cold; it came from the deepest, most elemental part of me. 'I'm not going crazy. I'm *not*.' But no matter how desperately I said it, I couldn't force it to be true. 'Oh my God. They're going to send me off to Happy Acres Funny Farm.'

'Sylvie.' Rhys gripped my shoulders, speaking in the same voice that he'd used to reach through my terror when I'd been hanging over the river. When I glanced up, his face was very close, and as the wind rustled the trees, enough starlight trickled through that I could see his eyes. 'You're not crazy.'

'How do you know?' I asked, more plaintive than accusing. 'Why should I trust you?'

He smiled, slightly. 'Saving your neck isn't enough?'

Well, I'd asked for a reason. It was convincing, but not satisfactory. 'I'm serious, Rhys. You've been secretive. *Sneaky,* even. And don't think I haven't noticed you call me names when you're trying to distract me. And how could you think I couldn't see through Shaw—'

He stopped me, a finger to my lips, and my breath caught at the presumptuous gesture. 'Don't invoke trouble,' he warned, as if saying Shawn's name would conjure him.

But I couldn't say anything – the startling familiarity of his touch held me transfixed. Wide-eyed, I watched his dawning realization of the intimacy of the moment stretching between us. His bemused gaze dropped to my mouth, and almost absently, he traced the curve of my lip, then brushed my hair from my cheek. My pulse jumped and skittered, and there was no reasoning with it.

'Why should I trust you?' I repeated the question in a whisper, not to him, but to myself.

He combed his hand through my hair, letting it drift through his fingers. It was full of dirt and pine needles, but he didn't seem to care. 'Because I couldn't stand it if I let anything happen this time.'

'This time?' I almost knew what he meant. I felt it often, that the rapport between us was as old as it was new. But here in the woods, the bewildering sensation didn't seem nearly as important as his proximity and the way the trees pushed away the rest of the world.

But my question shook him out of the moment. He blinked, seeming genuinely puzzled. 'Did I say "this time"?'

'Yes.' I focused on curiosity, to hide my disappointment. 'What did you mean?'

Rhys shook his head. 'I'm not sure.'

I had not so much a spark of insight as a wet fizzle. 'Does it have to do with your friend who was injured in the mine?'

His spine straightened, and he drew back from me in unhappy surprise. 'How did you know about that?'

I grimaced. It seemed I wasn't keeping anyone's secrets tonight. 'I told your dad I wouldn't let you know he told me.'

'It's not about Pembrokeshire.' He ran a hand through his hair. 'Or maybe it is, I don't know.' He climbed to his feet and looked towards the house, confusion and frustration clear in the set of his shoulders.

'Maybe if you told me what happened,' I ventured, not even – for once – demanding or sarcastic.

He gave me a dry look. 'Like you've told me what you're doing here?'

After so many weeks of angst over it, the ease of my answer surprised me. 'I chased a Vicodin with too many glasses of champagne at my mother's wedding and passed out in Central Park.'

Clearly, he hadn't expected me to answer. I hadn't either, but I wanted to hear his secret more than I wanted to keep mine. At least, that particular one. 'So?' I prompted.

He sighed, rubbing the furrow between his brows. 'I nearly got my best friend killed in a landslide.'

The depth of his guilt baffled me. 'How could that have been your fault?'

My heart softened with sympathy at his sad shrug. 'If I'd seen what was happening, maybe I could have done something.'

'Because you're a geologist?' I asked, confused. 'But you were just an intern, right?'

'Right.' It was somehow confirmation and denial at the same time. He turned to face me, his mood changing. 'Your turn. What is it you're seeing in the house and the woods?'

Gigi growled low. I thought she was reacting to my tension at the question. Then I heard distant voices calling my name, and saw the gleam of flashlights through the trees.

'Crap.' I tried to get up while holding Gigi, but when I put my right hand on the ground, pain raced from my skinned palm to my wrenched shoulder. I hissed out a curse, and Rhys jumped forward, taking Gigi and helping me to my feet.

'Does this at least convince you,' he said urgently, his eyes flicking towards the approaching lights, 'that you should stay out of things? You can't go blundering around—'

'Blundering!' Forget the undertones of chauvinism – mildly amusing while he was holding my fluffy designer-purse dog – 'blundering' was not a verb a ballerina took lightly.

But Paula was calling my name, and the fear of discovery flooded back. 'You're not going to tell them about the river, are you?'

He handed me Gigi and said in a bargaining tone that I didn't trust at all, 'Promise you'll stay out of the Teen Town Council's way?'

I intended to lie. I looked right at him and formed 'OK' in my mouth, but what came out was 'Not unless you tell me what's going on. I'm done doing whatever people tell me to without asking questions.'

With a growl of exasperation that would have been funny if I weren't so frustrated and angry and scared, Rhys caught my hand – the uninjured one – and turned towards the house and the searchers. 'You picked a fine time to rediscover your backbone, Sylvie Davis.'

❧ ❧

After we'd emerged, dirty and bedraggled, from the woods, Paula exclaimed over the state I was in, and I quickly found myself bustled off to the kitchen. Under the cheery lights, Clara made tea, and Rhys and his father sat at the table while Paula scrubbed the bark and dirt out of my palm and sprayed it with Bactine.

It stung like fire, but the archaic first-aid torture paled next to my worry over what Rhys would say. I managed a convincing story about how I'd gotten into the woods – Gigi chased something, I'd chased her – and into my muddy, scraped-up state – I'd tripped in the dark and fallen on my face. But Rhys, with a quick, you-brought-this-on-yourself glance at me, said, 'She was lucky. She *might* have gone over the embankment if she hadn't caught herself on that tree.'

'Good Lord in His heaven,' said Paula, a hand on her heart as she looked at me. 'You might have been—'

Then she stopped, as two and two added up to five in her head. Her eyes widened, and her fingers went to her lips. 'Oh, Sylvie, honey.'

Crap. I shot Rhys a betrayed glare as I rushed to

assure my cousin. 'It was an accident, Paula. It was so dark, I had *no idea* the river was so close.'

She reached across the table and clasped the hand she'd just tortured. 'Sylvie, honey. If there's *anything* you want to tell me . . . I know you've been troubled, about The Accident, about not being able to dance any more. Things can seem very hopeless.'

I snatched my fingers out of hers, the sting bringing fresh tears to my eyes, which made me even more furious – at Rhys, yes, but mostly that there wasn't one person in my family who trusted my mental health. 'Paula, I'm fine.' It didn't sound very convincing ground out through my teeth. 'I'm *not* depressed, and I'm *not* going to jump in the river.'

Professor Griffith cleared his throat and moved to stand, nudging Rhys as he did. 'We'll just get back to bed. This sounds like a family matter.'

'Oh no,' I said, pointing to Rhys in an angry demand. 'Tell them how dark it was, how easy it was to get lost.'

He met my gaze and, raising his uninjured eyebrow, reminded me silently of the bargain I'd rejected. A band of worry tightened around my chest, worry that he might still rat that it was me, not Gigi, who saw things. It was only a second or two, long enough to twist the knife of anxiety, then he turned to Paula and said earnestly, 'I don't think Sylvie would try and hurt herself, Miss Davis.'

'Thank you,' I said without a shred of gratitude, since he was only telling the truth.

He went on without looking at me. 'You know she

wouldn't do anything rash without making arrangements for her dog.'

'Dammit, Rhys!' The outburst popped free of the iron bands of stress. 'Don't joke about that.'

Clara made a sound, almost a laugh, despite the gravity on everyone's faces. 'He has a point, Paula. Don't write Sylvie off just yet.'

'Thank you, Clara.' I meant the words, though they came out petulant, because *I* didn't think it needed to be said at all.

'Still, it *was* dark,' said Rhys. 'And she *is* a city girl.' He shook his head in a ridiculous and theatrical way. 'Maybe you and Vicious should stay in after nightfall, Sylvie.'

I shot him another death glare, but Paula quickly reclaimed my attention, and my outrage, with her agreement. 'That's not a bad idea, honey. You're not used to all the things out there in the woods. You don't need to be out in the dark.'

Rhys's satisfaction gave him away; this was exactly what he'd meant to achieve. I kept my gaze on Paula, but my fury was scattershot. 'I'm not a child. Or an idiot.'

'Even Addie has a curfew,' she said firmly.

'Which she ignores!' I made a sweeping gesture towards the summerhouse, endangering the mug of tea Clara had poured me. Rhys caught it before it could fall over, but I was too angry to be impressed. 'She was out with the teen council till all hours on a school night. Do you even *know* how late they stay out there?'

The words had exploded angrily, without my

considering if it was smart to tell the world I was keeping tabs on the TTC. But the lack of reaction was a surprise.

'That's different.' Paula spoke briskly, in a way that implied she hadn't registered *any* of what I'd said. 'And beside the point. We're not talking about going to an extracurricular activity—'

'Extracurricular—' I broke off in disbelief. 'Do you guys even hear yourselves when you talk about this group?' I looked at Rhys, who was studying his mug intently, no help at all.

Clara sat on the other side of me, rubbing a soothing hand over my back. 'I guess you must be feeling excluded. I've asked Addie to invite you to some of their get-togethers.'

'If she's feeling excluded,' said Paula, 'she could have gone to the graduation party. Shawn did ask her.'

I bent over and gently banged my forehead on the table. It might as well be the wall I kept running up against. With all of them. Paula and Clara. Rhys. Shawn. This entire town.

Not the professor, though. He slid my mug across the scarred and polished table until it touched my fingers. 'Drink your tea, love.' When I raised my head, he met my eye with a sympathetic smile. 'It'll make you feel better.'

The drink was warm and bracing, but the pause had given Paula time to marshal her arguments. 'Sylvie, forget the woods. I'm worried that you don't seem to be sleeping. You're always up at night.' She paused, clueing me in to what was coming. 'Don't answer now, while you're so upset, but I want you to think about going to see your stepfather's friend in Birmingham.'

She meant the shrink, but didn't want to say it in front of the Griffiths. Like they couldn't figure it out. From the corner of my eye, I saw Rhys fidget, guiltily, I hoped.

Part of me must have suspected this would happen, no matter how I tried to cover things up. It was as if all my fears – falling, going nuts, psychiatrists – had checked their calendars and decided this was the night to gang up on me.

'Cousin Paula,' I started, holding onto my mug with both hands, 'the only thing wrong with me is that you won't let me sleep with my dog.'

Paula relented slowly. 'Will you talk to Reverend Watkins, at least?'

'If I can bring Gigi up with me tonight.' She'd been exiled to her crate, and I felt sick about it, since I'd let her take the blame for my being out in the woods.

'Go ahead, Paula,' said Clara, gently cajoling. 'There's not that much left of the night anyway.'

Sighing deeply in surrender, Paula sat back in her chair. 'Fine. Finish your tea and go on up. I'm going to take some aspirin, then I'll come check on you.'

A bed check was, all told, not that bad. I turned my head to glare at Rhys, but didn't say anything with Clara and his dad still there. He met my eye, silently communicating the same thing. It could have been worse, if he'd told them everything.

'We'd better go up too,' said Professor Griffith,

standing to put action to words. 'Sleep tight, Sylvie, love.'

Somewhere, I found a small smile for him. 'Thanks, Professor.'

'Come along, Rhys. You look like five miles of bad road.'

'Right, Dad. On my way.'

I almost missed his exhale of effort as he pushed himself up from the table. He did look bad. The bruises on his face had faded, but they were still there, mottled green and purple. In the light of the kitchen, I saw something else through the thin white T-shirt he wore with the same khakis from yesterday.

His father was on his way down the hall. Clara had gone with Paula when she left to get her aspirin. Still sitting, I grabbed the loose hem of Rhys's shirt and jerked it up.

He jumped a foot, which was gratifying. 'Jesus, Sylvie!' He strangled the curse down to a whisper, glancing around for witnesses as he tugged the cotton down over impressive abs and a seat-belt bruise the colour of raw meat.

'Oh my God.' I was frozen, still seeing in my head the livid mark that ran up and across his chest. A bruise like that, and I was surprised he was moving around at all. *And* he'd held me suspended over the river. Both of us, really, as he leaned out, tethered by his grasp on the tree.

I didn't even know what to say. On the scale from pissed to smitten, my emotions made a dramatic slide towards grateful wonder. Which is an awkward place to be while you're holding onto a guy by his shirt like he's a Chippendales dancer or something. Not that I knew anything about that, except that one of my class partners had paid his tuition that way and— *Oh my God,* I needed to stop thinking about that.

'I'd better get Gigi and go upstairs,' I blurted, and dropped his shirt like it was hot, retreating to the welcome cool air of the porch, and to my dog, who was spayed and therefore blissfully ignorant of how complicated emotions could get.

❦ ❦

The morning dawned bright and cheery, completely contrary to my mood. There was a shade on my window, but I'd forgotten to pull it when I'd finally fallen into bed the night before. Earlier that morning, really. Gigi burrowed under the covers to get away from the eastern glare, but I had pressing business for the day. Paula had reminded me when she came up to do her bed check. It was Sunday, and we were going to church.

I wouldn't have been able to get out of it even if I'd been the poster girl for spiritual and mental health. It was just what you did here.

So I stumbled to the bathroom, still messy from my quick wash the night before. Since I'd rolled in the mud in my last pair of pj's, Paula had lent me a nightgown. Apparently my practical cousin was a closet Southern belle. The white cotton gown had deep ruffles around the neck and it ended in another froth of ruffle below my knees. The sleeves kept slipping down, and I had to push them up, over and over, as I washed my face.

The image in the mirror was almost a stranger's. Instead of my neat ballerina bun, or even the scrunchie that usually held my hair while I slept, dark tangles fell around my shoulders. My face had more colour than usual, including a dusting of freckles across my nose and cheeks, and faint purple shadows under my eyes. The hollows in my cheeks were less pronounced. All those desserts were beginning to show.

I brushed my teeth and headed back to my room to dress. The door hit someone as I flung it open, and my nerves – complacent with sleep and the mundane tasks of the morning – jolted to stinging alert.

God, I was jumpy. The muffled and distinctly British curse assured me that, whoever was in the hall, it wasn't the Colonel suddenly made flesh.

Paula's reminder of my appointment with the reverend had nudged my mood to the irate side of the scale. But when I peered round the door and saw Rhys doubled over, clutching his already abused nose, I momentarily slid towards apologetic sympathy. 'Did I hurt you?'

'Yes, sod it all.'

He didn't sound like he was going to die, so I let myself feel some satisfaction at getting back at him for ratting me out about the river. 'Good.'

He straightened, giving his nose a last experimental wiggle. 'And my face was just getting better.'

That was true. The bruises had lightened to greenish

yellow, though the skin under his left eye was still a bit purple. Strange that his face had healed so much faster than his chest. If the door had hit him in the sternum, I'd have actually felt bad about it.

When he finally lowered his hand, his eyes swept over me, and he started to laugh. 'What the blazes are you wearing?'

I narrowed my gaze. 'Don't start with me. It's your fault I'm having bed checks and parochial counselling. If I wind up at the shrink—'

I caught myself. I'd said too much, spoken my fear aloud. Guilt flashed, just for a moment, in Rhys's purple-shadowed eyes. 'I am sorry about that.' He did sound contrite, but he ruined it by adding, 'But did you really think you were going to avoid any hassle from Paula?'

Hearing someone crossing the hall downstairs, I lowered my voice to an angry hiss. 'You could have helped me try.'

'Sylvie?' Paula called my name from the foyer. 'Are you up?'

'Just on my way to the bathroom, Paula.'

'Do you want some breakfast before we go?'

'No, ma'am.' There was a disapproving pause. Refusing food was always the wrong answer. 'Just some juice, maybe.'

'Be down in twenty minutes.' She called me to heel like I called Gigi. The difference was, I would actually obey, even if I didn't like it.

Rhys had stood silent during this whole exchange. I grabbed his arm, pulled him into the bathroom and shut the door. His eyebrows climbed in exaggerated shock. 'You Yankee girls are really very forward.'

'Shut up.' I didn't want to be charmed by his humour or distracted by the way his eyes followed my movements as I pushed up the ridiculous sleeves of my borrowed nightgown.

For God's sake, Sylvie. Focus.

'The night before you left,' I said, 'you let on there was something going on here.'

That seemed to startle him, before his expression turned wary. 'Did I say that?'

'"Strange dealings afoot".' I quoted it firmly, because lately I'd discovered a lot about evasive phrasing. 'And seriously, Rhys, you have no poker face.'

He allowed a rueful grimace. 'It used to be better. Before I met you.'

This relatively straightforward admission sent the undisciplined part of me – which I wasn't sure existed before I came to Alabama – rocketing skyward in delight. It struck me, as he seemed to be focusing intently on my left eyebrow to keep his eyes above my neck, that it wasn't only *him* getting under *my* skin.

Don't think about skin, you twit. Focus.

I forced a warning into my voice. 'I'm not a helpless princess or a moron, Rhys. I can find out what's going on here, if I dig deep enough.'

My I'm-playing-hardball tone snapped his gaze to mine, and the muscle in his jaw clenched for just a second before he lifted his uninjured eyebrow with deliberate composure. 'How are you going to manage that? It sounds like you're going to have some trouble finding unsupervised time in the future.'

Crap. He was right. I jammed my fists on my hips and glared up at him. 'Dammit, Rhys. Why do you get off the hook while I'm stuck with a nanny? You were out there with me.'

His mouth twisted in a self-mocking half-smile. 'Because I'm the knight and you're the maiden, and life is not fair.'

At least he admitted it, but it still made me mad. 'Is that what this is? Be a good girl and don't stick your nose in the menfolk's business?'

All humour disappeared. 'I'd tell you the same thing if you were a guy. Don't muck around where you don't know how deep the water is.'

'You don't think I know how to swim?' I grabbed the door handle and twisted, throwing a cold look over my shoulder. 'Don't let the Victorian ruffles fool you.'

His hand landed on the door, keeping it closed. As irritated as I was, my heart still stuttered, and not in an entirely bad way. I turned in the space allowed by his arm, and pressed my back against the door, more to keep myself from doing anything stupid than from fear – or hope – that he would. Do something stupid, I mean.

He must have read my thoughts, or maybe I had no poker face either, because his eyes dropped to my mouth, then moved back up to hold my gaze. 'Stay out of the woods, Sylvie. That's all I'm asking.' At the 'Oh, really' arch of my brows, he added, 'And stay away from Shawn and the teen council.'

There was a warning there, and worry. Chauvinism, maybe, but also genuine fear for my safety. 'I can't,' I said, dogged, but a bit daunted, too. 'I'm supposed to go to the Catfish Festival this afternoon.'

'Tell Paula you're sick.'

'I can't,' I repeated, a little plaintively. 'If I don't talk to Reverend Watkins, she'll take me to a shrink. Better Shawn and catfish than a psychiatrist and a couch.'

He grimaced, satisfyingly rueful. 'I *am* sorry about that.'

My irritation flared with the reminder. 'You should be.'

'I only thought she'd keep closer watch on you, keep your nose out of trouble.'

We were standing so close, I had to tilt my head to meet his eye. How could I be feeling so many things at once? My blood zipped through my veins, thrilled at his nearness, infuriated by his evasion. His scent, unique and exhilarating and natural, filled my head, and I had to force myself to stay on track.

'It's the teen council, isn't it?' I watched his face as I asked my nonquestion. 'They're doing something.'

He struggled for a moment, then dropped his arm. 'I can't say.'

'Can't or won't?' I snapped, chilled by his withdrawal.

'Both,' he admitted, sounding genuinely regretful at the distance he put between us. 'You'd better go. Unless you want to tell the reverend you're late because you were ambushing blokes in your nightgown.'

I gave an indelicate snort, letting him end the inquisition because he had a point. Any minute now, Paula would be jerking my leash. 'Right. Because all this old-fashioned splendour is so tempting.'

He looked to the ceiling, as if for patience, then back at me. 'Don't be obtuse, princess. It's only because I'm a gentleman that I haven't let you know that I find Victorian ruffles insanely hot.'

I'd think he was teasing me – except that Rhys really didn't have any poker face at all. So I made my second prudent retreat in less than twelve hours, this time, if I let myself admit it, more delighted than dismayed.

Chapter 24

Since I was in church anyway, I thanked God that Addie had spent the night with Kimberley, and was not around to witness the Incredible River Disaster and its aftermath. The morning was difficult enough with only the regular amount of speculation and staring.

The antique pews were not very comfortable. Davis backsides had suffered the same wooden torture for generations, and I wondered if it was any easier with voluminous skirts and petticoats. On one hand, you might have more padding under your bum, but on the other, you'd have to deal with a corset. In an unairconditioned Alabama summer. I decided I'd rather take my own miseries.

My imagination ran away with the thought of corsets and crinolines, and suddenly I was picturing a church full of a starched and buttoned congregation, sweltering through an hour-long sermon. Had Hannah sat here, laced into her whalebone corset, lilac-scented handkerchief dabbing at her modest décolletage? Was *he* here? The guy? The one for whom she would rather sleep with the fishes than sleep without? The guy who had knocked her up and left her?

I glanced across to where Shawn Maddox sat with his father. Naturally the Maddox pew was right across the aisle from the Davis one. Up front, of course.

Shawn, wearing the male-under-thirty uniform of button-down shirt, necktie and khaki trousers, seemed to sense my gaze and turned his head slightly to smile at me. How did he *do* that? I didn't trust him, wasn't even sure I liked him in the normal way, let alone the way everyone in town seemed to expect me to. I'd just been – well, it would be hard to call it flirting, but no other term fitted – with Rhys in the bathroom at Bluestone Hill. But I *still* found myself yanking my gaze forward and blushing like I was a nineteenth-century girl caught staring at a young gentleman in church. I wished I had a fan so I could cool my blush before the rumours got any worse.

❧ ❧

Once Reverend Watkins had given the benediction, Paula slipped out through the side to give him the scoop on my latest adventure. I dawdled to give her time, and wasn't terribly surprised when Shawn appeared in front of me as I exited the pew.

'Wow,' said Shawn. 'You clean up nice.'

'Gee, thanks.' My tone was dry, but I appreciated the compliment, even from Shawn, whose praise I'd realized needed to be cut by half. I was wearing a skirt for the first time since having my cast removed. I lived in jeans, which hid the bumps and craters of the scars where my tibia had broken through my skin, and the pins that held it while it healed. But Paula had put her foot down on wearing jeans to church.

'What time should I pick you up for the shindig?' he asked.

'I need to talk to Reverend Watkins about something, and then I'd like to go home and change.' It occurred to me that I could still come down with a sudden, violent stomach bug, and I left myself some wiggle room. 'I could ask Paula to bring me to the festival later—'

'Oh no.' Shawn flashed that grin, full wattage and full of open appreciation. 'I'm making the most of this date. I'll see you in an hour and a half?'

'Make it two.'

'Done!' he said, and with another broad grin, hurried off.

I obeyed orders and headed to where Paula was waving to me. I'll say one thing – she was efficient as she ushered me into Reverend Watkins's tiny, book-cluttered office. Even he seemed a little stunned by the whirlwind as we faced each other across his desk. 'So,' he said, looking me right in the eye, 'Paula says you haven't been sleeping well.'

I had my answer prepared. 'It's not the big deal she thinks it is. Now that she's letting Gigi stay in my room at night, it shouldn't be a problem.'

'But you were in the woods last night.' He raised his brows in a question. 'Near where you saw the girl jump in the river?'

I sighed, and with an air of confession, gave him the half-truth I'd decided would make me sound as normal as possible. 'I was meeting a guy in the woods. Do you think I should have told her that instead?'

He blinked, and cleared his throat. 'Were you . . . um . . .'

'No, no, no,' I assured him honestly. 'Just talking.'

Looking relieved, he sat back in his creaking chair. 'Do you like this boy?'

'Yes.' This was more candid than I'd ever been with my shrink. The old, Manhattan Sylvie would have shrugged, or said something cutting. The agreement slipped out easily now, though I couldn't voice all my feelings because I didn't understand them, or why they seemed to run so deep when I'd only known Rhys a week. 'But it's complicated.'

'Don't answer if you don't want to, but . . . is it Shawn Maddox?'

I eyed him, gauging his reaction. 'No.' His guarded expression slipped away, and he looked relieved. The realization surprised me into saying, rather tactlessly, 'You seem to be the only one in town that doesn't seem to think the sun rises and sets on him.'

Reverend Watkins bit back a smile and said, with exaggerated gravity, 'Maybe it's because I already have a saviour.'

'Ha!' He'd surprised a braying laugh out of me. Since I felt like I'd get an honest opinion out of him, I floated an observation. 'You may have noticed that people around here seem to have some expectations of us. Shawn and me, that is.'

'Just a bit.'

His irony gave me hope – finally – for some refreshing candour. 'Can I ask you a question?'

'Certainly.' Glancing at the clock, he said, 'We might need another few minutes to convince Paula you've unburdened all your troubles.'

'What do you think of this Maddox Point deal? It keeps coming up whenever I talk to people from town.'

He steepled his fingers in front of his chin. 'I think that when the price tag makes things exclusive, the people it tends to exclude . . .'

I filled in the blanks of his tactful omission. 'You end up with a place as homogenized as a carton of milk. But the town is in favour of the place. I mean, everyone I've met is.'

He shrugged. 'Folks believe it will bring in rich people to spend their money on the weekends. Which it might.'

'Which would be good, right?' One of Shawn's win-win situations. 'The town could use the money. I mean, there are some nice houses in Maddox Landing, but out in the country . . .' I trailed off, and didn't mention the single-wide mobile homes and tumble-down shacks.

'Right.' He followed my gist with a sober nod. 'People who will pay with their taxes if the bond that Zachary Maddox wants is voted in. Call me a raging liberal, but I don't think people should have to fund the sewage system of a place that's too exclusive for them to afford.'

He stopped, looking a little embarrassed. 'Sorry. I thought I was done preaching for the day.'

'It's OK. I didn't know there was a bond up for a vote.' That put the town's rampant one-sided opinion on the matter in a different light. As usual, I hadn't thought about money.

'Anyway,' said the reverend as he stood to escort me the three steps to the office door. 'Revenue is nice, but I like looking out over a multicultural congregation. I don't want to go backwards, just to get more money in the collection plate.' He winced. 'That's just between you and me.'

'Of course.' I grinned. 'Sanctity of the confessional and all.'

The reverend smiled in return, and opened the door. 'You're thinking of the Catholics, but I'll take it.'

I went to meet Paula knowing I wasn't going to get a sudden case of the flu. I had to go to the festival. I took Rhys's warnings seriously – vague as they were – but when was I going to get a better chance to dissect the layers of mystery around the Teen Town Council and its connection to Maddox Landing and Maddox Point? Not to mention Bluestone Hill.

Chapter 25

I'd seen the banner over Main Street announcing the festival, but I hadn't known what to expect. I had a bit of a clue as Shawn drove past cars and pickups parked two deep on the town's side streets and in the lots of stores that appeared to be closed for the day.

'Where did all these people come from?' I asked. Gigi stood on my lap, her paws on the window, just as fascinated, but less flabbergasted.

Shawn slid me a smile as we pulled into a private parking lot right before the barricades across Main

Street. 'Did you expect twenty-five people at the high school gym?'

'Of course not. I was thinking a hundred or so in the National Guard armoury.' He laughed, but the truth was, I *had* underestimated the TTC. Through the windshield I could make out an enormous marquee shading long folding tables and chairs, and vendor booths set up around the town square. When Shawn killed the engine, I could hear a live band and happy crowd chatter. 'I didn't think Maddox Landing had this many people in it.'

'It doesn't. But people do know how to drive someplace when there's food, music and beer.' Flashing that grin, he got out of the truck and came round to help me down. When I'd gone back to the Hill, I'd discovered all my jeans were covered in garden dirt, so I was wearing another skirt. At least I wouldn't be able to tell if people were staring at me because I was a Davis, or because of the scars on my leg.

I put Gigi into her tote; I didn't want her to get stepped on in the crowd. She popped her head out the open top, nose twitching blissfully. I smelled at least part of what she did – plenty of fried food, both sweet and savoury. That, at least, was no surprise.

Shawn took my hand to steady me as I stepped over the kerb, and he didn't let go afterwards. I felt a tingle of reaction, but it was drowned out by the cynical voice in my head, pointing out how smoothly that was done.

What was I doing? I wasn't a girl detective. I was a ballerina who couldn't even trust her own senses. Last night I'd chased a ghost and nearly broken my neck. Was I running just as foolishly headlong now?

I was very aware I was doing the *exact* opposite of what Rhys had told me to do. It wasn't pure obstinacy, and it wasn't frivolous curiosity. I needed to dig at this mystery the way I needed to dig the weeds out of my garden. I kept thinking if I could just reveal the pattern, I would understand – I don't know – *something*.

'You look so serious,' said Shawn, nudging my arm with his elbow as we reached the square. 'It's supposed to be a party.'

Come on, Sylvie, get in gear. I might not be much of a detective, but when I had my game on, I could smile through *anything* – bleeding toes, wardrobe malfunctions, clumsy partners. I could handle this.

'Sorry,' I told Shawn, deliberately relaxing the furrow of concentration between my brows. We'd arrived with the festivities in full swing. The tables under the awning were already crowded, and the band was covering the only Lynyrd Skynyrd song I could name. It gave me an excuse for an arch smile. 'Is it in the state constitution that you have to play "Sweet Home Alabama" at every event?'

He laughed. 'Only at ones with more than fifty people.'

The streets around the town green (Maddox Green, of course) had been blocked off, and vendors were selling arts, crafts and every kind of fried food imaginable. It wasn't high-toned – 'booth' in some cases meant a barbecue and a card table stacked with paper plates and condiments – but in addition to the music and laughter, there was an energetic pulse in the air. I could feel it catching me up in its wave, maybe a little against my will.

'The Teen Town Council did all this?' I couldn't keep the marvelling wonder out of my voice.

'We spearheaded it, I guess you'd say.' Shawn downplayed the accomplishment. 'The real town council – mostly my dad and Ms Brewster – helped. For some reason people don't trust teenagers when it comes to forking over money for sponsorships and advertising.'

I would wager Shawn could convince anyone to trust him with anything. But there were probably logistical considerations if most of his workforce was under eighteen.

'I think you can tentatively call it a success,' I said.

He nodded. 'I'm thinking maybe next year it will be a two-day festival, maybe advertise in Selma and Montgomery. And of course by then, we'll have people in Maddox Point.'

'So soon?' I spoke without thinking, not shocked by his optimism, but by the timing. 'Don't you have to finish the surveys and see if the bond passes?'

His brows shot up in surprise, and he stopped walking. I was aware of the audience – hyper-aware, since I had my game on – but standing with Shawn always felt a little like standing in a bubble, just he and I, everyone else looking in.

'You've put your ear to the ground, I see.'

Crap. That was stupid, showing my hand that way. Even if Shawn were as straightforward as his public image, he was bound to take my interest the wrong way.

'Sylvie!' Hugely relieved for the distraction, I turned at my squealed name, then heard, even louder and more thrilled, 'Gigi!'

Caitlin and Kimberly ran up to us, and I felt almost flattered that they hugged me in welcome before petting my dog. Gigi, of course, was ecstatic, licking their hands like they were coated in bacon.

'Are you having a good time?' Caitlin asked.

It was a little hard to tell whether she was talking to me or the dog. I took a chance and answered. 'We just got here.'

Kimberly gestured across the tent. 'We've got a table by the band. One of the perks of helping to set up. Come sit with us.'

I was grateful for the invitation. I could feel out the TTC and have some respite from Shawn's full attention.

'We were about to get something to eat,' said Shawn. 'We'll head over after we hit the booths.'

Caitlin looked up from scratching Gigi's chin. 'Can we hold onto Gigi for you?'

A quick pinch of unease made a liar out of me. I wasn't *that* comfortable with them. 'It's awfully crowded. I'd better keep her close, in case she gets anxious.'

At the moment, she was closer to nirvana than a nervous breakdown. But Caitlin took it in stride, and Kimberly said, 'Bring your food over. We're right by the dance floor.'

They took off at full speed, red curls and black braids bouncing in tandem. I looked at Shawn, feeling ambushed. 'No one said there was going to be dancing.'

He raised his hands, holding off the bite in my accusation. 'I'm so sorry, Sylvie,' he said, sounding contrite. 'I didn't even think.'

Did I believe him? On the one hand, I suspected Shawn didn't spit without a plan. On the other, how could he know how much it still hurt to watch other people let music move them. It wasn't about skill, or style, or talent. It was about the kinetic joy of motion. The worst dancer in the world was happy shuffling his feet to the beat. How could I ever be happy shuffling, when I used to soar?

Shawn touched my shoulder, let his hand trail down my arm to again clasp my hand, this time with a reassuring squeeze. My defences were low, and the warm comfort of his touch spread through me, the cat-in-the-sunshine glow unknotting the tight knot at the base of my skull.

Game face, Sylvie. I needed to keep my head about me, to make good on my boast to Rhys that I knew how to swim in deep waters.

'Come on,' he said. 'Let's get something to eat. What will you have? Cheese fries? Elephant ear?'

'No fried green tomatoes?' I asked, the closest I could come to a disarming quip.

He grinned. 'I'll bet I can swing something for you.'

Almost more amused than cynical, I bet he could, too.

❧ ❧

By the time Shawn and I joined the rest of the TTC, I'd seen almost everyone I knew – south of the Mason-

Dixon Line, anyway – and met a lot more. I recognized some from the church, and some from the Daisy Café, but they all seemed to know me, or at least *of* me.

It was no longer a surprise, but my ballerina smile was getting a workout. Especially at the similarity of everyone's sentiments. 'Welcome home.' Or, 'It's great to see a young Davis back at Bluestone Hill.' It quickly went from irritating to unnerving.

By the time Shawn introduced me to his father, I was glad for the distraction. Mr Maddox was standing with Ms Brewster, who gave me a hug as if we were old friends, then, holding my hands at arm's length, looked me over.

'Sylvie, you look lovely. Alabama is certainly agreeing with you!' Her smile turned slyly teasing, but she stopped short of a wink. 'Or something is.'

'Clara's cooking,' I said dryly, turning aside her implication more politely than I was inclined to.

I couldn't pretend I didn't know this would happen. It was impossible to ignore the buzz of speculation about Shawn and me together, all subliminal, in smiles and nods that I couldn't address without seeming paranoid.

But I'd woefully underestimated its effect on me. The overlap of my present and Hannah's past seemed to flicker at the corner of my vision so I wasn't just seeing women in slacks and shorts smiling at Shawn, but ladies whispering behind fans, distracting themselves from the heat and their corsets with gossip about the latest Maddox/Davis merger.

An expectant pause brought me firmly back to the

present, and I realized that Shawn's dad had said something to me. Zachary Maddox was slick and modern, and surprisingly young. I guessed early forties, unless he just moisturized very well. He had charisma, too, but it was less Tom Sawyer and more politician, bringing to mind what Dr Young had said in the Old Cahawba cemetery. That seemed a lifetime ago.

And they were still waiting. It seemed like a 'How do you do?' sort of pause, so I smiled and said, 'I'm having a wonderful time. You must be so proud of Shawn for organizing the TTC on this festival. And he is so enthusiastic about Maddox Point . . .'

I left an open-ended pause for him to fill. Another trick of my mother's – it was hard to go wrong complimenting someone's offspring and business ventures.

Mr Maddox clapped his son on the shoulder and grinned. I definitely saw the similarity. 'Yes, he's a real entrepreneur,' he said, without any sarcasm. 'And not quite nineteen yet.'

'Dad,' said Shawn, in the aw-shucks voice.

'How is Maddox Point coming along?' I asked, hopefully sounding more sincere. 'Everyone has been talking about it.'

'Well enough.' Mr Maddox certainly seemed to take my interest as genuine. 'We had a few delays with some survey reports, but it's moving forward now. So, if I can just convince your cousin's friends over at Old Cahawba that we're no threat to them . . .'

He nodded over my shoulder, and I turned to see Dr Young sitting with a handful of young people – college students, from their University of Alabama

T-shirts. His dig crew, I guessed. Professor Griffith sat across from him, and they'd been looking my way. Gigi saw them too and wiggled impatiently in her bag. She'd been getting her share of attention from the people we met, but she knew the professors were soft touches for little dogs.

Both of them waved, but it was hard to interpret their expressions. Easier to read was that of one of the girls in the group; stiletto glares tend to carry better over distances, I guess.

I registered the lack of love between the Cahawba crew and the Maddoxes, and scanned the folding tables to see who else I'd missed. Paula and Clara were there – they also waved, though with more obvious encouragement. But no sign of Rhys. I was equally disappointed and relieved. It was hard enough to concentrate without the stress of his disapproval.

Mr Maddox was speaking again. 'You should take Sylvie out to the Point, Shawn. Take her round on the ATV, and talk about your plans.'

'Sounds great,' said Shawn, turning to me under the beaming approval of Ms Brewster and his dad's more restrained smile. 'What do you say, Sylvie? This week sometime?'

It sounded like it would be informative but exhausting, physically and mentally. Was I willing to date Shawn to find out why he wanted to date me? And what would Rhys say about that?

'I'm not much for ATVs,' I said, leaving the door open for me to wiggle out.

'Vehicles are negotiable.' Shawn grinned, as if the

matter had been settled, and said to his dad, 'We're going to join the gang. See you later, Ms Brewster.'

'Have a great time, kids!'

I didn't see it, but I knew her grin widened as Shawn slipped his arm around my shoulders.

❦ ❦

Even with my misgivings about the TTC, it was hard not to like them, at least a little bit. Whatever had the town thinking Shawn and his friends walked on water, as I sat with them at the table by the band, my leg propped up and my back to the empty space cleared for dancing, I was surprised at how *normal* they seemed. For instance, if Caitlin had been deliberately faking her welcome, she would have paid more attention to me than to my dog.

I'd taken Gigi out of her tote, and she was enjoying being passed among some of the girls, practising her wiles on them. The guys were talking about sports – one kept checking the baseball scores on his cell phone, to his girlfriend's annoyance – and about making the renovation of a swimming hole downriver their next project.

Addie was there too, and I expected her to be as annoying and antagonistic as usual. But oddly, in the full circle of her friends, she seemed not to mind my presence so much. She was the queen bee, and I was just a gnat. I found it more curious than annoying. At least for the moment.

When the guys suggested the swimming-hole

endeavour, she snorted. 'Y'all can work on whatever you want, but the next TTC project is getting the Maddox Point bond passed.'

'Are you campaigning for that?' I asked, not to challenge her, but in surprise. 'Isn't that a conflict of interest?'

Rather than snap back, she merely arched her brows. 'Are you going to report us?'

She had a point, but her words sent a small shudder of disquiet down my spine. I couldn't even say why, since, as she implied, who would care if twelve teens campaigned for something that was in the interest of their leader?

I glanced at Shawn, who'd moved a few places down the table to chat with the guys about who should be quarterback next year, now that he'd graduated. It sounded like an old argument, one so boring and benign, it made me doubt my own doubts. As if I needed any help second-guessing my instincts.

Kimberly startled me by plopping into Shawn's empty chair and grabbing my arm. Leaning in, she lowered her voice so I had to edge forward to catch her words under the music and chatter. 'Girl, I'm dying to ask about the other night. I can't believe you really saw the Colonel. I would have keeled over right in my tracks.'

My composure slipped, my shoulders stiffening warily. I'd known Addie would gleefully tell that tale, but I wasn't eager for it to spread further. 'I don't know *what* I saw, Kimberly.' I tried to keep the tightness out of my voice. 'I was mostly asleep. It was just a bad dream.'

Her face drooped in disappointment. 'But Shawn said—'

'*Shawn* said?' I shot a surprised and angry glare his way, but he was talking to one of the teen council guys. My look got his attention, though he didn't break off what he was saying.

'Yeah,' said Kimberly, looking confused. 'Shawn said that you must be really sensitive to the ghosts, because no one has seen them since his aunt Rainbow was here, back in the day.'

Her again. Before I could ask what Rainbow had supposedly seen, Kimberly's shift in mood distracted me.

'My granny has another theory, though.' Some of her enthusiasm had darkened. 'She says the spirits are getting more active. The mirror by her door cracked the other day.'

I frowned, leaning in to match her posture. 'What does that mean?'

Kimberly chewed her lip. 'She thinks maybe there's something in the air, stirring them up. Maybe it's a young Davis back at the Hill. She told me to tell you to be careful.'

There was something in that pause before she spoke, and I jumped on it. 'Kimberly. Do *you* believe what your grandmother said?'

Her eyes slid to the side. 'Well, *I* haven't seen anything, so I can't say.'

Before I could pursue her evasive answer, a movement caught my eye, derailing my train of thought. Reverend Watkins was trying to flag my attention.

You'd think someone in his profession would have more innate discretion.

'Would you excuse me for a minute, Kimberly?' She agreed amiably, but when I stood, the rest of the council looked at me curiously. 'I need to walk my dog,' I improvised. Of course Shawn offered to go with me, but I waved him back into his seat. 'It'll just take a minute.'

'You sure?' he asked, and though I gauged his expression as carefully as I could, I didn't see any suspicion.

'Definitely.' Whatever the reverend wanted to say to me, he obviously didn't want an audience.

I collected Gigi and slung the empty tote over my shoulder. Once I was away from the council, I saw the the reverend nod towards an empty table behind some speakers and headed there to meet him. As the afternoon had gone on, more people had clustered near the band, so we would have some privacy.

'What's going on, Reverend?'

'Nothing dire,' he said immediately, though the frowning slashes of his brows didn't exactly reassure me. 'I just came across something I knew you'd want to see, especially after our discussion this morning.'

'OK.' It felt like a long time ago. We'd talked about Shawn, and my feeling of expectation in that direction. Something the afternoon had certainly borne out.

'I found that journal you were interested in, by Reverend Holzphaffel.' He took a thin leather-bound book from under his arm.

'And you brought it to me here?' What could be in a hundred-and-fifty-year-old book that couldn't wait?

My question seemed to shake him out of his worry, and he smiled sheepishly, the furrows easing from his forehead. 'Well, I was coming anyway, and I knew you'd be here.'

He was wearing civilian clothes – a polo shirt instead of his clerical collar. But my anxiety didn't ease as quickly as his. 'What was in the journal?'

Gesturing to the table and chairs, he waited until I settled with Gigi in my lap before answering. 'I'd forgotten how uncensored Holzphaffel's opinions were. Which is what makes them such a valuable historical resource, of course, but remember, it was a long time ago, and people took some things very seriously.'

'What things?' I asked. His procrastinating preface was making me even more nervous. As he spoke, he flipped through the volume to a page marked with a sticky note. I guessed the book wasn't an original; I was horrified by the idea of a Post-it on Hannah's journal.

'Folklore. Spirits.' He looked at me, cynical, at least on the surface. 'Holzphaffel was from the Old World. Germany. He uses the word *hexen* a lot.'

Even though I didn't speak German, the word raised the hair on the back of my neck. 'As in "hex"? You mean witchcraft?'

He cleared his throat. 'I mean, people were very superstitious back then.' He laid the book on the table in front of me. 'It turns out Hannah Davis had a similar problem to yours.'

The book was a facsimile of handwritten pages, and

the cramped, old-fashioned script would have been hard to read from a good copy. But as I deciphered the passage he indicated, the distractions faded, until I was alone with the reverend, the book and the ideas that the words sent spinning through my brain.

The conviction with which the townspeople believe that Miss Davis and Mr Ethan Maddox should marry takes on an unsettling fervour, setting an almost magical importance to this union that recalls the archaic traditions of the Old Country, very out of place in the enlightened New World.

'"Archaic traditions".' I looked up at Reverend Watkins. 'What does that mean?'

He sat back in his chair. 'The South was devastated by the war, in a way that's hard for us to imagine. Maybe people put a . . . mystical significance on the match, because they badly needed to believe *something* would make things better.'

I nodded, making a rational argument to hide how shaken I was by that passage. 'Coming off the fact that Davis/Maddox marriages sealed business deals that were good for the community.'

He smiled wryly. 'Superstitions have to start from something.'

'But . . .' I let the word hang leadingly. Something that simple – something that everyone had already told me – wouldn't have made him seek me out here.

Shaking his head, he answered with obvious reluctance. 'It sounds ridiculous. But the archaic tradition he's talking about . . . In many pagan religions, the, er, marriage of certain parties – king and queen, priest and priestess – symbolized the joining of male and female deities to bless the earth. Make it abundant and prosperous.'

I couldn't believe he didn't spontaneously combust explaining that. *My* face flamed with embarrassment – I got that 'er, marriage' wasn't referring to the legal ceremony. But slowly the heat drained away, as what he was saying sank to the pit of my stomach.

'So . . . there's a real basis for this superstition?'

He demurred with a frown. 'I don't know about *real*.'

'I mean historical.' I don't know why that made it seem less silly and annoying, less dismissible.

'What you're going for,' said the reverend, 'is that there is a basis in folklore.'

Folklore. *Hexen*. Witchcraft. People of Holzphaffel and Hannah's day hadn't just thought a Davis/Maddox union was lucky, but something more than that. Something magical.

I stroked Gigi's fur with one hand and traced the cover of the book with the other. I found myself picturing the mazelike pattern of my garden circle and remembering what Professor Griffith said about the plants there, and their lore.

'May I borrow this?' I asked, indicating the book.

'Certainly.' He slid it towards me. 'That's why I brought it to you. I figured you'd want to read more of Hannah's story.'

'Reverend . . .' I began hesitantly, 'you don't believe this *hexen* idea, do you? That there's some kind of magic at work when a Davis and Maddox get together?'

Contemplating his answer, he said, 'I don't know

what to tell you, except there's power in belief. So tread carefully, Sylvie.'

His carefully phrased warning didn't ease my mind. Was it that far a stretch from the notion of ghostly echoes to the spine-chilling idea of magic? Maybe not sword-and-sorcery stuff, but the subtle influencing of events?

Gigi licked my face, and I realized I'd said goodbye to the reverend and hardly noticed he'd left. I was sure that made a great impression.

I'd not noticed a lot of things. Like how my guard came down and my uneasiness disappeared while I'd been sitting with the council. How the sway that Shawn had over people really was more than his charm could account for.

Gigi pawed my knee. In a distracted daze, I set her on the ground, slipped the reverend's journal into her carrier tote and walked her to a strip of grass beside the bank, away from the crowds. I wished I was back in my garden, where I could take off my shoes. My control was fisted tight around too many emotions – fear and disbelief and hysteria. If I loosened the knot even a little, they might all come bursting out, and then I *would* end up in a mental ward.

The summer sun was sinking slowly, painting everything in a golden glow. Methodically I traced the pattern of inexplicable events to their beginning. What was the *first* thing? The aproned woman in the kitchen? The scent of lilacs in my room? Or the shadow at the window?

With a start, I realized I had to go back further than that. To Central Park. What had changed that night?

I cast through my very fuzzy memory. I'd been loaded. I'd been talking about my dad. I said something stupid about believing in magic, and then demonstrated—

My knees folded up under me, and I sat down hard on the kerb. Gigi ran to me and jumped in my lap, anxiously licking my chin, and I hardly noticed.

The world as I knew it didn't change that night. *I* did, when I'd admitted – sheepishly, jokingly, with only a small part of myself – that magic could be real.

Superstition, ghosts, magic. What linked these things together? Was it me, or was it Alabama, or was it both?

Chapter 26

When I returned to the TTC table, I must have looked convincingly wan, because no one questioned me when I said I needed to go home. Kimberly in particular was solicitous, offering to chauffeur me, but of course Shawn insisted.

I stayed quiet on the drive, petting Gigi and thinking. The late-afternoon glow had turned to purple dusk, and Shawn switched on the headlights in the shadows of the tree-lined road. He was savvy enough to let the silence stand, but at the turnoff to the Hill, he finally spoke. 'I hope Kimberly didn't upset you.'

That was an unexpected tack, and I glanced at him in surprise. 'Why would she upset me?'

'I saw y'all talking, and . . . well, I know you're touchy about the ghost thing.'

'I'm touchy' – anger got the better of my sense, but it was good to feel something besides dazed and confused – 'because you keep putting words in my mouth, telling people I've *seen* things.'

'Do I?' His brow wrinkled in confusion. 'I thought you said you did.'

That might have worked, made me doubt myself, if Addie hadn't tried the exact same thing. 'I know I didn't.' Say it, that is. 'Are you trying to make people think I'm crazy? Or maybe just a little kooky?'

He did a double take between me and the curving road. 'Why would I want to do that?'

My sense of self-preservation kicked in before I blurted my first thought. If it got around that I saw ghosts, then I would be the girl who cried wolf if I ever tried to tell anyone that a bunch of high school students were influencing the success of the Maddox Point development. And that was *without* mentioning magic.

But if I said that aloud, I might as well go jump in the river myself. So I said, convincingly, 'I have no idea.'

Pulling the truck into his usual spot at the side of the house, he set the parking brake and turned to me. We were out of sight of any of the windows, and the deepening twilight made the cab seem more close, more intimate. 'Can I walk you in?'

The low rumble in his voice implied something more lingering than a handshake on the porch.

I counted cars, and seized on an excuse. 'Paula's here. And my leg really hurts, Shawn. It's been a long day.'

'All right.' He picked up a strand of hair that had escaped from my ponytail, and twirled it around his finger. 'I just don't want to end our first date on an argument.'

'It's our second date,' I said thoughtlessly. *Stupidly*. He grinned, and I realized my mistake.

'In that case,' he said, and leaned forward, with a slow, tempting smile – tempting in spite of *everything* – and brushed my lips with his.

Gigi stirred in my lap and sat up, putting a puppy barrier between us. Wilful, wonderful dog.

Shawn sat back with a disappointed laugh, and I opened the truck door, trying not to look like I was making a break for it, running from him, and from my own reaction to him.

'I'll call you about going out to the Point this week,' Shawn said, when I'd extracted Gigi and myself from the truck. 'And maybe we can talk about the TTC.'

That stopped the 'don't call me, I'll call you' on my lips. 'What about it?'

'Well, I know you're not here for long.' He propped a hand on the steering wheel, still turned to face me. 'But I hope you'll be back to visit. Maybe you'd like to have some say in how things go here.'

I was too stunned to say anything more committal than 'Maybe.'

'Great.' Shawn flashed his smile, and released the

parking brake. I closed the truck door, and wondered what the hell *that* invitation meant.

❧ ❧

Everyone was in their usual spots around the table when I came in – Clara and Paula, Rhys and his dad. The kettle was steaming, the tea canisters were out and it was all very domestic and cosy. The adults watched me with a paternal sort of expectation that would have been amusing if I didn't feel like someone had wrung out all my emotions and left me as limp as one of Clara's dishrags.

Rhys looked me over critically, but before I could register more than that, Gigi ran in behind me and made a flying leap into Professor Griffith's lap.

'Sylvie!' barked Paula, about to harp on me about the dog. But after another glance at me, she softened her tone. 'Lord, honey. You look done in. I'll bet today was just too much for your leg.'

Clara put her hands on the table to push herself up. 'Come sit down. I'll make you some tea.'

Crap. I must have looked as bad as I felt. It wasn't my leg, though it did ache. I was completely spent, like I'd done three shows in a day. But in a way, I'd been onstage since the church bell rang that morning.

'I'll make it,' I told her. 'Then, if you don't mind, I'll take it upstairs and go to bed.'

'That's an excellent idea,' said Paula. 'A warm drink and an early turn-in.'

Her agreement was a little pointed, but she didn't

need to worry about nocturnal wanderings. No ghost chasing for me tonight. At least, not in the woods. I planned to read more of Hannah's diary, and maybe the reverend's. *If* I could keep my eyes open long enough.

Rhys followed me on the pretence of refilling his own cup, though from his father's passing smile, he wasn't fooling anyone. At least, not about the fact he wanted to talk to me. While I refilled the kettle, he stood close by, letting the running water cover his voice. 'How was your date?'

As tired as I was, I managed to find the retort I wished I'd made that morning. 'You know, it's not as if you gave me a reason to turn Shawn down. Like, say, asking me yourself.'

He grimaced ruefully. 'By the time I thought of that, it was too late.'

'Nice.' I was glad to know that asking me out wasn't something that leaped quickly to his mind. The bruise to my ego made me cranky. 'For someone so concerned about me, you were nowhere to be seen this afternoon.'

His gaze slid from mine, and he became very intent on opening the tin of cookies on the counter. 'I had something to do.' Then he looked at me again, gaze narrowing. 'What happened to "I can swim, don't worry about me"?'

How did I admit that I'd had no idea how deep the waters were without inviting an 'I told you so'? Besides, it wasn't just depths, it was riptides and maybe sharks. That was a lot to deal with.

'Your kettle is overflowing,' he said, interrupting my thoughts.

I said a word that made Paula chide me from the table. Setting the kettle on the flame to boil, I turned back to Rhys. 'I don't suppose you're going to tell me where you were.'

'Not rock hunting.' He took a mug from the cabinet and handed it to me. I dropped in a tea bag, then handed him one for his own refill.

It was a small thing, but we moved as if completing each other's motions. If Shawn and I were supposed to be some kind of Davis/Maddox superteam, why did *this* feel so natural?

Rhys was asking me a question. 'Did you learn anything that was worth eating catfish for?'

'Nothing is worth eating catfish for.' A nice evasion, I thought. But from his expression, not an effective one. I glanced at the table to make sure the adults were caught up in their own conversation. 'Why are you asking me, when you obviously know everything?'

'If I knew everything,' he said, 'you wouldn't be such a huge variable.'

I found enough energy to be outraged at the unfairness of that. 'That makes me this kettle and you a pot.' The kettle wasn't black, but he took my point.

It occurred to me that maybe I wasn't asking the right questions. Given the incredible possibilities I was juggling, maybe I needed to be wondering not *what* he knew, but *how*.

At the table, Professor Griffith talked in his lilting accent about his theory that the settlers he was looking for had integrated into the tribes of Kansas and the Mississippi Valley. I listened absently until the simmering of the water on the stove drowned him out, then turned to Rhys, knowing the sound would hide our voices, too.

'How do you know there's something weird up with the TTC?' I asked softly, reaching for one of the cookies in the tin as an excuse to stay close and keep my voice down.

His look said I wasn't as subtle as I thought. 'Because I have eyes, and ears. And a bit of horse sense. *You* knew there was something out of kilter, even before I said anything.'

Yes, but my mind didn't leap to supernatural possibilities. It still wasn't quite making the stretch. But was his?

Just to see what he would say, I swallowed a bite of cookie, then casually mentioned, 'Shawn talked about my joining the TTC meetings while I'm here.'

Rhys's gaze sharpened to a razor's edge. 'Don't,' he said, a clipped demand, all teasing gone. I froze, not just with shock, but with a tremor of something darker. The single word was harsh, and it seemed to come from the deeper part of himself that he was so careful to keep hidden.

Something in my immobile face made him twitch, as if cursing himself, and he continued, just as urgently, but without the iron edge of a command. 'Sylvie, do not get involved any more than you already are. I know it must seem to you like kids just messing about with stuff, but it's not.'

I stared at him, a piercing alarm going off in my ear and twisting the muscles of my shoulders into knots. His words confirmed everything and nothing, and raised new spectres to compete with my fear of the Colonel.

'Sylvie!' Paula's voice cut through the sound, and I realized it was real. 'For heaven's sake, turn off the kettle!'

With a shaking hand that echoed my rattled emotions, I turned off the flame on the stove, and the whistle faded out. Placing my hands on the counter, I let out a trembling breath and the part of my tension caused by the scream of the kettle. My back to the adults at the table, I let their resumed conversation cover my whispered question.

'Kid stuff. Like magic?'

I couldn't believe I'd said that aloud. If he laughed or called me out for being nuts, I didn't know what I would do. I didn't look at him, but his stillness was its own answer in a way. Then he reached across me and filled my cup as he spoke in my ear. 'Stay out of it, Sylvie. I don't want anything to happen to you.'

His breath stirred my hair, and I shivered as he moved away. Dimly I heard him saying goodnight and excusing himself. I may have said something automatically, keeping up the act of normalcy until I could get to my room and finally let down my guard.

I believed he didn't want me to be hurt, but there were a lot more people than me involved. I'd been assuming the council had been doing something bad, and Rhys knew about it. He and Shawn were obviously in opposition somehow, and I'd figured that meant one was 'bad' and one was 'good'. But they could be good and less good. Or bad and less bad.

From the beginning, my connection to Rhys had been eerie and inexplicable – the familiarity, and dizzying attraction, and heightened swing of my emotions around him. I'd suspected Shawn's charm of hiding his motives, but what about Rhys?

Maybe I really couldn't trust anyone.

'Sylvie, honey, are you going to stare at that tea until it's cold?' asked my cousin.

I was too numb with fatigue and confusion to be irritated at her for scolding me like a stern governess. 'No, ma'am.'

'Why don't you go to bed if you're so tired?'

That was a great idea. Saying goodnight, I picked up my mug and called for Gigi. She bounced off the professor's lap; he and Clara said goodnight, sounding sympathetic for what I suppose must have looked like complicated romantic problems. I followed Gigi's plumed tail up the stairs, where she checked the halls for me, the advance guard against ghosts.

There was no chill on the landing, and I thanked heaven for small favours, then went into my room and closed the door against the world.

Chapter 27

When Gigi woke me in the morning, my first thought wasn't about magic, or about Rhys or Shawn, or how much my romantic troubles were tied up in the mysteries of Bluestone Hill, or what that had to do with the ghosts, if anything. It was about my garden.

Sunday had been the first day I'd spent no time at all there. I'd become used to the invigoration of digging in the dirt, re-creating the generations-old pattern. Not to mention the almost meditative calm it gave me. If I could figure things out at all it would be in the garden.

I dressed hurriedly, anxious to get downstairs and to work – almost as anxious as Gigi, who was impatient for her morning pee, especially since we'd gone to bed so early. I grabbed my copied drawings and notes – satisfyingly grubby by now – and cast a quick, guilty look at the desk, where I'd set Reverend Holzphaffel's journal on top of the other books I'd accumulated. Hannah's journal was still hidden in the drawer. I promised Hannah that a few hours of work in the garden would make me much better able to concentrate on her mystery, and headed downstairs.

However, I hadn't counted on the rain.

The drizzle started as soon as Gigi had finished her business. The light coat of moisture didn't seem to bother her, so we went to the knot garden, where she flopped at the base of the rock and rolled in the wet herbs.

The bluestone lived up to its name when it was wet, turning a dark slate colour. Did it live up to the rest of its hype? Electromagnetic potential, mystical energy, lines of spiritual force making a web on the earth – what did those things have to do with ghosts and magic?

Think, Sylvie. With the exception of the incident in Central Park, I only saw and sensed things here at the Hill and in Old Cahawba, and they were so close I might as well think of them together. So there was something about this place.

But there was something about me, too. That was why Shawn was so excited by my arrival, and why Rhys was so confused when I knew nothing about the Hill. He must have expected that I'd arrive and meddle with – whatever he was doing. I just wished I knew what it was I was supposed to be able to do.

Everything about Bluestone Hill went back generations. Maybe to figure out my story, I first needed to figure out Hannah's.

'Sylvie Davis!' I jumped when Paula yelled at me from the porch. The startled slam of my pulse almost drowned out her annoyingly predictable admonition. 'Don't you even think about gardening in the rain. Do you want to catch your death?'

Definitely not. And I didn't want her irritated with me, either. So I called back, 'I'm coming, Cousin Paula,' in an obedient voice.

It looked like I'd be spending the morning in my room with Hannah after all.

❧ ❧

In a way, reading Hannah's journal was as absorbing as working in the garden. When Gigi whined and scratched at the door, I had to blink myself back to the present, disoriented by the modern things in the room.

I'd started reading the entries where I'd left off, about a quarter of the way in, and just a few months before the end of the war. Hannah didn't write every day, and the whole journal covered the last six years of her life. The older she got, the more interesting her entries, though they remained frustratingly vague about the things I wanted to know most.

Gigi became insistent. The rain had stopped, and I

knew that walking the dog would force me to stretch my legs and work the kinks out of my back.

My knotted muscles were going to require more exercise than a stroll to the garden. I put on my sneakers and grabbed Gigi's leash, a plan already half formed. Figuring Paula might have something to say about my heading out into the woods, even in the daytime, I avoided her on the way out. Following the forest's edge made a longer walk to Old Cahawba, but it meant I didn't have to pay such close attention to my feet. After some of the things I'd read, I had a lot to think about.

Hannah didn't have one suitor, she had two. She referred to them rather unhelpfully as E__ M__ and J__ M__. Reading between the lines, I'd figured out that EM was probably Ethan Maddox, referred to in Reverend Holzphaffel's journal. Hannah's own entries told me that JM was his brother. I was almost to the end of her story, and I still didn't know which of them was The One. Late in the tale, about nine months before her last entry, she merely wrote of seeing 'him' today, or of meeting 'him' on the street.

However, E and J had their own story. They fought side by side in the war, but now – Hannah's now, which, even as I walked through the woods, following the plume of Gigi's tail, seemed slightly more real than my own time – the brothers hated each other. It didn't seem to be merely romantic competition, either. Hannah wrote how much it troubled her that whole families of men and boys were lost (her brothers, for instance) to the battlefield, and E and J couldn't stop their fighting.

Gigi and I reached a dirt road with an open gate – the entrance to Old Cahawba. The rain hadn't been hard enough to turn the road to mud, but it made the red earth sticky, turning Gigi's white feet to a rusty tan that matched the rest of her.

The road led to the fenced 'new' cemetery. Dr Young had explained there was an 'old' graveyard on the other side of the ghost town, where, even in death, the residents were segregated. I glimpsed Dr Young with a couple of tourists, giving them his spiel. He waved when he saw me, but I didn't interrupt. I knew what I was looking for.

When he was free, he joined me at the Maddox plot. I'd found Ethan Maddox. He died an old guy in 1895. But I saw no J. Maddox born near the same time. Which didn't necessarily mean that J had been the one to run off on Hannah. He could have left, or Ethan could have returned, after the fact.

'Hey, little lady,' said Dr Young, then bent to pet Gigi, so I wasn't sure which of us he meant. 'You're not limping today, I see.'

I realized that was true, despite the long walk. Of course, I had taken the more level path, which was much easier on my leg. And as I pointed out to him, 'It's worst when I'm tired or the weather is changing.'

He chuckled. 'Well, you must be in a different climate than me. There's a front blowing in a storm up north of us, and all my joints are aching today.' He gave Gigi a last pat, then stood stiffly, proving his point. 'But enough of that. Here for the rest of the tour?'

On a different day, I would have indulged him, and myself, with the full history lesson, but I was on a mission. 'Actually, I have a question for you. Though I wouldn't mind seeing more of the site while you answer.'

'Excellent. I haven't been to check on the dig today. We can ride over together if you like.'

'Great.' We started towards the cemetery gate. Though it was hard to forget the eerier aspects of our problems, the exercise of deciphering the puzzle of Hannah's story had steadied my mind, and I was eager to fill the gaps in my knowledge.

'So my question is this: What's a scalawag?' The Colonel had called J that, which hurt Hannah greatly. 'I gather it's not a nice thing.'

'Oh, no. A scalawag was worse than a carpet bagger.' At my blank look he explained, 'A carpet bagger – Reconstructionist is the nice term – was an opportunistic Northerner who came down after the Civil War had yanked the foundations out from under folks here. Not only did the war tear up the land and decimate families, the entire economy had been destroyed.'

'By emancipation of the slaves,' I said pointedly, in case he was one of *those* Southerners.

He chuckled. 'Don't take that tone. I'm just telling you the facts. It was a rough time.'

I knew this from reading Hannah's journal. Her own situation hadn't been helped by her father coming home from the war a bitter, broken man. Not that he'd been a sweetheart before.

'So,' I prompted as we reached the truck and Dr Young opened the door for me, 'carpetbaggers bought up land for pennies and made a fortune on the South's misery.'

'Right.' He closed my door, walked round and got behind the wheel, then continued as if he hadn't paused. 'A scalawag was a Southerner who helped the carpetbaggers.'

I processed this in light of what Hannah had written, factoring in the complex emotions of the loser of a war forced to rely on the winner to rebuild the states they'd toasted in the first place. 'So, if a Confederate veteran was a scalawag, then a loyal Southern gentleman, like Colonel Davis, for example, might not like him courting his daughter.'

Dr Young laughed in disbelief. 'He'd have to have *cojones* of solid brass just to try.' He glanced at me as he backed up the truck and pulled onto the road. 'Where did you get all this?'

'Just some family papers.'

I knew he'd be fascinated by the diary, but I didn't want to share even the existence of it yet. I felt like I'd been reading Hannah's private thoughts over her shoulder, and it would be a betrayal of her to gossip about it. Our problems were different, though with some obvious parallels: liking two guys, not sure who was in the right. She was strongly drawn to J, the scalawag, but conflicted about his motivations. She liked E well enough, but he was entrenched in town politics – including a council that met behind closed doors at the Hill – and she was unnerved by the expectations, especially from the Colonel, that she marry him.

Dr Young turned on Capital, interrupting my thoughts. I shifted uneasily on the bench seat as we got closer to the site of the old prison. Gigi, however, was happy standing on my knees, front paws on the dash. 'Tell me about this archaeological dig,' I said, to distract myself from the anticipation of weirdness.

'Oh, there's a group of students from U of A who are doing an internship. Excavating the foundations of the church by the river.'

'I thought Saint Mary's over towards the town was the church by the river.'

'Well, it's *a* church by *a* river. Built and paid for by uppity country families who didn't want to come into town to go to services.' He took his eyes off the road long enough to wink at me as he turned east, away from the prison site.

I relaxed considerably at the change in direction, and saw a large excavation – it looked like a basement – where at one end two guys and a girl were working with trowels and screens to dig and shift through the dirt. 'I guess Rhys isn't here today,' said Dr Young.

He'd been absent from the kitchen when I'd come in from the rain, and I hadn't seen him upstairs. I hadn't checked to see if the rental car was there, either.

'What does a geologist do at an archaeological dig?' I asked as the truck pulled to a stop, glad he'd given me an opening.

'He isn't totally useless,' Dr Young said with a grin. 'Besides the extra hands, it's nice to have someone with an eye for telling when a stone is part of the foundation, and when it's just a rock.' Climbing out of the truck he called over to the students, 'You didn't have any trouble with the rain, did you?'

I got out too, noting the wet tarps over to one side. When I put Gigi on the ground, she ran to the edge of the pit, much too interested in the digging.

The girl, a blonde with short wisps of hair poking out of her baseball cap, looked at the dog askance, then at me. I recognized her from the Catfish Festival, mostly because she was giving me the dagger eye again, barely hidden as Dr Young provided an introduction. 'Annabeth, this is Sylvie Davis. She's a friend of Rhys's. Sylvie, this is Annabeth, Rob and Steve.'

'Hi.' I waved, feeling awkward under their curious stares.

'We saw you yesterday,' said Rob, as if he'd placed me in his mental database. 'You're that visiting girl who's dating Shawn Maddox.'

I inhaled slowly for patience, rolling my lips in between my teeth. Before I could collect myself to politely correct him, Annabeth spoke.

'You know, you could tell your boyfriend that if he really gives a crap about nature, he should think about what that boat dock and what all he's planning will do to the river.'

'He's not my boyfriend,' I said coldly, which I'm sure didn't make a good impression. 'But you're welcome to tell *me* what the hell you're talking about.'

She gestured vaguely. 'The Cahaba River is the most ecologically diverse waterway in North America. There are plants growing there that don't grow anywhere else in the world. And your friend wants to put motorboats on it.'

'I did not know that.' Her words had distracted me from my irritation at her tone. 'About the river, I mean.'

My response seemed to take some of the wind out of her sails, and her scowl lessened slightly. 'More people would, if the ecological surveyor who came here to rate the impact of the proposed building had finished his report before he got laid up.'

I looked at Dr Young. 'The guy who broke his leg was an environmental impact surveyor?'

'Yes indeed.' He brushed the dirt off his hands. 'The ecology of a place can be delicate. Get one thing out of balance, and you could have a disaster.'

'Like floods and yellow fever?' I asked, thinking of the region's turbulent natural history.

'Could be,' said Annabeth.

'That's a big extreme,' countered Dr Young, though he looked impressed I'd been paying attention. 'However, a lot of little things could lead to a big thing in ways we don't even realize.' He gave Annabeth a stern grandfatherly look. 'But I didn't bring Sylvie over here to get a lecture.'

She and Rob both laughed, breaking the tension, and Dr Young sheepishly admitted, 'Not a scolding one, anyway.'

Annabeth got out of the pit, carrying a box with a

screen bottom. 'Sorry, Sylvie. I get a little hot about environmental issues. Still, you might put in a polite word with your boyfriend.'

'I might,' I said testily, despite the genuineness of her apology, 'if you stop calling him that, since he's not.'

She laughed and said, 'Deal,' taking me at my word, then led the way to a folding table nearby, where an array of rocks and brick was laid out, many with tags and numbers. 'Want the nickel tour? We're basically excavating the basement of the church.'

Over her shoulder, I could see the crumbling brick chimney through the trees. 'Has there been any excavation of the old prison?'

She frowned. 'That would be a big, expensive project. I'd love to be on it, though!' She shouted that towards Dr Young, who waved to show he'd heard.

I sort of liked Annabeth's direct personality now that she wasn't scowling at me and painting me with Shawn's brush. What I didn't like was the shiver that ran down my back as I thought about digging in that particular ground.

Hannah had written about the prison, and her youthful language and ladylike reticence had made her horror both stark and evocative. Even thinking about it now, in the humid afternoon, I felt an echo of the fingers of cold that had gripped me in that empty spot. The shadow of the chimney seemed to stretch towards me, like it would pull me back into that well.

Hiding a shiver, I realized that, imagination aside, the shadows *were* lengthening. 'I should be heading to the Hill. My cousin will have kittens if I'm not back well before dark.'

'Do you need a ride home?' asked Dr Young.

'Thanks, but not this time.' As he'd mentioned, my leg was holding up well. And the walk would give me more time to think. 'I'd like to come back sometime, though. For that nickel tour,' I added to Annabeth.

She grinned. 'We can use an extra pair of hands. Rhys has been busy with his dad's project, and hasn't been logging many hours. Of course, he's not earning college credit.'

I caught myself before I blurted out, 'Really?' Because Old Cahawba had been his stated destination every morning, at least that I could recall. Had it only been an excuse for his rock hunting? Or was he up to something else?

'Speaking of college hours,' said Dr Young, joining us at the worktable, 'let's see what you've got, Annabeth.'

I took that as my cue to exit. I said goodbye and left them to their work.

❧ ❧

Paula was livid when I got back. 'Where have you been?' she demanded from the stairs of the back porch. 'I've been worried sick about you.'

I was too surprised to be as angry at this over-reaction as I ordinarily would. 'Why? I just walked out to Old Cahawba. And I had my phone.'

The part about the phone made her blink, since she

clearly hadn't thought to call me. Then she heated back up. 'You couldn't have told me you were going?'

Now irritation began to overtake confusion. 'I left a note. What's the big deal?'

She huffed, mirroring my annoyance, but I suspected some of it was aimed at herself. She'd flown off the handle, and I'd acted responsibly. Well, relatively. I *could* have told her I was going.

'Someone broke into the office trailer out at Maddox Point,' she said. 'That kind of thing just doesn't happen around here, not by local people. So no wandering in the woods by yourself. Not even in the daytime.'

This news tumbled my thoughts around like leaves in the wind. I answered with an absent 'Sure, Paula' and tried to remember where Rhys had said he was yesterday. Not at the Catfish Festival like everyone else in town, that was for sure.

Gigi bounded up the stairs, dirty from our walk, and Paula didn't even comment, so I knew she was distracted. 'Was anything taken?' I asked.

My lack of argument to her order to stay out of the woods seemed to have calmed her down, and she shook her head. 'They think it might have been a drifter looking for money. They don't keep any out there. And a good thing, too.'

I was baffled. What were the odds of a random break-in, with nothing taken? And obviously no one local would have robbed the *Maddoxes,* of all people. But what could Rhys have possibly wanted from the Maddox Point office?

My feelings could have been lifted from Hannah's journal. She liked J, and if he was a scalawag, she wanted to believe it was for the best of reasons. Whatever Rhys was up to, I wanted to believe he was in the right somehow. But how could I trust him when he never gave me an explanation for any of his actions?

Chapter 28

I finished reading Hannah's journal that night. It was as dissatisfying as a mystery novel with no ending, as unsettling as a symphony that doesn't resolve to a final chord.

Turning back a few pages from the ambiguous last entry, I read again her disjointed description of the 'spectre of a dishevelled man in a blue uniform' that she'd seen while cutting through the woods from Cahawba. Her handwriting – never that great – showed her tremors, as did her admission that she attributed the incident to her 'condition'.

Her prose had been extremely circumspect about her love life. She wrote in veiled references and no detail. This was the only indication that she was, as I had wildly guessed, pregnant.

Back in the chair, I stared out the window, the moonlit woods superimposed with the reflection of my own face, pinched with worry for a girl long dead.

Not only did she not indicate who the father was, she didn't even describe any kind of baby-making interlude. What girl keeps a diary and doesn't write about her first time?

I got up again, leaned over the desk and opened the window. It wasn't just reading Hannah's troubles that was putting me on edge. There was something about the night, the full moon on the river, the wind in the trees.

There were three ghosts. The Colonel. The girl in the woods – Hannah, I corrected myself. And the wailing cry of an infant. What did it mean? That the baby had died with her? Or was it crying *for* her?

Maybe that was why I couldn't face Reverend Holzphaffel's journal before I went to sleep. If Hannah had, by her suicide, abandoned her baby, I didn't want to know.

❦ ❦

Naturally, since I expected something extraordinary to happen now that my suspicions were boiling, and Rhys – or someone – had stirred the pot by messing with Shawn's precious Maddox Point project, and I was poking under the rocks of the family history, the house and even the woods stayed calm through the night.

It was unnerving, like waiting for a storm you know is coming, know is only going to build more strength the longer it takes to arrive.

In the morning I dressed in my least dirty gardening jeans and brought the others down to put in the washer. With Gigi trotting beside me, I entered the kitchen to find Clara alone, putting away the last of the dishes.

'Good morning, sleepyhead. Throw those clothes in the laundry basket and I'll wash them for you.'

'Oh, you don't have to do that,' I said.

'I wouldn't offer if I minded.'

I tossed the clothes in the basket on the porch, opened the door for Gigi and came back into the kitchen. 'Where is everybody?'

She waved a hand at the empty air. 'Paula is in town buying paint, the professor is at work in his room, and Rhys is off doing what Rhys does.'

The comment started my usual round of internal arguments. What was he doing, what were his motives, why the hell wouldn't he tell me unless he had something to hide? By the time I got a carton of yogurt out of the refrigerator, my head hurt from all the arguing.

I worked in the garden all morning. Feeling driven, I channelled all my emotion into pulling weeds and cutting vines. The reverend's journal waited for me upstairs, but Hannah's problems were too tangled with my own, and I needed a respite from that for a little while.

And I had catching up to do. Though I'd squeezed in some work before sundown, I'd lost most of the previous day to the rain and my walk to Cahawba. Not to mention the time I'd spent with Hannah in the past.

Eventually, Clara made me stop for lunch. Paula and the professor had already eaten, so I wiped Gigi's feet (and mine) and we both came in, safe from my cousin's dislike of dogs.

'That's enough work for the day,' Clara said firmly as she set a bowl of minestrone soup in front of me, a piece of fresh bread beside it.

'I just have a little more to do,' I said, washing down a bite with some iced tea. I was surprised how much progress I'd made in just a week, but this close to being done, it pained me to stop, even to eat.

Clara left her stove and stood across from me, arms folded. 'Girl, you don't have to prove anything. Paula thinks hard work would cure the devil, so bugging you is the only way she knows to show she cares.'

That explained a lot. I bet she'd never had a puppy as a kid, either. Still, I couldn't help but be a bit touched, feeling the truth in what Clara said.

'OK,' I agreed. 'I just want to finish uncovering the stone. I'm so close to being done with the centre section.'

Sweeping away my empty bowl, Clara said, 'Don't you have something else you could be doing this afternoon, other than obsessing over that garden?'

Was I obsessing? Maybe, but as long as I was working on the garden I didn't have to think about solving mysteries. Not Hannah's, not Rhys's, not my own.

'Just a little bit more,' I promised, going to the fridge for a refill of my iced tea before heading back outside with Gigi.

I was up to my elbows in meadowsweet when the dog barked an alert that someone was coming. I turned to see Shawn Maddox in the gap between the hedges.

'Well, now I'm glad I didn't call before I came over,' he said with a smile. His gaze took in all the work I'd done – a lot in a few days – and fastened with interest on the standing stone in the centre, over half clear of vines now and catching tiny flecks of sunlight. 'You're almost finished.'

'Finished clearing, anyway,' I said, that possessive feeling creeping over me again. 'What are you doing here?'

'I came to ask if you wanted to go to the Point,' he said, dragging his eyes from the rock and looking at me with a low-wattage smile. 'But I don't want to take you away from your work. I can see you're up to your knees.'

It was a feeble joke, since I was kneeling in the greenery. 'I hope you didn't drive all the way out here without calling.'

'Nope. This is on the way to the Point and I had to go anyway.' He came a few steps further in. Gigi got up with a stretch and walked over to sniff his shoes. Shawn squatted way down to pet her, and I tried not to be charmed by the picture. Big, handsome guy, bent double to pet a little bitty dog . . .

Watch it, Sylvie. Though I had to admit, he didn't need any special powers to charm me through my dog.

'I mostly just wanted to talk to you for a bit.' Nodding to the bench, he said, 'Want to take a break?'

'OK.' I climbed to my feet and moved my diagrams out of the way so we could sit. The action gave me a moment to make sure I didn't sound too wary, or too eager, to find out what he wanted to say. 'What did you want to talk about? You mentioned something about the TTC.'

His mouth curved in the softest version of his smile. 'Sort of.' He sat beside me, and I didn't realize until too late that the bench was a little small for him, me and the way he made me feel. 'I have this feeling, Sylvie, that something happened yesterday that put you off the council.' He paused with an uncharacteristic vulnerability. 'Or maybe just me.'

I rubbed at the grass stains on my jeans, looking for an honest answer, so he wouldn't see through a lie. 'It was overwhelming, Shawn. The town, all the attention.'

'You don't really think the TTC is doing wrong, do you? Helping get Maddox Point off the ground?'

Prickles of unease started up my neck, but I tried to hide them with a casual shrug. 'What's the big deal about a little campaigning? Stuffing flyers in mailboxes, that sort of thing.'

Shawn's laugh surprised me. 'Can't you think of anything bigger? More off the chart? I know that someone must have said something to you, because suddenly you looked at us like we had a three-headed dog guarding our clubhouse.'

His candid tone drew my gaze to his. 'What do you mean, bigger?' I asked, as if I didn't know.

'Like . . . you and me.' His eyes were all confirmation and warmth and persuasion. 'And what we could do together.'

I watched him warily, wondering where he was going with this new honesty tactic. 'You mean, the superstition.'

'What if it was true?' He rubbed his thumb over the back of my hand. 'But not just good luck. What if we could make good things happen for people?'

'You mean, like, grant wishes?' I was distracted by the stroke of his thumb on my skin. It lulled my curiosity, the way I lulled Gigi to sleep by petting her belly.

'Maybe not automatically or overnight.' Switching his grip, he interlaced our fingers. 'Davis and Maddox. Not every generation, but sometimes, when the timing works out, we can do incredible things here. Make this place what it once was. A centre of things.'

For a breathless moment, his words held me in their spell. Then Gigi jumped in my lap, and I jerked in surprise, and broke Shawn's gentle grip on my hand.

'That's nuts,' I said, not talking about the supernatural but the way I'd just sat there, drinking in what he was telling me. When had I made the leap from magic is possible to magic is *reasonable*?

Shawn laughed. 'I know. Like seeing ghosts, it sounds nuts.'

I uneasily remembered my theory about crying wolf. Had Shawn been establishing plausible deniability so that he could talk about these things to me, and I couldn't tell anyone?

'What are you saying, Shawn?' It was a demand

for him to be straight with me. Gigi's body seemed very warm in my arms. It made me realize how cold my skin had gotten. No ghostly chill – it was coming from inside.

'I'm not saying anything.' He stood, casually turning to walk out of the gap in the hedges as he fired one last shot. 'Except that you should think about it a day or two. If there *was* such a thing as magic, what would you do with it?'

I didn't need a day or two to know that. The answer took no thought, raised no moral dilemma. If it were within my power to do, I'd fix my leg so I could dance again.

Chapter 29

Clara finally won the battle, making me stop work in the late afternoon. I'd come in for some iced tea, and she swore if I didn't quit for the day, she'd tell Paula I needed that shrink after all. I suspected she was bluffing, but I didn't want to chance it.

As I closed the fridge, my eye fell on the calendar hung on the door. Clearly the master schedule. The Catfish Festival was marked, and my flight arrival. Also final exams, and cheerleading practice. Today's notation jolted me with wary excitement. 'There is a TTC meeting tonight,' I said.

'It seems like there's a TTC meeting every night,' Clara answered, but in a singsong 'What's a mom to do about it?' way.

The calendar *was* loaded with meetings, not necessarily on the same day of the week or month, but there was always one on the full and new moons. Tonight's moon was full.

Shawn hadn't mentioned it, despite a clear intention to invite me eventually, so he either thought I wasn't ready yet, or there was something he needed to do without me there.

Which meant that I absolutely needed to find out what was going on at those meetings.

I climbed the stairs slowly, Gigi bounding in front of me. I was strangely bubbling with energy too, but it was focused on making a plan. I'd have to act as normal as possible, then sneak out of the house right after Addie. I was getting better at managing Paula, but Rhys was the unknown factor.

I had a good game face, but this kind of subterfuge wasn't my strength. Still, a tide of determination carried me forward. I just hoped I wasn't hurtling over another bluff, because I couldn't rely on anyone to catch me this time.

❦ ❦

After dinner, I paced with waiting-backstage impatience in my room, watching for the arrival of the TTC. I couldn't see where they parked out on the drive, but I could see the glow of lights through the half-opaque screens of the summerhouse, and I could watch the path Addie would have to take to join them. When I saw her walking purposefully across the lawn, I scooped up Gigi and headed for the stairs.

The landing was quiet, and the gap under Rhys's door was dark. I walked downstairs and oh-so-casually went into the den, where Paula and Clara were watching TV while darning socks and folding towels, respectively.

Clara glanced at me and kept folding. 'Sylvie, your jeans are in the dryer. So you'll be all set to dirty them up again tomorrow.'

'Thank you, Clara.' I gestured with my thumb towards the kitchen. 'I'm going to take the dog for a walk, then call it a night.'

'That's a good idea,' she said. 'After all the work you did today.'

Paula lowered the sock she was darning and looked at me sternly. 'You stay close to the house, after what we talked about, OK?'

Clara snapped a towel open, then brought the corners together. 'She'll be OK. The kids are in the summerhouse for their meeting tonight. As long as she stays out of the woods, she'll be fine.'

I sincerely hoped so. My stomach fluttered nervously, but I kept my stage face on, asking, as if it didn't matter, 'Are the Griffiths still out?'

The women exchanged glances, Clara's amused and tolerant, Paula's less so. 'I don't keep tabs on them,' said Paula, in an 'I'm not your social secretary' tone. 'But the professor mentioned they might be back late.'

This was good for my plan, so I told myself not to be irked or disappointed that Rhys seemed to have abandoned me to my choice. He had to know the TTC was meeting tonight. Wasn't he curious what I would do? Or did he assume he knew?

First, I had to deal with Paula. If I swallowed her implied critique without comment, she would know something was up. 'I only asked,' I said testily, 'because I might have a nice long soak in the tub after I walk Gigi, and I don't want to feel guilty for tying up the bath.'

Paula gave a long-suffering sigh at my attitude. 'Don't use all the hot water. A second tank is still on the list of improvements for the place.'

Clara just chuckled and said, 'Have a nice walk, Sylvie.'

My groundwork laid, I said goodnight and headed to the back of the house, Gigi tucked under my arm. On the porch, I took a deep breath and slipped her into her crate. She tilted her head, questioning me, and my heart squeezed, as if I were leaving her behind for good.

But the only thing worse than splitting up our team was the thought of putting her in danger. Chihuahuas know no fear, even when they should. Maybe we had that in common.

'Not this time, girl,' I whispered. The position of the crate would hide her from a casual glance, and the big pile of laundry would keep Clara busy for a while.

The nervous flutters in my stomach spread to my knees as I left the concealment of the back yard. I couldn't approach the summerhouse directly, because it was all open lawn, so I headed for the tree line, moving quickly, but trying not to *look* like I was moving stealthily. Once I reached the cover of the trees, I changed direction.

I snuck up from the river side, away from the door. The soft, flickering glow in the gazebo was, thankfully, not enough to spill out onto the surrounding ground. The moon was bright but still low, and I could keep to the shadows of the trees almost right up to the raised foundation.

Breathing in shallow, silent huffs, I pressed against the peeling wood, hunkering below floor level so I couldn't be seen, but I could hear the low drone of voices.

The wordless chant was so eerie and out of place that I almost doubted my senses. But what lifted the hair on my neck and arms wasn't what I *heard,* but what I sensed. This was a *ritual* sound, full of potential, thick and opaque somehow, murky as the silt of a river bottom, hiding silent, swift things below.

It was *not* kid stuff. I should be feeling satisfied that I was right, or at least relieved that I wasn't crazy. But as I pressed myself tightly against the half-wall, inches from discovery, my heart pounded like a timpani.

I could smell candle wax and incense, or something like it. Burning greens and wood, like the bundle of herbs I'd found. What else was going on? Somehow it was more frightening not to be able to see but only imagine. *Oh God. Don't let there be snake handling involved.*

'All right,' said Addie's voice. 'We're convened.'

This was jarringly matter-of-fact, but the tingle of power still hung in the air, woven into the smoke and the echo of the chant. And Addie sounded different. Instead of petulant, her tone reflected the confidence I'd seen on Sunday.

She continued in the same tone. 'Everyone put your intentions in the bowl. You know what we're supposed to be doing here, so I don't want anyone putting in something selfish, like a new fishing boat, *Jeff.* We all agreed what's best for the town.'

A frown knotted my forehead. Really? I'd thought the TTC was just a cover. If Shawn and the circle were trying to do good by Maddox Landing, then what was Rhys so bent about?

Someone else spoke, and I thought it might be Jeff, just based on his tone. 'If we burn the slips of paper, how will we know you didn't put in something for yourself, *Addie*?'

'Keep on target, people,' said Shawn, his voice so deep with authority I almost didn't recognize it. No boyish Tom Sawyer charm here. This was powerful and mature, like – I struggled for a comparison – like the ancient stone in my garden.

'The circle involves trust,' he said, and I shivered, because the surface of his statement was reassuring, but there was a darker thread beneath. 'I put in my paper. I trust you all to stick to the plan. So let's get on with it.'

I could visualize the scene startlingly well, the TTC all putting their wishes in the pot, like votes at the Vatican. I steeled myself as the chant began again, the voices of the circle joining a bit raggedly, like you might expect from a bunch of teens. Then they knit together and intensified, and I heard Shawn start to speak. I couldn't understand what he was saying, but the words trailed down my spine like frigid drops of water, spreading the cold of fear.

My pulse beat light and fast under my prickling skin. Anything seemed possible in the building energy of the night. I started to rise from my crouch, just to peek, like looking under your bed when you were sure there was a monster there. I hadn't done more than shift my weight when someone reached out of the shadows and pulled me back down, covering my mouth as I sucked in a terrified breath to scream.

'Shh.' Rhys whispered in my ear, too softly to carry through the screen to the circle inside. 'Just stay here.'

I wasn't going anywhere with his arm holding me so tightly to his chest that I could feel his heart thudding against my back, as if he was as afraid as I was. His breath stirred my hair against my face, and I realized how still the night was.

'You're here,' I whispered inanely.

'So are you.' He didn't sound angry, though. He sounded relieved, and I realized that what he meant was 'You're not inside.'

Shawn's voice continued over the ebb and flow of the chant, raising gooseflesh on my skin. 'What language is that?' In the movies it was always Latin, but this was different.

Rhys listened for a moment. 'Really bastardized Welsh, I think.'

'You *think*?' Wouldn't he know?

'His accent is so bad it might as well be Greek.' His arm tightened around me in warning as the chant paused, as if for collective breath. I stayed still, muscles braced and tight, until the sound started again. After his one exhale of relief, Rhys spoke in my ear. 'Let's get out of here.'

I didn't argue as he tugged me to my feet, pulling me with him across the shadowed lawn until we were hidden in the rustic palace of the towering oaks. The woods seemed to knit around us, but not in the terrifying way they'd fooled me the other night, when I'd seen Hannah here. This was comforting shelter, not a claustrophobic maze.

When we were well into the trees, I shook my fingers free of his grip and came to a stop, panting even though we hadn't run very far or fast. 'What *was* that?' I asked in a ragged whisper.

Rhys ran a hand over his face, looking almost as shaken as I felt. 'You said it yourself the other night. Magic.'

'Thinking it is a lot different than feeling it.' My brain whirred with fight-or-flight adrenaline, trying to hold onto as many details as possible and fit them into theories, all while dealing with *holy crap, magic is real.* 'And you know about this stuff? I mean, not just this here, but—' I made a wide, encompassing gesture, since this was so much more than I could yet wrap my mind around.

He shook his head, scattered and distracted. 'My experience has been similar but different.'

'Different how?' My whisper was harsh with demand.

He paced a few steps, then back. 'Different like rugby is from American football.'

'Sports analogies aren't going to work for me, Rhys.'

With a long exhale, he seemed to collect himself, centre his thoughts on me and the here and now. 'They're both about running a ball through to a goal, but the details are different.'

'Like Russian and French schools of ballet.' Alike enough that if you were a novice, you couldn't tell the difference. Football was football, magic was magic. 'But *how* do you know about this at all?' We were standing close so we could whisper, and at my question, I felt his tension step up, even above the stress already vibrating between us. 'Rhys?'

'In Pembrokeshire,' he answered shortly. In the tree-filtered moonlight, it was hard to see his expression. 'You said Dad told you about the mine collapse.'

A new wave of shock rushed over me. 'That was caused by magic?'

'Indirectly.' His tone was taut with reluctance, as well as an obvious tight grip on a whole backlog of emotions. 'But that's how I recognized the signs, in the history and the . . . the atmosphere here. What Shawn is doing, it messes with the balance of things.'

The air was warm and humid, but my insides were icy, and I wrapped my arms around my middle. 'So even if Shawn and the council are doing good for the town, it might cause something bad to happen?'

He looked at me, still tense, his tone guarded, his shoulders braced. 'Do you think Shawn is doing right?'

Some part of me still wanted to think that Shawn's intentions were good. But put to the question, I had to say, 'No.'

From what I'd overheard, there was room for self-ish requests, though Shawn clearly held the reins tight, with Addie his second in command. But even if everyone asked for things with no downside, what if something bad had to happen to bring it about? Something like – an awful realization curdled in my stomach – a surveyor falling in the river.

'Oh my God.' I looked at Rhys, who waited, expectantly, warily, for me to work things out. The bruises on his face had almost healed, but I could see them vividly in my mind's eye. What if it was magically expedient to have Rhys out of the way too?

'And you thought I could be involved with this?' My voice rose indignantly, and I wrestled it back down to a whisper.

Rhys leaned forward, matching my challenging – but quiet – tone. 'What was I supposed to think, with Shawn awaiting your arrival like you were his ordained priestess. That's why Addie hates you so much. You were meant to take her place.'

'I didn't know *any* of this,' I protested.

'Which I realized,' he said, in that too-patient way that betrayed his impatience. 'Except that you were so obviously hiding something.'

I stiffened, amazed there was any room in my

tangled emotions for hurt or offence. 'I thought I was losing my mind, with all the things going on here. Like you, being all secretive—'

Rhys caught my arm and I broke off with a startled gasp. 'Let me finish, Sylvie.' He stepped close, where he could speak in an unvoiced whisper. 'You started working in the garden, and I saw the way it thrived and how you were flourishing too, and it seemed impossible that you could *not* know who you were and what you could do.'

'What are you talking about?' Frustration and fear tumbled together in my head. I was so confused, and his words were sprouting buried insights – the way I could soothe my anger with my hands in the earth, weed by touch, bring the garden back to life.

Rhys watched the play of realization on my face, and when I met his gaze, he asked gently, 'Sylvie, have you even noticed you're not limping any more?'

My mouth opened to speak, but there were no words.

His hand still grasped my arm, but lightly, and his thumb stroked the inside of my wrist in a way that perhaps he meant to be soothing, but which, with his words, sent shudders of reaction to the heart of me. 'There *is* magic here. Shawn is using it through his circle of friends. You're doing it through the garden. When I saw that happening, I knew you were the one that Shawn thought you were. Are.'

'So you thought I was planning to hook up with him and rule this little corner of the world with our Davis-Maddox superpowers?' We were standing very close, and my whispered indignation didn't have far to carry.

He didn't apologize. 'Wouldn't you do anything to dance again?'

His words punched me in the stomach, drove the breath out of me. Because they were true. Rhys mercifully went on, not making me acknowledge it aloud. 'In any case, the night at the river convinced me you were naïvely going on instinct.'

I looked up at him with a challenge. 'That's why you suddenly *liked* me after I proved my innocence by nearly plummeting to my death.'

His expression turned rueful, almost sheepish. 'I *liked* you before, but I didn't want to.'

My eyes narrowed. 'You let me think it was just me.' And I meant everything. The liking. The feeling of connection, of familiarity.

'I was an idiot,' he said, brushing back my tangled hair.

My pulse fluttered, and I fought the temptation to lean into him. He was so close I could feel the warmth of him even in the humid air. 'That much I did know.'

Nothing was settled, and few of my questions were answered, but it was a struggle to straighten my spine and stiffen my resolve. 'But what's *your* part in this?' I asked, too breathlessly. 'Why couldn't you just tell me, or ask me outright? Did you come here knowing about the TTC, or did you just stumble on them?'

He looked pained by my badgering, but not annoyed. 'That's a lot of questions, princess.' His fingers traced lightly down my arm, to skim over my palm and finally tangle with mine. 'Which will take a while to answer.'

A magical potential of our own was building, and my questions, while vitally important, seemed less *urgent* at the moment.

I asked one more, my eyes on his, looking for evasion. 'Are you trying to distract me?'

With a small smile, he admitted, 'Maybe a little bit.' He drew me closer by our linked fingers, until my arm was wrapped around his waist, his hand holding mine, unresisting, at his back. 'Would that be so bad?' he asked, brushing my cheek with his other thumb.

'Just this once,' I whispered, already knowing it was a lie. More than ever, there was the past, present and future in the touch of his lips to mine.

He kissed me softly, and after one gently enquiring pause, kissed me again. And that was the end of asking anything. I tugged my hand from his, but only so I could wrap my arms around him properly and he could draw me even closer, which he did, without hesitation. For all the confusion he'd caused me, there was nothing equivocal about the way his mouth caressed mine, the way his fingers slid into my hair to cradle the back of my head.

The timing was bad, but the kiss was so right. Not just the feel and taste of him, but everything – the sheltering woods, the water rushing nearby and the green, wet scent all around us.

Too soon, but too late for me to ever be the same again, Rhys pulled back, setting me away from him as if he needed to break the connection or go mad. I knew how he felt.

'We do not want to do this here,' he said, his hands still on my shoulders, his thumbs tracing my collarbones. My shirt was crooked and out of place, but not as much as I wanted it to be.

'OK,' I said, still breathless. 'Where do we want to do it?'

He accepted the invitation, pulling me close again, hands spanning my waist. I twined my arms around his neck like the vines that wrapped the standing stone in my garden. One endless kiss, new and familiar as the last, then the world spun and we were falling onto the thick carpet of pine needles and oak leaves. They scratched my skin as my shirt rode up, but the feeling anchored me to the earth, like Rhys's welcome weight, his arms still around me.

My head reeled with sensation and emotion, not all of which I could sort out. His and mine, and some memories that seemed overlaid from some other time. I felt a dread of being caught, but it paled next to this longing.

It was that specific dread, not of anyone living, that made me finally pull away – put cool, damp air between us. There was more in that moment somehow than my brain could hold, and I felt that if I let the kiss continue, if I let my *thoughts* continue, I might splinter.

'Don't,' I whispered, when he would have drawn me back down. 'I have to get back. The Colonel is watching.' I was oddly aware it was a nonsensical thing to say, that I was losing the division between myself and the echoes of the past.

'I don't care,' said Rhys. He ran his fingers through my hair, combing out the pine needles and letting the tangled strands fall around us like a curtain. 'He's just a ghost in a window. He can't hurt you now.'

'Then why am I so scared of him?' I breathed the question, trying not to let him distract me. 'Whenever I feel that awful, freezing cold in the stairs—'

My mind snagged on a thought, and I pushed my hair back so what moonlight filtered through the trees illuminated his face. 'Have you *seen* him?'

His eyes narrowed warily, as if he didn't like where this might be headed. 'Not exactly. A hint, maybe. A bit of cold.'

I pushed myself up with a hand on his chest. He winced, and I remembered his bruises, but didn't let remorse dull my anger. 'It would have saved me a world of anxiety if you had mentioned that sooner.'

'I *did* tell you that you weren't crazy.' He propped himself on his elbows. 'If *you'd* told me you were seeing things, I would have reassured you sooner.'

'Now I remember why I was irked with you.' I sat up, straightening my clothes, wishing I could do the same with my dignity. 'Even after the river, you *still* didn't trust me.'

'Sylvie,' he began. I thought – hoped – he would try and smooth things over, but he just said, 'Keep your voice down.'

That was the pin that popped the last bubble of the dreamlike interlude. The right answer was 'I trust you now,' or even better, 'I was a jerk.' It was *definitely* not 'Be quiet.'

'I'll do better than that,' I retorted – in a whisper – as I pulled myself up off the forest floor. 'I'm out of here.'

I flounced off in a truly prima ballerina exit, too furious to think about what might be waiting. Too angry to listen for his footsteps behind me. When I reached the edge of the woods, though, I stumbled to a shocked halt. Rhys almost ran me over, and caught my shoulders to steady us both. Then his fingers tightened, and I knew he felt it too.

The cold was distinct and bitter next to the humid night and my heated emotions. I'd never felt the chill so strong outside the house. Fear wrapped an icy fist around my heart, and I felt the full brunt of the supernatural imprint, one hundred and fifty years of furious waiting, aimed like a naked spotlight from the upstairs window.

'He's not watching the summerhouse,' I whispered. My stomach knotted until I thought I might throw up. 'He's watching the woods for her. Hannah.'

Rhys stepped closer to my back, a sheltering, protective action, and a possessive one. 'He's watching for them both.'

I didn't ask whom he meant. Hannah and her lover. Had they met here in the woods, where Rhys and I kept meeting? Had Hannah stood here, with her sweetheart's hands on her shoulders, and known she'd been caught? Or did they say goodnight, thinking their secret was safe, while the Colonel watched and seethed?

As awful as the malevolent attention was, the suddenness with which it turned away was even more jarring. 'It's never moved from the window before,' I said, a whole new level of fear twisting my heart.

There was a cry, a shriek of bone-deep terror, not from the woods, but from the house.

The sound broke our stasis. I might not have been limping any more when I walked, but running was another thing. Rhys slowed as I hobbled over the uneven lawn, but I urged him ahead. 'Go on. Run.'

He took me at my word and lengthened his stride. I followed, dread pushing me up the hill to the house. It wasn't nearly as late as it felt. The downstairs windows were still mostly lit. I could hear Gigi barking, rising to a frenzy as I hurried through the porch, past her crate, then through the kitchen towards the front of the house.

When I reached the foyer, Paula and both Griffiths were already there. Clara lay crumpled at the bottom of the stairs, like a rag doll thrown down the steps, the impression of a cast-off toy heightened by my jeans scattered around her. She must have dropped them when she fell.

Paula knelt in her pyjamas, her face ashen, her hands trembling. Professor Griffith was restraining her from moving her friend, talking in soothing, crisis tones about paramedics and neck braces, while Rhys carefully checked to make sure Clara was breathing.

He stayed with them while I pushed away my shock and hurried to the den, where I grabbed the phone and dialled with trembling fingers.

'Nine-one-one,' said the calm woman on the other end of the line. 'What's your emergency?'

Where to start. Somehow, I managed to block out ghosts and secret rites and magic spells, and concentrate on the facts. 'There's been an accident. My friend has fallen down the stairs, and she's unconscious. We need an ambulance.'

Chapter 30

Paula rubbed her arms against the chill in the foyer. The professor fetched a crocheted afghan from the back of a sofa in the parlour, and covered Clara with it while they waited for the paramedics.

I didn't wait. Handing the phone to Rhys, I said, 'I'm going to get Addie.' Shock had chased away my fear. Besides the cold, which the others seemed to feel but not acknowledge, there was no sign of the Colonel.

'Sylvie!' Rhys met my eye with a warning. 'Play it cool.'

With a quick flash of anger, I thought he meant I shouldn't bait Addie when her mom was injured, as if I would. Then reason kicked in, and I got that he was advising me not to let on what I knew about the council. As if I would be that stupid.

I nodded and cut through the den to the side door. The route took me into my garden, and to the stone monolith that marked it. Immediately I could sense that whatever the circle had been doing, it was done. The same way I could feel the energy moving before, I could sense its stillness now. Not gone, not dissipated, but resting. Now that I was attuned to it, I didn't know how I'd ever *not* felt it.

Out on the road, car headlights were coming to life as some of the council left straight from the summerhouse. A smaller group walked towards me, their silhouettes distorted by backpacks and book bags, as if they were coming in from a late-night study session.

But the energy level gave them away. It was the intangible aura of stage presence, the indefinable glow that made certain people rivet attention. All four had it, but Shawn's was so bright, it cast the others in shade.

I waited for them, stewing in suspicion. I couldn't imagine why anyone would want to hurt Clara. Especially her daughter. Maybe Clara was only collateral damage, but the timing of her fall was too coincidental, and it was hard to keep the blame from my face as the group – Shawn and Addie, Kimberly and Caitlin – reached me.

Shawn seemed amused by my expression, and I

wondered what I'd given away. 'You could have just asked to join us,' he said.

His complacency ratcheted up my anger. But I turned to Addie, who stood at his side. She stared back with a challenging lift of her chin and I forced myself to keep my voice even. 'Your mother's had an accident. The ambulance is on its way.'

Her face went slack with shock, the kind you can't fake. It was too dim to see her colour drain, but in the charged air I sensed it. *All* my senses seemed to be on high alert, supercharged. Addie staggered a step, and Kimberly steadied her with a sympathetic arm around her shoulders.

Just for a moment, I *had* considered how, if something happened to Clara, it might bring Addie her wish. No one would tell her to stay in school instead of becoming the next Naomi Campbell. But her stunned expression, the dawning horror and worry, cleared her in my mind. At least of any intentional harm.

'She's in the foyer,' I told her more gently. 'At the bottom of the stairs.'

Addie took a few unsteady steps, then broke into a long-legged run. Kimberly touched my arm, get?ting my attention. 'Is her mom hurt bad? What happened?'

I cast my gaze over them, reassured by how stunned they looked. All except Shawn, who seemed concerned but not genuinely surprised. 'She fell down the stairs.'

Kimberly and Caitlin exchanged a worried glance. I turned to leave them, heading through the garden. Dimly I heard Shawn tell them to go on home, which didn't register until I caught the sound of his footsteps on the gravel path behind me.

Turning back, I tried to play it cool, like Rhys had told me. 'This is a family matter, Shawn.'

He seemed surprised, and a little hurt. 'I am family.'

I didn't know what to believe from him any more, and it came through in my tone. 'Fourth cousins twice removed is not close enough.'

As I turned to go, he snagged my hand in his. I whirled, spoiling for a fight, but he did nothing but grasp my fingers, our arms at their full extension, and run his gaze over me.

His eyes narrowed and I wondered what had given me away – the pine needles in my hair, my rumpled shirt or the scalding blush that raced to my cheeks.

He seemed to wrestle with thwarted anger, then tamp it down behind a mask of imperturbability. I marvelled that I could see it all so clearly, as if some filter had been lifted.

'Well,' he said, with an unconvincing echo of his easygoing charm. 'Someone has been a little naughty.'

The words were teasing, his tone amused. But there was a thread of steel underneath, possessive yet oddly cold. The way he'd examined me at arm's length, impassively evaluating, reminded me of the Colonel at the window. And that gave me the creeps more than an innuendo would have.

'I don't see how that's your business,' I said, trying for cool, and failing.

Shawn laughed, and it was genuine. 'Don't be

stupid, Sylvie. I told you this afternoon. You and I could be an amazing team, if you don't go messing it up by messing around with someone else.'

That was the final twist that snapped the rubber band of my temper. 'Maybe I don't want to be a team with you, Shawn. Does the circle even understand what's going on? Or are you playing them like everyone else in town?'

Annoyance flashed over his face. 'I don't know what your boyfriend has been telling you, but I'm just trying to do what's right for this place. Like my ancestors. And yours.'

'I don't do *magic spells*.'

'Of course you do.' His hand squeezed mine, drawing me a reluctant step towards him. 'I see it. Rhys sees it. And I know you feel it too.' He gestured to the garden, to the stone, encompassing all my work. 'You could do amazing things with your connection to the earth, your elemental abilities. *He* won't show you. But I will. All you have to do is ask.'

I could hear Gigi barking on the porch, as if she knew I was in trouble, that even with my eyes fully open, I could still feel that pull of temptation. 'You need to leave now,' I said, wrenching my hand from his grasp.

Shawn reached down and picked up the backpack he'd dropped earlier, slinging it over his shoulder with a lack of concern, as if my surrender were inevitable. 'You could do anything, Sylvie. Remember that.'

'Just go,' I said, dredging up all the pack-leader authority I could muster. My voice hardly shook at all.

His voice, however, played inside my head, all the way back into the house, rising and falling in time to the approaching siren. *You could do anything.*

❧ ❧

The moulded plastic chairs in the waiting room of the county hospital ER must have been designed by a chiropractor trying to drum up future business. They were, impossibly, making my body even edgier than my nerves.

Rhys and his father sat on either side of me. After the ambulance had whisked Clara off, the professor had driven my shaken cousin and Clara's ashen daughter in the station wagon, and Rhys and I had followed in the rental car. When we'd arrived, Paula instructed us to leave her car and return home, but, without even talking about it, the Griffiths and I took seats in the plastic torture devices while Paula and Addie were allowed into the treatment area.

I'd been forced to reevaluate Addie. After her initial tears and shock, she had pulled herself together and had the presence of mind to grab Clara's purse with her insurance and health information. Paula had barely remembered her own bag.

On the drive to the hospital and even in the waiting room, Rhys and I had been mostly silent. I had plenty to think about, and from the way the muscle in Rhys's jaw kept flexing, I could guess his mind was working overtime as well.

Finally, Professor Griffith had had enough waiting

and stood up stiffly. 'I'm off to search – in vain, I'm sure – for a cup of tea. Call my mobile if Paula comes out with news.'

He wandered down one of the antiseptic tile hall-ways; he'd dressed hastily in a blue knit shirt and a black pair of trousers. Rhys still wore his jeans and rugby shirt, both rather dirty, and I'd grabbed a cardigan from the back of the desk chair in the den to cover the grass stains on my clothes. Fortunately, everyone had more important things on their minds than our incriminating condition.

I wrapped the sweater more tightly around myself and said miserably, 'I wish I could have brought Gigi.'

Rhys reached for my hand, holding it in both of his. My head spun, adjusting to the changes in the past few hours. No argument about who didn't trust whom seemed very important any more. 'She'll be fine in your room. We checked all the locks and windows before we left. You've never felt anything weird in there, right?'

'Nothing bad.' The dread and bone-biting cold had only manifested on the landing and in the hall, reaching down the stairs. The only other ghosts that bothered me were the crying in the woods, and the girl. Hannah.

As for the rest, I'd come to accept that the house was permeated with the past, and all the half-sensed things – glimpsed shirttails and apron strings dis-appearing round corners, caught whiffs of perfume or tobacco, snatches of a tune on the pianoforte – were just imprints of life, like Professor Griffith had suggested.

Except for the prison area at Cahawba. Those imprints were darker, the deep footprints of a lot of misery.

I'd been trying to fit together all the puzzle pieces I'd gathered. My standing stone must mark some kind of energy spot – metaphysical, electromagnetic, geo-whatever – that made what Shawn and the circle were doing possible. But what about the ghosts? If the ley line thing Professor Griffith had talked about extended from Bluestone Hill to the ruins of Old Cahawba on the north side, then could that make it a hot spot for ghosts as well as magic?

Eyeing the distance between us and our near?est companions, a whispering prayer circle in the corner, I lowered my voice and asked Rhys, 'If you've experienced' – I was hesitant to say 'magic' in public, no matter how quietly – 'strange things before, why do you say the power of rocks and crystals is pseudo-science?'

'Because it is,' he said, jaw tightening. 'Most of the time. But on the one-in-a-thousand chance that someone might stumble on something real, I'm going to say nonsense. Can you imagine how out of balance the world would be if every neo-druid crystal hugger who read something on the Internet started trying to do magic with rocks and twigs? Chaos.'

He'd alluded to that in the woods, and I hadn't pursued it. 'I don't understand what you mean by "out of balance".'

'Good and bad things happen, and there's a sort of equilibrium to it. We're not really meant to mess with it.' He still held my hand, and I noticed he was rubbing his thumb along mine in an agitated sort of way.

'What about . . .' I nodded towards the people praying in the corner.

Rhys smiled slightly. 'Not the same thing, as far as I can tell. The universe – or whatever – keeps things balanced according to criteria we can't wrap our heads around. It's when you muck about with it in a big way that bad things happen.'

'Like mine collapses,' I guessed.

The muscle in his jaw jumped, and then he sighed in admission. 'Yes, exactly.'

I stared at his profile, wondering what that tension had to do with his taking it on himself to correct what Shawn was doing. All on his own. That was either quixotic as hell, or crazier than I ever thought of being.

'Why did you break into the office at Maddox Point?' I asked.

He grimaced, looking more sheepish than guilty. 'I knew they'd have a decent map, maybe satellite pictures of the area. It was a bit of a ditch effort, really.'

'For what?' Then insight flashed – he had already admitted to looking for more bluestone. 'Are you searching for another standing stone in the woods?'

His scowl lacked his usual edge. 'You have gotten very nosy for a girl who didn't even ask where she was going when she got on the plane from New York.'

I ignored that, refusing to be drawn off course. 'Here's my theory,' I said, lowering my voice. 'There's something about my rock in the garden. You said in the woods – there's magic in that place. Maybe it's one of those ley lines or something.'

He glanced warily at a stodgy-looking couple who seemed to be taking a lot of interest in our whispers. 'Maybe.'

'You're not just hunting for any old rock. You're looking for another power spot.'

With clear reluctance, he admitted, 'If Shawn has his circle, then a powerful position might even things up.'

Unaccountably furious with this *insane* idea, I leaned forward and hissed, 'Why? So you can get into a battle of magical one-upmanship? Do you want to *die* in the next car accident? Or maybe you want to prove yourself his equal in being completely conscienceless when it comes to what you think is right!'

My voice had risen at the end, to the point where the stodgy old couple stared in disapproval and the prayer circle was probably now praying for me. But the only thing that hurt worse than the thought of Rhys turning into Shawn was the thought of Rhys dead.

He choked back a retort and glanced in frustration at our audience. With an impatient sound, he pulled me out of the waiting room and into the empty hallway. 'Do not,' he said in a harsh, quiet voice, 'compare me to Shawn. He doesn't care about the consequences of his actions. I do.'

There was anger in his tone, and in the flush on his face. But there was also hurt, and beneath that the guilt I hadn't been able to get at yet.

'I believe you, Rhys.' I kept a tight clasp on his

hand, wanting to hold onto this new partnership. 'I can't even say *why* I trust you, except that you're such a bad liar and apparently not much of a burglar, either.'

He laughed softly, embarrassed but not offended. 'It's not my strong suit, no.'

'Why do I feel, ever since we first met, that I know you, that I'm connected to you somehow? This is crazy.'

'I don't know, love.' His gaze dropped, lingered on our entwined fingers as he traced the lines of my palm with his thumb. 'The world is full of patterns that repeat, and they're particularly alive there in your bend in the river. Maybe we've been pulled into the pattern.' I shivered, an electric thrill running up my arm and all through me, the way it had when we'd first touched in the airport. But this caress was deliberate, and the easy intimacy of his touch was thrilling and new. I didn't – couldn't – keep that from my face when he lifted his eyes to meet mine. 'Just believe that I care about what happens to you.'

While I still struggled to form words, he glanced into the waiting room, and released my hand. 'There's Paula and the doctor. Go talk to her while I ring my dad.'

Anxiety returned in a rush as I wove through the maze of plastic chairs and attached tables. But I could see from my cousin's weary relief that the news wasn't as bad as it could be. The tall, dark-skinned doctor by her side confirmed it. Clara had cracked several ribs, dislocated her shoulder and broken her hip.

Paula gave a tired laugh. 'You should hear her.

She's mad as hell. Only old women break their hips, she says.'

'From the bruises,' said the doctor wryly, 'it's lucky she didn't break her neck.'

On this sobering note, he took his leave as the Griffiths reentered the waiting room. Paula gave them the recap and told us we could go home. 'Addie and I will follow shortly.'

'Are you sure?' asked Professor Griffith in concern.

'Yes.' She drew herself up, moving towards steel magnolia mode, but not quite reaching it. 'You've already done so much. Thank you, both. You feel more like family than guests.'

'That's how we feel as well.' He rather gallantly leaned down and kissed her cheek. 'If you promise to be careful on the road, then I will take these two youngsters home and we'll all get some rest.'

Rhys didn't make a face at the word 'youngster', but I did. Then I sent my love to Clara, and dragged myself out after the Griffiths. Adrenaline had run its course and left me drained. Father and son chatted quietly as we crossed the parking lot, and when we got to their rental car, I crawled into the back seat, and was asleep before the engine even turned over.

Chapter 31

I woke late, to a very cloudy day.

Gigi was still curled in the crook behind my knees; there wasn't enough sunlight to wake her. What filtered in through the deep casement looked watery and grey.

'It's time to get up, Gee.'

Her answer was a grumbling growl. She moved to the warm spot on the pillow, in the curve of my neck, and went back to sleep. I couldn't help but think she had the right idea.

The ringing of my cell phone jolted me out of a complacent doze. After a stumbling search, I found my jeans in a heap on the floor and dug the phone out of the pocket.

'Hey, John.'

'Are you still asleep?' he asked. 'What time is it there?'

'Uh . . .' I had no idea. It couldn't be too late, or Gigi would have demanded a walk by now. 'We had a really long night. My cousin's business partner and friend had a horrible fall. We were at the hospital.'

'That's awful! Is she going to be all right?'

'She broke her hip. But it could have been a lot worse.' I sat on the bed and tried to get my thoughts together. Gigi rearranged herself on the centre of the pillow, figuring I wasn't coming back. 'Are you calling to check up on me?'

'Sort of. There are all kinds of torrential rains on the news. I just wanted to make sure you weren't getting washed away.'

I glanced at the window. 'It's not raining here, but it looks like it might be somewhere close.'

'You could turn on the news. There *is* television out in the sticks, right?'

A knock on the door prevented my answering that in the way it deserved. 'Hang on,' I told John, and stumbled to the door. I was wearing a T-shirt that said BALLET DANCERS SPEND ALL DAY AT THE BARRE. The shirt covered everything important, but I stood behind the door when I opened it, anyway.

Rhys was in the hall, pulling on a rain slicker and looking distracted. 'Hey.'

'Hi.' The phone was still in my hand, and I

wondered if I should push Mute. But despite a softening of his gaze when he first saw me, Rhys was all business.

'You need to get downstairs. It's raining bloody hell upriver, and they're worried about flooding. Paula and Addie are packing bags before they go to the hospital, in case they get stranded. Dad is going into town to make sure the larder is stocked up, and I'm headed out to Cahawba. They'll need help sandbagging the excavation.'

A spark of worry made me forget about the phone, my stepbrother and my half-dressed state. 'Is it dangerous?'

'You'll be safe here,' he assured me. 'The mansion is on high ground. It's stood through floods before. Just stay up near the house.'

'I mean, will you be safe out at Old Cahawba?' Anxiously, I stepped out from behind the door. 'It's been washed out twice.'

'I'll be fine.' He smiled, in a warm way that made my insides knot. 'But you could give me a kiss for luck if you want.'

I was actually a little afraid of how much I wanted to, which was the only thing that kept me where I was. That and worry I might have morning breath.

And, oh yeah, my stepbrother on the phone. I pointed to the cell and said, 'I have a chaperone.'

'In that case, get a move on, love.' There was still a trace of humour in his back-to-business tone. 'Get dressed and get downstairs. There's work to be done.'

He headed down the hall, and I shut the door, marvelling at how much things had changed in a night.

Then I spoke into the phone, 'I know you heard all that.'

'I don't even know where to begin,' said John. 'What is going on there? Who is that guy?'

Cradling the phone against my shoulder, I grabbed my jeans and pulled them on. 'You haven't known me nearly long enough to go all protective big brother on me, John.'

'Who else is going to? Sylvie, please tell me you're not getting involved with someone while you're in a . . . a—'

'A what?' I snapped. 'A third-world country? Or are you talking about my fragile mental state?'

'Come on, Sylvie.'

I sighed and sat on the edge of the bed. 'I'm not involved. Exactly. I'm not sure what you'd call it. But trust me when I say that if I was, it would be the least weird thing going on.'

'What are you talking about?'

'Gotta run, John. I'll catch you up later. God willing and the creek don't rise.'

'Oh my God. You've gone native.'

'Bye, John.' I hung up, slipped on a pair of shoes, grabbed my sleepy dog and then headed downstairs. Rhys was right. If the waters were rising, there were things that needed to be done. I hoped somebody would tell me what they were, or I'd be no help at all.

❧ ❧

Paula wanted me to go with her and Addie, but I assured her I would be fine in the house. It wasn't as if

I'd be alone – the Griffiths would be back – and if the waters did rise, someone – a Davis – should be here to monitor, handle it or call the authorities. That was the argument that swayed her, but I was stunned how strongly I felt that I shouldn't leave Bluestone Hill with the uncertainty of the rains upriver.

Paula and Addie pulled out in the Mom Mobile, accompanied by the distant roll of thunder. Overhead the sky was uniformly grey and dismal, but nonthreatening. As I stood on the porch watching the taillights of the wagon, Professor Griffith joined me, shrugging into his rain jacket.

'The water is still hot in the kettle if you want to make yourself a cup of tea,' he said. 'Is there anything in particular you want from the market? Bearing in mind I'll have to take what I can get.'

'You probably won't have any competition for the soy milk.'

'True.' He took a step down, then glanced back at me in careful study. 'You'll be all right while I'm gone? You can call my mobile if you need to. Or Rhys's – he trekked over to the dig site on foot, but he can get back in a trice if you need him.'

I hid my nervousness with sarcasm. 'I realize that an apartment in a city of eight million people hasn't prepared me for staying in a big country house by myself, but I think I can manage. It's not even raining.'

He glanced at the sky. 'It's not the rain here that's the problem. It's all the storms upriver. The water has to go somewhere.'

On that cheerful note, he left in the rental, and for

the first time since I came to Alabama, I was alone in the house. Technically speaking.

Before, when I needed to regroup, to think, or most important to *not* think, I headed to the ballet barre. The repetitive pattern of the exercises, the concentration on placement, extension, turnout and pointe were a physical mantra to clear my brain whenever it was too full.

Now I went to the garden. But it was different today. As Gigi and I stepped into the circle, the unfinished pattern around the rock called to me, not with a promise of mental peace, but with an urgent demand. With the same visceral certainty I'd had about not leaving the house, I knew I needed to finish this. The work was too close to being done.

I had no clue what that meant in terms of the things I'd learned last night, about the garden and about myself. But the garden was one place where I'd never had trouble listening to my instincts.

❧ ☙

The work went quickly, and soon, tired but satisfied, I sat back on my heels, gazing at the results of my labour. The corner beds were still an overgrown mess, but I'd cleared the central planting area of choking weeds, revealed its original shape and uncovered the full beauty of the bluestone centrepiece.

It stayed damp today, looking truly blue. When the sun would occasionally peek through the clouds, the flecks of quartz caught the light, looking like scattered stars on an indigo sky.

Uncluttered by rampant weeds, not to mention the insidious kudzu, the bare hint of the labyrinth motif that wound into the four-foot-tall stone in the centre was now visible. The herbs and foliage, skimpy when I'd first cleared them, had become thick and lush, some of them already flowering.

My effect on the garden was obvious and tangible. But what about its effect on me? Had I really instinctively tapped into the energy here and made myself healthier, like one of these plants? There seemed to be a difference between what I felt here and what I sensed from the circle in the summerhouse. This was reciprocal somehow, and my progress was like the plants' – natural but accelerated.

But what would happen if I actually tried to connect with the energy here? What could I do then?

Gigi, lying under the stone bench, jerked her head up with a growl. Automatically, I looked towards the house, but couldn't see anything other than the corner of the balcony and the top of the spiral staircase. The Colonel didn't have the dog upset. It must be something else.

'You've made a lot of progress.'

With a start, I turned towards Shawn's voice. He stood in the opening of the hedge, his hands shoved in the pockets of his cargo pants. When my eyes narrowed in suspicion, he pulled them out, as if to show me they were empty. 'Truce. I came for a report on Clara.'

Since I couldn't figure out how he'd be served by her injury, I decided to give him the benefit of the doubt. 'She's going to be all right.' But I couldn't let him off the hook entirely, so I added, with an edge of accusation: 'Eventually.'

He nodded, looking so contrite that I frowned, wondering suddenly if I'd been mistaken about him. 'I know. That's all I could think about while I was trying to sleep last night. What if our spell had somehow accidentally hurt Clara. It just kills me to think that, Sylvie. It kills me that *you* think that.'

Turning my back on him, I shook the dirt from one last weed and threw it into the basket I would take out back for compost. Maintaining, for him at least, a facade of normalcy. 'I don't see what I have to do with anything.'

'Don't be coy,' he chided with his usual easy humour. 'You know you have everything to do with it. Hasn't Rhys explained that to you?'

Unease tightened my stomach, and I forced myself to relax my shoulders, despite the weight of his gaze on me. Why mention Rhys? Was he trying to raise my suspicions? 'He may have mentioned,' I said with understatement, 'that my connection to the magic here was important to you.'

Sitting on the bench, Shawn leaned forward, elbows on his knees so he was level with me as I knelt in the greenery. 'We're supposed to meet again tonight. Addie won't be able to be there, so you can take her spot.'

Outraged, I twisted to look at him, fists propped on my thighs. 'Is that what breaking Clara's hip was supposed to accomplish? Get Addie out of the way?'

He met my eye, and grimaced with uncharacteristic

candour. 'The stuff the circle does is imprecise. That's why I need you. It will work better with a Davis. I thought Addie'd get a modelling job or something. Everyone wins.'

That honesty was disarming, but I forced my guard up. 'Does your circle know you're just using them? That you'd blow them off like you're blowing off Addie, as soon as they're no more use to you?'

'The council knows we're doing what's right for the town. If Maddox Point goes through and brings growth to the area, it won't be a thirty-minute wait for an ambulance. It will be ten.'

Gigi grumbled from under the bench; I didn't need her prompt to call bullshit on that. 'Aren't you just Humanitarian of the Year.'

He ignored my sarcasm, pressing his own argument. 'The council has been going on for a long time, Sylvie. Since our families first came here. But every now and then, there's someone like you, and someone like me, who can connect with the elements. Just look at this place.' He gestured to my work. The overcast skies kept the dew from burning off, and the smell of the herbs was thick and vibrant. He knelt beside me and picked off a grey-green leaf of sage. 'These plants? They're for healing. See how well they've worked, and you didn't even know what you were doing. Just think what you can do if you learn more about your instincts.'

This was a different Shawn, as if the gilt of his surface charm had been rubbed off to reveal the compelling power beneath it. It pulled at something inside me, and when he took my dirty hands in his, I let him, just to see where this offer was going.

'I'll teach you how to use your connection,' he said. 'Do you think Rhys will do that? He's been trying to keep you in the dark, right?'

That was overplaying his hand. I tugged my fingers free – or tried to. 'Not any more.'

'Yes, but he doesn't belong here.' Shawn gestured to the standing stone. 'That rock was brought here by *our* ancestors and put there to mark this spot, where earth energy is strong. This whole area, where the two rivers converge.'

'That's very poetic, Shawn.' I made my voice wry, despite the spell he wove, the tugging I could feel on the part of me that wanted to be this special, magical person he described. Like the special, magical person I'd been when I danced.

'Come on, Sylvie.' He rubbed the dirt on my fingers. 'I know you can feel it. It's in your blood. That's why I need you.'

'So you can get what you want,' I said, to remind myself more than to accuse him.

'And so can you.'

Would that be so bad? Temptation hissed in my ear, made my heart race with anticipation of the mere possibility.

'What's the trade-off?' I asked, thinking about what Rhys had said about consequences. 'Do you even care?'

'The trade-off is, the town improves, things go well for me, you get to dance again. It's a win-win situation.'

I desperately wanted to ignore my instincts. But I'd worked so hard for my success as a dancer – of course, genetics had given me long legs and natural ability, but I'd sweated and bled and ached to achieve what I'd had. Hell, I hadn't eaten a dessert in six years until I came here. Even without Rhys's warnings, even without my gut feeling at the summerhouse, I knew in my heart that you just didn't get things for free.

The thought snapped Shawn's hold on me, and I pulled my hand loose before my resolve weakened. 'You'd better go,' I said, rising to my feet.

He stood as well. 'Will you at least think about it?'

His reasonable tone irritated me, as if I were being irrational. 'Just get out of here, Shawn.'

Gigi, picking up on my mood, started to growl again. Shawn laughed, raising his hands in surrender. 'Fine, fine.' He seemed so normal, it was hard to believe he'd just been trying to seduce me into using magic for his – and *my* – selfish ends. 'I'll see you around.'

I scooped Gigi up so she didn't run after him. 'Not if I see you first,' I murmured, to no one but the dog. Shawn hadn't bothered to wait for my reply.

No way had he given up that easily. Though I guess he figured he had time to bring me around. And he must have seen that I was temptable. Not by him, but by what I might reclaim.

I walked to the bluestone monolith, Gigi still tucked in the crook of my arm. I stared for a moment, then pressed my palm to the stone's surface. Time had dulled the texture, but not smoothed it. And it did feel warm, or at least warmer than I could account for on the grey day.

When my dad took me to the Metropolitan Museum when I was a kid, he would talk about balance in art. I understood it on a more practical, physical level. Staying balanced while dancing was about equal and opposite movements. If I extended my leg in a *développé devant* – to the front – then I had to tighten my centre of balance and lean backwards slightly to stay upright.

If I took what Rhys had said, and applied what I knew from art and ballet to magical, mystical energy, didn't that mean that for everything that happened, something opposite had to happen too? Maybe not one for one, but something to balance the equation.

Dr Young had said that ecology was fragile, and if things got off kilter, the effects could be big. The Maddox and Davis families had apparently been messing around with the natural balance throughout our history here. When that happened to a dancer, she fell on her face. What happened when the energy of a geographical area was out of whack? Something had to correct for it.

Was this what Rhys had meant when he said bad things happen when you mess with the balance? Yellow fever? Floods? Horrible prisons? Mine collapses?

What about ghosts? Shawn had said this whole region was powerful, up to the junction of the rivers, which included Old Cahawba. Was Shawn's messing around with the natural order of things skewing the energy here, making the echoes of the past resonate more loudly, making the intangible more real?

As I went inside, I noticed the Colonel's chill wafting down the stairs, and wondered what had him stirred up in the middle of the day. Maybe Shawn unsettled him as much as he did me.

Despite my weak joke, I climbed the stairs warily, but the cold seemed to be fleeting. A thought stuck with me, though, about Shawn's effect on people: If I had this elemental affinity for the garden, what was Shawn's superpower? Charm was obviously part of it. That was blindingly obvious in retrospect. It worried me what he might be capable of. My scruples were susceptible to temptation, but at least I had some.

Chapter 32

Still unsettled by my conversation with Shawn, I distanced myself from the garden a bit, and brought both Hannah's diary and the reverend's journal downstairs and into the den. With the big-screen TV and the modern furniture, I felt grounded in this century and less likely to lose myself. I brought a glass of iced tea for myself and a chew for Gigi, which she promptly took to the love seat and started gnawing.

As soon as I sat down, the lights went off. My heart stopped for a painful, panicked second. Then reason kicked back in – along with my pulse – and I registered that the light on the satellite receiver box was black, the LED on the answering machine was dark and I couldn't hear the hum of the refrigerator down the hall.

The power had gone out. Paula had warned me that might happen if there were storms in the area, and had pointed out where the flashlights and candles were. I found a flashlight and nervously put it beside me on the couch. Expected or not, it was unnerving.

To distract myself, I picked up the Reverend Holzphaffel's journal. Gigi left her chew and pranced down the length of the cushions, then climbed into my lap, licked my chin and went to sleep. I petted her silky fur and tried to relax. One or both Griffiths would be back soon.

The dates on Hannah's headstone had been December 21, 1852, and June 20, 1870. I realized, with a start, that it was almost midsummer, the anniversary of her death. Opening the Reverend Holzphaffel's journal to 1869, about nine months before Hannah's end, I read to see if he mentioned young Miss Davis's suitors.

The facsimile of the handwritten pages wasn't any easier to read than Hannah's scrawled entries, but at least they were more detailed. Reverend Holzphaffel didn't hold much with Thou Shalt Not Gossip About Your Neighbour. There was the reference to Mr Ethan Maddox I'd read the other day, which I scanned again with new understanding. It didn't take me long to find the answer that Hannah hadn't bothered writing for herself. Ethan's brother, the scalawag, was named Jacob.

He *was* trying to bring investors to the area – even ones from the North – but he didn't seem like a profiteer. Just the opposite, in fact. He was an outspoken young man who pointed out some hard truths about his own family, like how Davis Ironworks and Maddox Shipping were leaving their neighbours in the dirt as far as recovery from the war was concerned.

It was clear that the reverend liked the guy, even though everyone else was pushing Hannah towards Ethan. I didn't want Jacob to be the one who left her in the lurch, but having read Hannah's journal, that seemed more than likely.

I remembered the blistering animosity radiating from the window last night, aimed at the spot where Rhys and I came out of the woods. Was *I* some kind of trigger for the Colonel? I certainly identified with Hannah. If she had been meeting Jacob on the sly, her father would certainly have been seething as he watched from the window.

I filed those questions away and kept reading. The story, even without my personal connection to it, engrossed me. I lost track of time, squinting until my eyes ached. Gigi shifted positions twice, getting up, stretching, sinking back into my lap with a sigh.

Then the bottom of one page ended in the middle of a sentence about Easter services, and the top of the next one talked about the fall harvest. Confused, I flipped back and forth, and found that the entries skipped from March to September 1870.

I carried the book to the window and angled it to catch what light the clouds hadn't cut off. Inside, near the binding, was a shadow of the tattered edges of the missing pages. But it was flat, just a copied image. The pages had been torn out before the journal had been reproduced.

Lowering the book, I looked out the window, surprised at how dark it had gotten. Even with the distraction of Hannah's story, and the missing months, my disquiet came back in a rush. Shouldn't one or both of the Griffiths be back?

The phone rang from the kitchen, the only one that wasn't cordless and worthless with the power out. I was stiff after sitting curled on the couch for hours, and by the time I reached the phone, I'd lost count of the rings. When I finally picked up, Professor Griffith sounded relieved.

'Sylvie! Are you watching the news?'

'The power went out a little while ago.' I had tried to stay calm about it, since I'd lived through a power outage before, and it was a lot scarier in the city, where the whole world stopped. But the worry in his voice turned up the volume on my nerves.

'Call Rhys,' the professor instructed me, in a no-arguments tone. 'The water is headed downriver much faster than anyone thought. I don't know if I'm going to be able to get back to you two. The state police are already putting up road barricades.'

Maybe some part of me had anticipated this, but it was much smaller than the part that wondered what I'd been thinking, staying by myself.

Deep breaths, Sylvie. Don't panic. I felt safe in the house. I just had to trust my instincts. Bluestone Hill had stood through floods before. Gigi and I would be all right.

'OK,' I said, surprising myself with my calm. 'Don't risk coming back here if it looks dicey.'

'There's a torch in my room, and Rhys should have one, too. You've still got a good bit of daylight left, but it won't hurt to be prepared.'

'Yes, sir.' I looked at the clock on the wall. How had it gotten so late? Had I lost that much time in the past?

'You have Rhys's mobile number? It's on the tablet by the phone in the foyer.'

'OK.'

It was starting to be my mantra. Everything was going to be all right. Storms had come before, and they would come again. That was nature.

But so was the destruction they left in their wake.

The professor rang off, and I went to find my cell phone. I'd plugged it in after I talked to John that morning, so it should have charged before the power went out. At least *something* had worked out.

At the bottom of the steps I paused, one hand on the banister. The stairwell was cool, in a way that had nothing to do with the overcast skies and the distant storms. Defiantly, I put a foot on a stair, gripping the railing tightly, telling myself the ghost couldn't startle me like it had Clara. It couldn't hurt me unless I let it.

I braved it out, but my heart was pounding when I reached the top landing and saw the sheer curtains of the French doors shifting in an unearthly breeze. My knuckles went white on the banister and I held my breath in dread, but there was no shape or form.

I'd never seen the Colonel during the day, so maybe he had limits. But what had stirred him up?

Think, Sylvie. I'd first glimpsed him when I'd been out on the lawn. Then again from the same place. Then I'd sensed him from inside after I'd seen Addie going to meet the TTC – out on the grounds.

So someone must be out on the grounds.

I forced myself forward, ignoring the prickle of fear on my neck. When the cold didn't get worse, I held my breath and pushed through the spot that nothing occupied. I threw the latch and flung open the windows, stepping onto the balcony to scan the storm-coloured twilight.

The wind was cool and damp, tangling my hair around my face. It smelled of distant rain but also of the river, of everything that was washing down with it. Of fish and industry. Of decaying vegetation and urban storm drains. What was coming was the flip side of the coin of progress.

The wind carried a noise as well – the first ghost I'd sensed, and the last I'd identified. I knew the high-pitched cry now, and I could hear the hunger and fear and loneliness in it. It was far off, and so was the sound that came with it: the faint, brave bark of a tiny dog.

My stomach knotted with a painful yank. I'd left Gigi on the couch with her chew when I'd gone to answer the phone. I hadn't heard her growl at the cold on the stairs.

Rushing back inside, I was so chilled with panic, I

could have walked right through the Colonel fully manifest and I wouldn't have known it. In my room, I grabbed Gigi's favourite toy and squeaked it as I ran through the upstairs hall, calling her name, listening for the jingle of her tags.

I dashed down the stairs, for once without a single thought of falling. In the den, I squeaked the toy and called her again. The parlour was empty, and so was the dining room. I got to the kitchen and found the back door standing open, sick dread halting me at the sight.

It hadn't been like that when I was on the phone. All the doors were closed tight. Rhys and Professor Griffith had checked before they left.

I ran out into the yard, without a jacket, without a flashlight, and sprinted to the edge of the terrace, looking out on the rolling drop of terrain to the woods, and beyond that, the river.

'Gigi!' I yelled her name into the wind. The faint wisp of a baby's cry came back to me and, with nothing to guide me but a hunch, I desperately followed it. Since that first night, my dog had been determined to track down that sound.

I didn't go into Hannah's woods. I kept heading north, parallel to the river, weaving in and out through the trees until I stumbled onto a trail, and realized I was on the path to the ruins of Old Cahawba. Maybe Gigi remembered the way, and it had made her bold in her pursuit.

Seizing that hope, I ran along the path, stopping every hundred feet or so to rest my leg and call into the trees for my dog. I'd given up trying to use an alpha-

478

dog voice. My yells were frantic, and hoarse with my terror for her.

When I reached the Cahawba graveyard, it was almost dusk. The thin cover of clouds diffused the light to a uniform glow, turning the trees into towering monsters and the moss dripping from their branches into vampire cloaks.

Suddenly one seemed to come alive in front of me. I screamed, my nerves stretched to their limit. The figure raised its arms, like flapping wings, and spoke.

'Sylvie! What are you doing here?'

I recognized his voice and would have felt foolish if I hadn't been so upset. You would think I would've known by now that if someone was going to grab me or loom out of the dark, it was going to be Rhys.

'Gigi's gone,' I said, wheezing with fear and exhaustion. 'I followed a noise this way. I have this horrible feeling—'

He took my shoulders in a steadying grip. 'We'll find her. You said you followed a sound?'

I nodded, then shook my head. I'd trailed the faint cry at first, but hadn't heard it in a while. Yet my instincts had carried me this way, and they kept proving smarter than I was.

'Shawn came to the house earlier,' I said. My teeth had started to chatter once I'd stopped moving. It hadn't been this cold up on the Hill. Rhys rubbed my arms, warming me outside with friction, and inside with his careful attention. 'He wanted me to work with him. Make this crazy magic dynasty. And when I told him to leave . . .' I shivered too hard to talk.

His fingers tightened in anger, but not at me. 'Did he hurt you?'

I shook my head. 'No. He didn't even get mad, which was worse. Maybe he took Gigi or lured her away.'

'Sylvie, this is where the two rivers converge, and there's a flood coming down both of them. We need to get out of here.'

Determination burned off fear, and maybe good sense, too. 'I can't leave without Gigi!'

We were yelling over the wind now, which moaned and growled like a living thing. But it carried something else with it, a real growl, from a real animal.

I shook off Rhys's hold and ran towards the sound. It led me towards the bluff where the joined rivers curved around, and the chimney marking the space that had once housed the prison.

Shock made me stumble. I could *see* the ghosts now. In the dusk was a cloud of suggestion, formless hints in pillars of sickly grey light. Even more appalling were the sounds, wretched moans that pulled at every dark, miserable part my soul.

Rhys came up beside me as I stared into the cold mist of suffering. 'Can you see her?'

'No.' Only masks of horror floating in and out of the cloud, faces with hopeless eyes, hungry to drag me down with them. Terror stole away my breath, and my chest burned, as if I were drowning, too.

Then, from the midst of them, I caught a small dog's ferocious barks, and desperation buoyed me back up. I grabbed Rhys's arm, afraid even to hope, and somehow dug below the horror for my voice. 'Gigi, come here.'

Her next bark was sharp, distinct. Obedient. Standing at the very edge of the invisible wall that imprisoned the ghosts, so close that the frigid mist dampened my skin and my hair, I called her again.

Her excited panting reached out from the fog, as if she was running to me. But then I heard a horrible snap, and a yelp, and a heartrending cry of pain.

Without thinking, I plunged into the icy haze, feeling Rhys's grasp just miss me. He called my name, and I knew why Gigi hadn't come to me sooner. Once inside the cloud of ghosts, I could barely hear anything but their misery. My heart beat against my ribs and an overwhelming despair clawed through my insides.

The fog was resilient. It had weight and substance, like flabby flesh. I heard Gigi's frantic cries, and I pushed forward with renewed resolve.

They are only ghosts. They can't hurt you. I didn't even know if this was true – it didn't *feel* true – but I clung to the thought single-mindedly, or I wouldn't have been able to make myself move.

Reaching, stretching, I grasped something solid and warm. A hand. A real hand, pulling me out of the fog. Rhys, of course. It always was.

We stood in perfectly normal darkness. I was freezing and soaked to the bone, and there was ice on my hair. Steam rose from my skin. I'd come all the way through the prison and out the other side, leaving the ghosts behind their invisible wall.

But I hadn't found my dog. Rhys wrapped me up in

his rain jacket, a cocoon of warmth which crinkled noisily in my ears as I pushed loose from him. 'Where's Gigi? I was following her barks.'

He held onto my arms, and I realized with a jolt how close I'd come the edge of the bluff. A few steps more, and I would have tumbled into the river. 'Look down,' he said, and dread curdled in my gut.

I peered over the side and saw Gigi lying about four feet down a sheer drop. Her tongue hung out, and she panted heavily. Something inside me twisted and came undone – the parts the stubborn dog had held together all these months.

She saw me and tried to get up, but she couldn't. Her whines were so soft, I could hardly hear them over the rush of the river. 'Stay,' I told her, my voice breaking along with my heart. I tried to make it more emphatic so she would obey, but could only manage a sob. 'Stay, Gigi.'

Rhys's arm was around my waist, keeping me steady as the edge threatened to crumble under my feet. 'Sylvie,' he said with gentle force, getting my attention. There was an anxious warning in his voice. 'Look at the water.'

It was rising as we stood there. In maybe five minutes, Gigi would be carried away in the flood.

'I have to get her.' Pushing away my anguish, my fear for her, I readied myself for an argument, but Rhys didn't protest.

All business, he stripped off his top layer – a long-sleeved shirt – and handed it to me. 'Use this to make a sling for her. I'll lower you down.'

'Anchor me above the knee,' I told him, to save my tibia the stress. I crouched in position at the drop-off with a dizzying sense of déjà vu and a rush of familiar phobia. I tamped it down and kept my eyes on Gigi.

'Careful,' Rhys said as I walked my hands down the embankment. Whining piteously, Gigi tried to wag her tail as I got nearer. I hadn't thought I had any heart left to ache, but I was wrong. Slithering down, I pushed my belly over the edge, then my hips. Rhys's hands tightened on my knees, holding them securely as he lay on the ground above, counterbalancing my dangling weight.

By stretching my arms, I was just able to reach Gigi. She cried as I slipped her into the sling I'd made of Rhys's shirt, and I crooned soothing nonsense to her. I could barely hear myself above the river. The water had reached the bottom of the rock that had broken her fall. It splashed us both as I looped the tied sleeves of the shirt around my neck, cradling Gigi with one hand, holding myself away from the cliff with the other.

I had no way to fend off the corpse-white hand that came up out of the water and grabbed my trailing hair. It was indistinct but solid, and it was definitely, *definitely* not Rhys.

Chapter 33

I screamed like I was being murdered, frenzied terror seizing me as hard as the dead-cold fingers coming out of the river.

Rhys moved lightning fast, jerking me back. My hair slipped through the grip of the thing under the water, and my stomach lurched with revulsion. My elbows left huge patches of skin on the dirt and exposed roots as Rhys dragged me up the embankment; enough reason reached through my panic that I tried to shelter Gigi the best I could. Rhys and I landed in an awkward tangle of arms and legs that might have embarrassed me on any other occasion. But not when something drowned and horrible had tried to drag me to my death.

'How did it grab me?' I shouted, somewhere between hysteria and a psychotic break. 'How did it *touch* me?'

'I don't know.' Rhys hauled me to my feet, wrapped the discarded slicker around me and the dog shivering in the sling against my chest. 'But we have got to go. Right now.'

I felt a rumble, and heard a roar, and looked up to see a wall of water rushing downstream, pushing the river up and over its banks, taking lumber and dirt and debris with it.

That wasn't all that came with the water. As the river rose, so did the ghosts. I watched in sick, frozen horror as they flowed, unearthly, ahead of the waves. Drowned ghosts, their shapes waterlogged and bloated. Plague ghosts, their spectres gaunt with fever and pocked with disease. They overran the invisible prison walls, hanged ghosts with broken necks and bulging tongues, figures with limbs missing, or swollen with sickness.

Rhys pushed me into motion, past the wall of exhaustion and shock. I tried not to look back as we ran. The air had turned so cold that it seared my throat, but we kept going. I cradled Gigi, wrapped in the makeshift sling, trying not to jar her. She'd gone quiet, stopped whining. My own shivers were so bad, I couldn't tell if she was still shaking or not.

Rhys, holding my hand, headed for a line of sandbags, where we paused for breath.

'Is everyone gone from this site?' I asked, between painful attempts to fill my lungs. 'Annabeth and Dr Young are safe?'

He nodded, reassuring me there'd be no collateral damage, but dashing any hope of a ride or help.

We were going to have to move in a moment, but I grasped for a clue, the chance he knew some magic to stop this. Maybe not the water, but the ghosts. 'This is what you meant when you said bad things happen when you mess around with the natural balance of things?'

He was working to catch his breath too. 'I admit, "bad things" may have been an understatement.'

I struggled to understand. 'And this is the backlash for what the TTC has been up to?'

Shaking his head, Rhys peered over the sandbags, checking the advance of the water. 'This could be fifty years of previous councils, previous Maddoxes.'

'How does using earth magic give you floods and ghosts?'

'It's all energy, all tied together. They're not entities, they're just – imprints.' He shook his head in confusion. 'I don't know why they're so strong. This is different.'

I could feel Gigi now, panting in quick, shallow breaths. When I stroked her with light fingers, she barely moved, barely whined. 'How far to the house?'

Rhys checked the rising tide again. 'It's close, if you go through the woods. But we'll be closer to the river.'

'Let's risk it.' I'd been sitting too long; we needed the rest, but urgency gripped me, tightening the knot of my nerves.

I stumbled a bit when I got up, the muscles of my weak leg going noodly for a moment. Rhys was ready, steadying me until I had both legs under me. 'Thanks.'

On the run through the woods, I was so intent on

Gigi, I noticed nothing else. If Rhys hadn't been leading me, I would have ended up in the river again – especially as the river was so much wider than it used to be. In the corner of my eye I could see it creeping up through the woods, carrying the pine needles like flotsam.

I wasn't even sure when I'd made up my mind what to do. But as we emerged from the trees, stumbling up the hill and away from the water, I headed straight for the side garden, and the standing stone.

'Sylvie' – Rhys caught the sleeve of my coat – 'we need to get inside. If it starts to rain—'

He broke off as I unwrapped the sling from around my neck, cradling my tiny dog in the crook of my arm. 'I have to do something, Rhys.' My frantic urgency had become steely determination. 'I can't let her die.'

'You want to do more magic, in the middle of all this?' His voice was hard, incredulous. But searching my expression, his gaze softened with pity. 'I know you love her, but you'll be adding fuel to the fire.'

'But nothing!' All my fury at the world when I broke my leg solidified to a sharp, painful point. 'Bad magic hurt my dog. How is it *balance* to let that happen?'

When he didn't have an answer, I pulled away. Stepping into the centre of the garden, I wound through the faint labyrinth pattern and laid Gigi gently in her favourite spot, on a springy bed of herbs. The damp air thickened their scent around us, chasing away the smell of the river, the image of the horrors that came out of it.

I bent my ear to Gigi's side. Her ribs hardly moved and her breath was faint on my cheek.

Sitting back on my heels, I realized, with sinking desperation, that I didn't know what to do. I knew this place was important. I knew that working here in this ground had healed me in several ways. But how to evoke that, I had no clue.

Gigi's breath ran out in a deep sigh. It was a long moment before she breathed back in, and it didn't come easily. Anguish shredded the last bit of my heart. I couldn't lose her. What would keep me sane in this new, strange world of magic?

I raised imploring eyes to Rhys and wiped at the tears I hadn't noticed I'd shed. 'Please, please help me. She's all that I have left.'

He turned his own gaze to the veiled sky, as if seeking answers or trying to hold onto his resolve. I held my breath in hope as he came to a decision and sank to his knees facing me. 'Sylvie, love. You have everything and the whole world, and you don't realize it.'

I couldn't speak. My throat clenched with emotion. Rhys took my hands in his, smearing my tears across my fingers with his thumbs. 'You've got everything you need here. I've watched you work in this garden and build yourself a healing sanctuary. How did you know what to do?'

'Accident.' He looked at me, chiding, impatient. Provoking. 'And . . . I thought about my dad.'

I heard Dad's voice again – another ghost, but this one alive in my head. *Every day I put my hands in the earth, Sylvie, I feel like I cheat the cancer out of one more day.*

Plunging my hands into the earth on either side of Gigi, I spoke to my dad, to Mother Nature, to God. To

488

whatever force of the universe had made this impossible thing possible. *Please. I know it's another selfish wish. But I'll give up whatever it takes to restore the balance.*

The smell of clean dirt filled my head. My fingers seemed to grow and lengthen; I seized on the imagery, picturing them seeking help, like roots after water. Instinct drove me, and I let myself be directed.

Doubling over, I breathed onto Gigi's still muzzle, stirring her tiny whiskers with life drawn from the ground. I envisioned her bones knitting, like minute green branches growing together and hardening into wood, and her poor little heart beating steadily in my hand.

Then, like the slow creep of the dawn, I realized I could feel her pulse against my palm, and her breath tickling my cheek. I sat up in surprise, in spite of everything not quite able to believe it.

'It worked.' I laughed in amazement, and looked up at Rhys, my heart full now with joy and wonder and bursting to share it with him. 'I did it! I fixed her, Rhys.'

'I know you did, love.' He sounded sad, which didn't make sense when I had just done this *incredible* thing.

Giddy with excitement, I stroked my dirty hands over Gigi's fur, feeling her stir gently and without pain. 'She's going to be OK.'

'He doesn't get it.' I jumped at the voice that came from above us, from the corner of the balcony. With everything else going on, I'd forgotten about Shawn, but he leaned on the balustrade, looking very at ease.

'Rhys doesn't *use* his talents. Or so he said when I asked him to join us.'

I climbed warily to my knees, angling myself protectively over Gigi's still prone body. 'What are you doing here, Shawn?'

'Waiting for you.' He ambled to the spiral staircase and descended it in a couple of jumps.

I shot a questioning glance at Rhys. 'What's going on? What does he mean, he asked you to join him?'

Rhys got to his feet and stepped out of the greenery surrounding the standing stone. 'He recognized my potential like I recognized yours. He wasn't gracious about his offer, but he could have kept watch on me if I was part of the circle. Which isn't the reason I said no.'

Shawn reappeared through the hedges, walking into my garden like he owned it, and I felt a surge of possessiveness so fierce that my hands curled into fists. 'It's been like reality TV,' he said. 'Alliances, challenges, double-dealing. Him watching us, us watching him. Y'all watching each other.'

I rubbed my forehead with gritty fingers, wondering when the figurative floor was going to stay level beneath me. I kept learning new things that I had to fit into the pattern. 'What was it that kept you from telling me what was going on, Rhys?'

He sighed, resigned. But his gaze met mine unflinchingly, full of guilt and self-recrimination. 'The mine in Pembrokeshire.'

I added up my fragments of clues on the subject. I knew he felt responsible, only I had figured it was because he couldn't stop what he saw happening. But this was more than that. My sinking heart made the leap a few seconds before my brain. 'You didn't just come across a circle like this one,' I accused. 'You were part of one.'

'Started it, actually.' The admission was brittle, as if he was braced for my anger. 'With a girl from the village, based on their old traditions. Probably like Shawn started his here.'

Why hadn't he told me this? After I told him I trusted him, and believed he wasn't like Shawn. Betrayal knifed through me, and I stabbed back with an accusation. 'So the mine collapsed because of you.'

He flinched, but held my gaze. 'We had the best intentions. Parts of Wales are – well, they're like parts of the American South. Very poor. The mines peter out, or no one needs what they produce any more, and towns simply die. We were just trying to bring some prosperity back to the region.'

'Funny how alike our stories are,' said Shawn, so smugly I wanted to punch him in the nose.

'Did you tell him?' I demanded of Rhys, surging to my feet, careful of Gigi still sleeping in the circle. 'Did you warn Shawn what would happen if the council continued to throw things out of whack?'

'Of course I did,' he snapped. 'Why do you think I came here with my dad? When I came across an old article about the monolith at Bluestone Hill and read about the cycle of prosperity and disaster, I recognized the pattern. The first thing I did when I realized what Shawn was doing was warn him. And when he didn't care, I had to figure out what to do to stop him.'

'And you, Sylvie,' said Shawn, standing opposite Rhys in the garden. 'He knew how powerful you'd be. So did I. Look at what you just did. You're amazing.'

Well, that was true.

'But the water is still rising,' I said, wondering now, too late, what healing Gigi had added to the unbalanced equation. I had no call to throw stones at Rhys, except that he'd told such a huge lie by omission.

Shawn continued what Shawn did best – sweet-talking me out of my scruples. 'And when the river recedes, think of all the good you can do.' He stepped over the green border of the circle and reached for my hand. I looked at Rhys, but he didn't move. 'You can heal this land and make it better than it was.'

Why didn't Rhys *say* anything? Why didn't he try and convince me to be on his side?

'You could speed Clara's healing,' said Shawn. 'The council is down in the summerhouse waiting. Whatever you say, goes.'

I could do this. There was that tempting pull again, but it didn't come from Shawn. It came from some place deep inside me. Some part of me that said I could control this where neither of them could. The circle went way back, and so did the cycle of prosperity and disaster. I could reverse the process; when disaster struck, speed the healing, like I'd done my leg.

'Can Rhys join the circle?' I asked. Because if I was going to be part of some kind of ancient dynastic male-female yin-yang tradition, it was *not* going to be with Shawn Maddox.

'Sure thing,' said Shawn. Which confirmed he was

lying. That was way too easy. 'Do you know what this means, Sylvie? You can fix your leg. Really fix it, not just make it feel better, the way you have here. You can dance again.'

His words reached into my heart like ten clawed, covetous fingers. I could dance again. I could have back the only thing I'd ever cared about. I could be whole.

Rhys still watched me in silence, but I saw the flicker in his eyes, the steeling of his own heart. He thought I was going to say yes. Well, I couldn't blame him. In that instant *I* thought I was going to say yes.

The water was still rising. We were running out of time for me to decide what I was going to be when I grew up. As usual, it was easier to know what I was *not* going to be more than what I was.

The decision hurt as if I'd shattered my leg all over again, only it was my whole being, the person I was, breaking apart. I turned to Shawn, pulling myself up, poised like the ballerina I would never be again. 'There is no win-win situation here. And I believe you know that.'

From the corner of my eye, I saw Rhys shift, a nearly imperceptible breath of released tension. But Shawn still gripped my hand, and his fingers tightened as he realized he'd lost his thrall over me. 'That's what you think—'

'Here's what I *know*, Shawn. If the archaeological park is washed under by this flood, the state might sell it to Maddox Point pretty cheap. That's one win for you.

'And I'm the last Davis. I inherit all of this, eventually. If the bulldozer matchmaking going on here worked, a Maddox would finally have ownership of Bluestone Hill.' That was my theory, anyway. I didn't know if Alabama was a common-law state, but it was a pretty good guess that a wife's property became joint on her marriage. Talk about a long-term plan on the part of the Maddox men.

'It must be really inconvenient for you that I sort of hate your guts right now.'

My mouth was running now without any sense of self-preservation. I knew Shawn was more calculating than he appeared. But part of me still believed he was just trying to play the odds in his favour and that he would give in easily when I stood up to him.

That was a miscalculation. He proved his viciousness in the grip on my hand. It tightened until I felt the bones grind together, and I gave a surprised gasp of pain.

Rhys jumped forward, but not before Shawn yanked me out of the green circle and up against him, twisting my arm around behind my back until I cried out and went up on my tiptoes, trying to relieve the pressure on the joint.

'Stop there, English, or we'll see if you can fix her broken arm.'

I made another sound, this one not of pain but of fear, because when Shawn spun me round, I faced the river. 'Rhys, look. The lawn. The water.'

He glanced behind him and his shoulders stiffened as he saw what I meant. The water was creeping up towards the summerhouse. And bringing its unearthly entourage with it.

'I think he's bringing them,' I said with horrified awe. I knew Shawn had an uncanny ability to charm and sway people. The spectres would be even easier because they had no will of their own. 'He's controlling them. Oh my God. You *did* make the Colonel's ghost throw Clara down the stairs.'

'Shut up!' Shawn wrenched my arm up higher, twisting a cry of pain from me.

And then, suddenly, *he* was screaming. Shawn let go of my wrist and I slipped out of his hold, stunned to see a six-pound ball of muddy fluff attached to his leg. Gigi was awake. She'd gotten up under his jeans and clamped onto his Achilles tendon. And she was *not* letting go.

Rhys didn't waste the opportunity. He jumped Shawn and they went down with a hard crash into the gravel. Gigi let go, and I scooped her up in my good arm and scrambled out of the way. Rhys's fists were flying and I had to wonder where a professor's son had learned to fight like that.

Unfortunately, it looked like Shawn Maddox knew what he was doing, too, as my shoulder could attest. I didn't even see how he did it – magic? Oh my God, anything was possible – but he threw Rhys into a hedge, then went after him.

My mind was spinning through the past few minutes, checking lost bits of conversation. The council was in the summerhouse, which was going to be underwater in a few minutes. Not to mention overrun by the ghost army. Why weren't they running and screaming in fear? Where they in a similar thrall?

In a decisive burst of insight, I knew what to do. While the boys tore through my garden and the drowned legion advanced, I ran for the standing stone.

The rock seemed to hold onto the moisture in the air, staying dark and wet the whole day. It should have been cold to the touch, but it felt warm and alive. The stone wasn't magic, but it was the focal point of something huge and mystical, and I opened myself up to that idea and flung myself off the cliff of reason and logic, into the swirling ocean of I-might-be-crazy-but-I-don't-care.

And I didn't fall.

A tide of energy rose and caught me. It seemed to carry me to a dizzying height, until I was looking down at the land from far above, a satellite image of this earth. My earth. I could see lines of energy running through it like a net of light, dim and broken in places, shining too bright and hot in others, like a fuse about to go out.

Too high. Too far.

The dancer who flings herself around the stage ends up injured or unemployed. She always *places* herself. That's what gives her balance. That's what gives her control.

I came back down, in my body but still with the extra layer of awareness. I could see the lines of power that connected Shawn to the ghosts. With a wave of my hand, I cut the cords that bound them, surprised at how easy it was. Of course, that was setting things to rights. What I did next was more difficult. I pointed at the grass at Shawn's feet and tripped him as he ran at Rhys again.

He hit the ground and Rhys grabbed his arm, taking a page from Shawn's own book, and twisted it up behind his back. Shawn thrashed and cursed, but couldn't move.

Leaving the stone, I felt the connection stretching along with me, unthinned by distance. I crouched in front of Shawn, grabbed a handful of purple flowers from the herbs beneath him, and dropped them over him, picturing a blanket of sleep. He stopped thrashing.

Rhys looked at me, breathing hard, bleeding from his nose and his lip. 'You are taking to this rather quickly.'

'I'm a natural,' I said, oddly calm. I didn't think it was shock. I felt too *right*.

Trusting my spell to hold, Rhys stood and offered his hand to help me up. I stood without it. 'How could you believe that I would go along with him?' I accused.

He looked at me levelly. 'Weren't you thinking of it?'

'That's—' Completely true. 'Completely beside the point.'

Screams from the summerhouse interrupted what was probably a dead-end argument. When Shawn had gone unconscious, it must have released whatever hold he had on the council. They seemed to be only now noticing what was going on, and I was amazed at his ability. It must have taken a lot of power to keep nearly a dozen people as complacent as he'd kept the town about the TTC's activities.

'Come on,' said Rhys, and we ran for the spiral

staircase at the corner of the balcony, Gigi still in the crook of my arm. I climbed quickly, and Rhys and I assessed the situation from the better vantage point.

The water was already up around the bottom of the summerhouse, and there were still ghosts, milling about as if they had nowhere to go now that they had lost their direction.

Kimberly and the others leaned out the door, but understandably didn't want to come further as the water swirled and eddied around the steps. That, and the ghosts.

Rhys wiped the blood from under his nose and rubbed his hand on his jeans. 'This is going to be a big job. Are you up for it?'

'Are you?' I asked, since all I'd seen him do tonight was use his fists.

He turned to me, his face beat up, his clothes filthy, his expression wary. 'We'll have to really trust each other.'

'I can probably fake it for long enough.' It wasn't really the time for jokes. But it also wasn't the time for a long discussion on how trust involved telling your ally – that was accurate, if incomplete – everything pertinent before the bad guy forces you to. It wasn't his error in judgement that made me wonder if I could trust him again, but that he hadn't *told* me about it.

'No, Sylvie,' Rhys said, urgent, but careful to catch and hold my gaze. 'I trust you, now more than ever. You have to trust me like you'd trust your old partner not to drop you on your head.'

I studied him for as long as I dared, with the crisis

all around us. Then I admitted, 'I trust you, Rhys. My heart is smarter than my brain, and I should listen to it.'

He smiled, just a quick acknowledgement, and I faced the river, offering him my hand. Rhys took it, my left in his left, and stood behind me. Then he surprised me by putting an arm around my waist, like we were starting a pas de deux. My senses expanded again, my awareness of the world, but this time Rhys's hold kept me grounded, linking realities, focusing my perceptions like a lens.

I saw the web lines of power, the hot nodes and the sickly dim ones, but now I was able to relate them to where we were. There was a line connecting the ruins of Old Cahawba, the Hill, the church and the town, and all along the line the energy was off. Out of proportion. It skewed the beauty of this unseen, extra?sensory landscape.

With water imagery on my mind, I pictured myself opening dams where the line connected to others, equalizing the pressure. Evening the flow of the earth's energy.

'Can we hold back the water so they can get out of the summerhouse?' Rhys's voice was low in my ear.

I blinked, and saw that the ghosts had gone. Nothing but shades, they'd disappeared as shadows did when you flicked on the light.

'OK,' I said. With our linked hands I made a motion, like pushing back a curtain. The wave swept back – I couldn't help a gasp of amazement – and the Teen Town Council made a run for it. They helped one another up the wet and slippery slope, towards the house and high ground.

Defying physics was more difficult than righting the natural order of supernatural energy. My knees began to shake, and Rhys's arm tightened around my waist, flooding me with strength. Even he was breathing hard, though, when the last boy was out of the gazebo and running for the house.

We let go together, and the water swept forward, taking the summerhouse with it. But everyone inside was safe. And the ghosts were – mostly – laid to rest.

The very last thing was done quickly. But a deal was a deal, and you don't get something for nothing. As Gigi looked up at me, monitoring everything with a serene doggy calm, I took a sad but resolute breath, laced my fingers with Rhys's and balanced the last equation.

I knew my leg would continue to heal without help. What I didn't realize was how much the garden's energy was keeping me propped up. The night's worth of stress and running and fighting surged through me, and with a cry of pain and surprise, I went crashing down, neither leg supporting me any more.

It was a good thing Rhys was there to catch me.

Chapter 34

There were some seriously frantic parents by the time things were all over. The sheriff showed up, kids were ferried home, there were a lot of tears on all sides. Now that decades of accumulated imbalance had been reset, Shawn didn't have the same power to draw on. If I needed proof of that, I found it in Shawn's face as the sheriff read him the riot act for endangering all the teens with his prank.

None of the kids could recall how they got there. And most of them were also fuzzy on the details of what they did during their normal meetings. Kimberly did remember that Clara was in the hospital, and told me to tell Addie to call her.

Rhys's dad arrived just as the last car pulled away. The waters were receding almost as quickly as they'd risen, and the state police had opened up the roads that were out of danger. Professor Griffith made tea – naturally – and we ate by candlelight – cold cereal with tepid soy milk – while I gave him the official version of the evening's events: Rhys had been busy at the archae- ological park, I'd been reading in my room, and we had no idea that Shawn Maddox had organized a get- together of thrill-seeking teens in the summerhouse. That is, until they barely escaped serious injury as the floodwaters knocked down the building.

'I never had a good feeling about that Maddox boy,' said the professor. 'Despite his last name.'

'What about his last name?' I asked, recalling the conversation vaguely.

'Maddox. It's an anglicization of Madoc. Quite the coincidence, isn't it?'

'Yes. But you said it was unrelated.' I wondered if other people would be realizing things about the Mad- doxes that they hadn't before, now that Shawn's charm had run out. He would still have his natural good looks, though, so perhaps not.

Rhys held his watch to the light of one of the candles. 'Isn't it getting late, Dad? I'll bet you're knackered.'

Professor Griffith checked his own watch. 'Heavens. It feels much later than it is. I'll bet you youngsters are done in as well.'

'A bit,' I admitted in a colossal understatement. I could barely move, and my leg hurt like someone had been hammering on it. 'I really want a bath, though. Is the water heater gas, do you know?'

'You could try it and see.' The professor rose from the table with a stretch. 'There will be some cleanup to do in the morning, so let's get an early start. We don't want Paula to come home to any more of a disaster than she has to.'

I smiled slightly, imagining that Paula would have a lot to say about the mess. Her ordered life had been anything but since I'd gotten here.

❧ ❧

The water heater, thank heavens, worked just fine. I sank my aching body into the scalding water and felt every scratch, scrape and bruise sting and protest. I lay in the water, thinking, until it was cool enough to give Gigi a quick rinse. She seemed to have no lingering effects from her adventures, but I didn't let her paddle or play.

I was startled by how much I didn't regret my trade-off. My leg would continue to heal, at its own rate, and if simply working in the garden helped it along, I would take that. But the help I'd gotten tonight – running through the woods, rescuing Gigi, facing Shawn – had been extraordinary. I mean extra-extraordinary, and I didn't regret giving up that step towards temptation.

Besides soaking my aching body, there was another motive behind my leisurely bath. When I came out, the house was quiet and dark – no flicker of candlelight from downstairs or the professor's room. Holding Gigi's tags to keep them quiet, I snuck down the hall to Rhys's door, but he didn't answer my quiet tap. Returning to my own room, I wasn't at all surprised to find him waiting for me.

He sprawled on the bed, looking cleaner than when I'd left him in the kitchen. 'You took long enough,' he said, checking out my latest borrowed sleepwear – a set of plaid flannel pyjamas. I practically swam in them, but I was still chilled, and they were perfect and warm. Not to mention modest.

'I needed the soak.' I set Gigi on the floor, and she immediately jumped on the bed to greet our visitor.

'*I* had to make do with a cold splash in my room,' said Rhys, bringing all kinds of pictures to mind. He'd left a candle burning on the nightstand, and it cast appealing shadows on his sculpted face.

'It's a good thing it's so dark in the house,' I said. 'Or your dad would have wondered about your newest bruises.'

'Oh, he asked me. I told him I got in a fight over a lady's honour.'

I pulled the towel from my head and combed through my hair with my fingers. 'Are we going to talk about what really happened?'

Rhys paused in petting Gigi. 'We were both there.'

'Let's compare notes.' I sat on the very edge of the bed, unaccountably shy now that we weren't in the middle of life-and-death crises. 'Tell me about Prince Madoc.'

He sat up and took a length of my hair between his fingers, toying with it idly as he spun the tale. 'Once upon a time, there was a Welsh nobleman named Madoc. He had a brother, and both of them were in contention for their father's throne. Rather than risk a civil war, Madoc went exploring and found new lands to conquer, with no one to contest him. He sailed back to Wales, and gathered up a group of men and women to return with him to this New World.'

'Simple enough.'

'You would think so.' He kept playing with my hair, winding it around his finger. 'But there was a princess involved.'

'Of course there was.' Women always complicate things. That was what made stories, and life, interesting.

'She was meant to marry the brother, but Madoc persuaded her to come away with him to this undiscovered country. Some say he kidnapped her; others say they were truly in love.'

'But it's the same pattern as Hannah and her suitors.' At his blank look, I had to explain the whole thing from the diary. Then, more reluctantly, I pointed out, 'And there's you, and me, and Shawn. Even though you're not brothers. Is it coincidence? Or were we cast in these roles when we got here? Did we never have a choice in how we felt?'

He caught my anxious gaze with his own steady one. 'We always have choices, Sylvie. And patterns can be broken.'

'But' – I wasn't done yet – 'what if we leave here, and I don't feel this way any more? About you.'

He didn't look worried. 'Do you think that's going to happen?'

I studied his face, which wasn't impassive at all. With the smallest flickers of expression, I could read his calm confidence in the future. That was different than when we'd met. I'd gotten better at reading him, but he'd also let me in. Maybe not by choice at first. But here we were, sitting on my bed in the middle of the night.

'No,' I said, answering his question, then turning it around. 'Do you?'

Taking two handfuls of my hair, like pigtails, he pulled me close, laying his forehead against mine. 'I think I loved you before I ever got here. So no, I don't think that will change when we leave.'

Wetting my lips, I could feel his breath kissing them, from just inches away. 'So,' I whispered, 'what are we going to do now?'

'I suggest we stop asking questions,' he said, and shut me up very effectively.

After a few minutes – by which I mean a blissful, long, unhurried span of undetermined time – we lay on top of the covers of my lumpy bed and exhaustion took over. I fell asleep between kisses, but not so deeply that I didn't grab Rhys when he tried to leave. He gave in, curled around me and flipped the quilt up over us both.

❧ ❧

I woke, freezing cold, despite my flannel pj's, and being sandwiched between Rhys and Gigi, who'd managed to take her usual place behind my knees. The icy

506

air seemed to creep in under the door and through the keyhole.

The Colonel did not approve. I closed my eyes again against a wave of guilt. I'd forgotten something important. I still didn't know why Jacob had left Hannah or what had happened to her baby.

❦ ❦

The next morning when I woke, Rhys was gone, back in his own room before his lousy chaperone of a father was awake, and before all the excitement began.

When the flood took out the summerhouse, it revealed something else. A ring of standing stones, bluestone, like the one in the garden, each about two feet high. They'd been under the summerhouse. Which, in retrospect, made great sense.

Rhys, once he got over beating himself up for scouring half the county for something right under his nose, was giddy with excitement. Not because of the magical implications, but because Paula gave him permission to take a sample and compare all the rocks to the ones native to Wales, so he could find out if they really had come from there, like the Stonehenge stones.

It wouldn't mean anything to his father's research unless he could prove how long they'd been at the Hill, but it was interesting to find out that Rhys was a complete nerd about rocks, for no other reason than that he thought they were cool.

The resolution to Hannah's story wasn't so quick or dramatic as the destruction of the summerhouse. It took me getting up the nerve for a thorough search of the Colonel's office for the missing pages of Reverend Holzphaffel's diary. I came up empty, but it gave me the idea to go into Rhys's room and check the desk there – the twin to the one in mine.

In the matching secret compartment, I found the missing pages, read them, then carried them back to my room and put them in Hannah's desk, along with her diary. I knew what Hannah was searching for in the woods, and she wasn't looking for death.

And Dad must have known too. Who else could have secreted those pages there? It was only speculation – the way my connection with Hannah was only speculation – but I imagined Dad going through a journey similar to mine his last summer here. Paired up with Rainbow by the town, discovering the potential in the earth here, rousing the ghosts.

I didn't know where he'd found the pages from the reverend's journal. They were the originals, so someone must have torn them out and hidden them long before Holzphaffel's relative ever got hold of the books. I was guessing Dad discovered them in the Colonel's office, where I expected to find them. He'd read what Holzphaffel had suspected happened at Bluestone Hill, the story that I'd just read. Dad had seen what the manipulation of power could lead to, the kind of thing our family was capable of, and he had walked away to start his own life.

But I wasn't my dad, and I wasn't really about sticking

secrets in drawers. So I read the reverend's pages again, and made a plan for how to reveal the secrets written in them.

※ ※

On the day the river receded from the woods, I took Gigi and Rhys with me and went searching.

'What are we looking for?' Rhys asked, helping me over a spot where the water had left the ground crumpled like the front of a wrecked car.

'I think Gigi was on the trail of it the night of the flood,' I said, watching her plumed tail like a beacon as she trotted ahead of us. 'Before she got turned round by too many ghosts.'

For this, my new senses came in handy. I knew when we were close, and hurried after Gigi when she started running. My limp was back – not always, but definitely on long, uneven treks like this one.

Rhys and I found Gigi quickly, sitting under a bedraggled lilac tree. I dropped to my knees and dug in the soft mud with my fingers. Even if I'd thought about bringing any of my gardening tools, I wouldn't use them for this.

Surprisingly close to the surface, I touched something hard yet porous. By this time, Rhys had put my actions together with the story I'd told him, and leaned over my shoulder to see. 'Is that it?'

'Yes.' All that was left of the tiny skeleton was the skull and a few of the bigger bones. I left them all where they were.

Rhys took out his phone. 'Dr Young will know what to do. What do you want me to tell him?'

'That the flood uncovered these, and Gigi found them on our walk.' I paused. 'Let's leave the fact that my great-great-grandfather was a murderer out of the story.'

'It could have been Ethan Maddox,' he offered, as if that would make me feel better.

I shook my head. 'I think he may be responsible for his brother disappearing. But it's not Ethan who watches Hannah search for her baby.'

❧ ❧

Reverend Watkins agreed to let the bones be interred next to Hannah Davis's exiled grave, even though they were never really identified. There's not much left of a newborn to test for a DNA match.

I was content. Hannah could stop looking for the child her father had left out in the woods to die, and the baby could finally rest with the mother it barely knew.

And with nothing to watch, the Colonel disappeared, too. I would attribute it to shame that his deed had been discovered, but he was just a shade, repeating a pattern that had now been broken.

Epilogue

On the day I turned eighteen, I received access to the Davis trust fund. On the day after that, I made my cousin Paula and her partner a no-interest loan sufficient to renovate Bluestone Hill and (finally) open it as an inn. She could even hire someone to do the work for her – including the painting.

Which was fortunate, because the bluestone monolith and stone circle made the Travel Channel's list of 'Mysterious Places to Stay Overnight', and the inn was booked up before the paint was even dry.

Professor Griffith finished his book, and it was about as widely read as you would expect. One of his colleagues called it 'well researched but absurd'. I think the professor considered that a compliment.

Maddox Point was built, but it became Cahawba Point, a village of rustic rental lodges, where people could enjoy the unspoiled beauty of the Cahaba River. No ATVs or powerboats allowed.

Shawn Maddox missed the cutoff for his college paperwork, and ended up getting a job at the Daisy Café. I didn't expect that would last, because he was still Tom Sawyer, even without the magic charm. But it gave me satisfaction for the moment.

I saw Addie in an ad in *Seventeen* recently. She looked gorgeous, sulky and petulant, and I'm sure it will sell a ton of perfume.

Mother and Dr Steve are unaccountably happy. He really loves her, and she really loves that he loves her. So it all works out.

I told John about my adventure, and he didn't think I was crazy. I'm not sure what made me trust him, except that he used to be the only one who cared what happened to me.

But not any longer. Now there's Rhys.

Because of Rhys, I found out what a hassle it is to get a student visa to the UK. Apparently the British like something more definite than 'undeclared' as a major. I know I have a lot to learn, but where does helping the world with your supernatural green thumb fit into a traditional course of study?

At least they no longer have a quarantine on dogs.

Rhys says we'll figure it out.

Eighteen may be young to know you want to spend the rest of your life with someone, but I felt like this had been several lifetimes coming, and didn't want to waste a moment of this one.

Author's Note

Cahawba (often spelled Cahaba) is a real place, and I've worked a lot of its history into Sylvie's story. The Davis and Maddox families are entirely fictional, there is no Bluestone Hill or Maddox Landing, and I've tweaked the geography a bit. And though, as far as I know, there is no nexus of earth magic at the junction of the Cahaba and Alabama Rivers, if you walk around Old Cahaba Park, it takes only a little imagination to see the ghosts of the houses and bustling streets of Alabama's first state capital. For more information on the park and the preservation efforts there, visit www.cahawba.com.

Acknowledgements

Thanks to the staff of Old Cahawba Park for answering my questions (and for maintaining such a useful bookstore and website). Liberties and outright mistakes in history and geography are all my own.

This book is my friend Cheryl Smyth's fault. She introduced me to Old Cahawba, and to the natural beauty of a state I'd long assumed was all about Confederate flags in the back of pickups at NASCAR races. Also, it's handy having a mad scientist on call.

Credit also goes to my friends and critique partners, Candace Havens and Shannon Canard, who suffered through some very rough drafts and a few hysterical phone calls. And to Mom, who let me drive her car through some really rutted Alabama roads in the name of research. And to my husband, Tim, who has come to take so much in stride.

Much gratitude goes to my agent, Lucienne Diver, who totally gets where I come from, because she comes from there, too. But this time I have to give extra kudos to my editor, Krista Marino, who pushed Sylvie (and me) out of our comfort zones to make this book (even) better. I'm so lucky to work with her, and with all the folks at Random House.

And, as always, I'm grateful to teachers and librarians for their support, and to my readers, who are awesome.

Silver Screen Photography

ROSEMARY CLEMENT-MOORE lives and writes in Arlington, Texas. *The Splendour Falls* is her first book published in the UK for teenage readers. You can visit Rosemary at www.readrosemary.com.

DARK TOUCH

SHADOWS

AMY MEREDITH

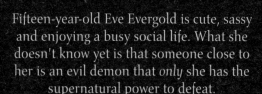

Fifteen-year-old Eve Evergold is cute, sassy and enjoying a busy social life. What she doesn't know yet is that someone close to her is an evil demon that *only* she has the supernatural power to defeat.

She needs to work out who it is — and fast! Because although there's something very attractive about the dark side . . . dating a demon? Pure *hell*!

Shadows is the first book in the brilliant new **Dark Touch** series.

RED FOX: 978 1 849 41051 9